ALSO BY AMERICA'S TEST KITCHEN

More Mediterranean

The New Cooking School Cookbook: Fundamentals

The Complete Autumn and Winter Cookbook

Five-Ingredient Dinners

One-Hour Comfort

The Complete Plant-Based Cookbook

Cook for Your Gut Health

The Complete Salad Cookbook

Vegetables Illustrated

Bowls

The Ultimate Meal-Prep Cookbook

The Chicken Bible

Meat Illustrated

The Complete One Pot

Foolproof Fish

Cooking for One

How Can It Be Gluten-Free Cookbook Collection

The Complete Summer Cookbook

The Side Dish Bible

100 Techniques

Easy Everyday Keto

Everything Chocolate

The Perfect Pie

The Perfect Cake

The Perfect Cookie

How to Cocktail

Spiced

The Ultimate Burger

The New Essentials Cookbook

Dinner Illustrated

America's Test Kitchen Menu Cookbook

Cook's Illustrated Revolutionary Recipes

Tasting Italy: A Culinary Journey

Cooking at Home with Bridget and Julia

The Complete Mediterranean Cookbook

The Complete Vegetarian Cookbook

The Complete Cooking for Two Cookbook

The Complete Diabetes Cookbook

The Complete Slow Cooker

The Complete Make-Ahead Cookbook

Just Add Sauce

How to Braise Everything

How to Roast Everything

Nutritious Delicious

What Good Cooks Know

Cook's Science

The Science of Good Cooking

Bread Illustrated

Master of the Grill

Kitchen Smarts

Kitchen Hacks

100 Recipes: The Absolute Best Ways to Make the True Essentials

The New Family Cookbook

The Cook's Illustrated Baking Book

The Cook's Illustrated Cookbook

The America's Test Kitchen Family Baking Book

The Best of America's Test Kitchen (2007–2022 Editions)

America's Test Kitchen Twentieth Anniversary TV Show Cookbook

The Complete America's Test Kitchen TV Show Cookbook 2001–2022

Healthy Air Fryer

Healthy and Delicious Instant Pot

Mediterranean Instant Pot

Cook It in Your Dutch Oven

Vegan for Everybody

Sous Vide for Everybody

Toaster Oven Perfection

Air Fryer Perfection

Multicooker Perfection

Food Processor Perfection

Pressure Cooker Perfection

Instant Pot Ace Blender Cookbook

Naturally Sweet

Foolproof Preserving

Paleo Perfected

The Best Mexican Recipes

Slow Cooker Revolution Volume 2: The Easy-Prep Edition

Slow Cooker Revolution

The America's Test Kitchen D.I.Y. Cookbook

THE COOK'S ILLUSTRATED ALL-TIME BEST SERIES

All-Time Best Brunch

All-Time Best Dinners for Two

All-Time Best Sunday Suppers

All-Time Best Holiday Entertaining

All-Time Best Soups

COOK'S COUNTRY TITLES

Big Flavors from Italian America

One-Pan Wonders

Cook It in Cast Iron

Cook's Country Eats Local

The Complete Cook's Country TV Show Cookbook

FOR A FULL LISTING OF ALL OUR BOOKS

CooksIllustrated.com

AmericasTestKitchen.com

PRAISE FOR AMERICA'S TEST KITCHEN TITLES

"The book's depth, breadth, and practicality makes it a must-have for seafood lovers."
PUBLISHERS WEEKLY (STARRED REVIEW) ON *FOOLPROOF FISH*

"Another flawless entry in the America's Test Kitchen canon, *Bowls* guides readers of all culinary skill levels in composing one-bowl meals from a variety of cuisines."
BUZZFEED BOOKS ON *BOWLS*

"*The Perfect Cookie* . . . is, in a word, perfect. This is an important and substantial cookbook. . . . If you love cookies, but have been a tad shy to bake on your own, all your fears will be dissipated. This is one book you can use for years with magnificently happy results."
THE HUFFINGTON POST ON *THE PERFECT COOKIE*

Selected as the Cookbook Award Winner of 2017 in the Baking category
INTERNATIONAL ASSOCIATION OF CULINARY PROFESSIONALS (IACP) ON *BREAD ILLUSTRATED*

"With 1,000 photos and the expertise of the America's Test Kitchen editors, this title might be the definitive book on bread baking."
PUBLISHERS WEEKLY ON *BREAD ILLUSTRATED*

"True to its name, this smart and endlessly enlightening cookbook is about as definitive as it's possible to get in the modern vegetarian realm."
MEN'S JOURNAL ON *THE COMPLETE VEGETARIAN COOKBOOK*

"Diabetics and all health-conscious home cooks will find great information on almost every page."
BOOKLIST (STARRED REVIEW) ON *THE COMPLETE DIABETES COOKBOOK*

"This book upgrades slow cooking for discriminating, 21st-century palates—that is indeed revolutionary."
THE DALLAS MORNING NEWS ON *SLOW COOKER REVOLUTION*

"Foolproof and high proof, this thoroughly researched and easy to follow volume will steady the hand of any home mixologist."
PUBLISHERS WEEKLY ON *HOW TO COCKTAIL*

"The book offers an impressive education for curious cake makers, new and experienced alike. A summation of 25 years of cake making at ATK, there are cakes for every taste."
THE WALL STREET JOURNAL ON *THE PERFECT CAKE*

"Offers a real option for a cook who just wants to learn some new ways to encourage family and friends to explore today's sometimes-daunting vegetable universe. This is one of the most valuable vegetable cooking resources for the home chef since Marian Morash's beloved classic *The Victory Garden Cookbook* (1982)."
BOOKLIST (STARRED REVIEW) ON *VEGETABLES ILLUSTRATED*

"Here are the words just about any vegan would be happy to read: 'Why This Recipe Works.' Fans of America's Test Kitchen are used to seeing the phrase, and now it applies to the growing collection of plant-based creations in *Vegan for Everybody*."
THE WASHINGTON POST ON *VEGAN FOR EVERYBODY*

"Some books impress by the sheer audacity of their ambition. Backed up by the magazine's famed mission to test every recipe relentlessly until it is the best it can be, this nearly 900-page volume lands with an authoritative wallop."
CHICAGO TRIBUNE ON *THE COOK'S ILLUSTRATED COOKBOOK*

"The 21st-century *Fannie Farmer Cookbook* or *The Joy of Cooking*. If you had to have one cookbook and that's all you could have, this one would do it."
CBS SAN FRANCISCO ON *THE NEW FAMILY COOKBOOK*

"The go-to gift book for newlyweds, small families, or empty nesters."
ORLANDO SENTINEL ON *THE COMPLETE COOKING FOR TWO COOKBOOK*

"A one-volume kitchen seminar, addressing in one smart chapter after another the sometimes surprising whys behind a cook's best practices. . . . You get the myth, the theory, the science, and the proof, all rigorously interrogated as only America's Test Kitchen can do."
NPR ON *THE SCIENCE OF GOOD COOKING*

"An extensive guide to grilling and barbecueing with 692 recipes, ratings, tips and techniques for outdoor cooking. There is plenty of information for those new to grilling, those into serious barbecue and grilling or those who want new recipes."
DETROIT FREE PRESS ON *MASTER OF THE GRILL*

THE
SAVORY
BAKER

150 Creative Recipes, from Classic to Modern

AMERICA'S TEST KITCHEN

Library of Congress Cataloging-in-Publication Data

Names: America's Test Kitchen (Firm)
Title: The savory baker : 150 creative recipes, from classic to modern / America's Test Kitchen.
Description: Boston, MA : America's Test Kitchen, [2022] | Includes index. | Summary: "Full PDF of book has been provided"-- Provided by publisher.

Identifiers: LCCN 2021049637 (print) | LCCN 2021049638 (ebook) | ISBN 9781948703987 (hardcover) | ISBN 9781948703994 (ebook)
Subjects: LCSH: Baking. | LCGFT: Cookbooks.
Classification: LCC TX763 .S29 2022 (print) | LCC TX763 (ebook) | DDC 641.81/5--dc23/eng/20211026
LC record available at https://lccn.loc.gov/2021049637
LC ebook record available at https://lccn.loc.gov/2021049638

AMERICA'S TEST KITCHEN
21 Drydock Avenue, Boston, MA 02210

Printed in Canada
10 9 8 7 6 5 4 3 2 1

Distributed by Penguin Random House Publisher Services
Tel: 800.733.3000

Pictured on front cover **Gruyère and Herb Buttermilk Biscuits (page 56)**

Pictured on back cover **No-Knead Tarts with Zucchini and Crispy Prosciutto (page 134), Caramelized Onion Flatbread with Blue Cheese and Walnuts (page 194), Broccoli Cheese Cornbread (page 44), Sausage and Chive Pull-Apart Rolls (page 274)**

Editorial Director, Books **Adam Kowit**

Executive Food Editor **Dan Zuccarello**

Deputy Food Editor **Stephanie Pixley**

Executive Managing Editor **Debra Hudak**

Book Editor **Valerie Cimino**

Senior Editors **Camila Chaparro, Leah Colins, Joseph Gitter, Sara Mayer, and Russell Selander**

Associate Editor **Sarah Ewald**

Test Cook **Carmen Dongo**

Assistant Editor **Sara Zatopek**

Design Director, Books **Lindsey Timko Chandler**

Deputy Art Director **Janet Taylor**

Photography Director **Julie Bozzo Cote**

Photography Producer **Meredith Mulcahy**

Senior Staff Photographers **Steve Klise and Daniel J. van Ackere**

Staff Photographer **Kevin White**

Additional Photography **Carl Tremblay and Joseph Keller**

Food Styling **Joy Howard, Catrine Kelty, Chantal Lambeth, Kendra McNight, Ashley Moore, Christie Morrison, Marie Piraino, Elle Simone Scott, Kendra Smith, and Sally Staub**

Photoshoot Kitchen Team

Photo Team and Special Events Manager **Allison Berkey**

Lead Test Cook **Eric Haessler**

Test Cooks **Hannah Fenton, Jacqueline Gochenouer, and Gina McCreadie**

Assistant Test Cooks **Hish Hassan and Christa West**

Senior Manager, Publishing Operations **Taylor Argenzio**

Imaging Manager **Lauren Robbins**

Production and Imaging Specialists **Tricia Neumyer, Dennis Noble, and Amanda Yong**

Lead Copy Editor **Rachel Schowalter**

Copy Editors **Christine Campbell and April Poole**

Proofreader **Kelly Gauthier**

Indexer **Elizabeth Parson**

Chief Creative Officer **Jack Bishop**

Executive Editorial Directors **Julia Collin Davison and Bridget Lancaster**

CONTENTS

WELCOME TO AMERICA'S TEST KITCHEN

This book has been tested, written, and edited by the folks at America's Test Kitchen, where curious cooks become confident cooks. Located in Boston's Seaport District in the historic Innovation and Design Building, it features 15,000 square feet of kitchen space, including multiple photography and video studios. It is the home of *Cook's Illustrated* magazine and *Cook's Country* magazine and is the workday destination for more than 60 test cooks, editors, and cookware specialists. Our mission is to empower and inspire confidence, community, and creativity in the kitchen.

We start the process of testing a recipe with a complete lack of preconceptions, which means that we accept no claim, no technique, and no recipe at face value. We simply assemble as many variations as possible, test a half dozen of the most promising ones, and taste the results blind. We then construct our own recipe and continue to test it, varying ingredients, techniques, and cooking times until we reach a consensus. As we like to say in the test kitchen, "We make the mistakes so you don't have to." The result, we hope, is the best version of a particular recipe, but we realize that only you can be the final judge of our success (or failure). We use the same rigorous approach when we test equipment and taste ingredients.

None of this would be possible without a belief that good cooking, much like good music, is based on a foundation of objective technique. Some people like spicy foods and others don't, but there is a right way to sauté; there is a best way to cook a pot roast; and there are measurable scientific principles involved in producing perfectly beaten, stable egg whites. Our ultimate goal is to investigate the fundamental principles of cooking to give you the techniques, tools, and ingredients you need to become a better cook. It is as simple as that.

To see what goes on behind the scenes at America's Test Kitchen, check out our social media channels for kitchen snapshots, exclusive content, video tips, and much more.

You can watch us work (in our actual test kitchen) by tuning in to *America's Test Kitchen* or *Cook's Country* on public television or on our websites. Listen to *Proof*, *Mystery Recipe*, and *The Walk-In* (AmericasTestKitchen.com/podcasts) to hear engaging, complex stories about people and food. Want to hone your cooking skills or finally learn how to bake—with an America's Test Kitchen test cook? Enroll in one of our online cooking classes. And you can engage the next generation of home cooks with kid-tested recipes from America's Test Kitchen Kids.

Our community of home recipe testers provides valuable feedback on recipes under development by ensuring that they are foolproof. You can help us investigate the how and why behind successful recipes from your home kitchen. (Sign up at AmericasTestKitchen.com/recipe_testing.)

However you choose to visit us, we welcome you into our kitchen, where you can stand by our side as we test our way to the best recipes in America.

facebook.com/AmericasTestKitchen
instagram.com/TestKitchen
youtube.com/AmericasTestKitchen
tiktok.com/@TestKitchen
twitter.com/TestKitchen
pinterest.com/TestKitchen

AmericasTestKitchen.com
CooksIllustrated.com
CooksCountry.com
OnlineCookingSchool.com
AmericasTestKitchen.com/kids

GETTING STARTED

INTRODUCTION

Cookbooks on sweet baked treats abound, but baking is about so much more than just desserts. Consider the savory side. From skillet cornbread to cheesy pizza, the world of savory baking is diverse and wide-ranging, welcoming those items and so many more under its umbrella: scones, muffins, and biscuits; pies, tarts, and galettes; turnovers, Danish, and other pastries; and flatbreads, crackers, and pancakes. This unique collection, your sourcebook for savory baking, includes all of these categories—and then some.

And when it comes to flavoring opportunities, why should sweet desserts have all the fun? The 150-plus recipes here showcase aromatic herbs and spices, fresh vegetables (and sometimes fruits), crunchy nuts and seeds, and rich cheeses and meats. You'll find these ingredients stuffed into fillings, incorporated into doughs, layered on as crusts and glazes, and blended into accompanying butters and sauces.

No matter your skill level, this cookbook will also serve as your trustworthy guide. When it comes to baking of any stripe, reliable recipes are as good as gold, and America's Test Kitchen puts the full weight of its test kitchen talent behind every recipe in this book. We teach you all the methods and techniques you need, complete with step-by-step photos and instructions, to master everything from one-bowl quick breads to pinwheel pastries to boulangerie-worthy breads. We also offer our foolproof recipes for homemade doughs without hesitating to let you know when you can substitute store-bought doughs instead, along with other flexible preparation tips to achieve these irresistible baked goods.

Some of our favorite everyday recipes are quick breads that simply use baking powder or baking soda, but here we've taken the flavors to a whole new level with Manchego and Chorizo Muffins, Panch Phoran Scones, and Whole-Wheat Soda Bread with Walnuts and Cacao Nibs. Another way to satisfy your baking cravings fast is with store-bought puff pastry, and we had lots of fun in the kitchen with this hero ingredient, upending the expected notion of sweet pastries to create savory goodies. Goat Cheese, Sun-Dried Tomato, and Urfa Danish may fool your eyes, but one taste will turn you into a believer. Beet and Caramelized Onion Turnovers are filled with a gorgeous ruby beet "jam," and the accompanying fuchsia-colored Beet-Yogurt Sauce is equally stunning.

Puff pastry is also ideal for turning out speedy full-size tarts such as our Asparagus and Goat Cheese Tart. Or turn to one of our easy press-together pastry doughs to bake a whole range of tarts, galettes, and pies, including Potato and Parmesan Tart; Corn, Tomato, and Bacon Galette; and Vegetable Pot Pie. For even more creations that will look like you spent far more time on them than you did, check out our pointers for mastering phyllo to turn out crispy, golden Lamb Phyllo Pie, Hortopita, or Eggplant and Tomato Phyllo Pie.

Pizza dough (either made from scratch or store-bought) is fantastic for crowd-pleasing snacks and great family meals like Za'atar Monkey Bread, Thin-Crust Whole-Wheat Pizza with Pesto and Goat Cheese, and Cast-Iron Skillet Calzone. Another fun and flavorful way to eat with your hands are pull-apart baked goods. Besides our monkey breads, we've got Sausage and Chive Pull-Apart Rolls, a reimagined take on sweet breakfast buns. Prosciutto and Fig Pinwheel Bread is an absolute showstopper that seems too beautiful to tear into—but trust us, you won't be able to resist. And while you could slice into a loaf of Saffron-Rosemary Challah, it's customary on holidays (and so gratifying) to tear and share this beautifully braided aromatic bread.

Savory baking doesn't even have to happen in the oven. Before you protest, consider all the savory pancakes and flatbreads that come together on the stovetop. This collection just wouldn't be complete without our takes on scallion pancakes, kimchi pancakes, buckwheat blini, chickpea socca, bánh xèo, cheese pupusas, and alu parathas.

Last but hardly least, any savory baking book worth its salt must include some true artisan breads, the kind that you might buy in a fancy boulangerie that cause you to say, How can I get that crispy crust, that so-satisfying chewy crumb, at home? While there's no doubt that these breads are labors of love, we guide you step by step through proofing, kneading, shaping, and baking so you can turn out bakery-style breads like Cheddar and Black Pepper Bread and Focaccia with Caramelized Red Onion, Pancetta, and Oregano.

It's time to satisfy your savory tooth. So let's dive into the overflowing cornucopia of savory baking.

THE FRESH FLAVORS OF SAVORY BAKING

There are so many creative ways to incorporate fresh produce, herbs and spices, and meats and cheeses into savory baked goods. Here are some of our favorite tried-and-true methods.

VEGETABLES

Just as with fruits in sweet baking, vegetables bring loads of flavor and mouthwatering moistness to savory baking. And, as with fruits, managing the water content of vegetables is critical to using them successfully. Here are some ways we do that.

Salt and Drain

Salting vegetables draws out excess liquid. Sliced and salted tomatoes for the Fresh Tomato Galette (page 147) drain off in a colander. A similar approach works with No-Knead Brioche Tarts with Zucchini and Crispy Prosciutto (page 134): Thinly sliced and salted zucchini drains on paper towels before it's nestled into the tartlet dough and baked.

Starch It Up

Drying freshly mashed potatoes on the stovetop ensures that Potato-Dill Sandwich Bread (page 288) and Potato Knishes (page 272) are light, not leaden. Microwaving potatoes can also dry them out, as for Sweet Potato Cornbread (page 43). And for Potato Biscuits with Chives (page 54), we skip fresh potatoes and start with dehydrated potato flakes.

Give It a Squeeze

Sometimes literally wringing out moisture-laden vegetables is what's needed. For Feta-Dill Zucchini Bread with Feta Butter (page 32), squeezing shredded raw zucchini in a kitchen towel does the trick. For Hortopita (page 126), blanching and then pressing fresh greens removes their excess moisture.

Start with Dried

Dried (and unrehydrated) porcini mushrooms and sun-dried tomatoes add huge hits of umami without liquid to items including Porcini and Truffle Crescent Rolls (page 251); Sun-Dried Tomato, Garlic, and Za'atar Biscuits (page 48); and Goat Cheese, Sun-Dried Tomato, and Urfa Danish (page 64).

Open a Can (or a Jar)

Canned and jarred ingredients can bring powerful flavor without too much moisture. Gochujang and Cheddar Pinwheels (page 61) roll up Korean red pepper paste and shredded cheese in puff pastry for superflavorful bite-size morsels. Tomato paste brings intense tomato flavor without excess moisture to Pizza Babka (page 326).

Cook It Down

Precooking vegetables evaporates water while concentrating flavor. In the Fresh Corn Cornbread (page 40), fresh corn kernels are pureed and then cooked down before being incorporated. Caramelizing onions eliminates moisture and adds a big flavor boost to Focaccia with Caramelized Red Onion, Pancetta, and Oregano (page 314) and Peppery Dinner Rolls with Caramelized Onion and Smoked Paprika (page 246).

FRUITS

Just because this is a savory baking book doesn't mean that fruit is banished. Both fresh and dried fruits can bring a subtle sweetness to savory baked goods.

Complement Savory with Sweet

Seeded Pumpkin Crackers (page 154), Cranberry-Walnut Bread (page 297), and Fig and Fennel Bread (page 302) all take advantage of the bright flavor and chewy texture of dried fruit. And fresh apples play well with savory flavors in the Butternut Squash, Apple, and Gruyère Turnovers (page 71).

10 Baked Goods That Swap Sweet for Savory

Manchego and Chorizo Muffins, page 24

Goat Cheese, Sun-Dried Tomato, and Urfa Danish, page 64

Beet and Caramelized Onion Turnovers with Beet-Yogurt Sauce, page 68

Butternut Squash, Apple, and Gruyère Turnovers, page 71

Smoked Salmon and Chive Mille-Feuille, page 73

Fennel-Apple Tarte Tatin, page 120

No-Knead Brioche Tarts with Zucchini and Crispy Prosciutto, page 134

Dutch Baby with Burrata and Prosciutto, page 236

Butternut Squash and Spinach Bread Pudding, page 242

Sausage and Chive Pull-Apart Rolls, page 274

SPICES AND HERBS

You might think of "baking spices" as skewing sweet, such as cinnamon and nutmeg. But decidedly savory spices, along with fresh and dried herbs, are delicious in baked goods.

Spice Things Up

Homemade or store-bought spice blends enliven Mana'eesh Za'atar (page 179), Furikake Japanese Milk Bread (page 322), and Panch Phoran Scones (page 31). A generous amount of a single spice can also make a bold statement, as in Asiago and Black Pepper Breadsticks (page 261) or Saffron-Rosemary Challah (page 332).

Herbs Are Heroes

Fresh parsley, chives, and sage are all packed into Gruyère and Herb Buttermilk Biscuits (page 56), which are dramatically topped with a whole sage leaf before baking. Blue Cheese and Chive Popovers with Blue Cheese Butter (page 235) double up on fresh chives, using them both in the popover batter and in the compound butter that you slather over them when they're hot from the oven.

Buttery Goodness

You can whip up an easy flavored butter using practically any herbs, spices, or other seasonings. To make ½ cup compound butter, beat 8 tablespoons softened unsalted butter in a bowl with a fork until fluffy. Mix in your ingredients (use these ideas or feel free to experiment) and season with salt and pepper to taste. Cover in plastic wrap and let rest so that the flavors blend, about 10 minutes, or roll into a log and either refrigerate in an airtight container for up to 1 week or freeze for up to 2 months.

Herb Butter: Use 2 to 3 tablespoons chopped fresh herbs of your choice. If you like, add either 1 minced garlic clove or 2 tablespoons minced shallot.

Herb-Mustard Butter: Use 3 tablespoons minced fresh herbs and 5 tablespoons whole-grain mustard.

Herb-Lemon Butter: Use 3 tablespoons minced fresh herbs and 4 teaspoons grated lemon zest.

Thai Curry Butter: Use ½ cup Thai red curry paste.

Nori Butter: Use 2 teaspoons nori powder.

Scallion Butter: Use 1 tablespoon finely chopped scallion.

Cheesy Butter: Use ¾ to 1 cup crumbled cheese such as feta or goat cheese.

NUTS AND SEEDS

Nuts and seeds give rich flavor and crunchy mouthfeel to savory baked goods just as much as they do to sweet baked treats.

Go Nuts

Toasted almonds infuse every bite of Chicken B'stilla (page 130) with their buttery richness, and Lamb Phyllo Pie (page 133) gets a crunchy topping of toasted pistachios.

Plant a Seed

Poppy seeds are integral to the filling for Onion-Poppy Bialys (page 262). Everything Bagel Grissini (page 162) are coated all over in a seasoning blend containing sesame and poppy seeds.

MEATS

Meat brings meal-worthy heartiness to savory baked goods, but harnessing the meat's fat content is important to avoid greasiness.

Render Equals Tender

Rendering fat before adding meat to doughs and batters is an effective way to avoid greasy, flabby baked goods. Precooking bacon in a skillet and draining most (but not all) of the fat brings bacony flavor to the French Onion and Bacon Tart (page 137). A similar approach works with prosciutto for the No-Knead Brioche Tarts with Zucchini and Crispy Prosciutto (page 134). Microwaving is another great way to render excess fat, as we do with the chorizo for Manchego and Chorizo Muffins (page 24).

CHEESES

Most cheeses adapt beautifully to savory baking, and we use all different kinds, from soft fresh goat cheese to shreddable cheddar to hard aged Parmesan. While it naturally provides flavor and texture, cheese's moisture and fat content perform practical functions in baked goods.

Insulate Your Dough

Shredded or grated cheese can act as an insulating layer between crusts and juicy toppings to keep crusts crispy while baking and serving. In the Eggplant and Tomato Phyllo Pie (page 122), sprinkling a layer of shredded mozzarella over the assembled phyllo layers prevents the vegetable topping from sogging out the delicately crisp pastry. In the Corn, Tomato, and Bacon Galette (page 144), you'll get similar results by sprinkling the galette dough with grated Parmesan before topping with corn kernels, cherry tomatoes, and cheddar.

Make It Crusty

Cheese toppings turn golden and crunchy in the oven. The Quick Cheese Bread (page 34) is plenty cheesy with little chunks of cheddar mixed into the batter. But the pièce de résistance is sprinkling shredded Parmesan over the top of the loaf before baking. This technique offers similarly delicious results for Garlicky Olive Bread (page 39).

Get Saucy

Soft cheeses can melt down during baking to form something wonderfully oozy. In the Camembert, Sun-Dried Tomato, and Potato Tart (page 139), an entire wheel of Camembert is cut and arranged over potatoes and onions in a tart shell. During baking, the rind turns crisp-chewy and the interior melts over the vegetables. The Adjaruli Khachapuri (page 208) is a soft-crusted bread "boat" filled with a pool of melted cheeses.

SAVORY BAKING
PANTRY STAPLES

Stock these essential ingredients in your kitchen and you'll be well on your way toward making any of the recipes in this book.

FLOURS

Different flour varieties contain varying amounts of protein. More protein leads to more gluten development; depending on what you're baking, that may or may not be desirable, so use what's specified in each recipe. Unless otherwise noted, we prefer unbleached flour because bleached flour can carry off-flavors. Here are the flours we use in this book.

ALL-PURPOSE FLOUR has a moderate protein content (10 to 11.7 percent) and is good when you want a relatively tender, soft crumb, as for Quick Cheese Bread (page 34); Garlic Knots (page 256); or Focaccia with Caramelized Red Onion, Pancetta, and Oregano (page 314). We develop our recipes using Gold Medal Unbleached All-Purpose Flour (10.5 percent protein). Pillsbury All-Purpose Unbleached Flour (also 10.5 percent protein) offers comparable results. If you use a higher-protein all-purpose flour (such as King Arthur Unbleached All-Purpose Flour, with 11.7 percent protein) in recipes that call for all-purpose flour, the results may be drier and chewier. Sometimes the higher protein content of King Arthur all-purpose flour is desirable, and those instances are noted. If you can't find King Arthur all-purpose flour in those cases, substitute bread flour.

BREAD FLOUR has a high protein content (12 to 14 percent), which ensures strong gluten development and chewy texture. Because of its structure-building properties, it's great for artisan breads such as Prosciutto Bread (page 298). Do not substitute all-purpose flour in these recipes; the bread will not be able to support an airy, chewy crumb. We prefer Gold Medal Bread Flour. For some recipes, we recommend King Arthur Unbleached Bread Flour, which has a higher protein content.

WHOLE-WHEAT FLOUR is made from the entire wheat berry, unlike white flours. Though whole-wheat flour is high in protein (about 13 percent), it doesn't form gluten as readily as similarly high-protein white flours thanks to the presence of the sharp bran, which can pierce the gluten structure as it forms, and peptides, which interfere with gluten development from the start. Because it behaves differently and can make baked goods dense, we usually rely on a mix of white and whole-wheat flours to get the best balance of structure and texture in items such as Whole-Wheat Quinoa Bread (page 290). We use King Arthur Premium Whole Wheat Flour. Whole-wheat flour goes rancid more quickly than white flour; store it in the freezer and bring it to room temperature before use.

RYE FLOUR brings an earthy, tangy flavor to items such as Rye Crepes with Smoked Salmon, Crème Fraîche, and Pickled Shallots (page 224). The darker the color, the more bran the flour contains. Rye flour is low in one of the proteins needed for developing gluten, so you need to cut it with white flour to avoid dense baked goods, as we do in Fig and Fennel Bread (page 302). Store rye flour like whole-wheat flour.

BUCKWHEAT FLOUR isn't related to wheat at all. Buckwheat is an herb belonging to the same family as rhubarb or sorrel. High in protein and fiber and gluten free, buckwheat flour is made by grinding its triangular seeds, which contribute a dark color and earthy flavor. It adds moistness and pliability to Galettes Complètes (page 226) and Blini (page 217).

CHICKPEA FLOUR is also known as besan, garbanzo flour, or gram flour. Beany-tasting chickpea flour is made from ground raw or roasted chickpeas and has a high protein content (20 percent). It's common in Indian, Middle Eastern, and European cooking and is used to make Socca with Caramelized Onions and Rosemary (page 212) and Farinata (page 215).

CORNMEAL comes in many different varieties. Because the texture and flavor vary, it's important to use the cornmeal variety specified in a recipe. For example, our Fresh Corn Cornbread (page 40) requires coarse-ground cornmeal to achieve its rustic texture and full flavor. Coarse-ground cornmeal doesn't soften, however, so we turn to regular cornmeal for a more delicate texture in things such as Corn Muffins with Rosemary and Black Pepper (page 27). We usually use yellow cornmeal, though white cornmeal can often be substituted.

MASA HARINA is flour made from cooked corn (whereas cornmeal is ground from uncooked dried corn). Corn kernels are nixtamalized (cooked and soaked in alkaline limewater), which breaks down and gels some of the carbohydrates. This mixture is dried and ground. We use it for Cheese Pupusas (page 172), Tomatillo Chicken Huaraches (page 176), and more.

TAPIOCA STARCH (also called tapioca flour) is often used in gluten-free baking. Made from the starchy tuberous root of the cassava plant, it gives elasticity and structure to baked goods and is an integral ingredient in Pão de Queijo (page 255).

LEAVENERS

YEAST comes in two forms: fresh and dry. Fresh yeast is highly perishable, so we don't use it in the test kitchen. There are two types of dry yeast: instant yeast and active dry yeast. Instant yeast (also called rapid-rise yeast) is our usual choice because it doesn't need to be proofed and can be added directly to dry ingredients—the result of undergoing a gentler drying process that doesn't destroy the outer cells. Active dry yeast is treated with heat, which kills the outermost cells. It must be proofed, or dissolved in liquid, before use to slough off the dead cells and render the yeast active. To substitute active dry yeast for instant yeast in a recipe, use 25 percent more of it to compensate for the greater quantity of inactive yeast cells. And you'll need to dissolve active dry yeast in a portion of the water from the recipe, heated to 110 degrees. Then, let it stand for 5 minutes before adding it to the remaining wet ingredients.

BAKING SODA is an alkali and therefore requires an acidic ingredient in the batter or dough, such as buttermilk or sour cream, in order to work. Used in combination with baking powder, it boosts leavening power in quick breads such as Sweet Potato Cornbread (page 43) and Rosemary and Olive Drop Biscuits (page 50). Because it raises the pH of dough, it can also help promote browning.

BAKING POWDER is a mixture of baking soda, a dry acid, and double-dried cornstarch, so it doesn't need an additional acidic ingredient to work as baking soda does. The cornstarch absorbs moisture and prevents the premature production of gas. Baking powder works twice—when it first comes in contact with a liquid and again in response to heat. It leavens quick breads such as Jalapeño and Cheddar Scones (page 28) and also helps fry breads like Bean and Cheese Sopaipillas with Green Chile Sauce (page 96) puff up.

FATS

BUTTER works better in baked goods when it's unsalted. The salt amount in different brands of butter varies, which affects flavor; plus, salted butters usually have a higher water content than unsalted butters, which can interfere with gluten development. The temperature of butter often matters in a baking recipe; see the handy chart opposite.

OIL is added in small quantities to add extensibility to doughs and to tenderize breads that don't need the rich flavor of butter. Neutral-tasting vegetable oil adds tenderness without altering flavor. Extra-virgin olive oil has a pronounced flavor, which is great in certain applications. For breads that are baked at superhot temperatures, especially flatbreads, a good amount of oil in dough can also result in a crisp crust: The oil essentially fries the dough in the oven for our Red Pepper Coques (page 186).

LARD brings a clean richness and subtle savoriness to baked goods. Because it has a higher melting point than butter, it remains solid for longer in the oven's heat. This allows more time for air pockets to form in dough, leading to flakiness. Lard also contains no water, unlike butter, so it doesn't encourage gluten development. We use lard in Bean and Cheese Sopaipillas with Green Chile Sauce (page 96) and Piadine (page 165).

Gauging Butter Temperature

CHILLED

TEMPERATURE	About 35 degrees
METHOD	Cut into small pieces and freeze until very firm, 10 to 15 minutes.
HOW TO TEST	It should not yield when pressed with a finger and should be cold to the touch.

SOFTENED

TEMPERATURE	60 to 68 degrees
METHOD	Let refrigerated butter sit at room temperature for 30 to 60 minutes.
HOW TO TEST	At 60 degrees, it should yield to slight pressure and crack when pressed. At 68 degrees, it should bend easily without breaking and give slightly when pressed.

MELTED & COOLED

TEMPERATURE	85 to 94 degrees
METHOD	Melt in small saucepan or microwave-safe bowl and let cool for about 5 minutes.
HOW TO TEST	It should be fluid and slightly warm to the touch.

EGGS

EGGS do a lot for baked goods. The yolks can provide a dense richness, while the whites can contribute extra structure. Adding extra whites to a batter can also provide moisture without a lot of liquid, helping our Gougères with Aged Gouda and Smoked Paprika (page 232) puff up. Extra yolks add fat and emulsifiers to make a stable custard in our Butternut Squash and Spinach Bread Pudding (page 242). We also brush a lot of our baked goods with egg wash, a mixture of egg and water, before baking. The protein in the white helps the exterior brown, and the fat in the yolk makes the crust shiny.

SALT

SALT isn't just for seasoning. In yeasted doughs, it tightens gluten strands to make them stronger. Salt also slows gluten development (which helps to develop flavor): If you forget it in a bread, the dough will rise very quickly and the flavor will be very dull. Salt also helps with browning by controlling yeast activity so that the yeast doesn't eat all the natural sugar (sugar is another component that helps make crusts brown). Salt can even change the electrical charges on egg proteins, letting them set up into a strong network early in the baking time, as in the Gougères with Aged Gouda and Smoked Paprika (page 232).

SUGAR

SUGAR has a place in savory baking, but it must be used judiciously—not only for the obvious reason but also because it attracts and traps moisture (it's hygroscopic), an advantage for tender sweet cakes and chewy cookies but not necessarily for flaky, crispy, savory baked goods. A little is needed for moistness in the Corn Muffins with Rosemary and Black Pepper (page 27), which would be too dry with none at all. Sugar also helps with browning: In the Fennel-Apple Tarte Tatin (page 120), a small amount helps to brown the fennel (and amplify its flavor) in the skillet before adding the apples, blanketing it with pastry, and baking. It also helps to brown the crust in Everything Bagel Bread (page 294), which gets a dunk in sugar-spiked boiling water. Last but not least, sugar can give yeast a snack to help its dough-proofing power, as in the Pletzel (page 188).

LIQUIDS

WATER is the default liquid in bread baking. When it mixes with flour, the proteins in the flour hydrate and begin to form gluten. When it comes to baking, the temperature is always important; for example, ice water can keep a dough from over-heating in a food processor, and too-hot water can kill yeast. We always specify water temperature in our recipes; see the chart below.

MILK AND CREAM also feature in a lot of the recipes in this book. They contribute richness; the fat tenderizes the crumb and can weaken the gluten structure in an advantageous way; and the proteins contribute to the browning of the outer crust in a manner similar to eggs. Because fat content is important, we always specify what type of milk or cream is best for a recipe.

Water Temperature

ICE WATER	About 35 degrees
ROOM TEMPERATURE	About 67 degrees
WARM	About 110 degrees
BOILING	212 degrees

TIME TO MAKE THE DOUGH

There's no need to feel intimidated by the idea of working with dough or pastry. Sometimes store-bought is the best approach! And when making your own doughs, follow our techniques and tips for impressively delicious results.

PUFF PASTRY POINTERS

Store-bought frozen puff pastry delivers all the advantages of homemade puff pastry without the hours of tricky, temperature-sensitive dough work, so we recommend it for the most consistent results. Puff pastry is available in versions made with vegetable shortening as well as all-butter versions, so try both and see which you prefer. Here are some of our best practices for working with this freezer-aisle favorite.

1   You can thaw puff pastry on the counter for 30 minutes to 1 hour if your kitchen is cool, but the safest bet is to thaw it in the fridge for 24 hours. That way, the pastry defrosts slowly, and there's no risk of it overheating.

2   When rolling the puff pastry sheet, try to avoid rolling over the edges of the sheet too much. Flattening the edges could inhibit the "puff" during baking.

3   A sharp knife edge will make clean, precise cuts that preserve the layers rather than pinch them together.

4   After you've shaped and cut your puff pastry, it can be a good idea to chill the dough for 15 to 30 minutes before baking to firm it up and help it retain flakiness.

5   If you thaw more puff pastry than you need, simply pop the leftovers back in the freezer. In testing, we've found that there is little difference between dough frozen once and dough frozen twice; all-butter pastry won't rise quite as high after a double freeze as pastry made with shortening will, but the effect is minimal.

TIPS FOR TAMING PHYLLO

Frozen packaged phyllo dough bakes up into delicate layers of light, flaky, crisp-crunchy pastry. These paper-thin sheets have a maddening tendency to tear, dry out quickly, or stick together. To master this delicate dough, follow our tips.

1   Thaw phyllo in the refrigerator overnight or on the counter for 4 to 5 hours; don't thaw it in the microwave. Allow phyllo to come to room temperature before using for the easiest handling.

2   To help prevent cracking, keep phyllo moist until you're ready to work with it. The usual approach is to cover the stack with a damp dish towel, but it's easy to overmoisten the towel and turn the dough sticky. We prefer to cover the stack with plastic wrap to protect the phyllo and then place a damp towel on top.

3   Because phyllo is so fragile, some sheets crack and even tear while still in the box. Don't worry about rips; just make sure to adjust the orientation of the sheets as you stack them so that cracks in different sheets don't line up.

4   When phyllo sheets emerge from the box fused at their edges, don't try to separate the sheets. Instead, trim and discard the fused portion.

CAPTIVATINGLY CRISPY CRUSTS

There are numerous techniques we use to achieve irresistibly crisp and crackly crusts, edges, and exteriors in pies, pizzas, and breads; here's a quick peek into our favorite methods.

Reduce Fat (or Brush It On Later)

Thin batters and lean doughs generally make for crisper exteriors. For the Blue Cheese and Chive Popovers with Blue Cheese Butter (page 235), making a relatively thin batter by leaving out butter and using low-fat milk instead of whole milk helps them emerge from the oven crispier. Also, brushing fat onto the surface of a dough before baking, such as egg wash on pie crusts or oil on phyllo dough, causes the surface to crisp right up in the oven.

Build a Steam Engine

Steam can help foster crispness from both within and without. For the Blue Cheese and Chive Popovers with Blue Cheese Butter (page 235), as the thin pastry shell rapidly expands in the hot oven, interior steam expands the batter, helping the outside form a crispy shell. Gougères with Aged Gouda and Smoked Paprika (page 232) incorporate an extra egg white into the batter to help create interior steam. Almost No-Knead Bread with Olives, Rosemary, and Parmesan (page 286) is baked in a covered Dutch oven to mimic the steamy environment of an artisan-bakery oven. Go even further in the artisan direction by pouring water over a pie plate filled with lava rocks when baking Sage-Polenta Bread (page 312).

Turn Up the Heat

A baking stone or steel is the easiest and most effective way to achieve crisp bottom crusts on flatbreads and pizzas. For recipes including Lahmajun (page 180) and our thin-crust pizzas (pages 196–199), preheating the stone or steel in a 500-degree oven for an hour practically turns your home oven into a professional bakery oven.

Recipes You Can Make Using Store-Bought Dough

FRENCH BAKERY–WORTHY FLAKINESS

Likewise, we use a few different techniques to achieve ultimate flakiness in galettes, biscuits, savory pancakes, and more. What they have in common is an understanding of how fat works.

Cut and Roll

Cutting chilled butter into dough lets the solid little lumps create separation in the dough structure when baked. We like to achieve this quickly in a food processor for flaky pie crusts such as those for Double-Crust Chicken Pot Pie (page 84) and Tourtière (page 88). But the fat doesn't always need to be in a solid form to take advantage of this technique. Cōngyóubing (page 170) are formed by rolling the dough into a round, brushing it with oil and sprinkling it with scallions, and then coiling it into a cylinder and rolling it into a round again. This creates layers of dough and fat that result in deliciously flaky shards when the scallion pancakes are cooked in a skillet.

Smear and Fold

A French technique called fraisage involves smearing flour and chunks of chilled butter together in long strokes across a counter to incorporate the butter and create long, thin layers of flaky pastry. We use this technique for our Galette Dough

(page 336). A similar but more refined approach is to give dough a series of rolls and folds to incorporate the butter. For the Gruyère and Herb Buttermilk Biscuits (page 56), frozen butter is grated into the dough and then the dough is rolled and folded repeatedly to create hundreds of flaky layers.

TRY A LITTLE TENDERNESS

It's probably no surprise: The versatile and reliable workhorses of fat and moisture can also help make breads and rolls melt-in-your-mouth tender.

Enrich Your Dough

Softened or melted butter coats gluten strands in dough to prevent them from forming a firm structure, making for tender pull-apart results in Porcini and Truffle Crescent Rolls (page 251), Prosciutto and Fig Pinwheel Bread (page 282), and more. Incorporating egg yolks into dough can have a similar effect, thanks to their fat content.

Make a Tangzhong

This technique involves heating a mix of water and flour until it forms a paste and then mixing the paste into the dough. This method helps the flour absorb the liquid it's cooked with, resulting in pillowy softness for baked goods including Furikake Japanese Milk Bread (page 322) and Saffron-Rosemary Challah (page 332).

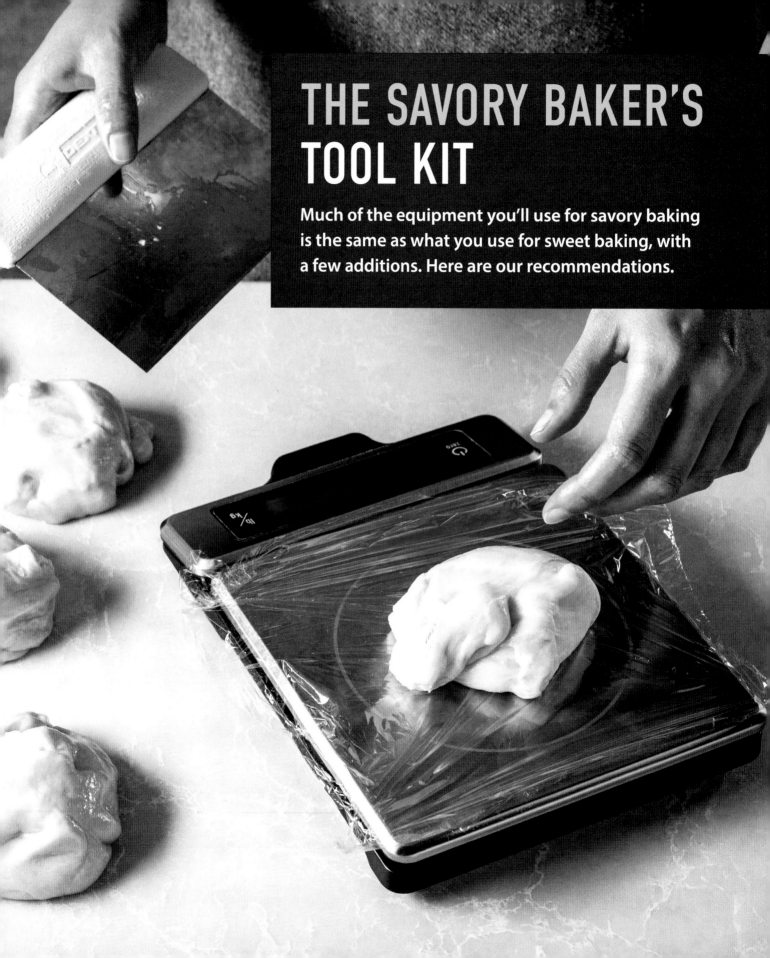

THE SAVORY BAKER'S TOOL KIT

Much of the equipment you'll use for savory baking is the same as what you use for sweet baking, with a few additions. Here are our recommendations.

BAKING BASICS

Here are the essentials for setting up a well-stocked kitchen for everyday savory baking (and for tackling most of the recipes in this book).

Measuring cups

It's helpful to have multiple sizes of liquid measuring cups for any kind of baking; the industry-standard **Pyrex Measuring Cup** is unbeatable.

You should be weighing the bulk of your ingredients, but you'll still need a set of measuring cups for small quantities of dry ingredients. Look for well-constructed, evenly weighted stainless-steel models with easy-to-read measurement markings and long, straight handles. We use the very accurate **OXO Good Grips Stainless Steel Measuring Cups**.

Measuring spoons

We prefer heavy, well-constructed stainless-steel measuring spoons with long, sturdy, well-designed handles. Choose deep bowls; shallow bowls allow more liquid to spill with the shake of an unsteady hand. **Cuisipro Stainless Steel 5-Piece Measuring Spoons** is our recommended set.

Digital kitchen scale

Weighing your ingredients ensures consistent results in baked goods. We prefer digital scales for their readability and precision. Look for one that has a large weight range and that can be tared or "zeroed," which discounts the weight of the container. We like the **OXO Good Grips 11 lb Food Scale with Pull Out Display**.

Bench scraper

A bench scraper is handy for transferring bread dough from one surface to another and for cleanly cutting dough into pieces without compressing the edges. Our winner is the **Dexter-Russell 6" Dough Cutter/Scraper—Sani Safe Series**. It has a comfortable handle, and the deeply beveled edge cuts through dough quickly.

Bowl scraper

The best way to remove or fold sticky dough is with a bowl scraper. This handheld spatula is curved, with enough grip to scrape the bowl clean and enough rigidity to move dough easily. Our favorite model, the **Fox Run Silicone Dough/Bowl Scraper**, is made of contoured silicone covering a metal insert.

Rolling pin

There are many styles of rolling pins; we prefer the control that comes with the classic French-style wood rolling pins without handles. These pins come straight and tapered. We tend to reach for straight pins, which make achieving even dough thickness and rolling out larger disks easy. The **J.K. Adams Plain Maple Rolling Dowel** has a gentle weight and a slightly textured surface for less sticking.

Pastry brush

We love to use silicone brushes for basting meat and poultry and for oiling hot pans. But for spreading egg wash or melted butter on delicate doughs or pastry, we prefer to use a pastry brush with natural-fiber bristles. Our favorite is **Winco Flat Pastry and Basting Brush, 1½ inch**.

Wire cooling rack

Cooling baked goods on a wire rack allows air to circulate so that the item dries properly and retains a crisp crust. The **Checkered Chef Cooling Rack** is an essential; plus, it fits neatly inside a rimmed baking sheet.

Stand mixer

A stand mixer, with its hands-free operation, numerous attachments, and strong mixing arm, is a must if you plan on baking regularly. Heft matters, as does a strong motor that can knead stiff dough with ease. Our favorite stand mixer is the **KitchenAid Pro Line Series 7-Qt Bowl Lift Stand Mixer**. Our Best Buy is the **KitchenAid Classic Plus Series 4.5-Quart Tilt-Head Stand Mixer**.

Baking sheets

We bake a number of savory pastries, flatbreads, and free-form loaves on rimmed baking sheets. An inverted rimmed baking sheet can also stand in for a baking peel or a baking stone or steel. The **Nordic Ware Baker's Half Sheet** is sturdy and warp resistant, producing evenly golden-brown crusts on all our baked goods.

Tart pan

Shallow, fluted tart pans give a home baker's tarts a professional look. The very best tart pan is the **Matfer Steel Non-Stick Fluted Tart Mold with Removable Bottom 9½"**. It produces perfectly even golden-brown tarts with crisp, professional-looking edges. Its nonstick coating makes the transfer from pan to platter a cinch.

Food processor

A food processor brings together many doughs, including pizza dough, in a flash. Look for a workbowl that has a capacity of at least 11 cups. With a powerful motor, responsive pulsing action, sharp blades, and a simple design, the **Cuisinart Custom 14 14-Cup Food Processor** aces all tests.

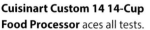

Pie plate

For crisp, flaky pie crusts that neither sog out on the bottom nor overbrown, we like the **Williams-Sonoma Goldtouch Nonstick Pie Dish**. You may also want to keep a deep-dish pie plate on hand.

Pie weights

Blind-baking pie dough before adding filling ensures that the crust cooks all the way through and doesn't get soggy after fillings are added. While you can use dried beans or raw rice as pie weights, we like **Mrs. Anderson's Baking Ceramic Pie Weights**. Four packages, equaling 4 cups, is enough to fill a pie shell, keeping the bottom from puffing and the sides from slumping during blind baking.

Loaf pan

We prefer 8½ by 4½-inch loaf pans to 9 by 5-inch pans; whether used for quick breads or yeasted breads, they produce tall loaves with rounder tops. For professional-looking results, we also like the squared-off corners of folded metal pans. The **USA Pan Loaf Pan, 1 lb Volume** is just right.

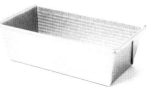

Muffin pan

Lighter-colored muffin tins produce lighter-colored baked goods, while darker muffin tins produce dark-colored baked goods. Gold tins turn out perfectly browned muffins right in the middle of the spectrum. Our favorite, the **OXO Good Grips Non-Stick Pro 12-Cup Muffin Pan**, also has a large rim, which makes it easy to maneuver.

Parchment paper

Lining your baking sheets with parchment paper is a simple way to keep dough from sticking. **King Arthur Flour Parchment Paper 100 Half-Sheets** are conveniently already cut to fit 18 by 13-inch baking sheets.

Digital thermometer

Although the visual cues provided in the recipes are the ultimate indicator of doneness, we also provide temperature ranges in many bread recipes to help guide you about when to pull loaves out of the oven. Use an instant-read thermometer to take the bread's internal temperature, sliding the probe all the way to the center of the loaf. We recommend the **ThermoWorks Thermapen ONE**; the **Thermoworks ThermoPop** is our winning inexpensive model.

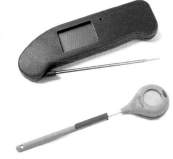

BEYOND THE BASICS

These items are helpful for some of our recipes, including popovers, crackers, pizzas, steamed buns, and some artisan loaves, and are well worth it if you have the space to store them.

Popover pan

To make our Blue Cheese and Chive Popovers with Blue Cheese Butter (page 235), you could use a muffin tin, but for the best rise, go for a popover pan. We like **Chicago Metallic 6-cup Popover Pan, Non-Stick**.

Mini loaf pan

If you want to make our Seeded Pumpkin Crackers (page 154), you can use a regular loaf pan, but mini loaf pans will give you professional-looking results. We like **Chicago Metallic Set of 4 Mini Loaf Pans**.

Cast-iron skillet

A cast-iron skillet creates the crispest crusts on flatbreads and cornbreads. You'll never replace the preseasoned **Lodge Classic Cast-Iron Skillet**. You'll want both the 10-inch and 12-inch pans.

Bamboo steamer

A bamboo steamer is the traditional and best way to make Lop Cheung Bao (page 266). We recommend the sturdy, durable **Juvale 10 Inch Bamboo Steamer with Steel Rings for Cooking**.

Baking stone or steel

A baking stone or steel conducts heat and transfers it evenly and steadily to baked goods, encouraging the development of a thick, crisp, nicely browned bottom crust. Look for a model large enough to accommodate a large pizza. We like The **Original Baking Steel** and the **Nerd Chef Steel Stone Standard ¼"**.

Baking peel

A peel is a wide, paddle-like tool made of wood, metal, or composite that looks like a giant spatula with a long handle that's useful for sliding pizza and free-form breads into and out of a hot oven. Our favorite is the **EXO Polymer Sealed Super Peel**.

Dutch oven

The steam-trapping environment created in a covered Dutch oven can mimic that of an artisan-bakery oven, helping to produce a dramatically open crumb structure and a shiny, crisp crust on breads. The **Le Creuset 7¼-Quart Round French Oven** is the gold standard of Dutch ovens. Our Best Buy is the 7-quart **Cuisinart Chef's Enameled Cast Iron Casserole**.

Proofing basket

Bakers achieve the symmetrical round loaves known as boules by transferring the dough to shallow woven baskets called bannetons (or brotforms) for the last rising step before baking. This helps them keep their shape, and the cloth lining absorbs moisture for a crisper crust. In this book, we achieve the same results by using a 5-quart colander (measuring about 11 inches in diameter and 4 inches deep) that has been lined with a 100-percent-linen dish towel (linen won't leave fibers on the dough). Our favorite colander is **RSVP International Precision Pierced 5 Qt. Colander**.

Garbage bags

Once you've got your dough in the colander, you still need to protect it from the surrounding environment to prevent the top from forming a tough skin (which will hinder rise and cause the interior crumb to be compressed). To protect the proofing loaf, make a simple homemade proofing box by fitting the colander inside a large plastic garbage bag and tying or folding the bag closed.

SPECIALTY EQUIPMENT

For some of the artisan-style bread loaves in Chapter 7, you'll get the most professional results using these tools.

Banneton

If you frequently bake the boule-style loaves found in Chapter 7, you might want to purchase one of these specialized shallow, woven, cloth-lined proofing baskets to use instead of using a towel-lined colander.

Flipping board

To move baguette-style loaves from the couche to the oven, professional bakers use a flipping board. We use the **Baguette Flipping Board** sold by **Breadtopia**. A homemade substitute, made by taping two 16 by 4-inch pieces of heavy cardboard together with packing tape, works equally well.

Couche

To proof baguette-shaped and torpedo-shaped artisan-style breads such as the ones found in Chapter 7, bakers use a couche, made from heavy linen, which keeps the loaf's shape intact and its surface uniformly dry as the dough proofs and rises. Only 100-percent-linen cloths will release the dough without sticking, leaving fibers behind, or tugging. Our favorite is the **San Francisco Baking Institute 18" Linen Canvas (Couche)**. You can substitute 100-percent-linen cotton towels (double them up to get enough structure to support the proofing loaves).

Lava rocks

A few of the recipes in Chapter 7 use lava rocks to create a boulangerie-quality crust. Pouring boiling water over a disposable pan full of preheated lava rocks creates an initial burst of steam; the irregularly shaped rocks absorb and retain heat to continue to produce steam, creating a moist oven environment that helps rustic breads develop a crisp crust. You can find lava rocks, which are also used for gas grills, at many hardware and home-improvement stores.

QUICK BREADS & SCONES

Manchego and Chorizo Muffins

MAKES 12 muffins | **TOTAL TIME** 45 minutes, plus 35 minutes cooling

4 ounces Spanish-style chorizo sausage, cut into ¼-inch pieces

3 cups (15 ounces) all-purpose flour

1 tablespoon baking powder

1 teaspoon table salt

¼ teaspoon pepper

¼ teaspoon cayenne pepper

4 ounces Manchego cheese, cut into ¼-inch pieces

⅓ cup finely chopped jarred roasted red peppers, patted dry

1¼ cups whole milk

¾ cup sour cream

¼ cup minced fresh parsley

3 tablespoons unsalted butter, melted and cooled slightly

1 large egg, plus 1 large egg beaten with 1 teaspoon water

Why This Recipe Works Who says muffins have to be sweet—or reserved only for breakfast? These savory beauties, studded with chunks of smoky Spanish-style chorizo, nutty Manchego cheese, and bright and sweet roasted red peppers, pair just as perfectly with a green salad for lunch as they do with a stew at dinnertime. Parcooking the chorizo in the microwave is an easy way to remove some of its fat, preventing orange streaks in the surrounding crumb of the muffin, and patting extra moisture from the roasted red peppers keeps them from weighing down the fluffy and tender crumb. A generous amount of minced parsley adds grassy, fresh flavors and pops of contrasting color, and a quick brush with egg wash before baking gives the tops of the muffins extra golden color and sheen. The texture of these muffins improves as they cool, so (try to) resist the urge to eat them while they're piping hot. Leftover muffins are excellent toasted; toast halved muffins in a toaster oven or on a baking sheet in a 425-degree oven for 5 to 10 minutes. You can substitute 2 percent low-fat milk for the whole milk, but don't use skim milk.

1 Adjust oven rack to middle position and heat oven to 375 degrees. Spray 12-cup muffin tin with vegetable oil spray. Microwave chorizo on paper towel–lined plate until chorizo starts to release fat, 30 to 60 seconds. Transfer chorizo to clean paper towels and press with paper towels to absorb excess oil.

2 Whisk flour, baking powder, salt, pepper, and cayenne together in large bowl. Using rubber spatula, stir in chorizo, Manchego, and red peppers until coated with flour mixture. Whisk milk, sour cream, parsley, melted butter, and whole egg together in separate bowl. Using rubber spatula, gently fold milk mixture into flour mixture until just combined (batter will be heavy and thick). Using ice cream scoop or large spoon, divide batter equally among prepared muffin cups and smooth tops. Brush muffin tops with egg wash.

3 Bake until muffins are light golden brown and toothpick inserted in center comes out clean, about 20 minutes, rotating muffin tin halfway through baking. Let muffins cool in muffin tin on wire rack for 5 minutes. Remove muffins from muffin tinc and let cool for 30 minutes. Serve.

Corn Muffins with Rosemary and Black Pepper

MAKES 12 muffins | **TOTAL TIME** 45 minutes, plus 10 minutes cooling

Why This Recipe Works While great sweet corn muffins are pretty easy to come by, delicious savory versions are less common. To bake up this golden-brown muffin, you'll use more cornmeal than is typical in the sweet variety: 2 parts cornmeal to 1 part flour. Muffins in general stay moist with the help of liquid, fat, and sugar; here a mix of milk, sour cream, and butter provides the right amount of liquid and fat, and there's just a little sugar (but not enough to make them sweet). To help make up for the moisture that a larger quantity of sugar normally creates, there's a unique mixing technique: Microwave some of the cornmeal with the milk until a thick, polenta-like porridge forms. The starch granules in cornmeal absorb only a limited amount of moisture (less than 30 percent of their own weight) when mixed into a cold liquid. But when the liquid is heated, it weakens the starch granules, so they are able to soak up and "trap" more fluid. Using this technique, you can add more liquid to the muffin batter without turning it too thin to form a domed muffin. Then it's just a matter of whisking in the rest of the ingredients, dividing the batter among the muffin tin cups, and baking. Don't use coarse-ground or white cornmeal here.

2 cups (10 ounces) cornmeal, divided

1 cup (5 ounces) all-purpose flour

1½ teaspoons pepper

1½ teaspoons baking powder

1 teaspoon baking soda

1¼ teaspoons table salt

1¼ cups whole milk

1 cup sour cream

8 tablespoons unsalted butter, melted and cooled slightly

3 tablespoons sugar

2 large eggs, beaten

1 tablespoon minced fresh rosemary

1 Adjust oven rack to upper-middle position and heat oven to 425 degrees. Spray 12-cup muffin tin with vegetable oil spray. Whisk 1½ cups cornmeal, flour, pepper, baking powder, baking soda, and salt together in medium bowl.

2 Combine milk and remaining ½ cup cornmeal in large bowl. Microwave milk-cornmeal mixture for 1½ minutes. Whisk thoroughly and continue to microwave, whisking every 30 seconds, until thickened to batter-like consistency (whisk will leave channel in bottom of bowl that slowly fills in), 1 to 3 minutes. Whisk in sour cream, melted butter, and sugar until combined. Whisk in eggs and rosemary until combined. Using rubber spatula, gently fold cornmeal-flour mixture into milk mixture until thoroughly combined. Using ice cream scoop or large spoon, divide batter equally among prepared muffin cups (about ½ cup batter per cup; batter will mound slightly above rim).

3 Bake until tops are golden brown and toothpick inserted in center comes out clean, 13 to 17 minutes, rotating muffin tin halfway through baking. Let muffins cool in muffin tin on wire rack for 5 minutes. Remove muffins from muffin tin and let cool for 5 minutes. Serve warm.

Variation

Corn Muffins with Cheddar and Scallions

Omit rosemary. Reduce pepper to ½ teaspoon. Add ¼ teaspoon dry mustard and pinch cayenne pepper to cornmeal-flour mixture in step 1. Whisk in 1½ cups shredded cheddar and 5 thinly sliced scallions with eggs.

Jalapeño and Cheddar Scones

MAKES 12 scones | **TOTAL TIME** 45 minutes, plus 40 minutes chilling and cooling

Scones

- 3 cups (15 ounces) all-purpose flour
- 12 tablespoons unsalted butter, cut into ½-inch pieces and chilled, divided
- ¼ cup (1¾ ounces) sugar
- 1 tablespoon baking powder
- 1¼ teaspoons table salt
- 6 ounces extra-sharp cheddar cheese, cut into ½-inch pieces
- ½ cup jarred sliced jalapeños, chopped
- 1 cup whole milk
- 1 large egg plus 1 large yolk

Honey Butter

- 3 tablespoons unsalted butter, melted
- 1½ tablespoons honey

Why This Recipe Works Just like muffins, scones need not be sweet. The bold and spicy mix of jalapeños and cheddar makes these savory scones most welcome as a hearty snack or an accompaniment to chilis or soups. They also make an outstanding breakfast sandwich with bacon, eggs, and (more) cheese. Start by mixing flour, baking powder, a little sugar, and salt with half of the butter in a food processor. The small amount of sugar in the dough balances some of the saltiness from the cheese and also helps with browning and crisping the exterior. Cutting some of the butter in with the flour prevents the flour from absorbing too much liquid later, which would make for dense scones. Then, for flakiness, add the remaining butter, along with some small chunks of extra-sharp cheddar cheese, and process until pea-size pieces form. Transfer this mixture to a bowl, toss in chopped jarred jalapeños, and gently stir in the wet ingredients. Kneading the dough only briefly minimizes gluten formation, which would make the scones tough. After shaping and cutting the scones, chill them and then slide them into the hot oven. Here's the kicker: After they're partially baked, slather the scones with honey butter and continue to bake them until they're a gorgeous golden brown.

1 **For the scones** Line rimmed baking sheet with parchment paper. Combine flour, 6 tablespoons butter, sugar, baking powder, and salt in food processor and process until butter is fully incorporated, about 15 seconds. Add cheddar and remaining 6 tablespoons butter and pulse until cheddar and butter are reduced to pea-size pieces, 10 to 12 pulses. Transfer mixture to large bowl. Stir in jalapeños until coated with flour mixture.

2 Beat milk and egg and yolk together in separate bowl. Make well in center of flour mixture and pour in milk mixture. Gently stir mixture with rubber spatula, scraping from edges of bowl and folding inward, until very shaggy dough forms and some bits of dry flour remain. Do not overmix.

3 Turn out dough onto well-floured counter and knead briefly until dough just comes together, about 3 turns. Using your floured hands and bench scraper, shape dough into 15 by 3-inch rectangle with long side parallel to edge of counter, dusting with extra flour if it begins to stick.

4 Using knife or bench scraper, cut dough crosswise into 6 equal rectangles. Cut each rectangle diagonally into 2 triangles (you should have 12 scones total). Transfer scones to prepared sheet, spacing them about 1 inch apart. Cover sheet with plastic wrap and refrigerate for at least 30 minutes or up to 24 hours. Adjust oven rack to middle position and heat oven to 425 degrees.

5 **For the honey butter** Meanwhile, combine melted butter and honey in small bowl.

6 Uncover scones and bake until lightly golden on top, 15 to 17 minutes, rotating sheet halfway through baking. Remove sheet from oven and brush tops of scones with honey butter. Return sheet to oven and continue to bake until scones are golden brown on top, 3 to 5 minutes. Transfer scones to wire rack and let cool for at least 10 minutes before serving.

Panch Phoran Scones

MAKES 8 scones | **TOTAL TIME** 35 minutes, plus 20 minutes cooling

Why This Recipe Works Simple, rich, and ultratender, cream scones (usually plain or dotted with currants) are a traditional accompaniment to afternoon tea. In this recipe we've kept them easy, rich, and tender (using butter as well as cream), but we've upped the sophistication level significantly by adding a savory spice blend. Panch phoran is an aromatic mixture of whole spices used in Indian and Nepali cooking; the spices are frequently tempered in hot oil or toasted in a dry skillet to intensify their flavors and aromas before they're added to dals and vegetable and meat dishes. This blend (the name translates as "five spices" in Bengali) can bring loads of complexity—the licorice notes of fennel, the allium fragrance of nigella, and the earthy muskiness of cumin and mustard—to baked goods such as these savory scones. Using just a tablespoon of sugar balances the assertive spice flavors without making the scones too sweet. They're a perfect savory companion to tea or an excellent alternative to sweeter breakfast or brunch treats.

1 Adjust oven rack to middle position and heat oven to 425 degrees. Line rimmed baking sheet with parchment paper. Toast mustard seeds, cumin seeds, fennel seeds, nigella seeds, and fenugreek seeds in 10-inch skillet over medium heat until fragrant, 2 to 4 minutes. Transfer seed mixture to plate to cool, about 10 minutes.

2 Pulse flour, baking powder, sugar, and salt in food processor until combined, about 3 pulses. Scatter butter evenly over top and pulse until mixture resembles coarse cornmeal, about 10 pulses; transfer to large bowl. Using rubber spatula, gently fold 1 cup cream and seed mixture into flour mixture until dough begins to form.

3 Turn out dough and any floury bits onto lightly floured counter and knead by hand until rough, slightly sticky ball forms, 5 to 10 seconds. Shape dough into 8-inch round of even thickness, then cut into 8 even wedges. Transfer wedges to prepared sheet, spaced 2 inches apart, and brush tops with remaining 1 tablespoon cream.

4 Bake until scones are light golden brown, 12 to 15 minutes, rotating sheet halfway through baking. Transfer scones to wire rack and let cool for at least 10 minutes. Serve warm or at room temperature.

1½ teaspoons brown mustard seeds

1½ teaspoons cumin seeds

1½ teaspoons fennel seeds

1½ teaspoons nigella seeds

¾ teaspoon fenugreek seeds

2 cups (10 ounces) all-purpose flour

1 tablespoon baking powder

1 tablespoon sugar

½ teaspoon table salt

5 tablespoons unsalted butter, cut into ¼-inch pieces and chilled

1 cup plus 1 tablespoon heavy cream, divided

Feta-Dill Zucchini Bread with Feta Butter

MAKES 1 loaf | TOTAL TIME 1½ hours, plus 2 hours cooling

Zucchini Bread

- 1 **pound zucchini, shredded**
- 2 **cups (10 ounces) all-purpose flour**
- ½ **cup (2¾ ounces) whole-wheat flour**
- 2 **teaspoons baking powder**
- 1 **teaspoon baking soda**
- ¾ **teaspoon pepper**
- ½ **teaspoon table salt**
- 3 **large eggs**
- 7 **tablespoons unsalted butter, melted, divided**
- 6 **ounces feta cheese, crumbled (1½ cups)**
- ⅓ **cup chopped fresh dill**

Feta Butter

- 2 **ounces feta cheese, crumbled (½ cup)**
- 4 **tablespoons unsalted butter, softened**

Why This Recipe Works Anyone lucky enough to have a vegetable garden is always looking for new ways to use up their surplus of zucchini, that notoriously abundant summer squash. But there's no reason why zucchini bread shouldn't be made year-round—and there's no reason why the squash's flavors should be hidden behind lots of sugar in a sweet bread. In this savory spin, the zucchini flavor really shines, complemented by assertively briny feta cheese, grassy fresh dill, and a touch of nutty whole-wheat flour mixed in with the all-purpose flour. If you've ever made zucchini bread, you know that the vegetable releases lots of moisture, so you must squeeze the shredded zucchini in a dish towel before incorporating it. The consistency of this quick-bread batter also helps control moisture, since it's actually more of a dough than a batter. Even after it's squeezed, the zucchini releases sufficient moisture during baking to turn what starts out as a stiff, dry dough into a perfectly tender loaf. Brushing the top with melted butter before baking creates a craggy, crunchy crust that offers textural contrast to the soft interior. To reinforce the feta's flavor, slather the rich feta butter onto slices of this hearty vegetable loaf. The test kitchen's preferred loaf pan measures 8½ by 4½ inches; if you use a 9 by 5-inch loaf pan, start checking for doneness 5 minutes earlier than advised in the recipe.

1 **For the zucchini bread** Adjust oven rack to middle position and heat oven to 350 degrees. Grease 8½ by 4½-inch loaf pan. Place zucchini in center of dish towel. Gather ends together and twist tightly over sink to drain as much liquid as possible.

2 Whisk all-purpose flour, whole-wheat flour, baking powder, baking soda, pepper, and salt together in large bowl. Whisk eggs and 6 tablespoons melted butter together in medium bowl, then stir in zucchini, feta, and dill. Using rubber spatula, gently fold zucchini mixture into flour mixture, then lightly knead batter with your oiled hands or bowl scraper until no dry spots remain (batter will be very thick).

3 Scrape batter into prepared pan, smooth top with rubber spatula, and brush with remaining 1 tablespoon melted butter. Bake until toothpick inserted in center of loaf comes out with few moist crumbs attached, 1 hour 5 minutes to 1¼ hours, rotating pan halfway through baking.

4 **For the feta butter** Meanwhile, using fork, mash feta and butter in bowl until combined. Set aside until ready to serve. (Feta butter can be refrigerated for up to 3 days. Let come to room temperature before serving.)

5 Let bread cool in pan on wire rack for 30 minutes. Remove bread from pan and let cool completely on wire rack, about 1½ hours. Slice and serve with feta butter.

Quick Cheese Bread

MAKES 1 loaf | **TOTAL TIME** 1¼ hours, plus 3¼ hours cooling

3 ounces Parmesan cheese, shredded (1 cup), divided

2½ cups (12½ ounces) all-purpose flour

1 tablespoon baking powder

1 teaspoon table salt

⅛ teaspoon pepper

⅛ teaspoon cayenne pepper

4 ounces extra-sharp cheddar cheese, cut into ½-inch pieces (1 cup)

1 cup whole milk

½ cup sour cream

3 tablespoons unsalted butter, melted

1 large egg

Why This Recipe Works One of the many joys of quick breads—whether savory or sweet—it that it's possible to make something special with just a mixing bowl and a little elbow grease. A case in point is this stellar bread that's rich and hearty, with a bold, cheesy crust. Simply mix the dry ingredients (using plenty of baking powder to lift this heavy mix) and then the wet ingredients (milk and sour cream for moisture and tangy flavor, melted butter, and an egg for structure) separately and then fold them together. Cutting the cheddar cheese into small chunks instead of shredding it makes for pockets of luscious cheesiness throughout the bread. For even more flavor and a crisp, browned crust, coat the bottom of the pan and sprinkle the top of the loaf with shredded Parmesan. You can substitute a mild Asiago, crumbled into ¼- to ½-inch pieces, for the cheddar. Use the large holes of a box grater to shred the Parmesan. The test kitchen's preferred loaf pan measures 8½ by 4½ inches; if you use a 9 by 5-inch loaf pan, start checking for doneness 5 minutes earlier than advised in the recipe. If, when testing the bread for doneness, the skewer comes out with what looks like uncooked batter clinging to it, try again in a different, but still central, spot. (A skewer hitting a pocket of cheese may give a false indication.) The texture of this bread improves as it cools, so resist the urge to slice the loaf when it's still warm.

1 Adjust oven rack to middle position and heat oven to 350 degrees. Grease 8½ by 4½-inch loaf pan, then sprinkle ½ cup Parmesan evenly in bottom of pan.

2 Whisk flour, baking powder, salt, pepper, and cayenne together in large bowl. Stir in cheddar, breaking up clumps, until cheddar is coated with flour mixture. Whisk milk, sour cream, melted butter, and egg together in second bowl.

3 Gently fold milk mixture into flour mixture using rubber spatula until just combined (batter will be heavy and thick; do not overmix).

4 Transfer batter to prepared pan and smooth top. Sprinkle remaining ½ cup Parmesan evenly over surface. Bake loaf until golden brown and skewer inserted in center comes out clean, 45 to 50 minutes, rotating pan halfway through baking.

5 Let bread cool in pan on wire rack for 15 minutes. Remove bread from pan and let cool completely on wire rack, about 3 hours. Slice and serve.

Variation

Quick Cheese Bread with Bacon, Onion, and Gruyère

Omit butter. Cook 5 slices bacon, cut into ½-inch pieces, in 10-inch nonstick skillet over medium heat until crispy, 5 to 7 minutes. Using slotted spoon, transfer bacon to paper towel–lined plate. Pour off all but 3 tablespoons fat from skillet. Add ½ cup finely chopped onion to fat left in skillet and cook over medium heat until softened, about 3 minutes; set aside. Substitute Gruyère for cheddar. Add bacon and onion to flour mixture with Gruyère.

Whole-Wheat Soda Bread with Walnuts and Cacao Nibs

SERVES 6 to 8 | **TOTAL TIME** 1¼ hours, plus 1 hour cooling

Why This Recipe Works What you usually find in the United States under the moniker "Irish soda bread" is a fairly sweet white bread made with butter, eggs, raisins, and caraway seeds. While delicious, it's not actually Irish (nor does it belong in a savory baking book). Traditional Irish soda bread, made with whole-wheat flour and without raisins, butter, or eggs, is the simple, savory counterpart to its sweeter Americanized cousin. It's craggy, hearty, and full of whole-wheat nuttiness, perfect for slathering with salted butter and enjoying alongside a cup of tea or pairing with soup or a wedge of cheese. Our rendition is true to this whole-wheat, not-sweet Irish ethos. Adding both wheat bran and wheat germ to the flour mixture creates complex flavor and a rustic, coarse texture. We still take some decidedly American liberties with the mix-ins, though, studding the bread with rich toasted walnuts and crunchy cacao nibs. The cacao nibs may give you pause (after all, what's chocolate doing in a savory baking book?), but the nibs provide the intense flavor of chocolate without any sweetness. If you need any more convincing, the simplicity of this bread will seal the deal: The dough comes together in just one bowl and requires a bare minimum of shaping before it's put in a cake pan and popped into the oven.

2 cups (11 ounces) whole-wheat flour

1 cup (5 ounces) all-purpose flour

1 cup wheat bran

¼ cup wheat germ

2 teaspoons sugar

1½ teaspoons baking powder

1½ teaspoons baking soda

1 teaspoon table salt

2 cups buttermilk

1 cup walnuts, toasted and chopped

6 tablespoons cacao nibs

1   Adjust oven rack to middle position and heat oven to 375 degrees. Lightly grease 8-inch round cake pan. Whisk whole-wheat flour, all-purpose flour, wheat bran, wheat germ, sugar, baking powder, baking soda, and salt together in large bowl.

2   Stir in buttermilk, walnuts, and cacao nibs until all flour is moistened and dough forms soft, ragged mass. Transfer dough to counter and gently shape into 6-inch round (surface will be craggy). Using serrated knife, cut ½-inch-deep cross about 5 inches long on top of loaf. Transfer to prepared pan. Bake until loaf is lightly browned and center registers 185 degrees, 50 minutes to 1 hour, rotating pan halfway through baking.

3   Remove bread from pan and let cool on wire rack for at least 1 hour. Slice and serve.

Garlicky Olive Bread

SERVES 8 to 10 | **TOTAL TIME** 50 minutes, plus 30 minutes cooling

Why This Recipe Works Fresh basil, olives, Parmesan, and garlic bring a sophisticated Italian flavor to this supersimple quick bread that's fast enough for a weeknight. You'll build flavor by making a potent garlic oil, which permeates the baked bread with garlic essence. A combination of whole milk and sour cream in the batter gives this bread extra richness and a lovely moist crumb. A generous amount of briny kalamata olives, halved to help them evenly disperse throughout the batter, offers juicy pops of flavor-packed texture. Shredded Parmesan both in the batter and generously sprinkled on top of the batter before baking contributes to the savory flavor profile while creating a crisp, golden top crust. The cast-iron skillet crisps the bottom and sides of the crust beautifully, producing an evenly browned loaf that is almost "fried" around the edges where the rich batter sizzles against the hot pan. Use the large holes of a box grater to shred the Parmesan. Do not substitute finely grated or pregrated Parmesan here. We prefer to use a well-seasoned cast-iron skillet in this recipe, but you can use an ovensafe 10-inch skillet instead.

2½ cups (12½ ounces) all-purpose flour

¼ cup chopped fresh basil

1 tablespoon baking powder

½ teaspoon table salt

4½ ounces Parmesan cheese, shredded (1½ cups), divided

1 cup whole milk

½ cup sour cream

1 large egg

5 tablespoons extra-virgin olive oil

3 garlic cloves, minced

1 cup pitted kalamata olives, halved

1 Adjust oven rack to middle position and heat oven to 450 degrees. Grease 10-inch cast-iron skillet.

2 Whisk flour, basil, baking powder, and salt together in large bowl. Stir in 1 cup Parmesan, breaking up any clumps, until coated with flour mixture. In separate bowl, whisk milk, sour cream, and egg until smooth.

3 Cook oil and garlic in 10-inch cast-iron skillet over medium heat until fragrant, about 3 minutes. Pour oil mixture into milk mixture and whisk to combine. Using rubber spatula, gently fold milk mixture into flour mixture until just combined, then fold in olives (batter will be heavy and thick; do not overmix).

4 Scrape batter into prepared skillet and smooth top. Sprinkle with remaining ½ cup Parmesan. Transfer skillet to oven and bake until loaf is golden brown and toothpick inserted in center comes out clean, 20 to 25 minutes, rotating skillet halfway through baking.

5 Using pot holders, transfer skillet to wire rack and let loaf cool for 10 minutes. Being careful of hot skillet handle, remove loaf from skillet, return to rack, and let cool for at least 20 minutes. Slice and serve.

Fresh Corn Cornbread

SERVES 8 to 10 | **TOTAL TIME** 1 hour, plus 25 minutes cooling

1⅓ cups (6⅔ ounces) coarse-ground cornmeal

1 cup (5 ounces) all-purpose flour

2 tablespoons sugar

1½ teaspoons baking powder

¼ teaspoon baking soda

1¼ teaspoons table salt

2 cups corn (2 to 3 ears corn)

6 tablespoons unsalted butter, cut into 1-tablespoon pieces, divided

1 cup buttermilk

2 large eggs plus 1 large yolk

Why This Recipe Works Cornbread falls into two primary styles: the sweeter, cakey Northern type and the more savory, crusty type more often found in Southern kitchens. Each has its die-hard fans, with good reasons. But typically, neither uses fresh corn—and that's where this recipe stands out. It's packed with 2 whole cups of fresh kernels for a quick bread bursting with fresh vegetable flavor. Putting it together is easy, though not quite as simple as just tossing fresh-cut kernels into the batter. Since fresh kernels are full of moisture, if you just add them whole, the kernels will turn tough as their moisture leaches out, and the crumb of the cornbread will end up riddled with unpleasant gummy pockets. Instead, you'll puree fresh kernels and then reduce the mixture on the stove until it thickens and turns a deep yellow, transforming into a concentrated corn "butter." The base of the cornbread uses slightly more cornmeal than flour and abandons the usual fine-ground cornmeal in favor of the coarse-ground type, which contains both the hull and the oil-rich germ of the corn kernel. The upshot: a more rustic texture and fuller flavor. Just a little sugar helps hold on to the liquid in the batter to keep the bread moist. We prefer to use a well-seasoned cast-iron skillet in this recipe, but you can use an ovensafe 10-inch skillet instead. Alternatively, in step 4, you can add 1 tablespoon of butter to a 9-inch round cake pan and place it in the oven until the butter melts, about 3 minutes.

1 Adjust oven rack to middle position and heat oven to 400 degrees. Whisk cornmeal, flour, sugar, baking powder, baking soda, and salt together in large bowl; set aside.

2 Process corn in blender until very smooth, about 2 minutes. Transfer to medium saucepan (you should have about 1½ cups). Cook puree over medium heat, stirring constantly, until very thick, deep yellow, and reduced to ¾ cup, 5 to 8 minutes.

3 Off heat, whisk in 5 tablespoons butter until melted. Whisk in buttermilk until incorporated. Whisk in eggs and yolk until incorporated. Using rubber spatula, gently fold corn mixture into cornmeal mixture until just combined.

4 Melt remaining 1 tablespoon butter in 10-inch cast-iron skillet over medium heat. Scrape batter into hot skillet and spread into even layer. Transfer skillet to oven and bake until cornbread is golden brown and toothpick inserted in center comes out clean, 23 to 28 minutes.

5 Using pot holders, transfer skillet to wire rack and let cornbread cool for 5 minutes. Being careful of hot skillet handle, remove cornbread from skillet, return to rack, and let cool for 20 minutes. Cut into wedges and serve.

Sweet Potato Cornbread

SERVES 8 to 10 | **TOTAL TIME** 1 hour, plus 1 hour cooling

Why This Recipe Works Sweet potato cornbread marries two favorite Southern ingredients to take cornbread in a colorful and flavorful new direction. This rendition, with its browned crust and brilliant orange-gold interior, is in a league of its own. As you might expect, introducing dense, moist sweet potatoes to cornbread affects the bread's texture, so they need to be handled properly to keep the bread light. Precooking and mashing the potatoes is a must, of course. Using a drier cooking method helps keep their moisture under control while intensifying the vegetable's flavor, and microwaving proves to be the easiest and most efficient way to achieve this. For corn flavor that stands up to the spuds, you'll use 1½ cups cornmeal to just ½ cup all-purpose flour for a light yet sturdy bread. The ¼ cup of brown sugar helps the bread develop deeper color and enhances the delicate sweet potato flavor without making the bread too sweet. Light or dark brown sugar works equally well in this recipe. We prefer to use a well-seasoned cast-iron skillet in this recipe, but you can use an ovensafe 10-inch nonstick skillet instead. Alternatively, in step 3, you can add 1 tablespoon of butter to a 9-inch round cake pan and place it in the oven until the butter melts, about 3 minutes.

1½ pounds sweet potatoes, unpeeled

½ cup whole milk

8 tablespoons unsalted butter, melted, plus 1 tablespoon unsalted butter

4 large eggs

1½ cups (7½ ounces) cornmeal

½ cup (2½ ounces) all-purpose flour

¼ cup packed (1¾ ounces) brown sugar

1 tablespoon baking powder

½ teaspoon baking soda

1¾ teaspoons table salt

1 Adjust oven rack to middle position and heat oven to 425 degrees. Prick potatoes all over with fork. Microwave on large plate until potatoes are very soft and surfaces are slightly wet, 10 to 15 minutes, flipping every 5 minutes. Immediately slice potatoes in half to release steam.

2 When potatoes are cool enough to handle, scoop flesh into bowl and mash until smooth (you should have about 1¾ cups); discard skins. Whisk in milk, melted butter, and eggs. Whisk cornmeal, flour, sugar, baking powder, baking soda, and salt together in separate large bowl. Using rubber spatula, gently fold potato mixture into cornmeal mixture until just combined.

3 Melt remaining 1 tablespoon butter in 10-inch cast-iron skillet over medium heat. Scrape batter into hot skillet and spread into even layer. Transfer skillet to oven and bake until cornbread is golden brown and toothpick inserted in center comes out clean, 25 to 30 minutes.

4 Using pot holders, transfer skillet to wire rack and let cornbread cool for 1 hour. Slide cornbread onto cutting board. Cut into wedges and serve.

Broccoli Cheese Cornbread

SERVES 8 to 10 | **TOTAL TIME** 1¼ hours, plus 1 hour cooling

6 tablespoons unsalted butter

1 onion, chopped fine

3 garlic cloves, minced

1 cup (5 ounces) cornmeal

1 cup (5 ounces) all-purpose flour

2 tablespoons sugar

1 tablespoon baking powder

¾ teaspoon table salt

8 ounces (1 cup) cottage cheese

3 large eggs

¼ cup whole milk

1 tablespoon hot sauce

12 ounces frozen broccoli florets, thawed, pressed dry with paper towels, and chopped coarse

8 ounces extra-sharp cheddar cheese, shredded (2 cups), divided

Why This Recipe Works To the uninitiated, the idea of putting broccoli in cornbread may sound like some kind of parental ploy to get a child to eat more vegetables. But you'll change your mind after one bite of this especially moist bread, which is sort of like a cross between cornbread and spoonbread. It's substantial enough to serve as a light lunch on its own and versatile enough to pair with any soup, stew, or chili. Frozen broccoli florets, thawed and pressed dry to remove excess water, add plenty of broccoli flavor without the extra time involved in trimming, blanching, draining, and chopping fresh broccoli. You'll use only a little bit of milk in the batter, letting most of the moisture come from the key ingredient: cottage cheese. Baking the cornbread right in the skillet you use to sauté the onion and garlic gives the bread a crusty browned bottom and sides. (Yes, garlic is unconventional for cornbread, but it nicely underlines the savory qualities of this version.) For a little extra pizzazz, stir in some shredded extra-sharp cheddar and a tablespoon of hot sauce, and sprinkle more cheddar on top before baking for a crisp top crust. Press the thawed broccoli as dry as possible before stirring it into the batter.

1 Adjust oven rack to middle position and heat oven to 375 degrees. Melt butter in 10-inch ovensafe nonstick skillet over medium-high heat. Add onion and cook until softened, about 5 minutes. Stir in garlic and cook until fragrant, about 30 seconds. Remove from heat; set aside.

2 Whisk cornmeal, flour, sugar, baking powder, and salt together in large bowl. Whisk cottage cheese, eggs, milk, and hot sauce together in separate bowl. Using rubber spatula, gently fold cottage cheese mixture into cornmeal mixture until just combined. Stir broccoli, 1½ cups cheddar, and onion mixture into batter until thoroughly combined (batter will be thick).

3 Scrape batter into now-empty skillet and spread into even layer. Sprinkle remaining ½ cup cheddar evenly over top. Transfer skillet to oven and bake until cornbread is golden brown and toothpick inserted in center comes out clean, 40 to 45 minutes.

4 Using pot holders, transfer skillet to wire rack and let cornbread cool for 1 hour. Slide cornbread onto cutting board. Cut into wedges and serve.

Savory Corn Spoonbread

SERVES 6 | **TOTAL TIME** 1½ hours, plus 15 minutes resting

Why This Recipe Works Spoonbread's history in the United States dates back to the 19th-century South, when batters of cornmeal and water were baked, fried, or griddled to make humble dishes such as johnnycakes and corn dodgers. With the later addition of milk and eggs, these dishes evolved into rich, spoonable custards called spoonbreads. Some later versions elevated the dish (literally) with baking soda, but the most refined recipes folded beaten egg whites into the batter, turning the spoonbread into a fluffy soufflé-like dish with a golden crust and a silky interior. And that's what we have here: This soufflé-style spoonbread is made by cooking cornmeal in milk, cooling the mixture, stirring in egg yolks, and then folding in beaten egg whites and baking. Soaking the cornmeal in milk for a few minutes before simmering it will eliminate any grittiness, and beating the egg whites with cream of tartar makes for a more stable foam and higher rise. To really intensify the corn flavor, you'll sauté the fresh kernels in butter, steep the cooked corn in milk, and then puree the mixture before combining it with the cornmeal. The silky mixture that comes out of the blender tastes like cream of corn soup—it's good enough to eat on its own! This "corn milk" creates a light, creamy texture and amazing corn taste that sets this spoonbread far apart from its workaday ancestors. You can substitute frozen corn, thawed and patted dry, for fresh.

1. Adjust oven rack to middle position and heat oven to 400 degrees. Grease 1½-quart soufflé dish or 8-inch square baking dish. Whisk cornmeal and ¾ cup milk together in bowl; set aside.

2. Melt butter in Dutch oven over medium-high heat. Add corn and cook until beginning to brown, about 3 minutes. Stir in sugar, salt, cayenne, and remaining 2 cups milk and bring to boil. Cover pot and let sit off heat for 15 minutes.

3. Transfer warm corn mixture to blender and process until smooth, about 2 minutes. Return to pot and bring to boil over medium-high heat. Reduce heat to low; add cornmeal mixture; and cook, whisking constantly, until thickened, 2 to 3 minutes. Transfer to large bowl and let cool completely, about 20 minutes. Once mixture is cool, whisk in egg yolks until combined.

4. Using stand mixer fitted with whisk attachment, whip egg whites and cream of tartar on medium-low speed until foamy, about 1 minute. Increase speed to medium-high and whip until stiff peaks form, 3 to 4 minutes. Whisk one-third of whites into corn mixture, then, using rubber spatula, gently fold in remaining whites until combined. Scrape batter into prepared dish and transfer to oven. Reduce oven temperature to 350 degrees and bake until spoonbread is golden brown and has risen above rim of dish, about 45 minutes. Serve immediately.

1 cup (5 ounces) cornmeal

2¾ cups whole milk, divided

4 tablespoons unsalted butter

2 cups corn (2 to 3 ears corn)

1 teaspoon sugar

1 teaspoon table salt

⅛ teaspoon cayenne pepper

3 large eggs, separated

¼ teaspoon cream of tartar

Sun-Dried Tomato, Garlic, and Za'atar Biscuits

MAKES 12 biscuits | **TOTAL TIME** 45 minutes

3 cups (15 ounces) all-purpose flour

1 tablespoon baking powder

¼ teaspoon baking soda

2 teaspoons sugar

1¼ teaspoons table salt

½ teaspoon pepper

2 cups heavy cream

3 garlic cloves, minced

1 cup oil-packed sun-dried tomatoes, rinsed, patted dry, and chopped fine, plus 4 teaspoons sun-dried tomato oil

3 teaspoons za'atar

Why This Recipe Works These flavor-packed cream drop biscuits are a dream to make: no cutting butter into the dry ingredients and no rolling out required. They're also a dream to eat. Fluffy, tender, and savory with umami-packed sun-dried tomatoes, pungent garlic, and earthy za'atar, they are just as at home on the brunch table alongside eggs as they are at dinner with a soup or stew. Their ease of preparation comes from an innovative technique that upends the traditional method for cream biscuits. Instead of adding cold liquid to the dry ingredients, you'll heat the cream first. The warm liquid makes the dough soft enough to be droppable, and using heavy cream ensures that you're adding just the right amount of both moisture and fat to create a tall, fluffy biscuit. Another advantage of heating the cream: You can infuse it with flavor, as we do by adding a few cloves of minced garlic to the cream before microwaving it. Brushing a bit of the sun-dried tomato oil on the biscuits before generously sprinkling them with za'atar reinforces the tomato flavor and also helps with browning. We prefer our Za'atar (page 179), but you can use store-bought, if you prefer.

1 Adjust oven rack to upper-middle position and heat oven to 450 degrees. Line rimmed baking sheet with parchment paper. Whisk flour, baking powder, baking soda, sugar, salt, and pepper together in large bowl. Microwave cream and garlic in separate bowl until just warmed to body temperature (95 to 100 degrees), 60 to 90 seconds, stirring halfway through microwaving. Using rubber spatula, gently fold cream mixture and tomatoes into flour mixture until soft, uniform dough forms.

2 Using greased ⅓-cup dry measuring cup, drop 12 level scoops of batter about 1 inch apart on prepared sheet. Brush biscuit tops with tomato oil, then sprinkle evenly with za'atar.

3 Bake until biscuits are starting to turn light golden brown, 14 to 18 minutes, rotating sheet halfway through baking. Transfer biscuits to wire rack and let cool for 5 minutes. Serve warm or at room temperature.

Rosemary and Olive Drop Biscuits

MAKES 12 biscuits | **TOTAL TIME** 45 minutes

2 cups (10 ounces) all-purpose flour

¼ cup pitted kalamata olives, chopped fine

2 teaspoons baking powder

½ teaspoon baking soda

1½ teaspoons minced fresh rosemary

1 teaspoon sugar

¾ teaspoon table salt

1 cup buttermilk, chilled

8 tablespoons unsalted butter, melted and cooled, plus 2 tablespoons unsalted butter

Why This Recipe Works In exchange for the ease of simple mix-and-drop biscuits, you often have to give up the great flakiness that comes with rolled biscuits, for which you must carefully incorporate solid fat into dry ingredients, add liquid, knead it all into a dough, and then roll the dough and cut the biscuits. These tangy, herbal drop biscuits, however, offer a similar flakiness to rolled biscuits, with none of the work. Our usual procedure for making drop biscuit dough is to melt butter, add the slightly cooled melted butter to room-temperature liquid ingredients, and stir that mixture into the dry ingredients. One time we got tired of waiting for the butter and liquid ingredients to reach the proper temperatures and went ahead and combined them. The too-warm butter clumped in the too-cold buttermilk, and no matter how much we whisked, the butter chunks wouldn't dissipate. So we stirred the lumpy mixture into the dry ingredients and baked the biscuits anyway. Amazingly, they came out higher and fluffier than those we'd been making with the ingredients at the "correct" temperatures. The chunks of butter melted in the oven, giving off steam that created rise and flakiness. Be sure to chill the buttermilk so that the melted butter clumps when the two are combined. These biscuits are best eaten still warm from the oven.

1 Adjust oven rack to middle position and heat oven to 475 degrees. Line rimmed baking sheet with parchment paper. Whisk flour, olives, baking powder, baking soda, rosemary, sugar, and salt together in large bowl. Stir buttermilk and melted butter in 2-cup liquid measuring cup until butter forms clumps.

2 Using rubber spatula, gently fold buttermilk mixture into flour mixture until just combined. Using greased ¼-cup dry measuring cup, drop 12 level scoops of batter 1½ inches apart on prepared sheet.

3 Bake until tops are golden brown, 12 to 14 minutes, rotating sheet halfway through baking. Melt remaining 2 tablespoons butter and brush on biscuit tops. Transfer biscuits to wire rack and let cool for 5 minutes before serving.

Variations

Mustard and Dill Drop Biscuits

Omit olives and rosemary. Add 1 tablespoon minced fresh dill to flour mixture and 2 tablespoons whole-grain mustard to buttermilk mixture.

Mixed Herb Drop Biscuits

Omit olives and rosemary. Add 2 tablespoons chopped fresh basil, 2 tablespoons minced fresh parsley, and 2 teaspoons minced fresh oregano to flour mixture.

Cheddar and Pimento Drop Biscuits

Omit olives and rosemary. Add ¾ cup shredded extra-sharp cheddar and ¼ cup finely chopped jarred pimentos to flour mixture.

Cornmeal and Black Pepper Drop Biscuits

MAKES 12 biscuits | **TOTAL TIME** 45 minutes

Why This Recipe Works Drop biscuits come together so quickly that they deserve to be a go-to weeknight staple, so here's another rendition for you to add to your rotation. As with the Rosemary and Olive Drop Biscuits (page 50), this dependable drop biscuit recipe produces tender biscuits using the inventive trick of stirring together cold buttermilk and melted butter until the butter clumps. These clumps of butter create steam during baking, and that steam (along with two leaveners) helps the biscuits rise to light and airy heights. This rustic version introduces cornmeal to the buttermilk batter. To enhance the cornmeal's natural sweetness, you'll add a little more sugar to this biscuit than the previous one while still keeping these little breads firmly in the savory category. A healthy amount of black pepper brings a warm pungency to the biscuits. The cornmeal batter is also a solid canvas for experimentation, ready to welcome flavorful stir-ins to suit a range of tastes. Chopped green chiles add Southwestern flair to one variation, and minced fresh sage makes a biscuit reminiscent of the festive flavors of stuffing. Be sure to chill the buttermilk so that the melted butter clumps when the two are combined. These biscuits are best eaten still warm from the oven.

1½ cups (7½ ounces) all-purpose flour

½ cup (2½ ounces) coarse-ground cornmeal

3 tablespoons sugar

2 teaspoons baking powder

½ teaspoon baking soda

1½ teaspoons coarsely ground pepper

¾ teaspoon table salt

1 cup buttermilk, chilled

8 tablespoons unsalted butter, melted and cooled, plus 2 tablespoons unsalted butter

1 Adjust oven rack to middle position and heat oven to 450 degrees. Line rimmed baking sheet with parchment paper. Whisk flour, cornmeal, sugar, baking powder, baking soda, pepper, and salt together in large bowl. Stir buttermilk and melted butter in 2-cup liquid measuring cup until butter forms clumps.

2 Using rubber spatula, gently fold buttermilk mixture into flour mixture until just combined. Using greased ¼-cup dry measuring cup, drop 12 level scoops of batter 1½ inches apart on prepared sheet.

3 Bake until tops are golden brown, 12 to 14 minutes, rotating sheet halfway through baking. Melt remaining 2 tablespoons butter and brush on biscuit tops. Transfer biscuits to wire rack and let cool for 5 minutes before serving.

Variations

Cornmeal and Green Chile Drop Biscuits
Omit pepper. Add ¼ cup canned chopped green chiles, patted dry, to flour mixture.

Cornmeal and Sage Drop Biscuits
Omit pepper. Add 1 tablespoon minced fresh sage to flour mixture.

Potato Biscuits with Chives

MAKES 12 biscuits | **TOTAL TIME** 55 minutes

2½ cups (12½ ounces)
    all-purpose flour

¾   cup (1¾ ounces) plain instant
    mashed potato flakes

⅓   cup chopped fresh chives

4   teaspoons baking powder

½   teaspoon baking soda

1   tablespoon sugar

1   teaspoon table salt

8   tablespoons unsalted butter,
    cut into ½-inch pieces and
    chilled, plus 2 tablespoons
    unsalted butter

4   tablespoons vegetable
    shortening, cut into ½-inch
    pieces and chilled

1¼ cups buttermilk, chilled

Why This Recipe Works Mashed potato biscuits might raise questions in your mind. If using leftover potatoes, what kind should you have, and what if they included butter or cream in the mash? If using freshly mashed potatoes, doesn't that labor take the ease out of biscuit making? And can potato biscuits turn out light and tender? Well, this recipe has all the answers. Adding potato to baked goods can produce a superlatively tender texture by interrupting the protein structure that forms when the proteins in wheat flour mix with liquid and link together. And there's an easy way to reap the benefits of potato starch without worrying about the moisture of the potatoes wreaking havoc: using instant mashed potato flakes. Dehydrated potato flakes have all the starch of whole potatoes but are devoid of water and thus more consistent than fresh spuds. Best of all, they're perfect for a speedy biscuit timeline. To compensate for the fact that potato starch has no gluten, you'll add a little more baking powder than usual, which helps these rolled-and-stamped biscuits rise tender and tall. The mix-ins are all classic potato flavor partners. We like the texture of these biscuits when they're made with both butter and shortening, but if you prefer to use all butter, omit the shortening and use 12 tablespoons of chilled butter in step 1. These biscuits are best eaten still warm from the oven.

1 Adjust oven rack to middle position and heat oven to 450 degrees. Line rimmed baking sheet with parchment paper. Process flour, potato flakes, chives, baking powder, baking soda, sugar, and salt in food processor until combined, about 15 seconds. Add chilled butter and shortening and pulse until mixture resembles coarse crumbs, 7 to 9 pulses.

2 Transfer flour mixture to large bowl. Stir in buttermilk with rubber spatula until combined, turning and pressing dough until no dry flour remains. Turn out dough onto lightly floured counter and knead briefly, 8 to 10 turns, to form smooth, cohesive ball. Roll out dough into 9-inch circle, about ¾ inch thick.

3 Using floured 2½-inch round cutter, stamp out 8 or 9 biscuits and arrange upside down on prepared sheet. Gather dough scraps and gently pat into ¾-inch-thick circle. Stamp out 3 or 4 biscuits and transfer to sheet.

4 Bake until biscuits begin to rise, about 5 minutes, then rotate sheet and reduce oven temperature to 400 degrees. Continue to bake until golden brown, 10 to 12 minutes. Melt remaining 2 tablespoons butter and brush on biscuit tops. Transfer biscuits to wire rack and let cool for 5 minutes before serving.

Variations

Potato Biscuits with Cheddar and Scallions

Omit chives. Process ¾ cup shredded extra-sharp cheddar and 4 thinly sliced scallions with flour.

Potato Biscuits with Bacon

Omit chives. Cook 6 slices bacon in 12-inch skillet over medium heat until crispy, 7 to 9 minutes; transfer to paper towel–lined plate. Crumble bacon when cool enough to handle. Process crumbled bacon with flour.

Gruyère and Herb Buttermilk Biscuits

MAKES 9 biscuits | **TOTAL TIME** 1¼ hours, plus 45 minutes chilling and cooling

3 cups (15 ounces) all-purpose flour

2 tablespoons sugar

2 tablespoons minced fresh parsley

2 tablespoons minced fresh chives

4 teaspoons baking powder

½ teaspoon baking soda

1 tablespoon minced fresh sage, plus 9 whole leaves

¾ teaspoon table salt

16 tablespoons (2 sticks) unsalted butter, frozen for 30 minutes

1¼ cups buttermilk, chilled

4 ounces Gruyère cheese, shredded (1⅓ cups), room temperature

Flake sea salt

Why This Recipe Works Crisp and crunchy on the outside, tender and as light as air on the inside, with hundreds of flaky layers flavored with cheese and fresh herbs, these are the most indulgent biscuits you'll ever eat. They rise up tall and true with strata that peel apart like sheets of buttery paper, thanks to our simplified lamination process. Rather than create a challenging butter "block" in the classic French style, coat frozen butter sticks in the flour mixture and then grate them directly into the flour. After adding buttermilk, take the dough through a sequence of rolling and folding to create the multitude of flaky layers. Using butter only (rather than incorporating shortening) ensures the right amount of hydration in the dough (butter contains water, whereas shortening does not). More hydration means a better gluten structure—the better to support all those layers. We prefer King Arthur brand all-purpose flour in this recipe, but other brands will work. Use sticks of butter. In hot or humid environments, chill the flour mixture, grater, and bowl before use. The dough will start out very crumbly and dry in pockets but will be smooth by the end of the folding process, so don't be tempted to add extra buttermilk. Flour the counter and the top of the dough as needed to prevent sticking, but be careful not to incorporate large pockets of flour into the dough when folding. You can use cheddar cheese in place of the Gruyère, if you prefer. For even more decadence, serve the biscuits with Herb Butter (page 5).

1 Line rimmed baking sheet with parchment paper. Whisk flour, sugar, parsley, chives, baking powder, baking soda, minced sage, and table salt together in large bowl. Coat sticks of butter in flour mixture, then grate 7 tablespoons from each stick on large holes of box grater directly into flour mixture. Toss gently to combine. Set aside remaining 2 tablespoons butter.

2 Using rubber spatula, gently fold buttermilk into flour mixture until just combined (dough will look dry). Transfer dough to liberally floured counter. Dust surface of dough with flour; using your floured hands, press dough into rough 7-inch square.

3 Roll dough into 12 by 9-inch rectangle with short side parallel to counter edge. Starting at bottom of dough and using bench scraper or metal spatula, fold into thirds like business letter. Press top of dough firmly to seal folds. Using bench scraper, turn dough 90 degrees clockwise. Repeat rolling into 12 by 9-inch rectangle, folding into thirds, and turning clockwise 3 more times, for a total of 4 sets of folds, sprinkling with extra flour as needed.

4 Roll out dough into 12 by 9-inch rectangle, then sprinkle with Gruyère, leaving bottom 4 inches and ½-inch border around top and sides clear of cheese. Using bench scraper, fold cheese-free bottom third of dough up over center, then fold center up over top, tucking any cheese that may have escaped back underneath top fold. Press to seal, then roll dough into 8½-inch square, about 1 inch thick. Transfer dough to prepared sheet, cover with plastic wrap, and refrigerate for 30 minutes. Adjust oven rack to upper-middle position and heat oven to 400 degrees.

5 Transfer dough to lightly floured cutting board. Using sharp, floured chef's knife, trim ¼ inch of dough from each side of square; discard. Cut remaining dough into 9 squares, flouring knife after each cut. Arrange biscuits at least 1 inch apart on now-empty sheet and place 1 sage leaf on top of each biscuit. Melt reserved 2 tablespoons butter, then brush sage leaves and tops of biscuits with melted butter.

6 Bake until tops are golden brown, 22 to 25 minutes, rotating sheet halfway through baking. Transfer biscuits to wire rack, sprinkle with sea salt, and let cool for 15 minutes before serving.

PASTRIES & PIES

Gochujang and Cheddar Pinwheels

SERVES 6 to 8 (Makes 18 pinwheels) | **TOTAL TIME** 40 minutes, plus 1 hour chilling

Why This Recipe Works Gochujang, a fermented soybean and red chile paste, lends spiciness, sweetness, and umami savoriness to many essential Korean dishes. But that magic combination of flavors also pairs well with less traditional ingredients, including cheese. While cheese has a shorter history in Korean cuisine than gochujang does, the combo does exist, including in one version of a popular street food called tteokbokki that features rice cakes in a spicy gochujang sauce topped with melted cheese. Taking a flavor cue from that, this easy and savory finger food pairs gochujang with sharp cheddar cheese, fresh chives, and sesame seeds to create a wildly delicious filling for puff pastry pinwheels. Sliced into thin rounds and baked, these two-bite swirls are crispy and cheesy and burst with umami, heat, nuttiness, and a touch of sweetness. They're so good that one bite will confirm that you'll return to this combination again and again. Be sure to use gochujang paste, which comes in a tub, instead of gochujang sauce, which comes in a bottle and has a different consistency. Convenient store-bought puff pastry works wonderfully for these quick pinwheels. See page 13 for more information on thawing frozen puff pastry.

1. Dust counter lightly with flour. Unfold puff pastry and roll into 10-inch square. Spread gochujang evenly over entire surface of pastry, leaving ½-inch border along top edge. Sprinkle evenly with cheddar, 2 tablespoons chives, and sesame seeds. Gently roll rolling pin over toppings to press into pastry.

2. Starting at edge of pastry closest to you, roll into tight log and pinch seam to seal. Wrap in plastic wrap and refrigerate until firm, about 1 hour. (Rolled pastry log can be refrigerated for up to 2 days before slicing and baking.)

3. Adjust oven rack to middle position and heat oven to 400 degrees. Line rimmed baking sheet with parchment paper and set inside second rimmed baking sheet. Using sharp serrated or slicing knife, trim ends of log, then slice into ½-inch-thick rounds (you should have 18 rounds) and space them about 1 inch apart on prepared sheet.

4. Brush pastries with egg wash and bake until golden brown and crispy, 14 to 16 minutes, rotating sheet halfway through baking. Transfer pinwheels to wire rack, sprinkle with remaining 1 tablespoon chives, and let cool for 5 minutes. Serve warm or at room temperature.

1 (9½ by 9-inch) sheet puff pastry, thawed

2 tablespoons gochujang paste

2 ounces sharp cheddar cheese, shredded (½ cup)

3 tablespoons minced fresh chives, divided

1 tablespoon sesame seeds

1 large egg beaten with 1 teaspoon water

Ham and Cheese Palmiers

SERVES 10 to 12 (Makes 34 palmiers) | TOTAL TIME 45 minutes, plus 1 hour chilling

1 (9½ by 9-inch) sheet puff pastry, thawed

2 tablespoons Dijon mustard

2 teaspoons minced fresh thyme

4 ounces thinly sliced deli ham

2 ounces Parmesan cheese, grated (1 cup)

Why This Recipe Works French palmiers have a superlative effort-to-outcome ratio; in other words, they are extremely simple to make, but they look extremely impressive—and they taste even better than they look. They're made from puff pastry that's rolled up and sliced into thin pieces that are said to resemble elephant ears (which they are sometimes called), palm leaves, or butterflies. The simplest and probably most familiar version of all is a sweet one, with granulated sugar sprinkled on the pastry before it's rolled up. For this savory twist, you'll brush a sheet of puff pastry with Dijon mustard, sprinkle it with fresh thyme, layer it with thinly sliced ham and Parmesan cheese, and roll it up into the signature double log. (For shaping instructions, see page 66.) To finish the pastries, simply slice the log and bake the palmiers until they turn golden brown and crispy. Store-bought puff pastry keeps these palmiers superquick to make. See page 13 for more information on thawing frozen puff pastry.

1 Dust counter lightly with flour. Unfold puff pastry and roll into 12-inch square. Brush evenly with mustard, sprinkle with thyme, lay ham evenly over top (to edges of pastry), and sprinkle with Parmesan. Roll up both sides of pastry until they meet in middle. Wrap pastry log in plastic wrap and refrigerate until firm, about 1 hour. (Rolled pastry log can be refrigerated for up to 2 days before slicing and baking.)

2 Adjust oven rack to middle position and heat oven to 400 degrees. Line rimmed baking sheet with parchment paper. Using sharp serrated or slicing knife, trim ends of log, then slice into ⅓-inch-thick pieces (you should have 34 pieces) and space them about 1 inch apart on prepared sheet.

3 Bake until golden brown and crispy, about 25 minutes, rotating sheet halfway through baking. Transfer palmiers to wire rack and let cool for 5 minutes. Serve warm or at room temperature.

Goat Cheese, Sun-Dried Tomato, and Urfa Danish

SERVES 8 (Makes 8 Danish) | **TOTAL TIME** 1 hour, plus 10 minutes cooling

8 ounces goat cheese

2 ounces cream cheese

1 large egg yolk, plus 1 large egg beaten with 1 teaspoon water

¼ teaspoon table salt

⅛ teaspoon pepper

1¼ cup oil-packed sun-dried tomatoes, chopped coarse, plus 2 tablespoons sun-dried tomato oil

4 teaspoons Urfa pepper, divided

2 garlic cloves, minced

2 (9½ by 9-inch) sheets puff pastry, thawed

1 teaspoon minced fresh thyme

Why This Recipe Works Danish pastries aren't just decadently sweet breakfast or brunch treats. Savory versions are unexpected, irresistible, and so much fun to make. For a savory cheese Danish to transcend breakfast, swap the more traditional cream cheese filling for a base of tangy goat cheese (but not entirely: adding a small amount of cream cheese makes the filling soft enough to spread easily but firm enough to hold its shape). Umami-rich sun-dried tomatoes complement the tart goat cheese when nestled together in the rich, flaky puff pastry. Mixing in some of the tomatoes' oil, garlic, and Urfa pepper (a dried Turkish chile pepper with a smoky, raisiny flavor) creates a supercharged topping that becomes pleasingly jammy in texture after it bakes. A final sprinkle of Urfa enhances the flavor of the lightly charred tomatoes with its unique sweet smokiness. If you can't find Urfa pepper, you can substitute ground dried Aleppo pepper or smoked paprika or forgo the pepper altogether. This recipe produces square-shaped Danish. If you'd like to try your hand at a fancier Danish shape, see page 66 for ideas and instructions. See page 13 for more information on thawing frozen puff pastry.

1 Adjust oven rack to middle position and heat oven to 400 degrees. Line 2 rimmed baking sheets with parchment paper and set aside. Process goat cheese, cream cheese, egg yolk, salt, and pepper in food processor until smooth, about 2 minutes, scraping down sides of bowl as needed; transfer to bowl. Stir tomatoes and oil, 1 tablespoon Urfa, and garlic together in second bowl.

2 Dust counter lightly with flour. Working with 1 piece puff pastry at a time, unfold pastry and roll into 10-inch square. Cut into four 5-inch squares. Space pastry squares evenly on prepared sheets. Divide goat cheese mixture evenly among pastry squares, mounding about 2 level tablespoons in center of each square and spreading into 3½-inch circle. Divide tomato mixture evenly over each goat cheese circle and sprinkle with thyme. Brush edges of puff pastry with egg wash.

3 Bake Danish, 1 sheet at a time, until edges are deep golden brown, 18 to 20 minutes, rotating sheet halfway through baking. Let Danish cool on wire rack for 10 minutes, then sprinkle with remaining 1 teaspoon Urfa. Serve warm or at room temperature.

Shaping Techniques for Pastry

Puff pastry is easy to work with and lends itself to many different shapes. After you try the Ham and Cheese Palmiers on page 62 and the simple square shape for the Goat Cheese, Sun-Dried Tomato, and Urfa Danish on page 64, have some fun with the crossover and diamond twist shapes here. The turnover fillings on pages 68–71 can also be used as Danish fillings.

PALMIERS

1 Layer desired fillings evenly over puff pastry sheet.

2 Tightly roll up pastry from opposite sides until they meet in middle.

3 After chilling, slice pastry into ⅓-inch-thick pieces using sharp serrated or slicing knife.

CROSSOVER DANISH

1 Cut each 10-inch square sheet puff pastry into four 5-inch squares. Space pastry squares evenly on 2 parchment paper–lined rimmed baking sheets. Divide base evenly among pastry squares, mounding about 2 level tablespoons in center of each square and spreading into 4 by 1½-inch oval, corner to corner. Divide topping evenly over base.

2 Brush edges of 1 pastry square with egg wash. Fold 1 corner of square over filling so pastry nearly covers filling. Brush pastry with egg wash.

3 Fold opposite corner of square over filling so corners overlap evenly, pressing gently to adhere. Brush pastry with egg wash. Repeat with remaining pastry squares.

DIAMOND TWIST DANISH

1 Cut each 10-inch square sheet puff pastry into four 5-inch squares. Space pastry squares evenly on 2 parchment paper–lined rimmed baking sheets. Fold 1 pastry square in half diagonally to form triangle.

2 Using paring knife, mark ½ inch from each edge along long side of triangle. Starting on right short side, cut straight line through both layers of pastry, maintaining ½-inch border, ending cut 1 inch from top of triangle where short sides meet. Repeat on left short side (2 cuts should never meet).

3 Unfold triangle.

4 Grasping 1 cut side of square, fold border over top of center and align edge flush with outside of center square.

5 Fold second cut side over top of center and align edge flush with opposite side of center square. Repeat with remaining pastry squares.

6 Divide base evenly among centers of each Danish (about 2 tablespoons each), spreading to cover in even layer, then divide topping evenly over each base. Brush edges with egg wash.

Beet and Caramelized Onion Turnovers with Beet-Yogurt Sauce

SERVES 8 (Makes 8 turnovers) | **TOTAL TIME** 1¾ hours, plus 15 minutes cooling

Beet-Yogurt Sauce

- ¾ cup plain yogurt
- 2 ounces shredded raw or cooked beets (½ cup)
- ¼ teaspoon table salt
- ⅛ teaspoon pepper

Turnovers

- 2 tablespoons vegetable oil
- 2 onions, chopped fine
- ¼ teaspoon table salt
- ¼ teaspoon pepper
- 10 ounces beets, trimmed, peeled, and shredded
- 1 tablespoon minced fresh thyme
- 1 tablespoon Dijon mustard
- 2 (9½ by 9-inch) sheets puff pastry, thawed
- 1 large egg beaten with 1 teaspoon water
- 5 teaspoons everything bagel seasoning

Why This Recipe Works It's rare that the humble beet gets to be the star of a dish. And you might not think of it as a baking ingredient at all. In these turnovers, however, this sweet, earthy root vegetable's true colors and flavors shine through—times two. And you barely have to precook the beets before using them. Add shredded raw beets to the skillet with caramelized onions just to wilt them, and then mix in woodsy fresh thyme and tangy mustard to create a gorgeous ruby-colored filling, which you'll use to stuff rectangular pockets of puff pastry. Sprinkle some everything bagel seasoning on top for an attractive finish; its toasted garlic and onion flakes echo the savory onions in the filling (use store-bought seasoning or make your own using the recipe on page 162). The turnovers bake up flaky and crisp, with a tender filling that almost fools your eyes into thinking it's a sweet jam when you cut into them. For a contrast in textures and temperatures, use additional shredded beets to make a tangy pink yogurt sauce that's as pretty as it is delicious and perfect for dunking or dolloping. Use the large holes of a box grater or a food processor fitted with a shredding disk to shred the beets. You can substitute 8 ounces cooked beets for the 10 ounces raw beets in the filling. See page 13 for more information on thawing frozen puff pastry.

1 **For the beet-yogurt sauce** Combine all ingredients in bowl. Refrigerate until ready to serve.

2 **For the turnovers** Adjust oven rack to middle position and heat oven to 400 degrees. Line rimmed baking sheet with parchment paper. Heat oil in 12-inch nonstick skillet over medium heat until shimmering. Add onions, salt, and pepper and cook, stirring often, until onions soften and are dark brown, about 20 minutes, adjusting heat if onions begin to scorch. Stir in beets and cook until just wilted, 2 to 3 minutes. Stir in thyme and cook until fragrant, about 30 seconds. Transfer beet mixture to bowl; stir in mustard; and let cool completely, about 20 minutes.

3 Dust counter lightly with flour. Working with 1 piece puff pastry at a time, unfold pastry and roll into 10-inch square. Cut into four 5-inch squares. Space pastry squares evenly on prepared sheet. Divide beet filling evenly among pastry squares, mounding about 3 tablespoons in center of each square, then brush edges of pastry with egg wash (reserve remaining egg wash). Fold pastry over filling to form rectangle. Using fork, crimp edges of pastry to seal. Cut two 1-inch slits on top of each turnover (do not cut through filling). (Unbaked turnovers can be frozen in airtight container for up to 1 month.)

4 Brush tops of turnovers with remaining egg wash and sprinkle with everything bagel seasoning. Bake turnovers until well browned, 22 to 25 minutes, rotating sheet halfway through baking. Let turnovers cool on wire rack for 15 minutes. Serve warm or at room temperature with sauce.

Butternut Squash, Apple, and Gruyère Turnovers

SERVES 8 (Makes 8 turnovers) | **TOTAL TIME** 1 hour, plus 15 minutes cooling

Why This Recipe Works Sweet butternut squash, tart apples, and earthy fresh sage are classic fall flavors, but crisp autumn air isn't required to enjoy these truly savory yet oh-so-slightly-sweet puff pastry turnovers. First, bloom the minced sage in some butter while simultaneously browning the butter to create a bold and deeply flavored infusion. Set that aside while you sauté the squash, apple, and shallot; adding some brown sugar to the vegetables and fruit promotes deeper, faster caramelization. A splash of cider vinegar ensures that the flavor is well balanced and not too sweet. Cooking the filling before assembling the turnovers also evaporates excess moisture from the produce, preventing the filling from leaking and turning the pastry soggy. Then, combine that luscious sage browned butter with the cooked filling; let it cool; and mix in shredded Gruyère for a nutty, melty binder. Sprinkling more Gruyère on top of the turnovers before baking adds a second level of cheesy goodness as it toasts in the oven and melts into the pastry. We prefer Granny Smith apples here, but you can substitute McIntosh. You can substitute cheddar cheese for Gruyère. See page 13 for more information on thawing frozen puff pastry.

1 Adjust oven rack to middle position and heat oven to 400 degrees. Line rimmed baking sheet with parchment paper. Melt 2 tablespoons butter in 12-inch skillet over medium-high heat. Add sage and continue to cook, swirling skillet occasionally, until butter is dark golden brown and has nutty aroma, about 2 minutes. Transfer browned butter mixture to large bowl; set aside.

2 Melt remaining 2 tablespoons butter in now-empty skillet over medium heat. Add squash, apple, shallot, sugar, salt, and pepper; cover; and cook, stirring occasionally, until squash and apple are softened and lightly browned, 13 to 16 minutes. Off heat, stir in vinegar and, using potato masher, mash half of mixture until mostly smooth. Add to bowl with browned butter mixture and stir to combine. Let cool completely, about 30 minutes, then stir in ¾ cup Gruyère. (Filling can be refrigerated for up to 24 hours.)

3 Dust counter lightly with flour. Working with 1 piece puff pastry at a time, unfold pastry and roll into 10-inch square. Cut into four 5-inch squares. Space pastry squares evenly on prepared sheet. Divide squash mixture evenly among pastry squares, mounding about 3 tablespoons in center of each square, then brush edges of pastry with egg wash (reserve remaining egg wash). Fold pastry over filling to form triangle. Using fork, crimp edges of pastry to seal. Cut two 1-inch slits on top of each turnover (do not cut through filling). (Unbaked turnovers can be frozen in airtight container for up to 1 month.)

4 Brush tops of turnovers with remaining egg wash and sprinkle with remaining ½ cup Gruyère. Bake until well browned, 22 to 25 minutes, rotating sheet halfway through baking. Let turnovers cool on wire rack for 15 minutes. Serve warm or at room temperature.

4 tablespoons unsalted butter, divided

1 tablespoon minced fresh sage

10 ounces butternut squash, peeled, seeded, and cut into ½-inch pieces (2 cups)

1–2 Granny Smith apples, peeled, cored, and cut into ½-inch pieces (2 cups)

1 shallot, minced

3 tablespoons packed brown sugar

½ teaspoon table salt

¼ teaspoon pepper

1 teaspoon cider vinegar

5 ounces Gruyère cheese, shredded (1¼ cups), divided

2 (9½ by 9-inch) sheets puff pastry, thawed

1 large egg beaten with 1 teaspoon water

Smoked Salmon and Chive Mille-Feuille

SERVES 4 to 8 (Makes 8 mille-feuille) | **TOTAL TIME** 1½ hours, plus 1½ hours chilling and cooling

Why This Recipe Works "Mille-feuille" translates from the French as "thousand leaves." This evocatively named pastry is classically sweet, involving a delicate stack of thin, crispy layers of puff pastry interspersed with decadent pastry cream. Here's our savory surprise, swapping the pastry cream for an airy, tangy blend of cream cheese, chives, and smoked salmon. The key to the shatteringly crisp puff pastry sheet lies in compressing it during baking: Within the sheet are hundreds of dough layers (created through a repetitive process of folds and turns) that puff up during baking when the butter in the dough melts and creates steam. Placing a baking sheet on top of the pastry while baking prevents the puffing and creates a thin sheet of crispy layers. For an elegant but simple presentation, create a layered stack by piping the salmon-chive cream cheese on the pastry base; topping it with a slice of smoked salmon and another layer of puff pastry; and decorating the top with more cream cheese, chives, and capers. If you don't have a pastry bag, you can use a zipper-lock bag with the corner snipped off. See page 13 for more information on thawing frozen puff pastry.

1 (9½ by 9-inch) sheet puff pastry, thawed

6 ounces smoked salmon (2 ounces chopped, 4 ounces whole)

2 tablespoons plus 2 teaspoons minced fresh chives, divided

1 tablespoon grated lemon zest

6 ounces cream cheese, softened

3 tablespoons heavy cream

1 tablespoon capers, rinsed

1 Dust counter lightly with flour. Unfold puff pastry and roll into 16 by 11-inch rectangle. Transfer to parchment paper–lined rimmed baking sheet and refrigerate until firm, about 1 hour.

2 Adjust oven rack to middle position and heat oven to 350 degrees. Prick pastry all over with fork, then cover with second sheet of parchment and set second rimmed baking sheet in first, compressing pastry. Bake until golden and crisp, 35 to 55 minutes, rotating sheet halfway through baking. Let cool completely between sheets on wire rack, about 30 minutes.

3 Process chopped salmon, 2 tablespoons chives, and lemon zest in food processor until finely chopped, about 10 seconds, scraping down sides of bowl as needed. Add cream cheese and cream and process until smooth, about 20 seconds, scraping down sides of bowl as needed. Season with salt and pepper to taste. (Salmon–cream cheese mixture can be refrigerated for up to 3 days.) Transfer salmon–cream cheese mixture to pastry bag fitted with round or star tip.

4 Transfer pastry to cutting board. Using serrated knife, trim to 13 by 9-inch rectangle. Cut pastry crosswise into four 3¼ by 9-inch rectangles, then cut each quarter crosswise into four 3¼ by 2¼-inch rectangles (you should have sixteen 3¼ by 2¼-inch rectangles).

5 Pipe half of salmon–cream cheese mixture decoratively over top of 8 pastry rectangles and top with whole salmon. Align remaining rectangles directly over topped rectangles. Pipe remaining salmon–cream cheese mixture decoratively over tops, then sprinkle with capers and remaining 2 teaspoons chives. Serve.

Spinach Pie for a Crowd

SERVES 10 to 12　　|　　**TOTAL TIME** 1½ hours, plus 1 hour cooling

2　tablespoons unsalted butter

2　shallots, minced

4　garlic cloves, minced

¼　cup all-purpose flour

1½　cups whole milk

3　ounces Parmesan cheese, grated (1½ cups)

1¼　pounds frozen whole-leaf spinach, thawed and squeezed dry

1　teaspoon table salt

½　teaspoon pepper

2　(9½ by 9-inch) sheets puff pastry, thawed, divided

1　large egg beaten with 1 teaspoon water

Why This Recipe Works Creamy, buttery, savory, and thoroughly satisfying, this easy spinach pie has showstopping good looks that will inspire you to plan your next party. Albanian spinach pies feature a more subtle, creamier spinach filling than Greek spanakopita does, and this recipe is closer to the former. The filling starts with a simple béchamel sauce boosted with shallots and garlic and enriched with a generous dose of Parmesan cheese. Frozen spinach works beautifully here and is easier to wrangle than the huge masses of fresh leaves that would be required. Assembling the pie on a baking sheet has a twofold advantage: It lets you make a large enough pie to serve a crowd, and it also allows plenty of space and airflow in the oven to crisp up the puff pastry on all sides. Scoring the top sheet of pastry before baking makes it easy to cut the pie into individual portions after it's baked. To dry the spinach after you thaw it, place the leaves in the center of a clean dish towel, gather the ends of the towel, and twist firmly. Letting the filling cool completely before assembling the pie ensures a crisp crust. See page 13 for more information on thawing frozen puff pastry.

1 Melt butter in medium saucepan over medium heat. Add shallots and garlic and cook until softened, about 2 minutes. Stir in flour and cook until golden, about 30 seconds. Slowly whisk in milk, scraping up any browned bits and smoothing out any lumps, and bring to simmer. Cook, stirring constantly, until thickened, about 3 minutes.

2 Off heat, stir in Parmesan until melted. Stir in spinach, salt, and pepper until combined. Transfer spinach mixture to bowl and let cool completely, about 30 minutes.

3 Adjust oven rack to lower-middle position and heat oven to 400 degrees. Grease rimmed baking sheet. Dust counter lightly with flour. Unfold 1 puff pastry sheet and roll into 14 by 10-inch rectangle. Loosely roll pastry around rolling pin and unroll it onto prepared sheet. Spread spinach mixture evenly over pastry, leaving ½-inch border. Brush border with egg wash (reserve remaining egg wash).

4 Dust counter lightly with flour. Unfold remaining pastry sheet and roll into 14 by 10-inch rectangle. Loosely roll pastry around rolling pin and unroll it over filling. Press edges of top and bottom sheets together to seal. Roll edges inward and use your fingers to crimp edges. Using sharp knife, cut top pastry sheet into 24 squares. Brush top pastry sheet evenly with remaining egg wash.

5 Bake until crust is golden brown, 30 to 35 minutes. Transfer sheet to wire rack and let pie cool completely, about 30 minutes. Transfer pie to cutting board and cut along guidelines. Serve.

Deep-Dish Quiche Lorraine

SERVES 8 to 10 | **TOTAL TIME** 3¼ hours, plus 3 hours 50 minutes chilling, freezing, and cooling

Crust

- 1¾ cups (8¾ ounces) all-purpose flour
- ½ teaspoon table salt
- 12 tablespoons unsalted butter, cut into ½-inch pieces and chilled
- 4–6 tablespoons ice water
- 3 tablespoons sour cream
- 1 large egg white, lightly beaten

Custard Filling

- 8 slices thick-cut bacon, cut into ¼-inch pieces
- 2 onions, chopped fine
- 1½ cups whole milk, divided
- 1½ tablespoons cornstarch
- 8 large eggs plus 1 large yolk
- 1½ cups heavy cream
- ½ teaspoon table salt
- ¼ teaspoon pepper
- ⅛ teaspoon ground nutmeg
- ⅛ teaspoon cayenne pepper
- 6 ounces Gruyère cheese, shredded (1½ cups)

Why This Recipe Works This is the ultimate quiche, with a supremely flaky, thick crust that's rich with butter cradling a satiny, creamy custard that's laced with hearty, satisfying fillings. You can get there with one simple tool you're bound to have in your kitchen: a cake pan. A 9-inch cake pan with 2-inch-tall straight sides is the ideal vessel to fit all these wonderful ingredients without overflowing. For extra insurance against the crust leaking or tearing (common problems when making deep-dish quiche), you'll use three tricks. First, line the pan with a foil sling, which will be invaluable when it's time to extract the finished quiche from the pan. Second, roll out a 15-inch round of dough and drape a generous amount of the dough up and over the sides of the pan. This, along with plenty of pie weights (3 to 4 cups), helps anchor the crust in place, preventing it from sagging or shrinking during blind baking. (If any part of the crust cracks or forms holes during blind baking, you can repair it with reserved dough scraps.) And third, glaze the baked crust with an egg white wash before adding the filling, which helps seal any would-be cracks. If you make the variation with mozzarella, use supermarket-style block mozzarella, not fresh. It is important to use ice water in the dough to prevent it from overheating in the food processor.

1 **For the crust** Process flour and salt in food processor until combined, about 3 seconds. Add butter and pulse until butter is size of large peas, about 10 pulses.

2 Combine ¼ cup ice water and sour cream in small bowl. Add half of sour cream mixture to flour mixture; pulse 3 times. Repeat with remaining sour cream mixture. Pinch dough with your fingers; if dough is floury and dry and does not hold together, add 1 to 2 tablespoons more ice water and pulse until dough forms large clumps and no dry flour remains, 3 to 5 pulses.

3 Turn out dough onto counter and flatten into 6-inch disk; wrap disk in plastic wrap and refrigerate until firm but not hard, 1 to 2 hours. (Dough can be refrigerated for up to 24 hours; let sit at room temperature for 15 minutes before rolling.)

4 Cut two 16-inch lengths of aluminum foil. Arrange foil pieces, perpendicular to each other, in 9-inch round cake pan, pushing them into corners and up sides of pan; press overhang against outside of pan. Spray foil lightly with vegetable oil spray.

5 Roll dough on generously floured counter into 15-inch circle about ¼ inch thick. Roll dough loosely around rolling pin and unroll into prepared pan. Working around circumference, ease dough into pan by gently lifting edge of dough with your hand while pressing into pan bottom with your other hand. Trim any dough that extends more than 1 inch over edge of pan. Patch any cracks or holes with dough scraps as needed. Refrigerate any remaining dough scraps. Refrigerate dough-lined pan until dough is firm, about 30 minutes, then freeze for 20 minutes.

6 Adjust oven rack to lower-middle position and heat oven to 375 degrees. Line dough with foil or parchment paper and fill completely with pie weights, gently pressing weights into corners of dough. Bake on rimmed baking sheet until exposed edges of dough are beginning to brown but bottom is still light in color, 30 to 40 minutes. Carefully remove foil and pie weights. If any new holes or cracks have formed in dough, patch with reserved scraps. Return dough to oven and bake until bottom is golden brown, 15 to 20 minutes. Remove crust from oven and brush interior with egg white. Set aside while preparing filling. Reduce oven temperature to 350 degrees.

7 **For the custard filling** Cook bacon in 12-inch skillet over medium heat until crispy, 5 to 7 minutes. Transfer bacon to paper towel–lined plate and pour off all but 2 table-spoons fat from skillet. Return skillet to medium heat; add onions; and cook, stirring frequently, until softened and lightly browned, about 12 minutes. Set aside to cool slightly.

8 Whisk 3 tablespoons milk and cornstarch together in large bowl to dissolve cornstarch. Whisk in eggs and yolk, cream, salt, pepper, nutmeg, cayenne, and remaining milk until smooth.

9 Scatter onions, bacon, and Gruyère evenly over crust. Gently pour custard mixture over filling. Using fork, push filling ingredients down into custard, then drag fork gently through custard to dislodge air bubbles. Gently tap pan on counter to dislodge any remaining air bubbles.

10 Bake until top of quiche is lightly browned, toothpick inserted in center comes out clean, and center registers 170 degrees, 1¼ to 1½ hours. Transfer to wire rack and let cool to touch, about 2 hours.

11 When ready to serve, use sharp paring knife to remove any crust that extends beyond edge of pan. Lift foil overhang from sides of pan and remove quiche from pan; gently slide thin-bladed spatula between quiche and foil to loosen, then slide quiche onto serving platter. Cut into wedges and serve warm or at room temperature.

Variations

Deep-Dish Quiche with Leeks and Blue Cheese

Omit bacon and onions. Melt 1 tablespoon unsalted butter in 12-inch skillet over medium heat. Add 4 large leeks, white and light green parts only, halved lengthwise, sliced ¼ inch thick, and washed thoroughly; cook until softened, 10 to 12 minutes. Increase heat to medium-high; continue to cook, stirring constantly, until leeks are beginning to brown, about 5 minutes. Transfer leeks to plate lined with triple layer of paper towels; press with double layer of paper towels to remove excess moisture. Increase salt in filling to 1 teaspoon. Substitute crumbled blue cheese for Gruyère; scatter blue cheese and leeks evenly over crust before adding custard. Reduce baking time to 1 to 1¼ hours.

Deep-Dish Quiche with Sausage, Broccoli Rabe, and Mozzarella

Omit bacon and onions. Cook 8 ounces hot or sweet Italian sausage, casings removed, in 12-inch skillet over medium heat, breaking sausage into ½-inch pieces, until no longer pink, 5 to 7 minutes. Transfer to paper towel–lined plate and pour off all but 2 tablespoons fat from skillet. Return skillet to medium heat; add 8 ounces broccoli rabe, trimmed and cut into ½-inch pieces; and cook until slightly softened, about 6 minutes. Transfer broccoli rabe to plate lined with triple layer of paper towels; press with double layer of paper towels to remove excess moisture. Increase salt in filling to 1 tea-spoon. Substitute shredded whole-milk block mozzarella for Gruyère; scatter mozzarella, sausage, and broccoli rabe evenly over crust before adding custard. Reduce baking time to 1 to 1¼ hours.

Pizza Chiena

SERVES 10 to 12 | **TOTAL TIME** 1¾ hours, plus 5¼ hours chilling and cooling

Dough

- 3 large eggs
- 3 tablespoons ice water
- 3 cups (15 ounces) all-purpose flour
- 1¼ teaspoons table salt
- 6 tablespoons unsalted butter, cut into ½-inch pieces and chilled
- 6 tablespoons vegetable shortening, cut into ½-inch pieces and chilled

Filling

- 1 tablespoon extra-virgin olive oil
- 12 ounces broccoli rabe, trimmed and chopped
- 8 ounces hot Italian sausage, casings removed
- ¼ teaspoon table salt
- 2 garlic cloves, minced
- 1 pound (2 cups) whole-milk ricotta cheese
- 4 ounces Pecorino Romano cheese, grated (2 cups)
- 2 large eggs
- 1 teaspoon pepper
- 8 ounces thinly sliced aged provolone cheese, divided
- 6 ounces thinly sliced hot capicola

- 1 large egg beaten with 1 teaspoon water

Why This Recipe Works Pizza chiena goes by many names: pizza ripiena, pizza rustica, torta pasqualina, and torta rustica, to name a few. Whatever you prefer to call it, one thing is certain: It's a very large, very rich, and very delicious meat and cheese pie in a pastry crust that's celebrated in Italian American homes during Easter. It's typically eaten at room temperature or chilled, so it's perfect to make ahead if you've got a crowd coming over. To stand up to the considerable fillings, this crust is reinforced with eggs, and after it's mixed in the food processor, the dough is kneaded to develop gluten and make it sturdy. As for the filling, many different meats can be included. We use hot capicola and Italian sausage; their subtle heat offsets the creaminess of the eggs and cheese. For the cheese, aged provolone and salty Pecorino Romano make a great pair, while creamy ricotta mixed with eggs holds it all together. Sautéed broccoli rabe adds freshness and a welcome touch of bitterness to further counter all the richness. Use a cake pan that's at least 2 inches deep. If your pan is light-colored, increase the baking time to 45 to 50 minutes. It is important to use ice water in the dough to prevent it from overheating in the food processor.

1 **For the dough** Whisk eggs and ice water together in bowl; set aside. Process flour and salt in food processor until combined, about 3 seconds. Scatter butter and shortening over top and pulse until only pea-size pieces remain, about 10 pulses. Add egg mixture and pulse until dough ball forms, about 20 pulses. Turn out dough onto lightly floured counter and knead until smooth and elastic, about 20 turns. Divide dough into one 1-pound ball and one 10-ounce ball (roughly two-thirds and one-third) and form each into 6-inch disk. Wrap disks tightly in plastic wrap and refrigerate for 1 hour. (Dough can be refrigerated for up to 24 hours.)

2 **For the filling** Heat oil in 12-inch nonstick skillet over medium-high heat until shimmering. Add broccoli rabe, sausage, and salt and cook, breaking up sausage with wooden spoon, until sausage is cooked through and broccoli rabe is tender, 5 to 7 minutes. Add garlic and cook until fragrant, about 30 seconds. Transfer to plate and let cool completely, about 15 minutes. Whisk ricotta, Pecorino, eggs, and pepper together in large bowl.

3 Adjust oven rack to middle position and heat oven to 375 degrees. Grease dark-colored 9-inch round cake pan. Roll 1-pound disk of dough into 14-inch circle on generously floured counter. Loosely roll dough around rolling pin and gently unroll it onto prepared pan, letting excess dough hang over edge. Ease dough into pan by gently lifting and supporting edge of dough with your hand while pressing into pan bottom and sides with your other hand. Leave overhanging dough in place.

4 Shingle half of provolone in bottom of dough-lined pan. Spread ricotta mixture over provolone. Scatter sausage mixture over ricotta mixture and press lightly into even layer. Shingle capicola over sausage mixture, followed by remaining provolone.

5 Roll remaining disk of dough into 10-inch circle on generously floured counter. Brush overhanging dough of bottom crust with egg wash (reserve remaining egg wash). Loosely roll 10-inch dough circle around rolling pin and gently unroll it over filling. Trim overhanging top and bottom doughs to ½ inch beyond lip of pan and pinch firmly together. Fold overhanging dough inward so folded edge is flush with edge of pan. Crimp folded edge of dough evenly around edge of pan with tines of fork.

6 Brush top of pie liberally with remaining egg wash. Using paring knife, cut eight 1-inch vents in top of pie in circular pattern. Bake until filling registers 150 degrees halfway between edge and center of pie and crust is golden brown, 35 to 40 minutes. Transfer pie to wire rack and let cool for at least 4 hours. Remove pie from pan, slice into wedges, and serve.

ASSEMBLING PIZZA CHIENA

1 Scatter sausage mixture over ricotta mixture and press into even layer. Shingle capicola over sausage mixture, then shingle remaining provolone over capicola.

2 After trimming top and bottom crusts and pinching them together, fold pinched dough inward until edge is flush with edge of pan.

3 Crimp folded edge evenly with tines of fork. Brush top of pie with egg wash and cut eight 1-inch vents in top of pie in circular pattern.

Chicken Pot Pie with Savory Crumble Topping

SERVES 6 | **TOTAL TIME** 1¾ hours

Crumble Topping

- 2 cups (10 ounces) all-purpose flour
- 2 teaspoons baking powder
- ¾ teaspoon table salt
- ½ teaspoon pepper
- ⅛ teaspoon cayenne pepper
- 6 tablespoons unsalted butter, cut into ½-inch pieces and chilled
- 1 ounce Parmesan cheese, finely grated (½ cup)
- ¾ cup plus 2 tablespoons heavy cream

Chicken and Filling

- 1½ pounds boneless, skinless chicken breasts and/or thighs
- 3 cups chicken broth
- 2 tablespoons vegetable oil, divided
- 1 onion, chopped fine
- 3 carrots, peeled and sliced ¼ inch thick
- 2 small celery ribs, chopped fine
- ¼ teaspoon table salt
- ¼ teaspoon pepper
- 10 ounces cremini mushrooms, trimmed and sliced thin
- 1 teaspoon soy sauce
- 1 teaspoon tomato paste
- 4 tablespoons unsalted butter
- ½ cup all-purpose flour
- 1 cup whole milk
- 2 teaspoons lemon juice
- 3 tablespoons minced fresh parsley, divided
- ¾ cup frozen baby peas

Why This Recipe Works Bursting with juicy chicken and tender vegetables, this easy pie gets to the table in just over 90 minutes—a rare feat for a from-scratch pot pie. It helps that there's no pastry to wrangle. Nor is there a whole bird to cut up: Here you poach boneless chicken breasts and/or thighs in broth and use the poaching liquid as the base of the velvety sauce. Sautéed mushrooms, soy sauce, and tomato paste create a deeply caramelized fond to boost the sauce's flavor. The other vegetables— a medley of onion, carrots, and celery—are sautéed while the chicken rests. In place of the traditional pastry crust, a crisp, buttery crumble is an unexpected (and easy) delight. It's plenty flavorful, thanks to additions of grated Parmesan and cream. To increase the crunch factor, bake the crumble separately from the filling, and then scatter it over the top and slide the dish into the oven until it's bubbling and fragrant. The soy sauce and tomato paste are secret weapons here, deepening the filling's flavor without conveying their distinct tastes, so don't omit them. When making the topping, do not substitute milk or half-and-half for the heavy cream.

1. **For the crumble topping** Adjust oven rack to upper-middle position and heat oven to 450 degrees. Combine flour, baking powder, salt, pepper, and cayenne in large bowl. Sprinkle butter over top of flour. Using your fingers, rub butter into flour mixture until it resembles coarse cornmeal. Stir in Parmesan. Add cream and stir until just combined. Crumble mixture into irregularly shaped pieces ranging from ½ to ¾ inch onto parchment paper–lined rimmed baking sheet. Bake until fragrant and starting to brown, 10 to 13 minutes. Set aside. (Crumble topping can be stored in zipper-lock bag at room temperature for up to 24 hours. Press out air before sealing bag.)

2. **For the chicken and filling** Bring chicken and broth to simmer in covered Dutch oven over medium heat. Cook until breasts register 160 degrees and/or thighs register 175 degrees, 8 to 12 minutes. Transfer chicken to cutting board, let cool slightly, then shred into bite-size pieces using 2 forks. Transfer chicken to large bowl. Pour broth through fine-mesh strainer into liquid measuring cup and reserve.

3. Heat 1 tablespoon oil in now-empty pot over medium heat until shimmering. Add onion, carrots, celery, salt, and pepper; cover and cook, stirring occasionally, until just tender, 5 to 7 minutes. Transfer vegetables to bowl with chicken.

4. Heat remaining 1 tablespoon oil in now-empty pot over medium heat until shimmering. Add mushrooms; cover and cook, stirring occasionally, until mushrooms have released their juice, about 5 minutes. Uncover and stir in soy sauce and tomato paste. Increase heat to medium-high and cook, stirring frequently, until liquid has evaporated, mushrooms are well browned, and dark fond begins to form on bottom of pot, about 5 minutes. Transfer mushrooms to bowl with chicken and vegetables.

5 Melt butter in now-empty pot over medium heat. Add flour and cook, stirring constantly, until golden, about 1 minute. Slowly whisk in reserved chicken broth and milk, scraping up any browned bits and smoothing out any lumps. Bring to simmer and cook until sauce thickens, about 1 minute. Season with salt and pepper to taste. Off heat, stir in lemon juice and 2 tablespoons parsley.

6 Stir chicken-vegetable mixture and peas into sauce. Pour mixture into 13 by 9-inch baking dish. (Dish can be wrapped tightly with plastic wrap and refrigerated for up to 24 hours.) Scatter crumble topping evenly over filling. Bake on rimmed baking sheet until filling is bubbling and topping is well browned, 12 to 15 minutes. Sprinkle with remaining 1 tablespoon parsley and serve.

Double-Crust Chicken Pot Pie

SERVES 6 to 8 | **TOTAL TIME** 1½ hours, plus 1½ hours resting, chilling, and cooling

1 recipe All-Purpose
Double-Crust Savory
Pie Dough (page 334)

4 tablespoons unsalted butter

1 onion, chopped fine

2 carrots, peeled and cut
into ¼-inch pieces

2 celery ribs, cut into
¼-inch pieces

½ teaspoon table salt

½ teaspoon pepper

6 tablespoons all-purpose flour

2¼ cups chicken broth

½ cup half-and-half

1 small russet potato
(6 ounces), peeled and cut
into ¼-inch pieces

1 teaspoon minced fresh thyme

1 (2½-pound) rotisserie chicken,
skin and bones discarded, meat
shredded into bite-size pieces
(3 cups)

¾ cup frozen peas

1 large egg beaten with
1 teaspoon water

Why This Recipe Works This classic double-crust chicken pot pie takes a shortcut, too, but it's a different path than the Chicken Pot Pie with Savory Crumble Topping (page 82). Here you make an easy and fast filling using flavorful rotisserie chicken, which needs only to be shredded and then stirred into the filling (you can cook chicken instead, if you prefer). Cutting all the vegetables—onion, carrots, celery, and potatoes—into small pieces allows for the filling to be made in one saucepan in less than 20 minutes. This frees you up to focus your time and energy on the savory, flaky crust. (We prefer our homemade All-Purpose Double-Crust Savory Pie Dough, but you can substitute store-bought pie dough.) When the golden-brown, piping-hot pie comes out of the oven, the aroma will be hard to resist. But the filling will be very loose and will run out all over the place if you cut into the pot pie right away. The 45-minute cooling time is necessary to let the filling set up and become firm enough to hold together during slicing. Don't worry; the pot pie will still be plenty hot even after it sets up. It's truly worth the wait.

1 Let chilled dough sit on counter to soften slightly, about 10 minutes, before rolling. Roll 1 disk of dough into 12-inch circle on lightly floured counter. Loosely roll dough around rolling pin and gently unroll it onto 9-inch pie plate, letting excess dough hang over edge. Ease dough into plate by gently lifting edge of dough with your hand while pressing into plate bottom with your other hand.

2 Roll other disk of dough into 12-inch circle on lightly floured counter, then transfer to parchment paper–lined rimmed baking sheet; cover with plastic wrap. Refrigerate both doughs for 30 minutes.

3 Meanwhile, adjust oven rack to lowest position and heat oven to 450 degrees. Melt butter in large saucepan over medium heat. Add onion, carrots, celery, salt, and pepper and cook until vegetables begin to soften, about 6 minutes. Add flour and cook, stirring constantly, until golden, 1 to 2 minutes. Slowly stir in broth and half-and-half, scraping up any browned bits and smoothing out any lumps, and bring to boil over medium-high heat.

4 Stir in potato and thyme. Reduce heat to medium and simmer until sauce is thickened and potato is tender, about 8 minutes. Off heat, stir in chicken and peas.

5 Transfer filling to dough-lined pie plate. Loosely roll remaining dough round around rolling pin and gently unroll it onto filling. Trim overhang to ½ inch beyond lip of plate. Pinch edges of top and bottom crusts firmly together. Tuck overhang under itself; folded edge should be flush with edge of plate. Crimp dough evenly around edge of plate using your fingers. Cut four 2-inch slits in top of dough. (Pie can be wrapped tightly in plastic wrap and then aluminum foil. Freeze for up to 1 month. When ready to bake, unwrap frozen pie, cover with foil, and place on rimmed baking sheet. Place sheet on middle rack of cold oven and set oven to 375 degrees.

Bake for 1¼ hours. Uncover pie and brush with egg wash. Rotate sheet and continue to bake until crust is golden brown and filling is beginning to bubble up through slits and registers at least 150 degrees, 55 minutes to 1¼ hours. Let cool for 45 minutes before serving.)

6 Brush top of pie with egg wash. Place pie on rimmed baking sheet. Bake until top is light golden brown, 18 to 20 minutes. Reduce oven temperature to 375 degrees; rotate sheet; and continue to bake until crust is deep golden brown, 12 to 15 minutes. Let pie cool on wire rack for at least 45 minutes. Serve.

Pub-Style Steak and Ale Pie

SERVES 6 to 8 | **TOTAL TIME** 3 hours, plus 20 minutes resting and cooling

Why This Recipe Works Any British pub worth its salt has a menu offering of a powerful steak and mushroom pie made with beer. It's classic English comfort food, and it isn't made with what Americans would call "steak" (British cooks use the term broadly to describe other cuts). Classically it has a top crust only and minimal vegetables. For this version, cook bacon and sauté mushrooms and onion in the rendered fat to build fond before sprinkling on flour to thicken and adding beer and broth to deglaze the pot. Then, stir in boneless beef short ribs and bake the filling, which produces fork-tender meat and a rich gravy. Transfer it to a pie plate, blanket it with a top crust, and bake until the filling is bubbling. English pale and brown ales work best here. Bitter, hoppy, or floral beers will have too pronounced a flavor, and lager-style beers will get lost. Don't substitute bone-in short ribs; their yield is too variable. We prefer our homemade All-Purpose Single-Crust Savory Pie Dough, but you can substitute store-bought pie dough.

1 Combine water and baking soda in large bowl. Add beef, salt, and pepper and toss to combine. Adjust oven rack to lower-middle position and heat oven to 350 degrees.

2 Cook bacon in large Dutch oven over high heat, stirring occasionally, until fat is partially rendered but bacon is not browned, about 3 minutes. Add mushrooms and ¼ cup broth and stir to coat. Cover and cook, stirring occasionally, until mushrooms are reduced to about half their original volume, about 5 minutes. Add onion, garlic, and thyme and cook, uncovered, stirring occasionally, until onion is softened and fond begins to form on bottom of pot, 3 to 5 minutes. Sprinkle flour over mushroom mixture and stir until all flour is moistened. Cook, stirring occasionally, until fond is deep brown, 2 to 4 minutes. Stir in beer and remaining 1¼ cups broth, scraping up any browned bits and smoothing out any lumps. Stir in beef and bring to simmer, pressing as much beef as possible below surface of liquid. Cover pot tightly with aluminum foil, then lid; transfer to oven. Cook for 1 hour.

3 Remove lid and discard foil. Stir filling; cover; return to oven; and continue to cook until beef is tender and liquid is thick enough to coat beef, 15 to 30 minutes. Transfer filling to 9-inch deep-dish pie plate. (Cooled filling can be covered and refrigerated for up to 2 days.) Increase oven temperature to 400 degrees.

4 Let chilled dough sit on counter to soften slightly, about 10 minutes, before rolling. Roll dough into 11-inch round on lightly floured counter. Using knife or 1-inch round cutter, cut round from center of dough. Drape dough over filling (it's OK if filling is hot). Trim overhang to ½ inch beyond lip of plate. Tuck overhang under itself; folded edge should be flush with edge of plate. Crimp dough evenly around edge of plate using your fingers or press with tines of fork to seal. Brush crust with egg (you won't need all of it). Place pie on rimmed baking sheet. Bake until filling is bubbling and crust is deep golden brown and crisp, 25 to 30 minutes. (If filling has been refrigerated, increase baking time by 15 minutes and cover with foil for last 15 minutes to prevent overbrowning.) Let cool for 10 minutes before serving.

3 tablespoons water

½ teaspoon baking soda

3 pounds boneless beef short ribs, trimmed and cut into ¾-inch pieces

½ teaspoon table salt

½ teaspoon pepper

2 slices bacon, chopped

1 pound cremini mushrooms, trimmed and halved if medium or quartered if large

1½ cups beef broth, divided

1 large onion, chopped

1 garlic clove, minced

½ teaspoon dried thyme

¼ cup all-purpose flour

¾ cup beer

1 recipe All-Purpose Single-Crust Savory Pie Dough (page 335)

1 large egg, lightly beaten

Tourtière

SERVES 6 to 8 | **TOTAL TIME** 1¾ hours, plus 4 hours resting, chilling, and cooling

1½ teaspoons table salt, divided

¾ teaspoon baking soda

2 tablespoons water

2 pounds ground pork

2 tablespoons unsalted butter

2 onions, chopped fine

3 garlic cloves, minced

1 teaspoon minced fresh thyme

1 teaspoon pepper

¼ teaspoon ground allspice

¼ teaspoon ground cinnamon

¼ teaspoon ground nutmeg

Pinch ground cloves

3 cups chicken broth

12 ounces russet potatoes, peeled and shredded

1 recipe All-Purpose Double-Crust Savory Pie Dough (page 334)

1 large egg beaten with 1 teaspoon water

Why This Recipe Works This warmly spiced, flaky-crusted pork pie is a traditional French Canadian dish to eat at Christmastime, after midnight mass. It's stick-to-your-ribs satisfying and is a great way to feed a hungry crowd. There are many different home versions of tourtière; this rendition uses ground pork mixed with shredded russet potatoes. Adding a bit of baking soda to the pork before cooking tenderizes it. The potatoes contribute moisture as well as their starch to the mixture as it bakes, giving the impression that there's a bit of gravy in the filling. Flavor the pork and potatoes with onions cooked in butter and then add the aromatics and warm spices customary to the dish: garlic, thyme, allspice, cinnamon, nutmeg, and cloves. Spreading the hot filling in a large baking dish helps it chill down more quickly in the refrigerator (or you can make it ahead). We prefer our homemade All-Purpose Double-Crust Savory Pie Dough, but you can substitute store-bought pie dough. Shred the potatoes on the large holes of a box grater just before cooking them, and don't soak the shreds in water or their starch will wash away and the filling won't thicken properly. Serve the pie just slightly warm.

1 Dissolve 1¼ teaspoons salt and baking soda in water in medium bowl. Add pork and knead with your hands until thoroughly combined. Set aside until needed, at least 20 minutes.

2 Meanwhile, melt butter in Dutch oven over medium-high heat. Add onions and remaining ¼ teaspoon salt and cook, stirring occasionally, until browned, 7 to 9 minutes. Add garlic, thyme, pepper, allspice, cinnamon, nutmeg, and cloves and cook until fragrant, about 1 minute. Add broth and potatoes, scraping up any browned bits, and bring to boil. Reduce heat to medium and simmer, stirring often, until potatoes are tender and rubber spatula leaves trail when dragged across bottom of pot, 15 to 20 minutes.

3 Add pork to pot, breaking up meat with wooden spoon, and cook until no longer pink, about 10 minutes. Transfer filling to 13 by 9-inch baking dish and refrigerate, uncovered, stirring occasionally, until completely cool, about 1 hour. (Cooled filling can be covered and refrigerated for up to 24 hours.)

4 Adjust oven rack to lowest position and heat oven to 450 degrees. Let chilled dough sit on counter to soften slightly, about 10 minutes. Roll 1 disk of dough into 12-inch circle on lightly floured counter. Loosely roll dough around rolling pin and gently unroll it onto 9-inch pie plate, letting excess dough hang over edge. Ease dough into plate by gently lifting edge of dough with your hand while pressing into plate bottom with your other hand. Wrap dough-lined pie plate loosely in plastic wrap and refrigerate until dough is firm, about 30 minutes.

5 Pour filling into dough-lined pie plate. Roll other disk of dough into 12-inch circle on lightly floured counter. Loosely roll dough around rolling pin and gently unroll it onto filling. Trim overhang to ½ inch beyond lip of plate. Pinch edges of top and bottom crusts firmly together. Tuck overhang under itself; folded edge

should be flush with edge of plate. Crimp dough evenly around edge of plate using your fingers. (If dough gets too soft to work with, refrigerate pie for 10 minutes, then continue.) (Assembled pie can be refrigerated for up to 24 hours before brushing with egg wash and baking.)

6 Cut four 1-inch slits in top of dough. Brush surface with egg wash. Bake until edges are light brown, about 15 minutes. Reduce oven temperature to 375 degrees and continue to bake until crust is deep golden brown and liquid bubbles up through vents, 15 to 20 minutes. Let pie cool on wire rack for 2 hours before serving.

Vegetable Pot Pie

SERVES 4 to 6 | **TOTAL TIME** 1½ hours, plus 10 minutes cooling

Why This Recipe Works This might be the best vegetable pot pie you'll ever eat. It features a rich gravy; a flaky, golden crust; and a hearty combination of sturdy vegetables—mushrooms, sweet potato, turnips, and Swiss chard—that can handle the baking time without turning to mush or developing muddy flavors. So that each vegetable comes out cooked just right, sauté the mushrooms, sweet potato, and turnips in butter first before stirring in the leafy chard. Since the vegetables leave behind a good amount of fond in the pot, when you whisk in the broth, the fond will be incorporated, lending the gravy deep, complex flavor. Stirring in some grated Parmesan cheese adds umami richness. Transfer it all to a deep-dish pie plate, add a top crust, and bake until it's golden. We prefer our homemade All-Purpose Single-Crust Savory Pie Dough, but you can substitute store-bought pie dough.

1. Let chilled dough sit on counter to soften slightly, about 10 minutes. Roll dough between 2 large sheets of parchment paper into 10-inch circle, flouring as needed. Remove top sheet of parchment. Fold over outer ½ inch of dough, then crimp into tidy fluted edge using your fingers. Using paring knife, cut four 2-inch oval-shaped vents in center. Slide bottom sheet of parchment with crust onto rimmed baking sheet and refrigerate until needed.

2. Adjust oven rack to middle position and heat oven to 400 degrees. Melt 2 tablespoons butter in Dutch oven over medium heat. Stir in onion, mushrooms, and ½ teaspoon salt and cook until mushrooms have released their liquid, about 5 minutes.

3. Stir in sweet potato and turnips. Reduce heat to medium-low; cover; and cook, stirring occasionally, until potato and turnips begin to soften around edges, 7 to 9 minutes. Stir in garlic and lemon zest and cook until fragrant, about 30 seconds. Stir in chard and cook until wilted, about 2 minutes. Transfer vegetables to bowl.

4. Melt remaining 2 tablespoons butter in now-empty pot over medium-high heat. Stir in flour and cook for 1 minute. Gradually whisk in broth, scraping up any browned bits and smoothing out any lumps. Bring to simmer and cook until sauce thickens slightly, about 1 minute. Off heat, whisk in Parmesan, parsley, lemon juice, and remaining ½ teaspoon salt. Stir in vegetables, along with any accumulated juices, and season with salt and pepper to taste.

5. Transfer filling to 9-inch deep-dish pie plate set on aluminum foil–lined rimmed baking sheet. Place chilled crust on top and recrimp edges. Brush surface with egg wash. Bake until crust is golden brown and filling is bubbling, about 30 minutes. Let cool on wire rack for 10 minutes before serving.

1 recipe All-Purpose Single-Crust Savory Pie Dough (page 335)

4 tablespoons unsalted butter, divided

1 onion, chopped fine

8 ounces cremini mushrooms, trimmed and quartered if large or halved if small

1 teaspoon table salt, divided

1 sweet potato (12 ounces), peeled and cut into ½-inch pieces

8 ounces turnips, peeled and cut into ½-inch pieces

3 garlic cloves, minced

½ teaspoon grated lemon zest plus 1 tablespoon juice

8 ounces Swiss chard, stemmed and cut into 1-inch pieces

2 tablespoons all-purpose flour

2 cups vegetable broth

1 ounce Parmesan cheese, grated (½ cup)

2 tablespoons minced fresh parsley

1 large egg beaten with 1 teaspoon water

Cast-Iron Skillet Calzone

SERVES 6 to 8 | **TOTAL TIME** 1½ hours, plus 30 minutes cooling

2 teaspoons extra-virgin olive oil

1 pound hot or sweet Italian sausage, casings removed

4 ounces thinly sliced pepperoni, quartered

2 garlic cloves, minced

1 recipe Pizza Dough (page 337)

8 ounces (1 cup) whole-milk ricotta cheese

2 tablespoons chopped fresh basil

1 teaspoon pepper

1 pound block mozzarella cheese, shredded (4 cups), divided

1 cup low-sodium marinara sauce

1 large egg beaten with 1 teaspoon water

2 teaspoons sesame seeds, toasted (optional)

Why This Recipe Works This is not a traditional Italian calzone. In fact, you could think of it as a more literal pizza pie. Rather than being folded like a turnover and sized to serve one or two, this calzone is reimagined as a double-crust, filled pie made in a 12-inch cast-iron skillet—enough to feed a horde of hungry diners. The high sides of a cast-iron skillet make assembly easy: Line the pan with pizza dough and add layers of mozzarella, garlicky sautéed sausage and pepperoni (mixed with ricotta and basil), marinara sauce, and more mozzarella. Then add a top crust of more pizza dough, brush it with egg, and bake. The excellent heat retention of the cast-iron skillet ensures a crust that's satisfyingly crispy on the outside and chewy inside. We like to use our Pizza Dough; however, you can use 1¾ pounds of ready-made pizza dough from the local pizzeria or supermarket. We call for low-sodium marinara sauce here to prevent the calzone from becoming overly salty. Serve with extra marinara sauce, if desired.

1 Adjust oven rack to lower-middle position and heat oven to 450 degrees. Heat 12-inch cast-iron skillet over medium heat for 3 minutes. Add oil and heat until shimmering. Add sausage and pepperoni and cook, breaking up meat with wooden spoon, until sausage is no longer pink, 5 to 7 minutes. Stir in garlic and cook until fragrant, about 30 seconds. Using slotted spoon, transfer sausage mixture to paper towel–lined plate. Wipe skillet clean with paper towels.

2 Place dough on lightly floured counter. Divide dough into one 22-ounce piece and one 10-ounce piece (roughly two-thirds and one-third). Press and roll larger piece of dough (keeping remaining dough covered with greased plastic wrap) into 16-inch round. Loosely roll dough around rolling pin and gently unroll it onto now-empty skillet, letting excess dough hang over edge. Ease dough into skillet by gently lifting and supporting edge of dough with your hand while pressing into skillet bottom and corners with your other hand. Some dough will overhang edge of skillet; leave in place.

3 Combine sausage mixture, ricotta, basil, and pepper in bowl. Sprinkle 2 cups mozzarella over surface of dough. Dollop sausage-ricotta mixture over mozzarella and press into even layer. Spread sauce over top, then sprinkle with remaining 2 cups mozzarella.

4 Brush overhanging dough of bottom crust with egg wash (reserve remaining egg wash). Press and roll remaining dough into 14-inch circle, then loosely roll dough around rolling pin and gently unroll it over filling. Trim overhanging dough to ½ inch beyond edge of skillet. Pinch edges of top and bottom crusts firmly together. Roll overhang to be flush with edge of skillet, then crimp with tines of fork.

5 Brush top of calzone with remaining egg wash and sprinkle with sesame seeds, if using. Using paring knife, cut eight 1-inch vents in top of dough in circular pattern. Transfer skillet to oven and bake until crust is golden brown, about 30 minutes, rotating skillet halfway through baking.

6 Using pot holders, transfer skillet to wire rack and let calzone cool for 30 minutes. Being careful of hot skillet handle, slide calzone onto cutting board using spatula and slice into wedges. Serve.

Vegetable Stromboli

SERVES 4 | **TOTAL TIME** 1½ hours

1 teaspoon extra-virgin olive oil

2 garlic cloves, minced

¼ teaspoon red pepper flakes

6 ounces broccoli florets, cut into ¼-inch pieces

2 tablespoons water

½ recipe Pizza Dough (page 337)

4 ounces thinly sliced aged provolone cheese

4 ounces block mozzarella cheese, shredded (1 cup)

½ cup chopped jarred roasted red peppers

¼ cup chopped pitted kalamata olives

1 large egg beaten with 1 teaspoon water

¼ cup grated Parmesan cheese

Why This Recipe Works Philadelphia-born stromboli are kissing cousins to Naples-born calzone. Whereas calzone are traditionally folded, somewhat like a pizza hand pie, stromboli are folded or rolled more in a jelly-roll fashion. For this stromboli, after rolling the dough into a rectangle, you'll layer provolone, mozzarella, roasted red peppers, kalamata olives, and sautéed broccoli evenly over the dough. Then you'll brush the borders of the dough with egg (to seal the seams) and fold the stromboli like a letter, pinching the edges to seal in all the filling ingredients. Brush the folded stromboli with egg, sprinkle it with Parmesan, and bake it in a 375-degree oven—that's hot enough to promote a golden-brown outer crust but moderate enough to allow the dough in the center of the stromboli to cook all the way through before the crust gets too dark. Stromboli is delicious eaten as is, hot or at room temperature, but feel free to serve your favorite tomato sauce alongside it. We like to use our Pizza Dough; however, you can use 1 pound of ready-made pizza dough from the local pizzeria or supermarket.

1 Adjust oven rack to middle position and heat oven to 375 degrees. Line rimmed baking sheet with aluminum foil and grease foil. Heat oil in 12-inch nonstick skillet over medium heat until shimmering. Add garlic and pepper flakes and cook until fragrant, about 30 seconds. Add broccoli and water; cover; and cook until just tender, about 1 minute. Uncover and cook until liquid has evaporated, about 1 minute. Transfer broccoli to dish towel; gather corners of towel and squeeze out excess moisture.

2 Roll dough into 12 by 10-inch rectangle on lightly floured counter with long side parallel to counter edge. Shingle provolone evenly over dough, leaving ½-inch border along top and sides. Sprinkle mozzarella, red peppers, olives, and broccoli evenly over provolone.

3 Brush borders with egg wash (reserve remaining egg wash). Fold bottom third of stromboli in toward middle. Fold top third of stromboli down to cover first fold, creating log. Pinch seam to seal. Transfer stromboli to prepared sheet, seam side down. Pinch ends to seal and tuck underneath.

4 Brush top of stromboli with remaining egg wash. Using sharp knife, make 5 evenly spaced ½-inch-deep slashes, 2 inches long, on top of stromboli. Sprinkle with Parmesan. Bake until crust is golden and center registers 200 degrees, 30 to 35 minutes, rotating sheet halfway through baking. Transfer stromboli to wire rack and let cool for 10 minutes. Transfer to cutting board and slice 2 inch thick. Serve.

CONSTRUCTING STROMBOLI

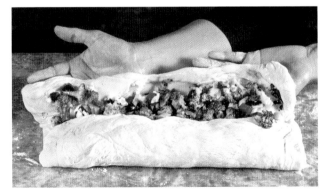

1 Layer the filling ingredients over the dough, leaving a ½-inch border along the top and sides. Brush perimeter with beaten egg. Fold the bottom third in toward the middle.

2 Carefully fold the top third down over the first fold. Pinch the seam firmly to seal the stromboli. Invert onto the baking sheet, pinch the ends to seal, and tuck the ends under. Brush with the remaining egg, cut vent holes, and sprinkle with Parmesan.

Bean and Cheese Sopaipillas with Green Chile Sauce

SERVES 8 (Makes 8 sopaipillas) | **TOTAL TIME** 3 hours, plus 40 minutes chilling and cooling

Dough

2¾ cups (13¾ ounces) all-purpose flour

1½ teaspoons table salt

½ teaspoon baking powder

6 tablespoons lard, cut into ½-inch pieces

¾ cup plus 2 tablespoons ice water

Refried Beans

4 tablespoons lard

1 cup finely chopped onion

2 (15-ounce) cans pinto beans, rinsed

1 cup chicken broth

1 teaspoon table salt

Green Chile Sauce

2 pounds Anaheim chiles

1 jalapeño chile

2 tablespoons lard

1 cup finely chopped onion

3 garlic cloves, minced

1 tablespoon all-purpose flour

1 cup chicken broth

1 teaspoon table salt

8 ounces mild cheddar cheese, shredded (2 cups), divided

2 quarts peanut or vegetable oil for frying

Why This Recipe Works Many versions of these fried breads are made throughout Latin America and the American Southwest. They can be stuffed or not and savory or sweet. This rendition is a stuffed turnover-style bread made with an easy home-made flour tortilla dough that uses lard for maximum flakiness and flavor plus a bit of baking powder to help the dough puff when it hits the hot oil. Use the flavorful lard again to make a batch of savory refried beans—first sauté some onion and then add two cans of drained and rinsed pinto beans, mashing them right in the skillet with a potato masher. After stuffing the beans and some cheddar cheese into the homemade dough, fold the turnovers into half-moon shapes. Sealing the dough with water and twisting the sealed edge keeps the filling from oozing out during frying, and a small steam hole poked into the top gives extra insurance against blowouts. For a lightly spicy green chile sauce, broil Anaheim chiles and a jalapeño to add smokiness while intensifying their tangy sweetness. Chopped and cooked with aromatics, flour, and chicken broth, they make an invigorating sauce to spoon over the sopaipillas. Use a Dutch oven that holds 6 quarts or more. We developed this recipe using John Morrell Snow Cap Lard. You can substitute vegetable shortening for the lard, if desired.

1 **For the dough** Whisk flour, salt, and baking powder together in large bowl. Rub lard into flour mixture with your fingers until mixture resembles coarse meal. Stir in ice water until combined. Turn out dough onto clean counter and knead briefly to form cohesive ball, 6 to 8 turns. Divide dough into 8 equal portions, about 2¾ ounces each (scant ⅓ cup), then roll into balls. Transfer dough balls to plate; cover with plastic wrap; and refrigerate until firm, about 30 minutes. (Dough balls can be refrigerated for up to 2 days.)

2 **For the refried beans** Heat lard in 12-inch skillet over medium heat until shimmering. Add onion and cook until softened, about 4 minutes. Stir in beans, broth, and salt. Cook, mashing beans with potato masher, until finely mashed and mixture is thickened, about 8 minutes. Season with salt to taste. Set aside and let cool completely.

3 **For the green chile sauce** Adjust oven rack 6 inches from broiler element and heat broiler. Line rimmed baking sheet with aluminum foil. Arrange Anaheims and jalapeño in single layer on prepared sheet. Broil until chiles are soft and mostly blackened, about 5 minutes per side, rotating sheet halfway through broiling. Transfer chiles to bowl and cover with plastic; let cool for 10 minutes.

4 Remove skins from chiles with spoon. Stem and seed Anaheims, then chop into ¼-inch pieces. Stem (but do not seed) jalapeño; chop into ¼-inch pieces.

5 Heat lard in large saucepan over medium heat until shimmering. Add onion and cook until softened, about 3 minutes. Stir in garlic and cook until fragrant, about 30 seconds. Stir in flour and cook for 1 minute. Stir in broth, salt, Anaheims, and jalapeño, scraping up any browned bits and smoothing out any lumps, and bring to simmer. Simmer until slightly thickened, about 6 minutes. Season with salt to taste; cover and set aside.

6 Keeping other dough balls covered with damp dish towel, roll 1 dough ball into 7-inch circle on lightly floured counter. Lightly squeeze ¼ cup cheddar in your palm to form ball. Place cheddar in center of dough round, followed by ¼ cup refried beans. Moisten edges of dough round with water. Fold dough round in half, creating half-moon shape to enclose filling, and press to seal.

7 Moisten sealed edge with water. Starting at 1 end, fold, slightly twist, and pinch dough diagonally across sealed edge between your thumb and index finger. Continue pinching and twisting dough around seam to create decorative rope edge. Transfer to parchment paper–lined baking sheet. Repeat with remaining dough balls, cheddar, and refried beans (reserve any remaining beans for another use). Using paring knife, poke ½-inch hole in center of each sopaipilla. (Filled sopaipillas can be covered and refrigerated for up to 24 hours.)

8 Line separate baking sheet with triple layer of paper towels. Add oil to large Dutch oven until it measures about 1½ inches deep and heat over medium-high heat to 375 degrees. Add 4 sopaipillas to oil and fry until golden brown, about 3 minutes per side. Adjust burner as needed to maintain oil temperature between 350 and 375 degrees. Transfer fried sopaipillas to prepared sheet. Return oil to 375 degrees and repeat with remaining 4 sopaipillas.

9 Reheat green chile sauce over medium-high heat until hot. Serve sopaipillas topped with chile sauce.

SHAPING SOPAIPILLAS

1 After placing cheddar and beans in center of dough round, moisten edges of dough round with water.

2 Fold dough round in half, creating half-moon shape to enclose filling, and press to seal.

3 Moisten sealed edge with water. Starting at 1 end, fold, slightly twist, and pinch dough diagonally across sealed edge between your thumb and index finger to create rope edge.

Jamaican Beef Patties

SERVES 8 (Makes 8 patties) | **TOTAL TIME** 1½ hours, plus 1¼ hours chilling and cooling

Dough

- ⅔ cup sour cream, chilled
- 1 large egg, lightly beaten
- 3 cups (15 ounces) all-purpose flour
- 1 tablespoon sugar
- 1¼ teaspoons table salt
- 1 teaspoon ground turmeric
- 16 tablespoons unsalted butter, cut into ½-inch pieces and chilled

Filling

- 1 tablespoon plus 1 cup water, divided
- ¾ teaspoon table salt
- ¼ teaspoon baking soda
- 1 pound 85 percent lean ground beef
- 1 tablespoon vegetable oil
- 12 scallions, chopped fine
- 4 garlic cloves, minced
- 1 habanero chile, stemmed, seeded, and minced
- 1 teaspoon dried thyme
- ¾ teaspoon curry powder
- ¾ teaspoon ground allspice
- ½ teaspoon pepper
- 1 slice hearty white sandwich bread, torn into 1-inch pieces

Why This Recipe Works Though versions vary from island to island, rich, spicy hand pies are a street-food staple across the Caribbean. The signature flaky golden pastry for these Jamaican patties uses either turmeric or curry powder; here you add turmeric to a buttery food-processor pie dough. Swapping in sour cream and an egg for the ice water that's usually in pie dough makes for an ultratender patty dough that won't crack during rolling and shaping. For the filling, treating the ground beef with a touch of baking soda softens its pebbly toughness and keeps it moist. Seasoning the beef with traditional Jamaican aromatics of scallions, garlic, curry powder, allspice, and chile makes for a heady spice profile. A slice of white bread added to the highly spiced beef mixture breaks down to form a velvety gravy that clings to the beef, and mashing it all together creates a cohesive filling that stays put within the patties. Scotch bonnet chile is a favorite local choice for these patties, so you can use one of those instead of the habanero, if you like. Whichever chile you use, it's a good idea to wear rubber gloves to protect your hands while prepping it. For a spicier filling, include the seeds and ribs of the chile.

1 **For the dough** Whisk sour cream and egg together in small bowl. Process flour, sugar, salt, and turmeric in food processor until combined, about 3 seconds. Scatter butter over top and pulse until butter is no larger than size of peas, about 10 pulses. Add half of sour cream mixture and pulse until combined, about 5 pulses. Add remaining sour cream mixture and pulse until dough begins to form, about 15 pulses.

2 Turn out dough onto sheet of plastic wrap and shape into 6-inch square, smoothing any cracks. Wrap tightly in plastic and refrigerate for 1 hour. (Dough can be refrigerated for up to 2 days.)

3 **For the filling** Combine 1 tablespoon water, salt, and baking soda in large bowl. Add beef and mix until thoroughly combined. Let sit at room temperature for 10 minutes.

4 Heat oil in 12-inch nonstick skillet over medium-high heat until just smoking. Add beef mixture and cook, breaking up meat with wooden spoon, until beginning to brown, 5 to 7 minutes. Add scallions, garlic, habanero, thyme, curry powder, allspice, and pepper and cook, stirring frequently, until scallions are softened, about 3 minutes.

5 Add bread and remaining 1 cup water and stir to incorporate. Bring to boil, then reduce heat to low and simmer, stirring occasionally, until sauce thickens and coats beef, 8 to 10 minutes. Off heat, mash beef mixture with potato masher until fine-textured and bread is fully incorporated, about 2 minutes. Transfer to clean bowl and let cool completely. (Filling can be covered with plastic and refrigerated for up to 24 hours.)

6 Adjust oven rack to upper-middle position and heat oven to 375 degrees. Line rimmed baking sheet with parchment paper. Remove dough from refrigerator and cut into 4 equal pieces (about 7½ ounces each). Working with 1 piece of dough at a time, sprinkle dough with flour and roll each dough piece on lightly floured counter into rough 11 by 9-inch rectangle about ⅛ inch thick, with long side parallel to counter edge, reflouring counter and dough as needed and covering each dough piece with plastic while rolling remaining dough.

7 Place 2 scant ⅓-cup mounds of filling on bottom half of dough, about 4 inches apart and about 2 inches from bottom edge of dough. Flatten mounds to roughly 3-inch rounds. Lightly brush bottom half of dough with water. Fold top half of dough over filling, pressing along sides, bottom edge, and between filling to adhere.

8 Cut between mounds and trim edges to form two 5 by 4-inch rectangles. Crimp edges with floured tines of fork to seal, then transfer patties to prepared sheet. (Patties can be transferred to freezer on sheet. Once frozen solid, patties can be transferred to zipper-lock bag and frozen for up to 1 month. To cook from frozen, extend baking time to 40 to 45 minutes, until bottoms are crisp.)

9 Bake until patties have puffed and exteriors have lightly browned, about 30 minutes. Transfer patties to wire rack and let cool for 10 minutes before serving.

SHAPING JAMAICAN BEEF PATTIES

1 Shape dough into 6-inch square, wrap in plastic wrap, and refrigerate for 1 hour.

2 Roll one-quarter of dough into rectangle and place 2 mounds of filling on top.

3 Fold dough over filling, press to adhere, and cut between mounds to make 2 patties.

Poblano and Corn Hand Pies

SERVES 8 (Makes 16 hand pies) | TOTAL TIME 1¾ hours, plus 1¼ hours chilling and cooling

Crema

- ½ cup mayonnaise
- ½ cup sour cream
- 2 tablespoons lime juice
- 2 tablespoons whole milk

Filling

- 1 (15-ounce) can pinto beans, rinsed with 3 tablespoons liquid reserved, divided
- 1½ cups frozen corn, thawed
- 6 ounces pepper Jack cheese, shredded (1½ cups)
- 3 scallions, white parts minced, green parts sliced thin
- 2 tablespoons vegetable oil
- 3 poblano chiles, stemmed, seeded, and cut into ¼-inch pieces
- 2 garlic cloves, minced
- 2 teaspoons minced fresh oregano or ½ teaspoon dried
- 1½ teaspoons ground cumin
- 1½ teaspoons ground coriander
- ½ teaspoon table salt
- ¼ teaspoon pepper

Dough

- 4 cups (20 ounces) all-purpose flour
- 2 teaspoons table salt
- 1 teaspoon baking powder
- 8 tablespoons vegetable shortening, cut into ½-inch pieces
- 1 cup vegetable broth
- 2 large eggs, lightly beaten
- 5 tablespoons vegetable oil, divided

Why This Recipe Works Stuffed with pinto beans, corn, poblano chiles, scallions, and pepper Jack cheese, these satisfying hand pies pack a belly-warming heat. They're also great to make ahead and keep on hand for portable meals or snacks. Vegetable shortening creates a dough that's easy to work with and sturdy enough to stuff with the filling mixture while baking up tender and flaky. Using vegetable broth instead of water enhances the dough's savory quality. For the filling, mashing a portion of the pinto beans with some of their canning liquid creates a moist binder so that it won't fall out messily when you take a bite. Oiling and preheating the baking sheets creates a searing-hot cooking surface for the hand pies, which helps give them crisp, golden-brown crusts without the need for deep frying. Poking each hand pie with the tines of a fork before baking creates a vent for the steam to escape. The tangy crema is wonderful for dolloping or dipping.

1 **For the crema** Whisk all ingredients together in bowl. Refrigerate until ready to serve (or for up to 2 days).

2 **For the filling** Place one-quarter of beans in large bowl; add bean liquid; and, using back of wooden spoon, mash until coarsely mashed. Stir in corn, pepper Jack, scallion greens, and remaining beans.

3 Heat oil in 12-inch nonstick skillet over medium-high heat until shimmering. Add poblanos and scallion whites and cook, stirring occasionally, until softened, 3 to 5 minutes. Stir in garlic, oregano, cumin, coriander, salt, and pepper and cook until fragrant, about 30 seconds. Transfer poblano mixture to bowl with bean mixture and stir well to combine. Season with salt and pepper to taste and let cool slightly. Refrigerate until completely cool, 45 minutes to 1 hour. (Filling can be refrigerated for up to 2 days.)

4 **For the dough** Meanwhile, process flour, salt, and baking powder in food processor until combined, about 3 seconds. Add shortening and pulse until mixture resembles coarse cornmeal, 6 to 8 pulses. Add broth and eggs and pulse until dough just comes together, about 5 pulses. Transfer dough to lightly floured counter and knead until dough forms smooth ball, about 20 seconds. Divide dough into 16 equal pieces. With your cupped hand, form each piece into smooth, tight ball. (Dough balls can be covered and refrigerated for up to 24 hours.)

5 Adjust oven racks to upper-middle and lower-middle positions, place 1 rimmed baking sheet on each rack, and heat oven to 425 degrees. Working with 1 dough ball at a time, roll each dough ball on lightly floured counter into 6-inch circle, covering each dough round with plastic while rolling remaining dough. Place heaping ¼ cup filling in center of dough round. Brush edges of dough with water and fold dough over filling. Press to seal, trim any ragged edges, and crimp edges with tines of fork. Pierce top of each hand pie once with fork.

6 Drizzle 2 tablespoons oil over surface of each hot baking sheet, then return sheets to oven for 2 minutes. Brush tops of hand pies with remaining 1 tablespoon oil. Carefully place 8 hand pies on each prepared sheet and bake until golden brown, 20 to 25 minutes, switching and rotating sheets halfway through baking. Transfer hand pies to wire rack and let cool completely, about 30 minutes. Serve with crema.

Picadillo Gorditas

SERVES 6 (Makes 12 gorditas) | **TOTAL TIME** 2¾ hours

Filling

- 1 pound 85 percent lean ground beef
- 1 russet potato, peeled and cut into ¼-inch pieces
- 1 teaspoon table salt
- 1 teaspoon pepper
- 1 onion, chopped fine
- 1 tomato, cored and chopped fine
- 3 garlic cloves, minced
- 1½ teaspoons ground cumin
- 2 teaspoons all-purpose flour
- ¾ cup water

Dough

- 5 cups (20 ounces) masa harina
- 2 teaspoons table salt
- 3⅔ cups water, room temperature
- 3 ounces Colby Jack cheese, shredded (¾ cup)
- 1½ quarts vegetable oil for frying

Why This Recipe Works Thanks to the everlasting popularity of certain fast-food items, the word "gordita" might conjure images of an overstuffed invention resembling a cross between a taco and a flatbread. Please set aside those images. Throughout central and northern Mexico, gorditas (Spanish for "little fat ones") are plump corn cakes with crispy exteriors and tender interiors that are split open like pitas and stuffed with various fillings, such as this ground beef picadillo. To make tender gordita shells, start with masa harina, which when combined with water forms a soft, putty-like dough with less structure than dough made with wheat flour. Then knead in a handful of shredded Colby Jack cheese for extra savoriness. A frequent cooking method for gorditas is griddling them without fat, although some cooks deep-fry them. In this version you'll fry the corn cakes in less than an inch of oil, which gives them a captivatingly crispy exterior cloaking a soft, moist interior. You can substitute Monterey Jack or cheddar cheese for the Colby Jack cheese. Add shredded iceberg lettuce, diced tomatoes, shredded cheese, and hot sauce to your filled gorditas, if desired.

1 **For the filling** Combine beef, potato, salt, and pepper in 12-inch nonstick skillet. Cook over medium-high heat until beef and potato begin to brown, 6 to 8 minutes, breaking up meat with wooden spoon. Add onion and tomato and cook until softened, 4 to 6 minutes. Add garlic and cumin and cook until fragrant, about 30 seconds.

2 Stir in flour and cook for 1 minute. Stir in water and bring to boil. Cook until slightly thickened, about 1 minute. Off heat, season with salt and pepper to taste. Cover and set aside.

3 **For the dough** Line rimmed baking sheet with parchment paper. Whisk masa harina and salt together in large bowl. Add room-temperature water and Colby Jack and knead with your hands until mixture is fully combined. (Mixture should have texture of Play-Doh and easily hold fingerprint.)

4 Divide dough into 12 level ½-cup portions and place on large plate; divide any remaining dough evenly among portions. Working with 1 portion at a time (keep remaining dough covered with damp dish towel), roll dough into smooth ball between your wet hands, then return it to plate. Cut sides of 1-quart zipper-lock bag, leaving bottom seam intact.

5 Enclose 1 dough ball in split bag. Using clear plate or dish (so you can see size of dough round), press dough into 4-inch round, about ½ inch thick. Smooth any cracks around edges of round; transfer to prepared sheet. Repeat with remaining dough balls, placing second sheet of parchment on top once sheet is filled so you can stack dough rounds as needed. Cover with damp dish towel. (Dough rounds can be covered tightly with plastic wrap, without dish towel, and refrigerated for up to 2 hours.)

6 Set wire rack in rimmed baking sheet and line with triple layer of paper towels. Add oil to Dutch oven until it measures about ¾ inch deep and heat over medium-high heat to 375 degrees.

7 Fry 4 dough rounds until golden brown on both sides, 5 minutes per side. Adjust burner, if necessary, to maintain oil temperature between 350 and 375 degrees.

Transfer fried rounds to prepared rack to drain. Return oil to 375 degrees and repeat with remaining dough rounds in 2 batches. Let fried rounds cool for 10 minutes. While rounds cool, reheat filling.

8 Insert paring knife into side of fried rounds and split 180 degrees to create pocket. Stuff each pocket with ⅓ cup filling and serve.

Lamb Fatayer

SERVES 12 (Makes 24 fatayer) | **TOTAL TIME** 1½ hours, plus 26½ hours chilling, resting, and cooling

Dough

- 3 cups (16½ ounces) bread flour
- 2 teaspoons sugar
- ½ teaspoon instant or rapid-rise yeast
- 1⅓ cups ice water
- 1 tablespoon extra-virgin olive oil
- 1½ teaspoons table salt

Filling

- 3 tablespoons extra-virgin olive oil, divided
- 1 pound ground lamb
- 1 onion, chopped fine
- 3 garlic cloves, minced
- 1 teaspoon table salt
- ¼ teaspoon ground cinnamon
- ¼ teaspoon ground nutmeg
- ¼ teaspoon pepper
- ⅛ teaspoon cayenne pepper
- ⅓ cup pine nuts, toasted
- 2 tablespoons tahini
- 1 tablespoon pomegranate molasses

Why This Recipe Works Fatayer are crispy triangular hand pies beloved throughout the Middle East but especially in Lebanon, where they originated. These individual little pockets can be filled with a wide assortment of greens, meat, or labneh, and they're often served on a meze platter or as a light meal at any time of day. Regardless of when or where they are eaten, fatayer are a bit of a labor of love but are well worth the time. The crust of this fatayer is a cold-fermented yeasted dough; giving it a long rest in the refrigerator lets it develop better flavor and structure, resulting in a crisp outer crust that maintains a slight chewiness. This method ensures that the fatayer holds its shape well during baking—which is necessary to keep all the luscious filling tucked inside. This juicy, ultrasavory filling features lamb sautéed with onion, garlic, traditional warm spices (cinnamon and nutmeg), and a pinch of cayenne for subtle heat. Toasted pine nuts are a classic addition and enrich the filling with pops of texture. Tahini and pomegranate molasses add delicious complexity while helping bind everything together. To ensure that the fatayer seal completely, be sure to tightly pinch the seams. It is important to use ice water in the dough to prevent it from overheating in the food processor.

1 **For the dough** Pulse flour, sugar, and yeast in food processor until combined, about 5 pulses. With processor running, slowly add ice water and process until dough is just combined and no dry flour remains, about 10 seconds. Let dough rest for 10 minutes.

2 Add oil and salt to dough and process until dough forms satiny, sticky ball that clears sides of bowl, 30 to 60 seconds. Transfer dough to lightly oiled counter and knead by hand to form smooth, round ball, about 30 seconds. Place dough seam side down in lightly greased large bowl or container, cover tightly with plastic wrap, and refrigerate for at least 24 hours or up to 3 days.

3 **For the filling** Heat 1 tablespoon oil in 12-inch nonstick skillet over medium heat until shimmering. Add lamb and onion and cook, stirring occasionally, until lamb is no longer pink and onion is lightly browned, 10 to 12 minutes. Stir in garlic, salt, cinnamon, nutmeg, pepper, and cayenne and cook until fragrant, about 30 seconds. Off heat, stir in pine nuts, tahini, and pomegranate molasses. Transfer to bowl and let cool completely, about 30 minutes. (Filling can be refrigerated for up to 24 hours.)

4 Press down on dough to deflate. Transfer dough to clean counter and divide into 24 equal portions (about 1¼ ounces each). Working with 1 dough portion at a time and keeping remaining dough portions covered with plastic wrap, cup dough with your palm and roll against counter into smooth, tight ball. Space dough balls 1 inch apart on counter, cover loosely with greased plastic, and let rest for 1½ hours.

5 Adjust oven rack to middle position and heat oven to 450 degrees. Line 2 rimmed baking sheets with parchment paper. Working with 1 dough ball at a time, generously coat with flour and place on well-floured counter (keeping remaining balls covered). Press and roll into 4-inch circle, then place 1 tablespoon lamb filling in center of circle. Grasping edges of dough at 4 and 8 o'clock, lift dough around filling and pinch tightly to seal. Grasp top of dough (12 o'clock) and lift around filling to meet at center seam, pinching tightly to seal. Pinch edges of dough where they meet to seal seam (dough should be rough triangle shape). Transfer to prepared sheet, evenly spacing 12 fatayer over each prepared sheet.

6 Brush fatayer with remaining 2 tablespoons oil. Bake, 1 sheet at a time, until deep golden brown, 12 to 15 minutes. Transfer sheets to wire rack and let cool for 15 minutes. Serve warm or at room temperature.

SHAPING FATAYER

1 Generously coat dough ball with flour and place on well-floured counter. Press and roll into 4-inch circle, then place 1 tablespoon filling in center of circle.

2 Grasping edges of dough at 4 and 8 o'clock, lift dough around filling and pinch tightly to seal.

3 Grasp top of dough (12 o'clock) and lift around filling to meet at center seam, pinching tightly to seal. Pinch edges of dough where they meet to seal seam (dough should be rough triangle shape).

Vegetable Samosas with Cilantro-Mint Chutney

SERVES 8 (Makes 24 samosas) | **TOTAL TIME** 2 hours, plus 1¼ hours chilling and resting

Filling

- 2 pounds russet potatoes, peeled and cut into 1-inch pieces
- 1 teaspoon table salt, plus salt for cooking potatoes
- 3 tablespoons vegetable oil
- 1 teaspoon fennel seeds
- 1 teaspoon cumin seeds
- 1 teaspoon brown mustard seeds
- ¼ teaspoon ground fenugreek
- ¼ teaspoon ground turmeric
- ⅛ teaspoon red pepper flakes
- 1 onion, chopped fine
- 3 garlic cloves, minced
- 1½ teaspoons grated fresh ginger
- ½ cup frozen peas, thawed
- ¼ cup minced fresh cilantro
- 1½ teaspoons lemon juice

Dough

- 2 cups (10 ounces) all-purpose flour
- ½ teaspoon table salt
- 3 tablespoons vegetable oil
- 2 tablespoons plain whole-milk yogurt
- 4–6 tablespoons ice water
- 3 quarts vegetable oil for frying

Why This Recipe Works With a pungently spiced potato filling in a thin, crispy pastry shell, these Indian fried turnovers are a deliciously indulgent snack or appetizer, especially when served with a tangy herbal yogurt chutney. First build a fragrant flavor base of fennel, cumin, mustard seed, fenugreek, turmeric, and pepper flakes in a skillet. Then add onion, ginger, and garlic and stir in chunks of parcooked potato to let their edges crisp and brown. Peas, cilantro, and lemon juice round out the flavors. Adding a generous amount of vegetable oil and some yogurt to the dough makes it nice and elastic so that it can easily be packed with filling; plus, the fat helps the crust turn out crispy and golden when fried. Whole fennel and cumin seeds bring great texture to the filling; however, you can substitute ½ teaspoon of ground fennel and ½ teaspoon of ground cumin. Likewise, whole-milk yogurt makes a richer, flakier dough and a more balanced chutney, but you can substitute low-fat yogurt (do not use nonfat). You will need a Dutch oven that holds at least 6 quarts for this recipe. A spider skimmer comes in handy when frying the samosas. It is important to use ice water in the dough to prevent it from overheating in the food processor. Serve with Cilantro-Mint Chutney (recipe follows).

1 **For the filling** Place potatoes and 1 tablespoon salt in large saucepan and add water to cover by 1 inch. Bring water to boil, then reduce heat to maintain simmer and cook until potatoes are tender and paring knife can be inserted into potatoes with little resistance, 12 to 15 minutes. Drain potatoes and set aside to cool slightly.

2 Heat oil in 12-inch nonstick skillet over medium-high heat until shimmering. Add fennel seeds, cumin seeds, mustard seeds, fenugreek, turmeric, and pepper flakes and cook until fragrant, about 10 seconds. Stir in onion and salt and cook until onion is softened, 5 to 7 minutes. Stir in garlic and ginger and cook until fragrant, about 30 seconds. Stir in potatoes and cook until beginning to brown around edges, 5 to 7 minutes. Stir in peas.

3 Transfer mixture to bowl; let cool completely; then refrigerate until completely cool, about 1 hour. Stir in cilantro and lemon juice and season with salt and pepper to taste. (Filling can be refrigerated for up to 2 days; reserve cilantro and lemon juice and stir in before shaping samosas.)

4 **For the dough** Pulse flour and salt in food processor until combined, about 4 pulses. Drizzle 3 tablespoons oil and yogurt over flour mixture and process until mixture resembles coarse cornmeal, about 5 seconds. With processor running, slowly add ¼ cup ice water until dough forms ball. If dough doesn't come together, add remaining 2 tablespoons ice water, 1 tablespoon at a time, with processor running, until dough ball forms. Dough should feel very soft and malleable.

5 Transfer dough to floured counter and knead by hand until slightly firm, about 2 minutes. Wrap dough in plastic wrap and let rest for at least 20 minutes. (Dough can be refrigerated for up to 24 hours.)

6 Divide dough into 12 equal pieces. Working with 1 piece of dough at a time, roll dough into 5-inch rounds; keep dough pieces covered with greased plastic wrap when not working with them. Cut each dough round in half to form 24 half-moons.

7 Moisten straight side of 1 half-moon with your wet finger, then fold in half. Press to seal seam on straight side only and crimp with fork to secure; leave rounded edge open and unsealed. Pick up piece of dough and hold gently in your cupped hand, with open, unsealed edge facing up; gently open dough into cone shape. Fill dough cone with 2 tablespoons filling and pack filling in tightly, leaving ¼-inch rim at top. Moisten inside rim of cone with your wet finger and pinch top edges together to seal. Lay samosa on flat surface and crimp sealed edge with fork to secure. Repeat with remaining half-moons and remaining filling.

8 Adjust oven rack to middle position and heat oven to 200 degrees. Line rimmed baking sheet with several layers of paper towels and set aside. Heat 3 quarts oil in large Dutch oven over medium-high heat to 375 degrees. Add 8 samosas and fry until golden brown and bubbly, 2½ to 3 minutes, adjusting burner, if necessary, to maintain oil temperature of 375 degrees. Using spider skimmer or slotted spoon, transfer samosas to prepared sheet and keep warm in oven. Return oil to 375 degrees and repeat with remaining samosas in 2 batches. Serve.

Cilantro-Mint Chutney

Serves 8 (Makes about 1 cup)

    2 **cups fresh cilantro leaves**
    2 **cups fresh mint leaves**
    2 **cups plain whole-milk yogurt**
    ¼ **cup finely chopped onion**
    1 **tablespoon lime juice**
 1½ **teaspoons sugar**
    ½ **teaspoon ground cumin**
    ¼ **teaspoon table salt**

Process all ingredients in food processor until smooth, about 20 seconds, scraping down sides of bowl as needed. Refrigerate until ready to serve (or for up to 2 days).

SHAPING SAMOSAS

1 Working with 1 half-moon of dough, moisten straight side with your wet finger, then fold in half. Crimp with fork to seal seam on straight side only; leave rounded edge open and unsealed.

2 Hold dough gently in your cupped hand, with open, unsealed edge facing up; gently open dough into cone shape. Pack with 2 tablespoons filling, leaving ¼-inch rim at top.

3 Moisten inside rim of cone with your wet finger and pinch top edges together to seal. Lay samosa on flat surface and crimp sealed edge with fork to secure.

TARTS
& GALETTES

Tomato and Mozzarella Tart

SERVES 6 to 8 (Makes one 16 by 7-inch tart) | **TOTAL TIME** 1¼ hours

2 (9½ by 9-inch) sheets puff pastry, thawed

2 ounces Parmesan cheese, grated (1 cup)

1 pound plum tomatoes, cored and sliced crosswise ¼ inch thick

½ teaspoon plus pinch table salt, divided

2 tablespoons extra-virgin olive oil

2 garlic cloves, minced

Pinch pepper

8 ounces whole-milk mozzarella cheese, shredded (2 cups)

2 tablespoons chopped fresh basil

Why This Recipe Works The trio of tomatoes, mozzarella, and basil might call pizza to mind, but this easy puff pastry tart is flakier and more delicate, and its rectangular shape makes a striking visual presentation. The key to using fresh tomatoes in baked goods is successfully managing their juiciness so that your creation doesn't turn out soggy. For a perfectly flaky crust here, use a simple two-step baking method—first, parbake the unfilled crust until golden; then bake it again after adding the fresh toppings. Before the first bake, brush the dough with water and sprinkle it with Parmesan; this helps to "waterproof" it. While the puff shell bakes, salt the sliced tomatoes and let them drain of their excess juice. Then assemble and finish with the second bake. For the best results, use authentic Parmigiano-Reggiano and very ripe in-season tomatoes. (The variation using sun-dried tomatoes is a wonderful year-round version.) Use low-moisture mozzarella sold in block form here, not fresh water-packed mozzarella. See page 13 for more information on thawing frozen puff pastry.

1 Adjust oven rack to lower-middle position and heat oven to 425 degrees. Line rimmed baking sheet with parchment paper. Dust counter lightly with flour. Unfold both pieces of puff pastry. Brush 1 short edge of 1 piece of pastry with water and overlap with second piece by 1 inch, forming 18 by 9-inch rectangle. Press to seal edges, then use rolling pin to smooth seam. Cut two 1-inch-wide strips from long side of dough and two more from short side. Transfer large piece of dough to prepared baking sheet and brush with water. Attach long dough strips to long edges of dough and short strips to short edges, then brush dough strips with water. Sprinkle Parmesan evenly over shell. Using fork, poke evenly spaced holes in surface of dough. Bake for 13 to 15 minutes, then reduce oven temperature to 350 degrees. Continue to bake until golden brown and crisp, 13 to 15 minutes longer. Transfer to wire rack; increase oven temperature to 425 degrees. (Tart shell can be stored at room temperature for up to 2 days.)

2 While shell bakes, place tomato slices in single layer on double layer of paper towels and sprinkle evenly with ½ teaspoon salt; let sit for 30 minutes. Place another double layer of paper towels on top of tomatoes and press firmly to dry tomatoes. Combine oil, garlic, pepper and remaining pinch salt in small bowl; set aside.

3 Sprinkle mozzarella evenly over baked shell. Shingle tomato slices widthwise on top of cheese (about 4 slices per row); brush tomatoes with garlic oil. Bake until shell is deep golden brown and cheese is melted, 15 to 17 minutes. Let cool on wire rack for 5 minutes. Sprinkle with basil, slide onto cutting board or serving platter, cut into pieces, and serve warm.

Variations

Tomato and Smoked Mozzarella Tart
Substitute 6 ounces smoked mozzarella for whole-milk mozzarella.

Sun-Dried Tomato and Mozzarella Tart
Substitute ½ cup oil-packed sun-dried tomatoes, drained, rinsed, and chopped fine, for plum tomatoes.

Tomato and Mozzarella Tart with Prosciutto
Place 2 ounces thinly sliced prosciutto in single layer on top of mozzarella before arranging tomato slices.

Asparagus and Goat Cheese Tart

SERVES 4 (Makes one 9-inch tart) | **TOTAL TIME** 45 minutes, plus 15 minutes cooling

Why This Recipe Works Fresh, grassy asparagus really shines as the main attraction of this impressive tart, which takes just minutes to assemble. Store-bought puff pastry—buttery, flaky, and easy to prep—is the baker's best friend here. The plentiful but light filling is predominantly flavored by the asparagus; cutting the spears into thin pieces ensures that the asparagus doesn't need any precooking and also makes the tart easier to eat. Toss the pieces with olive oil, garlic, lemon zest, scallions, and kalamata olives, and then scatter the mixture over the creamy base of goat cheese. Blending some olive oil in with the goat cheese makes it easier to spread evenly over the puff pastry. Dollop some more cheese on top, and then bake the tart to golden perfection. Look for asparagus spears no thicker than ½ inch. See page 13 for more information on thawing frozen puff pastry.

1 Adjust oven rack to upper-middle position and heat oven to 425 degrees. Line rimmed baking sheet with parchment paper. Combine asparagus, scallions, 1 tablespoon oil, olives, garlic, zest, salt, and pepper in bowl. In separate bowl, mix ¾ cup goat cheese and 1 tablespoon oil until smooth; set aside.

2 Dust counter lightly with flour. Unfold puff pastry and roll into 10-inch square; transfer to prepared sheet. Lightly brush outer ½ inch of pastry square with water to create border, then fold border toward center, pressing gently to seal.

3 Spread goat cheese mixture in even layer over center of pastry, avoiding folded border. Scatter asparagus mixture over goat cheese, then crumble remaining ¼ cup goat cheese over top of asparagus mixture.

4 Bake until pastry is puffed and golden and asparagus is crisp-tender, 15 to 20 minutes. Transfer tart to wire rack and let cool for 15 minutes. Drizzle with remaining 1 tablespoon oil, slide onto cutting board or serving platter, cut into 4 equal pieces, and serve warm or at room temperature.

6 ounces thin asparagus, trimmed and cut on bias ¼ inch thick (1 cup)

2 scallions, sliced thin

3 tablespoons extra-virgin olive oil, divided

2 tablespoons chopped pitted kalamata olives

1 garlic clove, minced

¼ teaspoon grated lemon zest

¼ teaspoon table salt

¼ teaspoon pepper

4 ounces (1 cup) goat cheese, softened, divided

1 (9½ by 9-inch) sheet puff pastry, thawed

Caramelized Onion, Tomato, and Goat Cheese Tart

SERVES 4 (Makes one 9-inch tart) | **TOTAL TIME** 1¼ hours, plus 15 minutes cooling

Why This Recipe Works Deeply savory caramelized onions offer a bold counterpoint to bright tomatoes and creamy goat cheese in this flavorful tart. The transformation of the pungent raw onions into meltingly tender strands typically involves very low heat and plenty of time. A few tricks shortcut that process without sacrificing flavor or texture: water, baking soda, and higher heat. Adding water at the outset of cooking softens the onions quickly. Adding baking soda at the end increases their pH, which speeds browning and helps turn the onions' inulin into fructose, which interacts with amino acids to create flavor. Since most of the effort here is in caramelizing the onions, the recipe makes more than you need; leftovers freeze beautifully, so the next time you crave this tart, you can get it to the table even faster. See page 13 for more information on thawing frozen puff pastry.

1 **For the caramelized onions** Bring onions, ¾ cup water, oil, and salt to boil in 12-inch nonstick skillet over high heat. Cover and cook until water has evaporated and onions start to sizzle, about 10 minutes.

2 Uncover, reduce heat to medium-high, and use rubber spatula to gently press onions into sides and bottom of skillet. Cook, without stirring, for 30 seconds. Stir onions, scraping fond from skillet, then gently press onions into sides and bottom of skillet again. Repeat pressing, cooking, and stirring until onions are softened, well browned, and slightly sticky, 15 to 20 minutes.

3 Combine baking soda and remaining 1 tablespoon water in bowl. Stir baking soda solution into onions and cook, stirring constantly, until solution has evaporated, about 1 minute. Transfer onions to bowl. Reserve ½ cup onions for tart, set remaining onions aside for another use. (Onions can be refrigerated for up to 3 days or frozen for up to 1 month.)

4 **For the tart** Adjust oven rack to upper-middle position and heat oven to 425 degrees. Line baking sheet with parchment paper. Dust counter lightly with flour. Unfold puff pastry and roll into 10-inch square; transfer to prepared sheet. Lightly brush outer ½ inch of pastry square with water to create border, then fold border toward center, pressing gently to seal.

5 Stir together reserved ½ cup onions and thyme. Spread onion mixture in even layer over pastry, avoiding folded border. Arrange tomatoes and goat cheese evenly over onions. Season with salt and pepper to taste. Bake until pastry is puffed and golden, 20 to 24 minutes, rotating sheet halfway through baking. Transfer tart to wire rack and let cool for 15 minutes. Slide onto cutting board or serving platter, cut into 4 equal pieces, and serve warm or at room temperature.

Caramelized Onions

- 3 pounds onions, halved and sliced through root end ¼ inch thick
- ¾ cup plus 1 tablespoon water, divided
- 2 tablespoons vegetable oil
- ¾ teaspoon table salt
- ⅛ teaspoon baking soda

Tart

- 1 (9½ by 9-inch) sheet puff pastry, thawed
- ¼ teaspoon minced fresh thyme
- 6 ounces cherry tomatoes, halved
- 2 ounces goat cheese, crumbled (½ cup)

Fennel-Apple Tarte Tatin

SERVES 4 (Makes one 10-inch tart) | **TOTAL TIME** 1¾ hours

1 (9½ by 9-inch) sheet puff pastry, thawed

3 tablespoons extra-virgin olive oil, divided

1 tablespoon sugar

½ teaspoon plus pinch table salt, divided

2 fennel bulbs, stalks discarded (1 bulb cut into 6 wedges, 1 bulb halved, cored, and sliced lengthwise ½ inch thick)

2 Granny Smith apples, peeled, cored, halved, and sliced ½ inch thick

4 teaspoons chopped fresh sage

2 teaspoons sherry vinegar

¼ teaspoon Dijon mustard

6 ounces (6 cups) watercress, torn into bite-size pieces

2 tablespoons chopped toasted and skinned hazelnuts

2 ounces goat cheese, crumbled (½ cup) (optional)

Why This Recipe Works Yes, tarte Tatin is traditionally a dessert, made by caramelizing apples in butter and sugar and then baking them with a pie dough top. After cooking, it's inverted and the juices seep deliciously into the crust. We developed a savory version, and we simplified the recipe while we were at it. The fennel is a revelation—cut into wedges before cooking, it quickly picks up beautiful caramelization on the outside while the center turns meltingly dense and silky. Arrange the wedges in an attractive pinwheel in the skillet, and then fill in the gaps with sliced fennel and set the pan over high heat to jump-start browning (adding a small amount of sugar helps with this). Then place some sliced apple and sage on top, blanket it with puff pastry, and finish it in the oven. The apples transform into a saucy sage-infused apple base for the fennel wedges once the tart is inverted. Look for fennel bulbs that are about 4 inches tall after trimming. Do not core the fennel bulb that is cut into wedges. See page 13 for more information on thawing frozen puff pastry.

1 Adjust oven rack to middle position and heat oven to 375 degrees. Dust counter lightly with flour. Unfold puff pastry and roll into 11-inch square. Using pizza cutter or sharp knife, cut pastry into 11-inch circle. Transfer to parchment paper–lined rimmed baking sheet, cover loosely with plastic wrap, and refrigerate while preparing filling.

2 Swirl 2 tablespoons oil in bottom of 10-inch ovensafe nonstick skillet, then sprinkle with sugar and ¼ teaspoon salt. Arrange fennel wedges in pinwheel shape, fanning out from center of circle. Fill in gaps with sliced fennel. Cook, without stirring, over high heat until fennel turns deep golden brown, 7 to 9 minutes.

3 Off heat, sprinkle with apple, sage, and ¼ teaspoon salt. Carefully transfer chilled dough to skillet, centering over filling. Being careful of hot skillet, gently fold excess dough up against skillet wall (dough should be flush with skillet edge). Using paring knife, pierce dough evenly over surface 10 times. Transfer skillet to oven and bake until crust is deep golden brown, about 45 minutes. Transfer skillet to wire rack and let cool for 10 minutes.

4 Meanwhile, whisk vinegar, mustard, remaining 1 tablespoon oil, and remaining pinch salt together in large bowl. Add watercress and hazelnuts and toss to coat. Season with salt and pepper to taste.

5 Run paring knife around edge of crust to loosen. Using dish towels or potholders, carefully place serving platter on top of skillet, and, holding platter and skillet firmly together, invert tart onto serving platter. Transfer any fennel slices that stick to skillet to tart. Sprinkle with goat cheese, if using, and serve immediately with salad.

ASSEMBLING FENNEL-APPLE TARTE TATIN

1 Arrange fennel wedges in pinwheel shape in skillet.

2 Fill in remaining gaps with sliced fennel.

3 Slide prepared puff pastry on top of cooked filling in skillet and press any excess dough up sides of skillet. Transfer to oven.

Eggplant and Tomato Phyllo Pie

SERVES 4 to 6 (Makes one 9-inch pie) | **TOTAL TIME** 1¾ hours, plus 15 minutes cooling

1 pound tomatoes, cored and sliced ¼ inch thick

1¼ teaspoons table salt, divided

1 pound eggplant, sliced into ¼-inch-thick rounds

½ cup extra-virgin olive oil, divided

12 sheets (14 by 9-inch) phyllo, thawed, room temperature

3 garlic cloves, minced

2 teaspoons minced fresh oregano

¼ teaspoon pepper

6 ounces mozzarella cheese, shredded (1½ cups)

2 tablespoons grated Parmesan cheese

1 tablespoon chopped fresh basil

Why This Recipe Works Phyllo dough is another route to an easy-to-assemble yet visually stunning tart, with the paper-thin dough layers baking to a beautiful golden brown color and shatteringly crisp texture. Here phyllo is paired with eggplant and tomatoes layered between mild mozzarella and nutty Parmesan. Broiling the eggplant slices before assembling the tart gives them deeper eggplant flavor and a delightful char. To capture the tomatoes' appealing juiciness while avoiding a soggy tart, salt the slices and let them sit in a colander to draw out excess moisture. Layering 12 sheets of phyllo dough creates a crust sturdy enough to stand up to the abundance of vegetables, and doing so in an offset pattern contributes to the beautiful presentation. The insulating layer of shredded mozzarella melts into the phyllo crust for a satisfyingly cheesy layer that also helps keep the crust from getting soggy. Fresh oregano and basil bring bold herbal flavor. See page 13 for more information on working with phyllo dough.

1 Adjust oven rack 6 inches from broiler element and heat broiler. Line rimmed baking sheet with aluminum foil. Toss tomatoes and ¾ teaspoon salt together in colander and set aside to drain for 30 minutes.

2 Meanwhile, arrange eggplant in single layer on prepared sheet and brush both sides with 2 tablespoons oil. Broil eggplant until softened and beginning to brown, 10 to 12 minutes, flipping eggplant halfway through broiling. Set aside to cool slightly, about 10 minutes.

3 Heat oven to 375 degrees. Line second rimmed baking sheet with parchment paper. Place ¼ cup oil in small bowl. Place 1 phyllo sheet on prepared sheet, then lightly brush phyllo with prepared oil. Turn baking sheet 30 degrees and place second phyllo sheet on first phyllo sheet, leaving any overhanging phyllo in place. Brush second phyllo sheet with oil. Repeat turning baking sheet and layering remaining 10 phyllo sheets in pinwheel pattern, brushing each with oil (you should have 12 total layers of phyllo).

4 Shake colander to rid tomatoes of excess juice. Combine tomatoes, garlic, oregano, pepper, 1 tablespoon oil, and remaining ½ teaspoon salt in bowl. Sprinkle mozzarella evenly in center of phyllo in 9-inch circle. Shingle tomatoes and eggplant on top of mozzarella in concentric circles, alternating tomatoes and eggplant as you go. Sprinkle Parmesan cheese over top.

5 Gently fold edges of phyllo over vegetable mixture, pleating every 2 to 3 inches as needed, and lightly brush edges with remaining 1 tablespoon oil. Bake until phyllo is crisp and golden brown, about 30 to 35 minutes. Let galette cool for 15 minutes then sprinkle with basil. Slide onto cutting board or serving platter, cut into pieces, and serve.

Weeknight Spanakopita

SERVES 6 to 8 (Makes one 14 by 9-inch pie) | **TOTAL TIME** 1½ hours, plus 10 minutes cooling

Filling

1¼ pounds curly-leaf
spinach, stemmed

¼ cup water

12 ounces feta cheese, rinsed,
patted dry, and crumbled
(3 cups)

¾ cup whole-milk Greek yogurt

2 large eggs, beaten

4 scallions, sliced thin

¼ cup minced fresh mint

2 tablespoons minced fresh dill

3 garlic cloves, minced

1 teaspoon grated lemon zest
plus 1 tablespoon juice

1 teaspoon ground nutmeg

½ teaspoon pepper

¼ teaspoon table salt

⅛ teaspoon cayenne pepper

Phyllo Layers

7 tablespoons unsalted
butter, melted

8 ounces (14 by 9-inch)
phyllo, thawed

1½ ounces Pecorino Romano
cheese, grated (¾ cup)

2 teaspoons sesame seeds
(optional)

Why This Recipe Works The roots of this flaky, crisp pastry filled with spinach and feta spiked with lemon, garlic, and herbs run deep in Greek culture. Mature spinach brings bold flavor and great texture; to prepare it, microwave and chop the leaves, and then squeeze them to remove water. Rinsing the feta before adding it removes some of its strong salty brine. Traditional recipes for spanakopita often include a sheep's-milk cheese called kefalograviera for complexity. Pecorino Romano is a good stand-in, and sprinkling it between the top sheets of phyllo helps the flaky layers hold together when sliced. Rather than shaping the spanakopita into triangles, pull out a baking sheet to make one impressive pastry; its short sides allow moisture to escape, crisping up the bottom crust nicely. Cutting the spanakopita into small pieces for serving also helps the pieces hold together. See page 13 for more tips on working with phyllo.

1 **For the filling** Place spinach and water in large bowl. Cover bowl with large dinner plate (plate should completely cover bowl and not rest on spinach). Microwave until spinach is wilted and decreased in volume by half, about 5 minutes. Remove bowl from microwave and keep covered for 1 minute. Carefully remove plate and transfer spinach to colander. Using back of rubber spatula, gently press spinach against colander to release excess liquid. Transfer spinach to cutting board and chop coarse. Transfer spinach to clean dish towel and squeeze to remove excess water. Place spinach in large bowl. Add feta, yogurt, eggs, scallions, mint, dill, garlic, lemon zest and juice, nutmeg, pepper, salt, and cayenne and mix until thoroughly combined. (Filling can be refrigerated for up to 24 hours.)

2 **For the phyllo layers** Adjust oven rack to lower-middle position and heat oven to 425 degrees. Line rimmed baking sheet with parchment paper. Using pastry brush, lightly brush 14 by 9-inch rectangle in center of parchment with melted butter to cover area same size as phyllo. Lay 1 phyllo sheet on buttered parchment and brush thoroughly with melted butter. Repeat with 9 more phyllo sheets, brushing each with butter (you should have 10 total layers of phyllo).

3 Spread spinach mixture evenly over phyllo, leaving ¼-inch border. Cover spinach with 6 more phyllo sheets, brushing each with melted butter and sprinkling each with about 2 tablespoons Pecorino. Lay 2 more phyllo sheets on top, brushing each with melted butter (do not sprinkle these layers with Pecorino).

4 Working from center outward, use palms of your hands to compress layers and press out any air pockets. Using sharp knife, score spanakopita through top 3 layers of phyllo into 24 equal pieces. Sprinkle with sesame seeds, if using. Bake until phyllo is golden and crisp, 20 to 25 minutes, rotating baking sheet halfway through baking. Let cool on baking sheet at least 10 minutes or up to 2 hours. Slide spanakopita, still on parchment, onto cutting board. Cut into squares and serve.

Hortopita

SERVES 4 to 6 (Makes two 10-inch pies)　｜　**TOTAL TIME** 1¾ hours, plus 15 minutes cooling

1¼ pounds kale, Swiss chard and/
or dandelion greens, stemmed

¼ teaspoon plus ⅛ teaspoon
table salt, divided, plus salt for
blanching vegetables

7 tablespoons extra-virgin olive
oil, divided

2 leeks, white and light green
parts only, halved lengthwise,
sliced thin, and washed
thoroughly

3 garlic cloves, minced

¼ teaspoon pepper, divided

6 ounces feta cheese, crumbled
(1½ cups)

2 large eggs, lightly beaten

⅓ cup minced fresh dill

3 tablespoons minced fresh mint

14 sheets (14 by 9-inch) phyllo,
thawed, room temperature

2 teaspoons sesame seeds and/
or nigella seeds (optional)

Why This Recipe Works While spanakopita may be the most iconic Greek phyllo pie, it is just one of many delicious choices. Its antecedent, hortopita, relies on a variety of wild greens (horta), including dandelion, mustard, chicory, and sorrel, as well as fennel and dill fronds, all traditionally foraged by Greek cooks. While we encourage you to experiment with your favorite greens, this recipe uses kale, Swiss chard, and/or dandelion greens for a pleasing combination of heartier and more tender greens and a balance of mild and assertive flavors. Supplemented with fresh dill and mint, sweet leeks, and a sprinkling of briny feta, the filling is complex and aromatic, perfect for encasing in tissue-thin sheets of phyllo that crisp up into flaky layers in the oven. Hortopita is often made as a square or rectangular pie, similar to our Weeknight Spanakopita (page 124), but this version resembles a strudel, making for a more elegant presentation. See page 13 for more information on working with phyllo dough.

1 Adjust oven rack to upper-middle position and heat oven to 400 degrees. Line rimmed baking sheet with parchment paper. Bring 4 quarts water to boil in large pot over high heat. Add greens and 1 tablespoon salt and cook until tender and bright green, 2 minutes for Swiss chard and dandelion greens and 4 minutes for kale. Drain in colander and run under cold water until cool enough to handle, about 1 minute. Using hands, firmly press cooled greens to release as much liquid as possible. Chop greens fine then transfer to large bowl and set aside.

2 Heat 3 tablespoons oil in now-empty pot over medium heat until shimmering. Add leeks, garlic, ¼ teaspoon salt, and ⅛ teaspoon pepper and cook until leeks are softened, 5 to 7 minutes. Transfer leeks to bowl with chopped greens and set aside to cool slightly, about 10 minutes. Stir in feta, eggs, dill, mint, remaining ⅛ teaspoon salt, and remaining ⅛ teaspoon pepper; set aside.

3 Place 16 by 12-inch sheet of parchment paper on counter with long side parallel to edge of counter. Place 1 phyllo sheet on parchment with long side parallel to edge of counter. Lightly brush sheet with oil. Repeat with 6 more phyllo sheets and oil, stacking sheets as you go.

4 Arrange half of greens mixture in 2½ by 10-inch rectangle 2 inches from bottom edge of phyllo and about 2 inches from each side. Using parchment, fold sides of phyllo over filling, then fold bottom edge of phyllo over filling. Brush folded portions of phyllo with oil. Fold top edge snugly over filling, making sure top and bottom edges overlap securely by about 1 inch. (If they do not overlap, unfold, rearrange filling into slightly narrower strip, and refold.) Press firmly to seal. Using thin metal spatula, carefully transfer to prepared sheet. Repeat process with remaining phyllo, oil, and remaining greens mixture, evenly spacing hortopita on prepared sheet. Lightly brush top and sides with oil. Using sharp knife, make 6 evenly spaced ¼-inch-deep slashes, 2 inches long, on top of each hortopita. Sprinkle with sesame and/or nigella seeds, if using.

5 Bake hortopita until golden brown, 35 to 40 minutes, rotating sheet halfway through baking. Let cool for 15 minutes. Slice and serve.

SHAPING HORTOPITA

1 Place 1 phyllo sheet on parchment paper and brush with oil. Repeat with 6 more sheets, stacking sheets as you go.

2 Arrange half of greens mixture in 2½ by 10-inch rectangle 2 inches from bottom edge of phyllo and about 2 inches from each side. Using parchment, fold sides of phyllo over filling, then fold bottom edge of phyllo over filling.

3 Brush folded portions of phyllo with oil. Fold top edge snugly over filling, making sure top and bottom edges overlap by about 1 inch. Press firmly to seal.

Chicken B'stilla

SERVES 10 to 12 (Makes one 12-inch pie) | **TOTAL TIME** 2¾ hours, plus 15 minutes cooling

½ cup extra-virgin olive oil, divided

1 onion, chopped fine

¾ teaspoon table salt

1 tablespoon grated fresh ginger

½ teaspoon pepper

½ teaspoon ground turmeric

½ teaspoon paprika

1½ cups water

2 pounds boneless, skinless chicken thighs, trimmed

6 large eggs

½ cup minced fresh cilantro

1 pound (14 by 9-inch) phyllo, thawed

1½ cups slivered almonds, toasted and chopped

¼ cup confectioners' sugar, divided

1 tablespoon ground cinnamon, divided

Why This Recipe Works The filling for this impressive Moroccan tart is customarily made with pigeon and richly flavored with almonds, cinnamon, and sugar. Here we swap the pigeon for chicken thighs, cooking them gently in a spiced broth. This rich cooking liquid is then used to create the thick filling, which traditionally has a custardlike consistency. Although b'stilla is usually made with layers of a paper-thin dough called warqa, phyllo also works perfectly. Assembling the pie in a 12-inch skillet (the same one you use to cook the chicken) creates a wide, thin pie. Traditionally the b'stilla is topped with a mixture of slivered almonds tossed with cinnamon and sugar. In this version, you encase the almond mixture in the phyllo to form the base of the pie; this lets it soak up the rich juices from the chicken. A final sprinkling of cinnamon sugar over the baked pie highlights the sweet and savory contrasts. See page 13 for more information on working with phyllo dough.

1 Heat 1 tablespoon oil in 12-inch ovensafe nonstick skillet over medium heat until shimmering. Add onion and salt and cook until softened, about 5 minutes. Stir in ginger, pepper, turmeric, and paprika and cook until fragrant, about 30 seconds. Add water and chicken and bring to simmer. Reduce heat to low; cover; and cook until chicken registers 175 degrees, 15 to 20 minutes. Transfer chicken to cutting board, let cool slightly, then shred into bite-size pieces using 2 forks; transfer to large bowl.

2 Whisk eggs together in small bowl. Bring cooking liquid to boil over high heat and cook until reduced to about 1 cup, about 10 minutes. Reduce heat to low. Whisking constantly, slowly pour eggs into broth and cook until mixture resembles loose scrambled eggs, 6 to 8 minutes; transfer to bowl with chicken. Stir in cilantro until combined. Wipe skillet clean with paper towels and let cool completely.

3 Adjust oven rack to middle position and heat oven to 375 degrees. Brush 1 phyllo sheet with oil and arrange in bottom of cooled skillet with short side against side of pan. Some phyllo will overhang edge of skillet; leave in place. Turn skillet 30 degrees. Brush second phyllo sheet with oil and arrange in skillet, leaving any overhanging phyllo in place. Repeat turning and layering with 10 more phyllo sheets in pinwheel pattern, brushing each with oil, to cover entire circumference of skillet (you should have 12 total layers of phyllo).

4 Combine almonds, 3 tablespoons sugar, and 2 teaspoons cinnamon in small bowl. Sprinkle mixture over phyllo in skillet. Lay 2 phyllo sheets evenly across top of almond mixture and brush top with oil. Rotate skillet 90 degrees and lay 2 more phyllo sheets evenly across top; do not brush with oil. Spoon chicken mixture into skillet and spread into even layer.

5 Stack 5 phyllo sheets on counter and brush top with oil. Fold phyllo in half crosswise and brush top with oil. Lay phyllo stack on center of chicken mixture.

6 Fold overhanging phyllo over filling and phyllo stack, pleating phyllo every 2 to 3 inches, and press to seal. Brush top with oil and bake until phyllo is crisp and golden, 35 to 40 minutes.

7 Combine remaining 1 tablespoon sugar and remaining 1 teaspoon cinnamon in small bowl. Let b'stilla cool in skillet for 15 minutes. Using rubber spatula, carefully slide b'stilla out onto cutting board or serving platter. Dust top with cinnamon sugar, slice, and serve.

ASSEMBLING CHICKEN B'STILLA

1 Brush 1 phyllo sheet with oil and arrange in bottom of skillet with short side against side of pan. Continue layering 11 more phyllo sheets in skillet in pinwheel pattern.

2 Sprinkle almond mixture over phyllo in skillet, then lay 2 phyllo sheets across top and brush with oil. Rotate skillet 90 degrees and lay 2 more phyllo sheets across top.

3 Spoon chicken mixture into skillet and spread into even layer. Stack 5 phyllo sheets and brush with oil. Fold in half, brush top with oil, and lay on chicken mixture.

4 Fold overhanging phyllo over filling and phyllo stack, pleating phyllo every 2 to 3 inches, and press to seal. Brush top with oil before baking.

Lamb Phyllo Pie

SERVES 8 (Makes one 12-inch pie) | **TOTAL TIME** 1¼ hours, plus 15 minutes cooling

Why This Recipe Works In this delectable pie inspired by the flavors of Greek cuisine, the layers of phyllo pastry absorb all the umami-rich drippings from the ground lamb while still retaining their crispy texture. A potent seasoning blend of coriander, cumin, paprika, cayenne, and cinnamon complements the lamb flavor and ensures that every bite is packed with spice. Sauté the lamb just enough to make sure that it's no longer pink; add the spices; and then stir in fresh cilantro, sweet raisins, and briny feta. To build the dish, create two distinct layers of lamb sandwiched between oil-brushed sheets of phyllo in a rectangular baking pan. After it comes out of the oven, sprinkle a mixture of toasted chopped pistachios, cilantro, and lemon zest over the crispy top. A straight-sided traditional metal baking pan works best to support the layers of this pie. See page 13 for more information on working with phyllo dough.

1 Adjust oven rack to lower-middle position and heat oven to 400 degrees. Heat 1 tablespoon oil in 12-inch nonstick skillet over medium-high heat until shimmering. Add onion and cook until softened, about 5 minutes. Stir in lamb and cook, breaking up meat with wooden spoon, until no longer pink, 5 to 8 minutes. Using slotted spoon, transfer lamb to large bowl; wipe out all but 2 tablespoons fat left in skillet. Cook 1 tablespoon lemon zest, coriander, cumin, paprika, salt, pepper, cayenne, and cinnamon in skillet until fragrant, about 30 seconds. Add mixture to bowl with lamb, along with feta, 1 cup cilantro, raisins, and lemon juice.

2 Stack 8 phyllo sheets in bottom of greased 13 by 9-inch baking pan, brushing sheets thoroughly with 5 teaspoons oil (a generous ½ teaspoon oil per sheet) before layering. Sprinkle half reserved lamb filling evenly over phyllo. Cover with 8 more phyllo sheets, brushing with 5 teaspoons oil (a generous ½ teaspoon oil per sheet), then sprinkle evenly with remaining lamb filling. Cover lamb filling with 8 more phyllo sheets, brushing all but final layer with 1 tablespoon oil (a scant ½ teaspoon oil per sheet). Working from center outward, use palms of your hands to compress layers and press out any air pockets. Brush top layer with remaining 2 teaspoons oil.

3 Using serrated knife with pointed tip, cut pie into 8 squares. Bake until golden and crisp, 30 to 40 minutes, rotating pan halfway through baking. Remove from oven and let cool for 15 minutes. Combine pistachios, remaining ¼ cup cilantro, and remaining 1 tablespoon lemon zest in small bowl. Sprinkle phyllo pie with pistachio mixture and serve.

- 6 tablespoons extra-virgin olive oil, divided
- 1 onion, chopped
- 2 pounds ground lamb
- 2 tablespoons grated lemon zest, divided, plus 3 tablespoons juice
- 1 tablespoon ground coriander
- 1 tablespoon ground cumin
- 1 tablespoon paprika
- 2 teaspoons table salt
- 1½ teaspoons pepper
- ¼ teaspoon cayenne pepper
- ¼ teaspoon ground cinnamon
- 8 ounces feta cheese, crumbled (2 cups)
- 1¼ cups chopped fresh cilantro, divided
- ½ cup golden raisins
- 1 pound (14 by 9-inch) phyllo, thawed
- ¼ cup pistachios, toasted and chopped fine

No-Knead Brioche Tarts with Zucchini and Crispy Prosciutto

SERVES 8 (Makes 8 tarts) | TOTAL TIME 1¾ hours, plus 20 hours resting

Dough

1⅔ cups (9⅛ ounces) bread flour

1¼ teaspoons instant or rapid-rise yeast

¾ teaspoon table salt

3 large eggs, room temperature, plus 1 large egg lightly beaten with 1 teaspoon water

8 tablespoons unsalted butter, melted

¼ cup water, room temperature

3 tablespoons sugar

Filling

1 (8 ounce) zucchini, halved lengthwise and sliced ⅛ inch thick

¾ teaspoon table salt, divided

6 ounces (¾ cup) whole-milk ricotta cheese

2 ounces whole-milk mozzarella cheese, shredded (½ cup)

3 tablespoons extra-virgin olive oil, divided

¼ cup chopped fresh basil, divided

2 garlic cloves, minced

¼ teaspoon pepper

2 ounces thinly sliced prosciutto, sliced ¼-inch-thick crosswise

Why This Recipe Works Elevate fluffy, tender brioche to the next level by turning it into a buttery nest for zucchini, a blend of cheeses, and prosciutto. Classic brioche bread has a tender crumb, a golden color, and a buttery, eggy flavor. Achieving these sumptuous results via traditional methods is laborious: Butter, softened to just the proper temperature, is kneaded into the dough in increments to ensure that it is completely incorporated. Only after one portion is fully incorporated can the next be added. We developed this much simpler no-knead method by using melted butter instead of solid butter for an enriched brioche that needs no kneading. The folding process and long resting time ensure success by encouraging the gluten to form correctly. For the savory filling, a blend of ricotta, mozzarella, garlic, and basil makes the creamy cheese base. To ensure that the zucchini slices won't leach moisture into the tart, you'll salt them and let them drain for half an hour on paper towels before shingling them on top of the cheese and baking the tarts. To finish these in style, give them a final sprinkle of salty crisped-up prosciutto and chopped fresh basil. We used King Arthur bread flour to develop this recipe.

1 **For the dough** Whisk flour, yeast, and salt together in large bowl. Whisk room temperature eggs, melted butter, water, and sugar together in second bowl until sugar has dissolved.

2 Using rubber spatula, gently fold egg mixture into flour mixture, scraping up dry flour from bottom of bowl, until cohesive dough starts to form and no dry flour remains. Cover bowl tightly with plastic wrap and let dough rest for 10 minutes.

3 Using greased bowl scraper (or your fingertips), fold dough over itself by gently lifting and folding edge of dough toward middle. Turn bowl 90 degrees and fold dough again; repeat turning bowl and folding dough 2 more times (total of 4 folds). Cover tightly with plastic and let rise for 30 minutes. Repeat folding and rising every 30 minutes, 3 more times. After fourth set of folds, cover bowl tightly with plastic and refrigerate for at least 16 hours or up to 48 hours.

4 Line 2 rimmed baking sheets with parchment paper. Transfer dough to well-floured counter and divide into 8 equal portions (about 2 ½ ounces each). Working with 1 piece of dough at a time (keep remaining pieces covered), form into rough ball by stretching dough around your thumbs and pinching edges together so that top is smooth. Place ball seam side down on clean counter and, using your cupped hand, drag in small circles until dough feels taut and round. Repeat with remaining pieces of dough.

5 Evenly space 4 rounds seam side down on each prepared sheet, about 3 inches apart. Cover loosely with greased plastic and let rise until rounds double in size and dough springs back minimally when poked gently with your knuckle, 1½ to 2 hours.

6 For the filling Toss zucchini with ½ teaspoon salt and spread over paper towel–lined plate. Let zucchini sit for 30 minutes, then gently blot dry with paper towels; set aside. Combine ricotta, mozzarella, 2 tablespoons oil, 2 tablespoons basil, garlic, pepper, and remaining ¼ teaspoon salt; set aside. Heat remaining 1 tablespoon oil in 12-inch nonstick skillet over medium heat until shimmering. Add prosciutto and cook, stirring frequently, until crispy, about 7 minutes. Using slotted spoon, transfer to paper towel–lined plate and set aside to cool.

7 Adjust oven racks to upper-middle and lower-middle positions and heat oven to 350 degrees. Grease bottom of flat-bottomed, round, 2 ½-inch-wide dry measuring cup or drinking glass. Press cup firmly into center of each dough round until cup touches sheet to make indentation for filling. Divide reserved ricotta mixture evenly among each indentation (about 2 tablespoons each) then spread into smooth layer. Divide reserved zucchini evenly among each tartlet, shingling zucchini decoratively on top of ricotta.

8 Gently brush dough with egg wash and bake until light golden brown, 15 to 20 minutes, switching and rotating sheets halfway through baking. Transfer tarts to wire rack and let cool for 15 minutes. Sprinkle with reserved crispy prosciutto and remaining 2 tablespoons basil. Serve warm or at room temperature.

French Onion and Bacon Tart

SERVES 6 to 8 (Makes one 9-inch tart) | **TOTAL TIME** 1 hour, plus 15 minutes cooling

Why This Recipe Works This elegant tart elevates the humble onion to a higher status by gently simmering it until meltingly soft, enriching it with an egg custard, and baking it in a buttery crust. With its slim tart shell and more onions than custard in the filling, this is a more refined version of a quiche. For a tart with so few ingredients, the top consideration is how best to prepare the onions so that they turn out fully tender yet not too sweet. Slicing the onions crosswise (against the direction of their fibers) allows them to soften and break down more readily than slicing them through the root end. Leaving the lid on the skillet the whole time the onions are cooking causes them to cook faster, in their own juices, so they become tender more quickly and retain their pure onion flavor, without too much browning. And they require minimal supervision—just a stir here and there. Though the onions are traditionally cooked in butter for this tart, we use the rendered fat left over from crisping up some bacon. Sprinkling the crispy bacon pieces on top of the tart offers a salty, smoky contrast to the creamy filling. Yellow or white onions work well, but avoid sweet onions, such as Vidalias, which will make the custard filling too watery and the tart too sweet. If you do not have 2 tablespoons fat left over from cooking the bacon, add vegetable oil as needed to make this amount.

1 Adjust oven rack to middle position and heat oven to 375 degrees. Cook bacon in 12-inch nonstick skillet over medium heat until crispy, 5 to 7 minutes. Using slotted spoon, transfer bacon to paper towel–lined plate. Pour off all but 2 tablespoons fat from skillet (add vegetable oil to supplement, if necessary).

2 Add onions, salt, and thyme sprig to skillet. Cover and cook until onions release liquid and start to wilt, about 10 minutes. Reduce heat to low and continue to cook, covered, until onions are very soft, about 20 minutes, stirring once or twice (if after 15 minutes onions look wet, remove lid and continue to cook another 5 minutes). Remove pan from heat and let onions cool for 5 minutes.

3 Whisk eggs, half-and-half, and pepper together in large bowl. Discard thyme sprig. Stir onions into egg mixture until just incorporated. Spread onion mixture over tart shell and sprinkle bacon evenly over top. Bake tart on sheet until center feels firm to touch, 20 to 25 minutes. Transfer sheet to wire rack and let cool for 15 minutes. Remove outer metal ring of tart pan, slide thin metal spatula between tart and pan bottom, and carefully slide tart onto cutting board or serving platter. Cut into wedges and serve warm or at room temperature.

4 slices bacon, cut into ¼-inch pieces

1½ pounds onions, halved through root end and sliced crosswise ¼ inch thick

¾ teaspoon table salt

1 sprig fresh thyme

2 large eggs

½ cup half-and-half

¼ teaspoon pepper

1 recipe Press-In Tart Dough (page 335), baked and cooled

Camembert, Sun-Dried Tomato, and Potato Tart

SERVES 6 to 8 (Makes one 9-inch tart) | **TOTAL TIME** 1¼ hours, plus 15 minutes cooling

Why This Recipe Works An entire wheel of soft, pungent Camembert cheese is the star of this decadent tart. Just slice the whole wheel horizontally through its middle, cut the halves into wedges, and then arrange the wedges cut side down over a potato and onion filling in the tart shell. As the tart bakes, the cheese rind forms a crisp-chewy crust and the cheese melts out over the filling and into all the crevices, melding everything together in delicious fashion. The flavor inspiration for this tart comes from the hearty French dish of cheese, potatoes, onions, and bacon called tartiflette. Here, though, sun-dried tomatoes take the place of bacon. Their concentrated, salty-sweet flavor and satisfying texture are fantastic with the rich cheese and potatoes and the buttery crust. If you can't find an 8-ounce wheel of Camembert, look for wedges that you can slice in half. Depending on the ripeness and style of the cheese used, it may have a different flavor intensity and level of meltability.

2 tablespoons unsalted butter

1 onion, halved and sliced ¼ inch thick

1 pound Yukon Gold potatoes, peeled and sliced ¼ inch thick

2 teaspoons minced fresh thyme

1 teaspoon table salt

¼ teaspoon pepper

½ cup oil-packed sun-dried tomatoes, rinsed, patted dry, and chopped coarse

1 recipe Press-In Tart Dough (page 335), baked and cooled

1 (8-ounce) wheel Camembert cheese

1 Adjust oven rack to middle position and heat oven to 375 degrees. Melt butter in 12-inch nonstick skillet over medium heat. Add onion and cook, stirring often, until golden brown, about 10 minutes. Stir in potatoes, thyme, salt, and pepper and cook, stirring occasionally, until potatoes are completely tender and lightly browned, 8 to 10 minutes. Stir in sun-dried tomatoes.

2 Spread potato mixture evenly into tart shell. Cut Camembert wheel in half horizontally to make 2 thin wheels, then cut each half into 4 wedges. Arrange wedges of cheese, rind side up, over top of tart. (Assembled tart can be refrigerated for up to 24 hours.)

3 Bake tart on rimmed baking sheet until crust is golden and cheese is melted and bubbling, 25 to 35 minutes, rotating sheet halfway through baking.

4 Transfer sheet to wire rack and let cool for 15 minutes. Remove outer metal ring of tart pan, slide thin metal spatula between tart and pan bottom, and carefully slide tart onto cutting board or serving platter. Cut into wedges and serve warm.

Smoked Salmon and Leek Tart

SERVES 6 to 8 (Makes one 9-inch tart) | **TOTAL TIME** 1 hour, plus 2 hours cooling

1 tablespoon unsalted butter

1 pound leeks, white and light green parts only, halved lengthwise, sliced thin, and washed thoroughly

½ teaspoon table salt

2 large eggs

½ cup half-and-half

1 tablespoon minced fresh dill

¼ teaspoon pepper

1 recipe Press-In Tart Dough (page 335), baked and cooled

6 ounces thinly sliced smoked salmon, cut into ¼-inch pieces

1 tablespoon extra-virgin olive oil

1 tablespoon minced fresh chives

Why This Recipe Works Scottish cooks have an arsenal of amazing dishes using smoked salmon caught and produced from the local waters, including this favorite, an elegant tart that makes a stunning presentation. The pink salmon and the green leeks embedded in the pale yellow egg-enriched custard create a gorgeous color contrast. And it's just as delicious as it looks, with all those textures in every bite, plus perfectly baked flaky tart crust. The tart has just enough silky, eggy custard to bind the ingredients together, acting as a supporting player to really showcase the rich smoked salmon. In fact, the preserve all the flavor of the seafood, you toss the chopped smoked salmon with a little olive oil and fresh chives and then sprinkle it over the tart *after* baking. Serve this showstopper with lemon wedges, if you like.

1 Adjust oven rack to middle position and heat oven to 375 degrees. Melt butter in 10-inch skillet over medium heat. Add leeks and salt and cook, covered, stirring occasionally, until leeks are softened, about 10 minutes. Remove pan from heat and let leeks cool, uncovered, for 5 minutes.

2 Whisk eggs, half-and-half, dill, and pepper together in bowl. Stir in leeks until just incorporated. Place tart shell on rimmed baking sheet and place in oven. Carefully pour egg mixture into shell and bake until filling has set and center feels firm to touch, 20 to 25 minutes. Transfer sheet to wire rack and let cool completely, at least 2 hours. (Baked tart can be refrigerated for up to 24 hours; bring tart to room temperature before continuing with step 3.)

3 Just before serving, toss salmon, oil, and chives together in bowl and season with salt and pepper to taste before sprinkling evenly over tart. Remove outer metal ring of tart pan, slide thin metal spatula between tart and pan bottom, and carefully slide tart onto cutting board or serving platter. Cut into wedges and serve at room temperature.

Potato and Parmesan Tart

SERVES 6 to 8 (Makes one 11 by 8-inch tart) | **TOTAL TIME** 1¼ hours, plus 30 minutes cooling

Why This Recipe Works With potatoes, Parmesan, and cream cheese packed into a buttery, crisp crust, this rustic and hearty free-form tart is a major crowd-pleaser. It uses our easy Galette Dough (although we call this a tart, since it's rectangular rather than round). The starchy quality of russets works great here; slicing the potatoes into thin rounds ensures that they cook evenly with no underdone spots (problems that can plague potatoes cut into chunks or wedges). Fold the sliced spuds into a mixture of softened cream cheese, mustard, shallot, and Parmesan; add an egg yolk for stability and extra richness; and add fresh rosemary (both in the filling and sprinkled on top) for a savory herbal quality. A light brush of egg white on the pastry dough before baking fosters a golden crust while acting as glue for anchoring a bit more sprinkled-on cheese, making the crust just as savory as the filling. You can substitute Yukon Gold potatoes for the russets, if desired. A baking stone helps to crisp the crust but is not essential; you can use a preheated rimless or overturned baking sheet instead.

1   1 recipe Galette Dough (page 336)
     4 ounces cream cheese
     2 ounces Parmesan cheese, grated (1 cup), divided
     2 tablespoons extra-virgin olive oil
     2 teaspoons Dijon mustard
     1½ teaspoons minced fresh rosemary, divided
     ½ teaspoon table salt
     ¼ teaspoon pepper
     1 large egg, separated
     1 pound russet potatoes, peeled and sliced ⅛ inch thick
     1 shallot, sliced thin

1   Adjust oven rack to lower-middle position, place baking stone on rack, and heat oven to 375 degrees. Line rimmed baking sheet with parchment paper. Roll dough into 14 by 11-inch rectangle on lightly floured counter, then transfer to prepared sheet.

2   Microwave cream cheese in large bowl until softened, 20 to 30 seconds. Whisk in ½ cup Parmesan, oil, mustard, 1 teaspoon rosemary, salt, and pepper until combined, about 20 seconds. Whisk in egg yolk. Add potatoes and shallot to cream cheese mixture and stir to thoroughly coat potatoes.

3   Transfer filling to center of dough and press into even layer, leaving 2-inch border. Sprinkle 6 tablespoons Parmesan and remaining ½ teaspoon rosemary over filling.

4   Grasp 1 long side of dough and fold about 1½ inches over filling. Repeat with opposing long side. Fold in short sides of dough, overlapping corners of dough to secure. Lightly beat egg white and brush over folded crust (you won't need it all). Sprinkle remaining 2 tablespoons Parmesan over crust.

5   Set sheet on stone and bake until crust and filling are golden brown and potatoes meet little resistance when poked with fork, about 45 minutes. Transfer sheet to wire rack and let tart cool for 10 minutes. Using offset or wide metal spatula, loosen tart from parchment and carefully slide tart onto wire rack; let cool until just warm, about 20 minutes. Slide tart onto cutting board or serving platter. Cut into slices and serve warm.

Variation

Potato and Blue Cheese Tart

Reduce Parmesan to ½ cup. Use ¼ cup in cream cheese mixture in step 4, 2 tablespoons to sprinkle over potatoes in step 5, and 2 tablespoons to sprinkle over folded crust in step 6. Add ¼ cup crumbled blue cheese to cream cheese mixture in step 4. Sprinkle additional ¼ cup crumbled blue cheese over potato mixture in step 5.

Corn, Tomato, and Bacon Galette

SERVES 4 to 6 (Makes one 8-inch galette) | **TOTAL TIME** 1¼ hours, plus 35 minutes cooling

3 slices bacon

1 cup frozen corn, thawed and patted dry

1 cup (6 ounces) cherry tomatoes, halved

½ cup shredded cheddar cheese (2 ounces)

1 garlic clove, minced

¼ teaspoon table salt

1 recipe Galette Dough (page 336)

¼ cup grated Parmesan cheese (½ ounce)

1 large egg, lightly beaten

1 scallion, dark green part only, sliced thin

Why This Recipe Works Galettes are essentially rustic and dramatic-looking free-form pies, assembled on a baking sheet rather than in a pie pan. The simple, buttery dough is rolled out into a circle and topped with a filling, and then the edges of the dough are partially folded over the filling, leaving the center exposed. Though they may be more common in fruit-filled dessert versions, savory galettes such as this one are perfectly at home on the table at any time of day. This simple, family-friendly galette screams summertime, but thanks to frozen corn kernels and always reliable cherry tomatoes, you can make it any time you need to bring some sunny summer vibes to the table. To prevent the corn and tomatoes from turning the crust soggy as the galette bakes, sprinkle a layer of grated Parmesan over the crust before topping it with the vegetable mixture—possibly the most delicious insulation material imaginable. For a festive presentation, pleat the crust as you fold over the dough. A baking stone helps to crisp the crust but is not essential; you can use a preheated rimless or overturned baking sheet instead.

1 Adjust oven rack to lower-middle position, place baking stone on rack, and heat oven to 375 degrees. Line rimmed baking sheet with parchment paper.

2 Spread bacon out over 2 layers of paper towels on plate, then cover with 2 more layers of paper towels. Microwave until bacon is crispy, 3 to 5 minutes. Let bacon cool slightly, then crumble.

3 In large bowl, stir together corn, tomatoes, cheddar cheese, garlic, and salt. Roll dough into 12-inch circle on lightly floured counter, then transfer to prepared sheet. Sprinkle Parmesan cheese evenly over dough, leaving 2-inch border (dough may run up lip of sheet slightly; this is OK). Spread corn-tomato mixture over Parmesan. Sprinkle cooked bacon over top.

4 Grasp 1 edge of dough and fold outer 2 inches over filling. Repeat around circumference of tart, overlapping dough every 2 to 3 inches; gently pinch pleated dough to secure but do not press dough into filling. Brush dough with egg (you won't need it all).

5 Set sheet on stone and bake until crust is golden brown, 45 to 50 minutes. Transfer sheet to wire rack and let galette cool for 15 minutes. Using offset or wide metal spatula, loosen galette from parchment and carefully slide tart onto wire rack; let cool until just warm, about 20 minutes. Slide tart onto cutting board or serving platter. Sprinkle scallion greens over filling, cut into wedges, and serve immediately.

PLEATING GALETTE DOUGH

1 Gently grasp 1 edge of dough and make 2-inch-wide fold over filling.

2 Lift and fold another segment of dough over first fold to form pleat. Repeat every 2 to 3 inches.

Fresh Tomato Galette

SERVES 4 to 6 (Makes one 8-inch galette) | **TOTAL TIME** 1½ hours, plus 50 minutes salting and cooling

Why This Recipe Works Whereas the Corn, Tomato, and Bacon Galette (page 144) will shine no matter what time of year you bake it, this galette is definitely best made with gorgeously ripe seasonal summertime tomatoes. The challenging part about baking with such precious jewels, though, is their unpredictable levels of juice. To draw out not only the tomatoes' excess juice but also their best, most concentrated flavor, salt the slices and let them sit in a colander to drain before building the galette. Shaking the colander after the 30-minute rest helps ensure that no stray liquid sneaks into the crust. Lining the inside of the galette dough with a layer of mustard and shredded Gruyère cheese provides added protection to ensure a crisp crust. Although the amount of overlapping crust is smaller in this recipe, the pleating technique is the same as on page 145. You can use sharp cheddar cheese instead of the Gruyère, if desired. A baking stone helps to crisp the crust but is not essential; you can use a preheated rimless or overturned baking sheet instead.

1 Toss tomatoes and 1 teaspoon salt together in large bowl. Transfer tomatoes to colander and set colander in sink. Let tomatoes drain for 30 minutes.

2 Adjust oven rack to lower-middle position, place baking stone on rack, and heat oven to 375 degrees. Line rimmed baking sheet with parchment paper. Roll dough into 12-inch circle on lightly floured counter, then transfer to prepared sheet (dough may run up lip of sheet slightly; this is OK).

3 Shake colander well to rid tomatoes of excess juice. Combine tomatoes, shallot, oil, thyme, garlic, pepper, and remaining ½ teaspoon salt in now-empty bowl. Spread mustard over dough, leaving 1½-inch border. Sprinkle Gruyère in even layer over mustard. Shingle tomatoes and shallot on top of Gruyère in concentric circles, keeping within 1½-inch border. Sprinkle Parmesan over tomato mixture.

4 Carefully grasp 1 edge of dough and fold up about 1 inch over filling. Repeat around circumference of tart, overlapping dough every 2 to 3 inches, gently pinching pleated dough to secure. Brush dough with egg (you won't need it all).

5 Set sheet on stone and bake until crust is golden brown and tomatoes are bubbling, 45 to 50 minutes. Transfer sheet to wire rack and let galette cool for 10 minutes. Using metal spatula, loosen galette from parchment and carefully slide onto wire rack; let cool until just warm, about 20 minutes. Slide tart onto cutting board or serving platter. Sprinkle basil over filling, cut into wedges, and serve immediately.

1½ pounds mixed tomatoes, cored and sliced ¼ inch thick

1½ teaspoons table salt, divided

1 recipe Galette Dough (page 336)

1 shallot, sliced thin

2 tablespoons extra-virgin olive oil

1 teaspoon minced fresh thyme

1 garlic clove, minced

¼ teaspoon pepper

2 teaspoons Dijon mustard

3 ounces Gruyère cheese, shredded (¾ cup)

2 tablespoons grated Parmesan cheese

1 large egg, lightly beaten

1 tablespoon chopped fresh basil

Mushroom and Leek Galette with Gorgonzola

SERVES 6 (Makes one 10-inch galette) | TOTAL TIME 1½ hours, plus 30 minutes cooling

1¼   pounds shiitake mushrooms, stemmed and sliced thin

5   teaspoons extra-virgin olive oil, divided

1   pound leeks, white and light green parts only, halved lengthwise, sliced ½ inch thick, and washed thoroughly (3 cups)

1   teaspoon minced fresh thyme

2   tablespoons crème fraîche

1   tablespoon Dijon mustard

1   recipe Whole-Wheat Galette Dough (page 337)

3   ounces Gorgonzola cheese, crumbled (¾ cup)

1   large egg, lightly beaten

2   tablespoons minced fresh parsley

Why This Recipe Works An umami-packed vegetable filling is tucked into a nutty whole-wheat crust in this galette. To make the filling both intensely flavorful and cohesive, pair the mushrooms and leeks with a potent triple binder of crème fraîche, Dijon mustard, and crumbled Gorgonzola. Mushrooms release a lot of liquid when cooked, so removing their excess moisture is crucial to both concentrating their flavor and preventing a soggy crust. To do that, simply microwave and drain the mushrooms before combining them with browned leeks and spreading them over the dough, topping everything off with crumbled Gorgonzola. You'll need a generous amount of flour (up to ¼ cup) to roll this dough out. Cutting a few small holes in the dough prevents it from lifting off the pan as it bakes. To pleat the dough, see page 145. A baking stone helps to crisp the crust but is not essential; you can use a preheated rimless or overturned baking sheet instead.

1 Microwave mushrooms in large bowl, covered, until just tender, 3 to 5 minutes. Transfer to colander and let drain; return to bowl. Meanwhile, heat 1 tablespoon oil in 12-inch skillet over medium heat until shimmering. Add leeks and thyme; cover; and cook, stirring occasionally, until leeks are tender and beginning to brown, 5 to 7 minutes. Transfer to bowl with mushrooms. Stir in crème fraîche and mustard. Season with salt and pepper to taste; set aside.

2 Adjust oven rack to lower-middle position, place baking stone on rack, and heat oven to 400 degrees. Line rimmed baking sheet with parchment paper. Roll dough into 14-inch circle about ⅛ inch thick on floured counter. (Trim edges as needed to form rough circle.) Transfer dough to prepared sheet. Using straw or tip of paring knife, cut five ¼-inch circles in dough (1 at center and 4 evenly spaced halfway from center to edge of dough). Brush top of dough with 1 teaspoon oil.

3 Spread half of filling evenly over dough, leaving 2-inch border. Sprinkle half of Gorgonzola over filling, cover with remaining filling, and top with remaining Gorgonzola. Drizzle remaining 1 teaspoon oil over filling. Grasp 1 edge of dough and fold outer 2 inches over filling. Repeat around circumference of tart, overlapping dough every 2 to 3 inches; gently pinch pleated dough to secure but do not press dough into filling. Brush dough with egg (you won't need it all).

4 Reduce oven temperature to 375 degrees. Set sheet on stone and bake until crust is deep golden brown and filling is beginning to brown, 35 to 45 minutes. Let tart cool on sheet on wire rack for 10 minutes. Using offset or wide metal spatula, loosen tart from parchment and carefully slide tart onto wire rack; let cool until just warm, about 20 minutes. Slide tart onto cutting board or serving platter. Sprinkle parsley over filling, cut into wedges, and serve warm.

Butternut Squash Galette with Gruyère

SERVES 6 (Makes one 10-inch galette) | **TOTAL TIME** 1½ hours, plus 10 minutes cooling

6 ounces (6 cups) baby spinach

1¼ pounds butternut squash, peeled and cut into ½-inch pieces (3½ cups)

5 teaspoons extra-virgin olive oil, divided

1 red onion, sliced thin

½ teaspoon minced fresh oregano

3 ounces Gruyère cheese, shredded (¾ cup)

2 tablespoons crème fraîche

1 teaspoon sherry vinegar

1 recipe Whole-Wheat Galette Dough (page 337)

1 large egg, lightly beaten

2 tablespoons minced fresh parsley

Why This Recipe Works A robust galette starring butternut squash and baby spinach is bound to be a favorite on any fall or winter table. The hearty filling is a great match for the sturdy whole-wheat crust. Just because this crust is sturdy, though, doesn't mean that you can add the vegetables without any parcooking. They'll leach too much moisture and render the crust soggy. As with the mushrooms in the Mushroom and Leek Galette with Gorgonzola (page 148), parcooking the spinach and squash in the microwave takes only a few minutes and helps get rid of excess liquid. Sautéed onion, a dollop of crème fraîche, shredded Gruyère, and a splash of sherry vinegar add rich, complex layers of flavor to the vegetables. You'll need a generous amount of flour (up to ¼ cup) to roll this dough out. Cutting a few small holes in the dough prevents it from lifting off the pan as it bakes. To pleat the dough, see page 145. A baking stone helps to crisp the crust but is not essential; you can use a preheated rimless or overturned baking sheet instead.

1 Microwave spinach and ¼ cup water in large bowl, covered, until spinach is shrunk by half, 3 to 4 minutes. Remove bowl from microwave and set aside, covered, for 1 minute. Transfer spinach to colander to drain. Using back of rubber spatula, gently press spinach to release excess liquid. Transfer spinach to cutting board and chop coarse. Return spinach to colander and press again with rubber spatula; set aside. Add squash to now-empty bowl and microwave, covered, until just tender, about 8 minutes; set aside.

2 Meanwhile, heat 1 tablespoon oil in 12-inch skillet over medium heat until shimmering. Add onion and oregano; cover; and cook, stirring frequently, until onion is tender and beginning to brown, 5 to 7 minutes. Off heat, add onion mixture to bowl with squash along with spinach, Gruyère, crème fraîche, and vinegar and stir gently to combine. Season with salt and pepper to taste and set aside.

3 Adjust oven rack to lower-middle position, place baking stone on rack, and heat oven to 400 degrees. Line rimmed baking sheet with parchment paper. Roll dough into 14-inch circle about ⅛ inch thick on well-floured counter. (Trim edges as needed to form rough circle). Transfer dough to prepared sheet. Using straw or tip of paring knife, cut five ¼-inch circles in dough (1 at center and 4 evenly spaced halfway from center to edge of dough). Brush top of dough with 1 teaspoon oil.

4 Spread filling evenly over dough, leaving 2-inch border. Drizzle remaining 1 teaspoon oil over filling. Grasp 1 edge of dough and fold outer 2 inches over filling. Repeat around circumference of tart, overlapping dough every 2 to 3 inches; gently pinch pleated dough to secure but do not press dough into filling. Brush dough with egg wash.

5 Reduce oven temperature to 375 degrees. Set sheet on stone and bake until crust is deep golden brown and filling is beginning to brown, 35 to 45 minutes. Let tart cool on sheet on wire rack for 10 minutes. Using offset or wide metal spatula, loosen tart from parchment and carefully slide tart onto cutting board. Sprinkle parsley over filling and cut tart into wedges. Serve.

CRACKERS & FLATBREADS

Seeded Pumpkin Crackers

SERVES 8 to 10 (Makes 50 crackers) | **TOTAL TIME** 2 hours, plus 5½ hours chilling and cooling

1 cup (5 ounces) all-purpose flour

1 teaspoon baking powder

¼ teaspoon baking soda

1 cup canned unsweetened pumpkin puree

1 teaspoon baharat

½ teaspoon table salt

¼ cup (1¾ ounces) sugar

2 tablespoons vegetable oil

2 large eggs

1 tablespoon grated orange zest

⅓ cup dried apricots, chopped

⅓ cup sesame seeds

⅓ cup shelled pistachios, toasted and chopped

2 tablespoons coarse sea salt

Baharat

Makes 3 tablespoons

1 tablespoon ground nutmeg

1 tablespoon paprika

1 teaspoon ground coriander

1 teaspoon ground cinnamon

1 teaspoon ground cumin

Combine nutmeg, paprika, coriander, cinnamon, and cumin in small bowl. (Baharat can be stored in airtight container at room temperature for up to 1 year.)

Why This Recipe Works These vibrantly flavored crackers take inspiration from biscotti, another crunchy delight made by forming dough into a loaf that is baked, then sliced into individual pieces and baked a second time. Here you'll season pumpkin puree with orange zest and baharat, a Middle Eastern and North African spice blend featuring ground red pepper, cardamom, cinnamon, and nutmeg. Once the dough comes together, fold in a blend of sesame seeds, pistachios, and dried apricots. Freezing the loaves after the first bake ensures that you can slice the crackers thin enough for the second bake. And here's a major bonus to that approach: You need only slice the number of crackers you want to serve at any given time, reserving the rest of the frozen loaves for another occasion. The crackers will continue to crisp as they cool; cooled crackers keep well in an airtight container at room temperature for up to 3 days. This recipe is best made in two 5½ by 3-inch loaf pans. You can use one 8½ by 4½-inch loaf pan instead; bake the loaf for the same amount of time and then slice the frozen loaf down the center before slicing crosswise to achieve the right size crackers. We prefer our homemade Baharat, but you can use store-bought, if you prefer. See the Thin-Crust Pizza with Pumpkin, Cashew Ricotta, and Apple-Fennel Slaw (page 198) to use up the remaining canned pumpkin.

1 Adjust oven rack to middle position and heat oven to 350 degrees. Grease two 5½ by 3-inch loaf pans. Whisk flour, baking powder, and baking soda together in large bowl; set aside. Combine pumpkin puree, baharat, and table salt in 10-inch skillet. Cook over medium heat, stirring occasionally, until reduced to ¾ cup, 6 to 8 minutes; transfer to medium bowl. Stir in sugar and oil and let cool slightly, about 5 minutes.

2 Whisk eggs and orange zest into pumpkin mixture then fold into reserved flour mixture until combined (some small lumps of flour are OK). Fold in apricots, sesame seeds, and pistachios. Scrape batter into prepared pans, smoothing tops with rubber spatula. Bake until skewer inserted in center comes out clean, 45 to 50 minutes, switching and rotating pans halfway through baking.

3 Let loaves cool in pans on wire rack for 20 minutes. Remove loaves from pans and let cool completely on rack, about 1½ hours. Transfer cooled loaves to zipper-lock bag and freeze until firm, about three hours. (Loaves can be frozen for up to 1 month before slicing.)

4 Heat oven to 300 degrees and line rimmed baking sheet with parchment paper. Using serrated knife, carefully slice each frozen loaf as thin as possible (about ¼ inch thick). Arrange slices in single layer on prepared sheet and sprinkle with sea salt. Bake until dark golden, 25 to 30 minutes, flipping crackers and rotating sheet halfway through baking. Transfer sheet to wire rack and let crackers cool completely, about 30 minutes. Serve.

Whole-Wheat Seeded Crackers

SERVES 12 | **TOTAL TIME** 2 hours, plus 2 hours resting and cooling

Why This Recipe Works These crisp, flavorful crackers take their inspiration from the sturdy Mediterranean lavash cracker, which is typically made with a mix of white, wheat, and semolina flours. For extra heartiness and nutty flavor, these use all whole-wheat flour. To give them plenty of texture to complement the wheaty flavor, stir sesame seeds and flaxseeds into the dough along with a touch of turmeric for its mild warmth (and color). Letting the dough rest for an hour after mixing makes it easier to roll out (between sheets of parchment paper for even greater ease). Prick the dough all over with a fork to prevent air bubbles; brush it with egg; and sprinkle it with chia seeds, sea salt, and pepper. Then bake the giant crackers until deep golden brown and let them cool before breaking them up into rustic pieces of your desired size. We like golden flaxseeds for their milder flavor, but you can also use brown flaxseeds. We also prefer the larger crystal size of sea salt or kosher salt for sprinkling on the crackers; you can substitute table salt, but reduce the amount by half. These keep well in an airtight container at room temperature for up to 2 weeks.

- 3 cups (16½ ounces) whole-wheat flour
- 2 tablespoons ground golden flaxseeds
- 2 tablespoons sesame seeds
- 1 teaspoon ground turmeric
- ¾ teaspoon table salt
- 1 cup (8 ounces) warm water
- ⅓ cup extra-virgin olive oil, plus extra for brushing
- 1 large egg, lightly beaten
- 2 tablespoons chia seeds, divided
- 2 teaspoons coarse sea salt or kosher salt, divided
- ½ teaspoon pepper, divided

1 Using stand mixer fitted with dough hook, mix whole-wheat flour, ground flaxseeds, sesame seeds, turmeric, and table salt together on low speed. Gradually add warm water and oil and knead until dough is smooth and elastic, 7 to 9 minutes. Turn dough out onto lightly floured counter and knead by hand to form smooth, round ball. Divide dough into 4 equal pieces, brush with oil, and cover with plastic wrap. Let rest at room temperature for 1 hour.

2 Adjust oven racks to upper-middle and lower-middle positions and heat oven to 400 degrees. Working with 1 piece of dough (keep remaining dough covered with plastic), roll between 2 large sheets of parchment paper into 15 by 11-inch rectangle (about ⅛ inch thick). Remove top sheet of parchment and slide parchment with dough onto baking sheet. Repeat with second piece of dough and second baking sheet.

3 Using fork, poke holes in doughs at 2-inch intervals. Brush doughs with egg, then sprinkle each with 1½ teaspoons chia seeds, ½ teaspoon sea salt, and ¼ teaspoon pepper. Press gently on seeds and seasonings to help them adhere.

4 Bake crackers until golden brown, 15 to 18 minutes, switching and rotating sheets halfway through baking. Transfer crackers to wire rack and let cool completely, about 30 minutes. Let baking sheets cool completely before rolling out and baking remaining 2 pieces of dough. Break cooled crackers into large pieces and serve.

Variation

Whole-Wheat Everything Crackers
Omit chia seeds. Reduce sesame seeds to 1½ teaspoons. Add 1½ teaspoons poppy seeds, 1½ teaspoons dried minced garlic, and 1½ teaspoons dried minced onion to flour mixture in step 2.

Gruyère, Mustard, and Caraway Cheese Coins

SERVES 10 to 12 (Makes 80 crackers) | **TOTAL TIME** 45 minutes, plus 1½ hours chilling and cooling

8 ounces Gruyère cheese, shredded (2 cups)

1½ cups (7½ ounces) all-purpose flour

1 tablespoon cornstarch

1 teaspoon caraway seeds

½ teaspoon table salt

¼ teaspoon cayenne pepper

¼ teaspoon paprika

8 tablespoons unsalted butter, cut into 8 pieces and chilled

¼ cup whole-grain mustard

Why This Recipe Works Having a simple, foolproof homemade cracker in your baking arsenal will make you the host with the most. All three of these choices are easy, cheesy, buttery, and just a little spicy—and best of all, you can stash all of them in the freezer for several weeks, ready to casually pull out at a moment's notice to wildly impress your guests. Using the food processor to mix everything together limits your handling of the dough, which helps to keep the cheese coins tender and flaky. The processor also makes it a snap to combine the dry ingredients with the shredded cheese. Adding a little cornstarch with the flour further ensures that the coins bake up nice and light. Process the blended dry ingredients and cheese with cut-up pieces of chilled butter until the mixture resembles wet sand, then add mustard and process until the dough comes together in a ball. Roll the dough into logs, refrigerate them until firm, and then slice them into thin rounds before baking until lightly golden and perfectly crisp.

1 Process Gruyère, flour, cornstarch, caraway seeds, salt, cayenne, and paprika in food processor until combined, about 30 seconds. Scatter butter pieces over top and process until mixture resembles wet sand, about 20 seconds. Add mustard and process until dough forms ball, about 10 seconds. Transfer dough to counter and divide in half. Roll each half into 10-inch log; wrap in plastic wrap; and refrigerate until firm, at least 1 hour. (Dough can be refrigerated for up to 3 days or frozen for up to 1 month; if frozen, thaw completely before continuing with step 2.)

2 Adjust oven racks to upper-middle and lower-middle positions and heat oven to 350 degrees. Line 2 rimmed baking sheets with parchment paper. Unwrap logs and slice into ¼-inch-thick coins, giving dough logs quarter turn after each slice to keep logs round. Place coins on prepared sheets, spaced ½ inch apart.

3 Bake until light golden around edges, 22 to 28 minutes, switching and rotating sheets halfway through baking. Let coins cool completely on sheets, about 30 minutes, before serving.

Variations

Blue Cheese and Celery Seed Cheese Coins
Omit mustard. Substitute 1 cup crumbled blue cheese and 1 cup shredded extra-sharp cheddar for Gruyère. Substitute celery seeds for caraway seeds. Increase paprika to 2 teaspoons and cayenne to ½ teaspoon.

Pimento Cheese Coins
Substitute garlic powder for caraway seeds. Increase paprika to 1 tablespoon and cayenne to ½ teaspoon. Substitute 3 tablespoons water for mustard.

Mini Cheese Crackers

SERVES 4 to 6 (Makes 64 crackers) | **TOTAL TIME** 1¼ hours, plus 15 minutes cooling

3 ounces sharp yellow cheddar cheese, shredded (¾ cup)

½ cup (2½ ounces) all-purpose flour

1 teaspoon cornstarch

⅛ teaspoon table salt

3 tablespoons unsalted butter, cut into 3 pieces and chilled

1 tablespoon cold water

Why This Recipe Works Here's a homemade version of cheesy, crunchy baked bite-size crackers that will awe and delight snackers of any age group. The dough for these crackers is extremely simple—just mix shredded cheddar cheese, flour, cornstarch, butter, a touch of salt, and a spoonful of water in the food processor. The butter will warm up during mixing, making it difficult to create crackers, but a half-hour stint in the refrigerator solves that problem, making the dough firm and easy to roll out, ready to be cut into perfectly shaped individual crackers. If you'd like to re-create the signature neon-orange look of the classic supermarket cheese snack cracker, use yellow cheddar cheese; white cheddar works just as well, of course. A fluted pastry wheel will give you the textured edges, but a sharp paring knife or pizza wheel gets the cutting job done, too. And don't forget to poke a small hole in the center of each cracker using the blunt side of a wooden skewer. These will stay satisfyingly crunchy in an airtight container at room temperature for up to 1 week.

1 Process cheddar, flour, cornstarch, and salt in food processor until combined, about 30 seconds. Add butter and process until mixture resembles wet sand, about 20 seconds. Add cold water and pulse until dough forms large clumps, about 5 pulses.

2 Transfer dough to counter and pat dough into 6-inch square. Wrap dough in plastic wrap and refrigerate until firm, about 30 minutes.

3 Meanwhile, adjust oven rack to middle position and heat oven to 350 degrees. Line rimmed baking sheet with parchment paper.

4 Discard plastic wrap and transfer dough to lightly floured counter. Roll dough into rough 9-inch square, about ⅛ inch thick. Use fluted pastry wheel, pizza wheel, or paring knife to trim dough into neat 8-inch square. Slice square into 8 strips, each 1 inch wide, then make 8 perpendicular slices, each 1 inch wide, to form 64 squares.

5 Place squares on prepared sheet (they can be close together, but not touching). Use blunt end of skewer to poke hole through center of each square. Bake until golden around edges, 16 to 18 minutes, rotating each sheet halfway through baking. Let crackers cool completely on sheet, about 15 minutes. Serve.

Everything Bagel Grissini

SERVES 8 to 10 (Makes 30 breadsticks) | **TOTAL TIME** 1 hour, plus 3½ hours rising and cooling

Everything Bagel Seasoning

- 1 **teaspoon sesame seeds**
- 1 **teaspoon poppy seeds**
- 1 **teaspoon dried minced garlic**
- 1 **teaspoon dried onion flakes**
- 1 **teaspoon kosher salt**

Grissini

- 1 **cup warm water (110 degrees)**
- 1 **tablespoon extra-virgin olive oil**
- 2 **cups (10 ounces) all-purpose flour**
- 1 **teaspoon instant or rapid-rise yeast**
- ¾ **teaspoon table salt**
- **Olive or vegetable oil spray**

Why This Recipe Works Long, thin, and appealingly scraggly, grissini have an ultracrisp texture and make an elevated accompaniment to practically any meal (they also make a perfect snacking choice while preparing said meal). They're often plain or have sesame seeds, but here we use pungent everything bagel seasoning to take them to the next level. The dough itself is similar to a pizza dough and is easy to pull together by kneading it in the food processor. After letting it rise, roll it out, cut it into strips, and shape each strip into a rope by hand. It's best to fold each strip in half vertically before rolling it; the doubled-up dough is less likely to break when stretched. A quick rest after folding the strips relaxes the dough so that it won't snap back when you stretch it. And then spray the ropes well with olive oil spray and sprinkle them with the seasoning before baking. The rustic nature of these hand-rolled breadsticks means that they will have thicker and thinner spots; extra cooling and drying time (about 2 hours) ensures that the thicker spots will become totally dry and crunchy. You can substitute store-bought everything bagel seasoning, if you prefer. These keep well in an airtight container for up to 2 weeks.

1 **For the everything bagel seasoning** Combine sesame seeds, poppy seeds, dried minced garlic, dried onion flakes, and salt in small bowl; set aside.

2 **For the grissini** Combine warm water and oil in 2-cup liquid measuring cup. Process flour, yeast, and salt in food processor until combined, about 3 seconds. With processor running, slowly add ¾ cup water mixture and process until dough forms ball, about 10 seconds. If dough doesn't readily form ball, add remaining liquid, 1 tablespoon at a time, and process until ball forms, about 3 seconds. Continue to process until dough is smooth and elastic, about 30 seconds. Transfer dough to lightly greased large bowl; cover bowl tightly with plastic wrap and let dough rise at room temperature until doubled in size, 1½ to 2 hours.

3 Adjust oven racks to upper-middle and lower-middle positions and heat oven to 350 degrees. Line 2 rimmed baking sheets with parchment paper. Press down on dough to deflate and transfer to lightly floured counter; divide dough in half with bench scraper. Working with 1 piece of dough at a time (keep second piece covered with plastic), roll dough into 12 by 8-inch rectangle. Using pizza wheel, cut rectangle crosswise into ¾-inch-wide strips (about 15 strips). Fold each strip in half and gently roll to form 4-inch-long log. Let logs rest, covered in plastic, for about 5 minutes.

4 On slightly damp counter, roll each log into thin rope, about 20 inches long, and transfer to prepared sheets. Spray ropes generously with oil spray and sprinkle evenly with everything bagel seasoning. Bake until breadsticks are golden brown, 25 to 30 minutes, switching and rotating sheets halfway through baking. Slide parchment with breadsticks onto wire racks; let cool completely, about 2 hours, before serving.

Piadine

SERVES 6 (Makes 6 sandwiches) | **TOTAL TIME** 50 minutes, plus 30 minutes resting

Why This Recipe Works You can make these rustic, tender-chewy flatbreads without yeast, lengthy rising times, or even your oven. Once a poor man's bread in the Emilia-Romagna region of Italian, piadine are now found at the table in most restaurants in the region. And when folded around various cheeses and cured meats and griddled, as in this recipe, they become the region's best street food. The texture is bready yet tender, with a short crumb. The traditional preparation method involves cutting lard into flour and then stirring in milk, but if you're not practiced at it, the piadine can come out too thin and chewy. This version has you mix the dough in the food processor and drizzle in melted lard so that it evenly coats the flour particles; this prevents too much gluten from forming. Adding a little baking soda to the flour helps puff the flatbreads ever so slightly. For the filling, choose prosciutto, mortadella, or coppa, all of which pair well with mild, melty mozzarella. Arugula provides a fresh, peppery counterbalance. You can substitute extra-virgin olive oil for lard but the flatbreads will be slightly chewier. You can also use a nonstick skillet instead of the cast-iron skillet; preheat the nonstick skillet with 1 teaspoon oil, then wipe out the oil before proceeding.

2 cups (10 ounces) all-purpose flour

½ teaspoon salt

¼ teaspoon baking soda

1 tablespoon lard, melted

¾ cup whole milk

6 ounces thinly sliced prosciutto, mortadella, or coppa

6 ounces mozzarella cheese, shredded (1½ cups)

2 ounces (2 cups) baby arugula

1 Pulse flour, salt, and baking soda in food processor until combined, about 5 pulses. With processor running, slowly add lard until incorporated, then add milk and process until dough forms tacky ball, about 5 seconds. Transfer dough to lightly floured counter and knead by hand to form smooth, round ball, about 3 minutes.

2 Divide dough into 6 equal pieces and cover loosely with greased plastic wrap. Working with 1 piece of dough at a time (keep remaining pieces covered), place ball seam side down on clean counter and, using your cupped hand, drag in small circles until dough feels taut and round. Let dough balls rest for 30 minutes.

3 Roll 1 ball of dough into 8-inch round of even thickness (about 1/16 inch thick) on lightly floured counter. Cover loosely with plastic and repeat with remaining dough balls.

4 Heat 12-inch cast-iron skillet over medium heat for 3 minutes. Carefully place 1 dough round in skillet and prick in several places with fork. Cook until spotty golden, 1 to 3 minutes per side, popping any large bubbles that form with fork. Transfer piadina to rimmed baking sheet and cover with clean dish towel; repeat with remaining dough rounds, stacking them under towel as they finish. (Cooled piadine can be stored in zipper-lock bag for up to 2 days; microwave for 30 seconds to soften before proceeding with recipe.)

5 Heat now-empty skillet over medium-low heat for 2 minutes. Evenly layer prosciutto, mozzarella, and arugula on half of each piadina, leaving ½-inch border. Working with 2 filled piadine at a time, fold other half of flatbread over filling, then place cheese side down in skillet and press lightly with back of spatula to compress layers. Cook until cheese is melted and piadine are warmed through, 1 to 3 minutes per side. Repeat folding and cooking remaining piadine in 2 batches. Serve immediately.

Alu Parathas

SERVES 4 (Makes 8 flatbreads) | TOTAL TIME 2 hours, plus 1¼ hours cooling and resting

Onion Raita

- 1 cup plain whole-milk yogurt
- ¾ teaspoon ground cumin
- ½ teaspoon sugar
- ½ teaspoon table salt
- ⅓ cup finely chopped onion
- 1 tablespoon chopped fresh cilantro

Filling

- 1 pound russet potatoes, peeled and cut into 1-inch pieces
- 2 tablespoons minced fresh cilantro or ¼ teaspoon ground coriander
- 1 tablespoon grated fresh ginger
- 1 Thai green chile, stemmed and minced, or ¼ teaspoon chili powder
- 1½ teaspoons amchoor (dried unripe mango powder)
- 1 teaspoon ground cumin
- ¾ teaspoon table salt
- ¼ teaspoon nigella seeds
- ¼ teaspoon ajwain

Dough

- 1⅔ cups (8⅓ ounces) all-purpose flour
- ½ teaspoon table salt
- ½ teaspoon sugar
- 2 tablespoons vegetable oil
- ½–¾ cup water, room temperature
- ¼ cup ghee

Why This Recipe Works Stuffed with mashed potatoes seasoned with green chile, cilantro, nigella seeds, amchoor, and salt, this soft Indian bread is griddled until golden. Popular across north India, the potato-stuffed bread is one iteration of a beloved genre of griddle breads called paratha. Others can be plain or stuffed with horseradish, cauliflower, or ground lamb. This recipe is adapted from a recipe from Meera Marathé, the mother of one of our editors, Kaumudi. "Alu parathas were one of my favorite childhood dishes," Kaumudi said. "My mother spent much of her childhood in the Punjab, where her mother learned how to make alu parathas and then taught her." According to Meera, "The filling and dough need to be soft, and how you stuff the bread and roll the paratha out is critical to its success." Her tip: "Make the dough ball smaller than the potato ball and then stretch the dough tight around the stuffing, and roll carefully till it's very thin." Though Meera kneads her dough by hand, a food processor works very well. And while through long practice she adeptly cooks one paratha on a tava (Indian iron griddle) while stuffing and rolling out the next, stuffing and rolling out all the parathas before starting to cook them is easier if you haven't made these before. Meera's parting advice: "Don't cook each side more than twice so the paratha remains soft and pliable." It will be easier to form the breads into wide, thin rounds using a dowel rolling pin rather than a rolling pin with handles. Paratha is often served with raita and Indian mango pickle.

1 **For the onion raita** Whisk yogurt, cumin, sugar, and salt in bowl until well combined. Stir in onion and cilantro. Season with salt to taste and refrigerate until ready to serve.

2 **For the filling** Place potatoes in large saucepan, add cold water to cover by 1 inch, and bring to boil over high heat. Reduce heat to medium and simmer until potatoes are very tender, about 16 minutes; drain well and mash with potato masher or potato ricer until completely smooth. Set aside to cool, about 20 minutes.

3 Stir cilantro, ginger, Thai chile, amchoor, cumin, salt, nigella seeds, and ajwain into cooled potatoes, then season with salt to taste. Cover and set aside. (Filling can be refrigerated for up to 24 hours; bring to room temperature before using.)

4 **For the dough** Pulse flour, salt, and sugar together in food processor until combined, about 5 pulses. Add oil and pulse until incorporated, about 5 pulses. With processor running, slowly add room-temperature water and process until dough is combined and no dry flour remains, about 30 seconds. Transfer dough to clean counter and knead by hand to form smooth, round ball, about 30 seconds; transfer to bowl, cover with plastic wrap, and let rest for 30 minutes.

5 Divide filling into 8 equal portions and roll into balls (about 1½ inches wide); set aside covered with plastic. Divide dough into 8 equal pieces (about 1¾ ounces each) and cover loosely with plastic. Working with 1 piece of dough at a time, form into rough ball by stretching dough around your thumbs and pinching edges together so that top is smooth. Place ball seam side down on clean counter and, using your cupped hand, drag in small circles until dough feels taut and round. Let balls rest, covered, for 15 minutes.

6 Working with 1 dough ball at a time, roll into 4-inch disk on lightly floured counter. Place 1 filling ball in center of dough disk and fold dough around stuffing to enclose completely, pinching dough to seal. Place seam side down on lightly floured counter and roll gently to even ⅛-inch-thick round (about 8 inches wide). Transfer to parchment paper–lined rimmed baking sheet and cover loosely with plastic.

7 Heat 12-inch cast-iron skillet over medium heat for 5 minutes, then reduce heat to low. Brush any remaining flour from both sides of paratha, then gently place in hot skillet in one smooth motion. Cook until bubbles begin to form on surface and paratha is light blond and moves about freely in skillet, 30 to 60 seconds. (Paratha may puff.)

Using metal spatula, flip paratha onto second side, and brush with some of the ghee. Cook until paratha is spotty brown and moves about freely in skillet, 20 to 60 seconds, pressing edges firmly into skillet with spatula to ensure even contact.

8 Flip paratha back onto first side and brush top with more ghee. Cook until spotty brown and dough no longer looks raw, 20 to 45 seconds, pressing edges firmly into skillet with spatula to ensure even contact. Flip paratha once more and cook until spotty brown and dough no longer looks raw, 15 to 30 seconds. Transfer cooked paratha to second rimmed baking sheet, let cool slightly, then cover loosely with dish towel.

9 Repeat shaping and cooking remaining parathas, removing skillet from heat between batches if it begins to smoke or if parathas brown too quickly. Place parathas side-by-side on sheet until cooled, then stack between parchment. Serve hot with reserved onion raita. (Parathas can be refrigerated for up to 2 days; to refresh, heat 12-inch cast-iron skillet over medium heat for 5 minutes, then reduce heat to low. Add paratha to skillet and cook until warmed through, flipping three times, 10 to 15 seconds per side.)

SHAPING ALU PARATHAS

1 Working with 1 piece of dough at a time, form into rough ball by stretching dough around your thumbs and pinching edges together so that top is smooth. Place dough ball seam side down on counter and, using your cupped hand, drag in small circles until dough feels taut and round.

2 After dough rests, roll 1 dough ball into 4-inch disk on lightly floured counter. Place 1 paratha filling ball in center of dough disk and gently fold dough around filling to enclose completely, pinching dough to seal.

3 Place seam side down on lightly floured counter and gently press and roll to even ¼-inch thickness (round should be about 8 inches wide). Transfer to parchment-lined rimmed baking sheet and cover loosely with plastic.

Cōngyóubing

SERVES 4 to 6 (Makes two 9-inch pancakes) | **TOTAL TIME** 1¼ hours, plus 30 minutes resting

Dipping Sauce

- 2 tablespoons soy sauce
- 1 scallion, sliced thin
- 1 tablespoon water
- 2 teaspoons unseasoned rice vinegar
- 1 teaspoon honey
- 1 teaspoon toasted sesame oil
- Pinch red pepper flakes

Pancakes

- 1½ cups (7½ ounces) plus 1 tablespoon all-purpose flour, divided
- ¾ cup boiling water
- 7 tablespoons vegetable oil, divided
- 1 tablespoon toasted sesame oil
- 1 teaspoon kosher salt, divided
- 4 scallions, sliced thin, divided

Why This Recipe Works Chinese scallion pancakes are deep golden-brown flatbread wedges with crispy exteriors that break away in flaky shards to reveal paper-thin, delicately chewy, scallion-studded layers. To achieve this, the dough must be rolled very thin. A dough made with boiling water does the trick, for two reasons. First, the boiling water dissolves the flour's starch molecules to a greater extent than cooler water does, letting the starch absorb the free water in the dough. This means that the dough is less sticky and you don't have to use as much flour when rolling (which would stick to the exterior and burn during cooking). Second, the boiling water decreases the elasticity of the dough's gluten network, so the dough is more relaxed and less prone to springing back into a thicker pancake. To form alternating layers of dough and fat, roll the dough into a large, thin round; brush it with a mixture of oil and flour; and sprinkle it with scallions before rolling it into a cylinder. Coil the cylinder into a spiral and then roll it out into a round again. Making a small slit in the center of each pancake prevents steam from building up underneath, so it lies flat and cooks evenly. Cover the pan for the first few minutes of cooking; this helps the dough cook evenly. Then uncover the pan for the final moments to brown and crisp the exterior. The steady, even heat of a cast-iron skillet is ideal here; you can use a heavy stainless-steel skillet, but you may have to increase the heat slightly. For an accurate measurement of boiling water, bring a kettle of water to a boil and then measure out the desired amount.

1 **For the dipping sauce** Whisk soy sauce, scallion, water, vinegar, honey, sesame oil, and pepper flakes together in small bowl; set aside.

2 **For the pancakes** Using wooden spoon, mix 1½ cups flour and boiling water in bowl to form rough dough. When cool enough to handle, transfer dough to lightly floured counter and knead until tacky (but not sticky) ball forms, about 4 minutes (dough will not be perfectly smooth). Cover loosely with plastic wrap and let rest for 30 minutes.

3 While dough is resting, stir together 1 tablespoon vegetable oil, sesame oil, and remaining 1 tablespoon flour. Set aside.

4 Place 10-inch cast-iron skillet over low heat to preheat. Divide dough in half. Cover 1 half of dough with plastic wrap and set aside. Roll remaining dough into 12-inch round on lightly floured counter. Drizzle with 1 tablespoon oil-flour mixture and use pastry brush to spread evenly over entire surface. Sprinkle with ½ teaspoon salt and half of scallions. Roll dough into cylinder. Coil cylinder into spiral, tuck end underneath, and flatten spiral with your palm. Cover with plastic and repeat with remaining dough, oil-flour mixture, salt, and scallions.

5 Roll first spiral into 9-inch round. Cut ½-inch slit in center of pancake. Cover with plastic. Roll and cut slit in second pancake. (To make ahead, stack uncooked pancakes between layers of parchment paper, wrap tightly in plastic wrap, and refrigerate for up to 24 hours or freeze for up to 1 month. If frozen, thaw pancakes in single layer for 15 minutes before cooking.)

6 Place 2 tablespoons vegetable oil in skillet and increase heat to medium-low. Place 1 pancake in skillet (oil should sizzle). Cover and cook, shaking skillet occasionally, until pancake is slightly puffy and golden brown on underside, 1 to 1½ minutes. (If underside is not browned after 1 minute, turn heat up slightly. If it is browning too quickly, turn heat down slightly.) Drizzle 1 tablespoon vegetable oil over pancake. Use pastry brush to distribute over entire surface. Carefully flip pancake. Cover and cook, shaking skillet occasionally, until second side is golden brown, 1 to 1½ minutes. Uncover skillet and continue to cook until bottom is deep golden brown and crispy, 30 to 60 seconds longer. Flip and cook until deep golden brown and crispy, 30 to 60 seconds. Transfer to wire rack. Repeat with remaining 3 tablespoons vegetable oil and remaining pancake. Cut each pancake into 8 wedges and serve, passing dipping sauce separately.

SHAPING CŌNGYÓUBING

1 Roll up scallion-sprinkled dough round into cylinder.

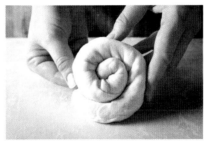

2 Coil cylinder, tucking end underneath, then flatten.

3 Roll out flattened spiral into 9-inch round; cut ½-inch slit in center of pancake.

Cheese Pupusas

SERVES 4 (Makes 8 pupusas)　│　**TOTAL TIME** 1¼ hours, plus 1½ hours chilling and resting

Curtido

- 1 cup cider vinegar
- ½ cup water
- 1 tablespoon sugar
- 1½ teaspoons table salt
- ½ head green cabbage, cored and sliced thin (6 cups)
- 1 onion, sliced thin
- 1 large carrot, peeled and shredded
- 1 jalapeño chile, seeded and minced
- 1 teaspoon dried oregano
- 1 cup chopped fresh cilantro

Pupusas

- 2 cups (8 ounces) masa harina
- ½ teaspoon table salt
- 2 cups boiling water, plus warm tap water as needed
- 2 teaspoons vegetable oil, divided
- 2 ounces cotija cheese, cut into 2 pieces
- 8 ounces Monterey Jack cheese, cut into 8 pieces
- 1 recipe Quick Salsa

Why This Recipe Works Pupusas have been sustaining Latin Americans since pre-Columbian times and are even the declared national dish of El Salvador. These enticing griddle cakes are made by stuffing cheese, beans, braised meat, or a combination thereof into a ball of masa harina dough. The ball is flattened into a disk and cooked on a cast-iron griddle (called a comal) until the tender cake forms a crisp, spotty-brown shell. Served with curtido (a pickled cabbage slaw) and a smooth, spicy tomato salsa, the result is irresistible. Hydrating the masa harina with boiling (rather than room-temperature) water lets the starches in the flour absorb it quickly and completely, resulting in an easy-to-handle dough. Properly hydrated masa dough should be tacky, requiring damp hands to keep it from sticking. If the dough feels the slightest bit dry at any time, knead in a little warm tap water until the dough is tacky. Pressing the stuffed pupusas between sheets of marked plastic ensures uniform size. An occasional leak while frying the pupusas is to be expected—and the browned cheese is delicious. For an accurate measurement of boiling water, bring a kettle of water to a boil and then measure out the desired amount. For a spicier curtido, add the jalapeño seeds.

1 **For the curtido** Whisk vinegar, water, sugar, and salt in large bowl until sugar is dissolved. Add cabbage, onion, carrot, jalapeño, and oregano and toss to combine. Cover and refrigerate for 1 hour. (Curtido can be refrigerated for up to 24 hours.) Toss slaw, then drain. Return slaw to bowl and stir in cilantro.

2 **For the pupusas** Using marker, draw 4-inch circle in center of 1 side of 1-quart or 1-gallon zipper-lock bag. Cut open seams along both sides of bag, leaving bottom seam intact.

3 Mix masa harina and salt together in medium bowl. Add boiling water and 1 teaspoon oil and mix with rubber spatula until soft dough forms. Cover dough and let rest for 20 minutes.

4 While dough rests, line rimmed baking sheet with parchment paper. Process cotija in food processor until cotija is finely chopped and resembles wet sand, about 20 seconds. Add Monterey Jack and process until mixture resembles wet oatmeal, about 30 seconds. Remove processor blade. Form cheese mixture into 8 balls, weighing about 1¼ ounces each, and place balls on 1 half of prepared sheet.

5 Knead dough in bowl for 15 to 20 seconds. Test dough's hydration by flattening golf ball–size piece. If cracks larger than ¼ inch form around edges, add warm tap water, 2 teaspoons at a time, until dough is soft and slightly tacky. Transfer dough to counter, shape into large ball, and divide into 8 equal pieces about 2¾ ounces each. Using your damp hands, shape 1 dough piece into ball and place on empty half of prepared sheet. Cover with damp dish towel. Repeat with remaining dough pieces.

6 Place open cut bag marked side down on counter. Place 1 dough ball in center of circle. Fold other side of bag over ball. Using glass pie plate or 8-inch square baking dish, gently press dough to 4-inch diameter, using circle drawn on bag as guide. Turn out disk into your palm and place 1 cheese ball in center. Bring sides of dough up around filling and pinch top to seal into rough ball. Remoisten your hands and roll ball until smooth, smoothing any cracks with your damp fingertip. Return ball to bag and slowly press to 4-inch diameter. Pinch closed any small cracks that form at edges. Return pupusa to sheet and cover with damp dish towel. Repeat with remaining dough and filling. (To freeze, wrap baking sheet in plastic wrap and freeze until pupusas are solid. Wrap pupusas individually in plastic, then transfer to zipper-lock bag. Freeze for up to 1 month. Cook directly from frozen, increasing cooking time by 1 minute per side.)

7 Heat remaining 1 teaspoon oil in 12-inch nonstick skillet over medium-high heat until shimmering. Wipe skillet clean with paper towels. Carefully lay 4 pupusas in skillet and cook until spotty brown on both sides, 2 to 4 minutes per side. Transfer to platter and repeat with remaining 4 pupusas. Serve warm with curtido and salsa.

Quick Salsa

Serves 4

For a spicier salsa, add the jalapeño seeds.

- ¼ small red onion
- 2 tablespoons minced fresh cilantro
- ½ small jalapeño chile, seeded and minced
- 1 (14.5-ounce) can diced tomatoes, drained
- 2 teaspoons lime juice, plus extra for seasoning
- 1 small garlic clove, minced
- ¼ teaspoon table salt
  Pinch pepper

Pulse onion, cilantro, and jalapeño in food processor until finely chopped, 5 pulses, scraping down sides of bowl as needed. Add tomatoes, lime juice, garlic, salt, and pepper and process until smooth, 20 to 30 seconds. Season with salt and extra lime juice to taste.

Tomatillo Chicken Huaraches

SERVES 4 (Makes 4 huaraches) | TOTAL TIME 1½ hours, plus 30 minutes resting

3 cups (12 ounces) masa harina

1¾ teaspoons table salt, divided

4 cups boiling water, plus warm tap water as needed

1 (15-ounce) can pinto beans, rinsed

¼ cup chicken broth

5 tablespoons lard, divided

½ onion, chopped fine

½ jalapeño chile, stemmed, seeded, and minced

2 garlic cloves, minced

1 teaspoon ground cumin

1 tablespoon chopped fresh cilantro plus ¼ cup fresh cilantro leaves

1 teaspoon lime juice

1 (2½-pound) rotisserie chicken, skin and bones discarded and meat shredded into bite-size pieces (3 cups)

3 cups tomatillo salsa

4 radishes, sliced thin

4 ounces queso fresco, crumbled (1 cup)

Why This Recipe Works Generously sized and utterly delicious, huaraches are named for their doppelgänger, the iconic huarache woven leather sandal. The hearty huaraches of Mexico City consist of masa dough filled and topped with varying proteins, vegetables, cheeses, and sauces. This version features a stuffing of rich refried beans with a topping of shredded chicken mixed with tomatillo salsa; it's all garnished with radishes and queso fresco. Using convenient store-bought rotisserie chicken lets you focus your time and efforts on making the masa flatbreads. Hydrating the masa harina with boiling rather than room-temperature water allows the starches in the flour to absorb it more quickly and completely, resulting in a well-hydrated dough that's easy to work with and won't dry out. This is important because you need to shape and flatten the dough twice: once before adding the stuffing and once after you fold the dough around it. Properly hydrated masa dough should be tacky, requiring damp hands to keep it from sticking. If the dough feels the slightest bit dry at any time, knead in warm tap water, 1 teaspoon at a time, until the dough is tacky. For an accurate measurement of boiling water, bring a kettle of water to a boil and then measure out the desired amount.

1 Whisk masa harina and 1¼ teaspoons salt together in large bowl. Add boiling water and mix with rubber spatula until soft dough forms. Cover with damp dish towel and let rest for 30 minutes.

2 Meanwhile, process beans and broth in food processor until smooth, about 30 seconds, scraping down sides of bowl as needed; set aside. Heat 1 tablespoon lard in 12-inch nonstick skillet over medium heat until shimmering. Add onion, jalapeño, and remaining ½ teaspoon salt and cook over medium heat until vegetables are softened and beginning to brown, 5 to 7 minutes.

3 Stir in garlic and cumin and cook until fragrant, about 30 seconds. Stir in reserved beans and cook, stirring often, until well combined and thickened slightly, about 5 minutes. Off heat, stir in chopped cilantro and lime juice and season with salt and pepper to taste; set aside to cool slightly. Once cool enough to handle, divide beans into 4 equal portions using greased ⅓-cup dry measuring cup. Transfer to large plate and set aside. Wipe out skillet.

4 Adjust oven rack to middle position and heat oven to 200 degrees. Set wire rack in rimmed baking sheet. Once the dough has rested for 30 minutes, test dough's hydration by flattening golf ball–size piece. If cracks larger than ¼ inch form around edges, knead in warm tap water by hand, 2 teaspoons at a time, until dough is soft and slightly tacky. Transfer dough to counter, shape into large ball, divide into 4 equal pieces, and place on parchment-lined second rimmed baking sheet. Cover dough with wet dish towel. Cut open seams along both sides of 1-gallon zipper-lock bag, leaving bottom seam intact.

5 Working with 1 piece of dough at a time, repeat testing hydration and add extra water as needed. Shape dough into rough oval, about 4 inches long, then enclose in split bag (oval should be perpendicular to counter edge and seam of bag should be on your right). Press dough flat into ½-inch-thick, 6-inch-long oval using flat-bottomed pot or pie plate. Peel away plastic, smooth any cracks around edges of round, and place 1 reserved refried bean portion in center of dough oval. (If at any time dough feels dry, moisten hands to smooth out any cracks and make dough pliable.)

6 Grasping side edges of zipper-lock bag, lift to bring sides of dough up around filling and press edges of dough to seal. Remoisten your hands, unfold bag, and smooth any cracks with your damp fingers. Flip dough seam side down, enclose in split bag, and press dough flat into a 9-inch oval about ¼ inch thick between split bag using flat-bottomed pot or pie plate. Return shaped dough to sheet, and cover with wet dish towel while shaping remaining dough.

7 Heat 1 tablespoon lard in clean, dry skillet over medium-high heat until shimmering. Gently place 1 dough oval in skillet and cook until dark spotty brown on first side, 4 to 6 minutes. Using 2 spatulas, gently flip huarache and continue to cook until second side is crispy and dark spotty brown, 4 to 6 minutes longer; transfer to prepared rack and hold in warm oven. Repeat with remaining lard and remaining dough ovals.

8 Meanwhile, microwave chicken and salsa in large bowl until warmed through, 1 to 3 minutes. Top huaraches with chicken-salsa mixture and sprinkle with radishes, queso fresco, and cilantro leaves. Serve.

SHAPING HUARACHES

1 Shape dough piece into 4-inch oval and enclose in split plastic bag. Using flat-bottomed pot or pie plate, press dough into 6-inch oval about ½ inch thick.

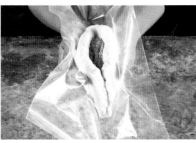

2 Smooth any cracks around edges of round and place bean mixture in center of masa. Grasping side edges of bag, lift to bring sides of dough up around filling; pinch top of dough to seal.

3 Remoisten your hands, unfold bag, and smooth any cracks with your damp fingers.

4 Flip dough seam side down, enclose in split bag, and press dough flat into 9-inch oval about ¼ inch thick between split bag using flat-bottomed pot or pie plate.

Mana'eesh Za'atar

SERVES 4 to 6 (Makes three 9-inch flatbreads) | **TOTAL TIME** 1¼ hours, plus 2¼ hours rising and resting

Why This Recipe Works In Lebanon, these flatbreads are a beloved street food and common addition to the daily at-home table. Dedicated bakeries prepare these flavorful breads using superhot ovens. Mana'eesh are typically topped with olive oil and za'atar, a combination of sumac; thyme; sesame seeds; and sometimes oregano, coriander, cumin, and salt. In Lebanese, the word "man'oushe" (the singular form of mana'eesh) means "engraved" and refers to the indentations in the bread made by tapping the dough with your fingertips before baking it. This keeps the dough from puffing too much in the oven and also creates pockets for the spice-and-oil mixture to pool. For this version, a food processor speedily mixes the simple dough. You can go a long way toward mimicking the superhot ovens of those professional bakeries by placing a baking stone on the middle rack of your oven and heating it at 500 degrees for a solid hour. The high heat encourages slight bubbles with delicate char to form on top of the bread while the bottom turns an even golden brown. If you don't have a baking peel, use a rimless or overturned baking sheet to slide the mana'eesh onto the baking stone. If you don't have a baking stone, you can use a preheated rimless or overturned baking sheet; however, the bread will be less crisp. We prefer our homemade Za'atar, but you can use store-bought, if you prefer.

1 **For the dough** Process flour, yeast, and salt in food processor until combined, about 3 seconds. Combine cold water and oil in liquid measuring cup. With processor running, slowly add water mixture and process until dough forms sticky ball that clears sides of bowl, 30 to 60 seconds.

2 Transfer dough to clean counter and knead into cohesive ball, about 1 minute. Place dough in greased bowl. Cover bowl with plastic wrap and let dough rise at room temperature until almost doubled in size, 2 to 2½ hours. One hour before baking, adjust oven rack to middle position, set baking stone on rack, and heat oven to 500 degrees.

3 **For the topping** Meanwhile, combine za'atar, oil, and salt in small bowl; set aside.

4 On clean counter, divide dough into 3 equal pieces, about 7 ounces each. Shape each piece of dough into ball; cover loosely with plastic and let rest for 15 minutes.

5 Working with 1 dough ball at a time on lightly floured counter, coat lightly with flour and flatten into 6- to 7-inch disk using your fingertips. Using rolling pin, roll dough disk into 9- to 10-inch circle. Slide dough round onto floured baking peel. Spread one-third of topping (about 1½ tablespoons) over surface of dough with back of dinner spoon, stopping ½ inch from edge.

6 Firmly tap dough all over with your fingertips, about 6 times. Slide dough onto baking stone and bake until lightly bubbled and brown on top, about 5 minutes. Using baking peel, transfer man'oushe to wire rack. Repeat with remaining dough and topping. Slice or tear and serve.

Dough

- 2½ cups (12½ ounces) all-purpose flour
- 1½ teaspoons instant or rapid-rise yeast
- 1 teaspoon table salt
- ¾ cup plus 2 tablespoons cold water
- 2 tablespoons extra-virgin olive oil

Topping

- 3 tablespoons za'atar
- 3 tablespoons extra-virgin olive oil
- ½ teaspoon table salt

Za'atar

Makes about ⅓ cup

- 2 tablespoons dried thyme
- 1 tablespoon dried oregano
- 1½ tablespoons sumac
- 1 tablespoon sesame seeds, toasted
- ¼ teaspoon table salt

Grind thyme and oregano using spice grinder or mortar and pestle until finely ground and powdery. Transfer to bowl and stir in sumac, sesame seeds, and salt. (Za'atar can be stored in airtight container at room temperature for up to 1 year.)

Lahmajun

SERVES 4 (Makes 4 flatbreads) | **TOTAL TIME** 1 hour, plus 17 hours resting and chilling

Dough

3¼ cups (16¼ ounces) all-purpose flour

⅛ teaspoon instant or rapid-rise yeast

1¼ cups (10 ounces) ice water

1 tablespoon vegetable oil

1½ teaspoons table salt

Vegetable oil spray

Topping

1 red bell pepper, stemmed, seeded, and cut into 1-inch pieces

¼ small onion

¼ cup fresh parsley leaves and tender stems

2 tablespoons mild biber salçası

1 tablespoon tomato paste

1 garlic clove, peeled

1 teaspoon ground allspice

1 teaspoon paprika

½ teaspoon ground cumin

½ teaspoon table salt

⅛ teaspoon pepper

⅛ teaspoon cayenne pepper

6 ounces ground lamb, broken into small pieces

Lemon wedges

Why This Recipe Works Thin and crispy lahmajun are meat-and-vegetable-topped Armenian flatbreads that are eaten whole, cut or folded in half, or wrapped around a salad to make a sandwich of sorts. This dough starts with a higher-protein all-purpose flour to create plenty of gluten for both crispness and tenderness (but not so much that it turns tough). Using very little yeast and letting the dough ferment slowly in the refrigerator minimizes the formation of gas bubbles that would make the dough difficult to roll and gives the yeast time to digest sugars in the dough and build up maximum flavor. The lengthy rest also allows the gluten to relax so that the dough can be stretched thin. The topping for lahmajun is more like a meaty veneer than a sauce—moist but not wet and concentrated in flavor so that each bite tastes vibrant despite the thin layer. It's heady from garlic; spices (allspice, paprika, cumin, cayenne); and biber salçası, a thick, cardinal-red Turkish pepper paste made from either sweet or a combination of sweet and hot peppers. Using umami-rich tomato paste and just a modest amount of onion and bell pepper further controls the moisture. Using plastic wrap to spread the topping over the dough rounds gives you the dexterity of using your fingers for a thin layer but avoids messy direct contact with the pasty topping. Then, borrow our technique for pizza: Set a baking stone on the upper-middle rack of the oven and heat it at 500 degrees for an hour. With this strategy, there's intense heat both underneath the flatbreads and reflecting onto them from above, guaranteeing crispness and browning in just a few minutes. If you don't have a baking peel, use a rimless or overturned baking sheet to slide the lahmajun onto the baking stone. If you don't have a baking stone, you can use a preheated rimless or overturned baking sheet; however, the breads will be less crisp. Use the mild variety of biber salçası; if it's unavailable, increase the tomato paste in the topping to 2 tablespoons and increase the paprika to 4 teaspoons. You can substitute 85 percent lean ground beef for the lamb, if desired. It is important to use ice water in the dough to prevent it from overheating in the food processor. We prefer King Arthur brand all-purpose flour in this recipe.

1 **For the dough** Process flour and yeast in food processor until combined, about 2 seconds. With processor running, slowly add ice water; process until dough is just combined and no dry flour remains, about 10 seconds. Let dough rest for 10 minutes.

2 Add oil and salt and process until dough forms shaggy ball, 30 to 60 seconds. Transfer dough to lightly oiled counter and knead until uniform, about 1 minute (texture will remain slightly rough). Divide dough into 4 equal pieces, about 6⅔ ounces each. Shape dough pieces into tight balls and transfer, seam side down, to rimmed baking sheet coated with oil spray. Spray tops of balls lightly with oil spray. Cover tightly with plastic wrap and refrigerate for at least 16 hours. (Dough can be refrigerated for up to 2 days.)

3 **For the topping** In now-empty processor, process bell pepper, onion, parsley, biber salçası, tomato paste, garlic, allspice, paprika, cumin, salt, pepper, and cayenne until smooth, scraping down sides of bowl as needed, about 15 seconds. Add lamb and pulse to combine, 8 to 10 pulses. Transfer to container, cover, and refrigerate until needed (topping can be refrigerated for up to 24 hours).

4 One hour before baking lahmajun, remove dough from refrigerator and let stand at room temperature until slightly puffy and no longer cool to touch. Meanwhile, adjust oven rack to upper-middle position (rack should be 4 to 5 inches from broiler element), set baking stone on rack, and heat oven to 500 degrees.

5 Place 1 dough ball on unfloured counter and dust top lightly with flour. Using heel of your hand, press dough ball into 5-inch disk. Using rolling pin, gently roll into 12-inch round of even thickness. (Use tackiness of dough on counter to aid with rolling; if dough becomes misshapen, periodically peel round from counter, reposition, and continue to roll.) Dust top of round lightly but evenly with flour and, starting at 1 edge, peel dough off counter and flip, floured side down, onto floured baking peel (dough will spring back to about 11 inches in diameter). Place one-quarter of topping (about ½ cup) in center of dough. Cover dough with 12 by 12-inch sheet of plastic and, using your fingertips and knuckles, gently spread filling evenly across dough, leaving ⅛-inch border. Starting at 1 edge, peel away plastic, leaving topping in place (reserve plastic for topping remaining lahmajun).

6 Carefully slide lahmajun onto stone and bake until bottom crust is browned, edges are lightly browned, and topping is steaming, 4 to 6 minutes. While lahmajun bakes, begin rolling next dough ball.

7 Transfer baked lahmajun to wire rack. Repeat rolling, topping, and baking remaining 3 dough balls. Serve with lemon wedges.

TOPPING LAHMAJUN

1 Place about ½ cup topping in center of rolled dough round. Cover dough with 12 by 12-inch sheet of plastic and, using your fingertips and knuckles, gently spread filling evenly across dough, leaving ⅛-inch border.

2 Starting at 1 edge, carefully peel away plastic, leaving topping in place.

Mushroom Musakhan

SERVES 4 to 6 (Makes two 15 by 8-inch flatbreads) | **TOTAL TIME** 2 hours, plus 20½ hours resting and cooling

Dough

1½ cups (8¼ ounces) whole-wheat flour

1 cup (5½ ounces) bread flour

2 teaspoons honey

¾ teaspoon instant or rapid-rise yeast

1¼ cups ice water

2 tablespoons extra-virgin olive oil

1¾ teaspoons table salt

Topping

½ cup extra-virgin olive oil, divided

2 tablespoons minced fresh oregano or 2 teaspoons dried

4 garlic cloves, minced

1½ tablespoons ground sumac

¼ teaspoon ground allspice

⅛ teaspoon ground cardamom

2 pounds onions, halved and sliced ¼ inch thick

2 teaspoons packed light brown sugar

1½ teaspoons table salt, divided

¼ cup pine nuts

2 pounds portobello mushroom caps, gills removed, caps halved and sliced ½ inch thick, divided

2 tablespoons minced fresh chives, divided

Why This Recipe Works Musakhan is a popular Palestinian dish featuring a flatbread that's usually topped with roasted chicken, caramelized onions, pine nuts, and tart ground sumac. This version includes the caramelized onions, pine nuts, and sumac, but it showcases mushrooms rather than chicken. Sautéed portobello mushrooms, with their robust flavor and meaty texture, make a satisfying savory topping. The traditional base for musakhan is taboon bread, a thick, crisp flatbread that is traditionally cooked in a clay oven called a taboon. To ensure crisp edges on these flatbreads, cook them on a preheated baking stone, and superheat the oven by briefly turning on the broiler before baking the musakhan. If you don't have a baking peel, use a rimless or overturned baking sheet to slide the musakhan onto the baking stone. If you don't have a baking stone, you can use a preheated rimless or overturned baking sheet; however, the breads will be less crisp. It is important to use ice water in the dough to prevent it from overheating in the food processor. Serve with plain yogurt for dolloping on top, if you like.

1 **For the dough** Pulse whole-wheat flour, bread flour, honey, and yeast in food processor until combined, about 5 pulses. With processor running, slowly add ice water and process until dough is just combined and no dry flour remains, about 10 seconds. Let dough rest for 10 minutes.

2 Add oil and salt to dough and process until dough forms satiny, sticky ball that clears sides of bowl, 30 to 60 seconds. Transfer dough to lightly oiled counter and knead by hand to form smooth, round ball, about 30 seconds. Place dough seam side down in lightly greased large bowl or container, cover tightly with plastic wrap, and refrigerate for at least 18 hours or up to 2 days.

3 **For the topping** Combine 1 tablespoon oil, oregano, garlic, sumac, allspice, and cardamom in bowl. Heat 2 tablespoons oil in 12-inch nonstick skillet over high heat until shimmering. Add onions, sugar, and ½ teaspoon salt and stir to coat. Cook, stirring occasionally, until onions begin to soften and release some moisture, about 5 minutes. Reduce heat to medium and continue to cook, stirring often, until onions are well caramelized, 35 to 40 minutes. (If onions are sizzling or scorching, reduce heat. If onions are not browning after 15 to 20 minutes, increase heat.) Push onions to sides of skillet. Add oregano-garlic mixture to center and cook, mashing mixture into skillet, until fragrant, about 30 seconds. Stir oregano-garlic mixture into onions.

4 Transfer onion mixture to food processor and pulse to jamlike consistency, about 5 pulses. Transfer to bowl, stir in pine nuts, and season with salt and pepper to taste; let cool completely before using.

5 Wipe skillet clean with paper towels. Heat 2 tablespoons oil in now-empty skillet over medium-high heat until shimmering. Add half of mushrooms and ½ teaspoon salt and cook, stirring occasionally, until evenly browned, 8 to 10 minutes; transfer to separate bowl. Repeat with 2 tablespoons oil, remaining mushrooms, and remaining ½ teaspoon salt; transfer to bowl and let cool completely before using.

6 One hour before baking, adjust oven rack 4 inches from broiler element, set baking stone on rack, and heat oven to 500 degrees. Press down on dough to deflate. Transfer dough to clean counter, divide in half, and cover loosely with greased plastic. Pat 1 piece of dough (keep remaining piece covered) into 4-inch round. Working around circumference of dough, fold edges toward center until ball forms.

7 Flip ball seam side down and, using your cupped hands, drag in small circles on counter until dough feels taut and round and all seams are secured on underside. (If dough sticks to your hands, lightly dust top of dough with flour.) Repeat with remaining piece of dough. Space dough balls 3 inches apart, cover loosely with greased plastic, and let rest for 1 hour.

8 Heat broiler for 10 minutes. Meanwhile, generously coat 1 dough ball with flour and place on well-floured counter. Press and roll into 12 by 8-inch oval. Transfer oval to well-floured baking peel and stretch into 15 by 8-inch oval. (If dough resists stretching, let it relax for 10 to 20 minutes before trying to stretch it again.) Using fork, poke entire surface of oval 10 to 15 times.

9 Spread half of onion mixture evenly on dough, edge to edge, and arrange half of mushrooms on top. Slide flatbread carefully onto baking stone and return oven to 500 degrees. Bake until bottom crust is evenly browned and edges are crisp, about 10 minutes, rotating flatbread halfway through baking. Transfer flatbread to wire rack and let cool for 5 minutes. Drizzle with 1½ teaspoons oil and sprinkle with 1 tablespoon chives. Slice and serve.

10 Heat broiler for 10 minutes. Repeat with remaining dough and toppings, returning oven to 500 degrees when flatbread is placed on stone.

Red Pepper Coques

SERVES 6 to 8 (Makes 4 coques) | TOTAL TIME 1¼ hours, plus 26¼ hours chilling, resting, and cooling

Dough

- 3 cups (16½ ounces) bread flour
- 2 teaspoons sugar
- ½ teaspoon instant or rapid-rise yeast
- 1⅓ cups (10⅔ ounces) ice water
- 3 tablespoons extra-virgin olive oil
- 1½ teaspoons table salt

Topping

- ½ cup extra-virgin olive oil, divided
- 2 large onions, halved and sliced thin
- 2 cups jarred roasted red peppers, patted dry and sliced thin
- 3 tablespoons sugar
- 3 garlic cloves, minced
- 1½ teaspoons table salt
- ¼ teaspoon red pepper flakes
- 2 bay leaves
- 3 tablespoons sherry vinegar
- ¼ cup pine nuts (optional)
- 1 tablespoon minced fresh parsley

Why This Recipe Works Thin and crunchy and topped with a myriad of savory (or sweet) toppings, these Catalan flatbreads are ubiquitous in Spanish tapas bars. Although coques are sometimes referred to as the Spanish version of pizza, that hardly does this dish justice. To get an extra-crisp flatbread, you'll use more olive oil than you typically would for a pizza dough, and you'll brush each coca with more olive oil before baking. Parbaking the dough before topping it further promotes an evenly crispy, sturdy base—all the better to support this deeply flavorful, sweetly tangy topping, made by cooking onions and roasted red peppers with olive oil, garlic, red pepper flakes, and sherry vinegar until the vegetables turn meltingly soft and sweetly savory. It is important to use ice water in the dough to prevent it from over-heating in the food processor. If you cannot fit two coques on a single baking sheet, bake them in two batches. We prefer King Arthur brand bread flour in this recipe.

1 **For the dough** Pulse flour, sugar, and yeast in food processor until combined, about 5 pulses. With processor running, slowly add ice water and process until dough is just combined and no dry flour remains, about 10 seconds. Let dough rest for 10 minutes.

2 Add oil and salt to dough and process until dough forms satiny, sticky ball that clears sides of bowl, 30 to 60 seconds. Transfer dough to lightly floured counter and knead by hand to form smooth, round ball, about 30 seconds. Place dough seam side down in lightly greased large bowl or container, cover tightly with plastic wrap, and refrigerate for at least 24 hours. (Dough can be refrigerated for up to 3 days.)

3 **For the topping** Heat 3 tablespoons oil in 12-inch nonstick skillet over medium heat until shimmering. Stir in onions, red peppers, sugar, garlic, salt, pepper flakes, and bay leaves. Cover and cook, stirring occasionally, until onions are softened and have released their juice, about 10 minutes. Remove lid and continue to cook, stirring often, until onions are golden brown, 10 to 15 minutes. Off heat, discard bay leaves. Transfer onion mixture to bowl, stir in vinegar, and let cool completely before using.

4 Press down on dough to deflate. Transfer dough to clean counter, divide into quarters, and cover loosely with greased plastic. Working with 1 piece of dough at a time (keep remaining pieces covered), form into rough ball by stretching dough around your thumbs and pinching edges together so that top is smooth.

5 Place ball seam side down on counter and, using your cupped hands, drag in small circles until dough feels taut and round. Space dough balls 3 inches apart, cover loosely with greased plastic, and let rest for 1 hour.

6 Adjust oven racks to upper-middle and lower-middle positions and heat oven to 500 degrees. Coat 2 rimmed baking sheets with 2 tablespoons oil each. Generously coat 1 dough ball with flour and place on well-floured counter. Press and roll into 14 by 5-inch oval. Arrange oval on prepared sheet, with long edge fitted snugly

against 1 long side of sheet, and reshape as needed. (If dough resists stretching, let it relax for 10 to 20 minutes before trying to stretch it again.) Repeat with remaining dough balls, arranging 2 ovals on each sheet, spaced ½ inch apart. Using fork, poke surface of dough 10 to 15 times.

7 Brush dough ovals with remaining 1 tablespoon oil and bake until puffed, 6 to 8 minutes, switching and rotating sheets halfway through baking.

8 Scatter onion mixture evenly over flatbreads, from edge to edge, then sprinkle with pine nuts, if using. Bake until topping is heated through and edges of flatbreads are deep golden brown and crisp, about 15 minutes, switching and rotating sheets halfway through baking. Let flatbreads cool on sheets for 10 minutes, then transfer to cutting board using metal spatula. Sprinkle with parsley, slice, and serve.

Pletzel

SERVES 6 to 8 | **TOTAL TIME** 1 hour, plus 3 hours resting and rising

3 cups (15 ounces) all-purpose flour

1⅔ (13⅓ ounces) cups water, room temperature

4 teaspoons kosher salt, divided

1½ teaspoons instant or rapid-rise yeast

1¼ teaspoons sugar

5 tablespoons extra-virgin olive oil, divided

3 onions, chopped fine

2 tablespoons poppy seeds

Why This Recipe Works It's only been in the past few decades that pletzel bread has fallen from fashion; it used to be that you could easily find it in Jewish bakeries across the country. This old-school flatbread featuring onion and poppy seeds deserves a renewed place at the table. Because it's a wet, sticky dough, the greatest challenge lies in how to handle it properly so that it bakes up with the airy interior that it should have. After mixing the dough in a stand mixer, let it rest for 20 minutes and then knead it at high speed for 10 minutes, until a glossy, smooth dough forms. Rather than rolling it out, you'll press the dough onto a rimmed baking sheet, let it rest, and then stretch it a final time. (If the dough resists stretching after you put it onto the baking sheet, let it relax for 5 to 10 minutes and then try again.) Top your pletzel with a mixture of sautéed onions, poppy seeds, and a bit of salt. After a stint in the oven, the flatbread will emerge superbly crisp yet chewy. When kneading this sticky dough in a stand mixer on high speed, the mixer might tend to wobble. To prevent this, place a towel or shelf liner under the mixer and watch it during mixing. Handle the dough with your lightly oiled hands and resist flouring your fingers or the dough might stick.

1 Place towel or shelf liner beneath stand mixer to prevent wobbling and fit mixer with dough hook. Add flour, room-temperature water, and 1½ teaspoons salt to bowl and mix on low speed until no patches of dry flour remain, about 4 minutes, occasionally scraping sides and bottom of bowl. Turn off mixer and let dough rest for 20 minutes.

2 Sprinkle yeast and sugar over dough. Knead on low speed until fully combined, about 2 minutes, occasionally scraping sides and bottom of bowl. Increase mixer speed to high and knead until dough is glossy, smooth, and pulls away from sides of bowl, 8 to 10 minutes. (Dough will only pull away from sides while mixer is on. When mixer is off, dough will fall back to sides.)

3 Using your fingers, coat large bowl and rubber spatula with 1 tablespoon oil. Using oiled spatula, transfer dough to bowl and pour 1 tablespoon oil over top. Flip dough over once so it is well coated with oil; cover bowl tightly with plastic wrap. Let dough rise at room temperature until nearly tripled in volume and large bubbles have formed, 2 to 2½ hours. (Dough can be refrigerated for up to 24 hours. Let dough come to room temperature, 2 to 2½ hours, before proceeding with step 4.)

4 Meanwhile, heat 1 tablespoon oil in 12-inch skillet over medium heat until shimmering. Add onions and 1 teaspoon salt and cook, stirring occasionally, until onions are golden brown, about 10 minutes. Remove from heat and stir in poppy seeds. Transfer to bowl; set aside. Adjust oven rack to lowest position and heat oven to 500 degrees.

5 Coat bottom and sides of rimmed baking sheet with 1 tablespoon oil. Using oiled rubber spatula, turn dough out onto prepared sheet along with any oil remaining in bowl.

6 Using your oiled fingertips, press dough out toward edges of sheet, taking care not to tear it. (Dough will not fit snugly into corners. If dough resists stretching, let it relax for 5 to 10 minutes before trying to stretch again.) Let dough rise, uncovered, at room temperature for 30 minutes. (Dough will increase but not quite double in volume.)

7 Using your oiled fingertips, press dough out toward edges of sheet once more. Using dinner fork, poke surface of dough 30 to 40 times. Brush top of dough with remaining

1 tablespoon oil and sprinkle with remaining 1½ teaspoons salt. Distribute onion–poppy seed mixture evenly over dough, leaving ½-inch border.

8 Bake until golden brown, 18 to 23 minutes, rotating sheet halfway through baking. Using metal spatula, transfer pletzel to cutting board. Slice and serve.

Pissaladière

SERVES 4 to 6 (Makes two 14 by 8-inch flatbreads) | TOTAL TIME 1¾ hours, plus 25½ hours resting and cooling

Dough

- 3 cups (16½ ounces) bread flour
- 2 teaspoons sugar
- ½ teaspoon instant or rapid-rise yeast
- 1⅓ cups ice water
- 1 tablespoon extra-virgin olive oil
- 1½ teaspoons table salt

Topping

- ¼ cup extra-virgin olive oil, divided
- 2 pounds onions, halved and sliced ¼ inch thick
- 1 teaspoon packed brown sugar
- ½ teaspoon table salt
- 1 tablespoon water
- ½ cup pitted niçoise olives, chopped coarse, divided
- 8 anchovy fillets, rinsed, patted dry, and chopped coarse, divided, plus 12 fillets for garnish (optional)
- 2 teaspoons minced fresh thyme, divided
- 1 teaspoon fennel seeds, divided
- ½ teaspoon pepper, divided
- 2 tablespoons minced fresh parsley, divided

Why This Recipe Works This savory Provençal bread is prized for its flavor and texture contrasts: salty black olives and anchovies on a backdrop of sweet caramelized onions and earthy fresh thyme, all laid over a crust that is part chewy pizza and part crisp cracker. You'll mix the dough in a food processor and knead it briefly by hand to build structure. Then let it have a long refrigerator rest to develop gluten and flavor slowly. After forming the dough into two balls, let them rest again and then roll them out and add the pungent toppings. Starting the onions covered and then uncovering them to finish leaves them perfectly browned and caramelized, and a bit of water stirred in at the end of cooking keeps them from clumping when spread over the crust. Chopping the anchovies keeps them from overpowering the other flavors (although you could opt to add more whole fillets on top). If you don't have a baking peel, use a rimless or overturned baking sheet to slide the pissaladière onto the baking stone. If you don't have a baking stone, you can use a preheated rimless or overturned baking sheet; however, the bread will be less crisp. We like to use our dough here; however, you can use 1¾ pounds ready-made pizza dough from the local pizzeria or supermarket. It is important to use ice water in the dough to prevent it from overheating in the food processor.

1 **For the dough** Pulse flour, sugar, and yeast in food processor until combined, about 5 pulses. With processor running, slowly add ice water and process until dough is just combined and no dry flour remains, about 10 seconds. Let dough rest for 10 minutes.

2 Add oil and salt to dough and process until dough forms satiny, sticky ball that clears sides of bowl, 30 to 60 seconds. Transfer dough to lightly floured counter and knead by hand to form smooth, round ball, about 30 seconds. Place dough seam side down in lightly greased large bowl or container, cover tightly with plastic wrap, and refrigerate for at least 24 hours or up to 3 days.

3 **For the topping** Heat 2 tablespoons oil in 12-inch nonstick skillet over medium heat until shimmering. Stir in onions, sugar, and salt. Cover and cook, stirring occasionally, until onions are softened and have released their juice, about 10 minutes. Remove lid and continue to cook, stirring often, until onions are golden brown, 10 to 15 minutes. Transfer onions to bowl, stir in water, and let cool completely before using.

4 One hour before baking, adjust oven rack 4 inches from broiler element, set baking stone on rack, and heat oven to 500 degrees. Press down on dough to deflate. Transfer dough to clean counter, divide in half, and cover loosely with greased plastic. Pat 1 piece of dough (keep remaining piece covered) into 4-inch round. Working around circumference of dough, fold edges toward center until ball forms.

5 Flip ball seam side down and, using your cupped hands, drag in small circles on counter until dough feels taut and round and all seams are secured on underside. (If dough sticks to your hands, lightly dust top of dough with flour.) Repeat with remaining piece of dough. Space dough balls 3 inches apart, cover loosely with greased plastic, and let rest for 1 hour.

6 Heat broiler for 10 minutes. Meanwhile, generously coat 1 dough ball with flour and place on well-floured counter. Press and roll into 14 by 8-inch oval. Transfer oval to well-floured baking peel and reshape as needed. (If dough resists stretching, let it relax for 10 to 20 minutes before trying to stretch it again.) Using fork, poke entire surface of oval 10 to 15 times.

7 Brush dough oval with 1 tablespoon oil, then sprinkle evenly with ¼ cup olives, half of chopped anchovies, 1 teaspoon thyme, ½ teaspoon fennel seeds, and ¼ teaspoon pepper, leaving ½-inch border. Arrange half of onions on top, followed by 6 whole anchovies, if using.

8 Slide flatbread carefully onto baking stone and return oven to 500 degrees. Bake until bottom crust is evenly browned and edges are crisp, 13 to 15 minutes, rotating flatbread halfway through baking. Transfer flatbread to wire rack and let cool for 5 minutes. Sprinkle with 1 tablespoon parsley.

9 Heat broiler for 10 minutes. Repeat with remaining dough, oil, and toppings, returning oven to 500 degrees when flatbread is placed on stone. Slice and serve.

Cauliflower Chickpea Flatbread with Romesco

SERVES 4 to 6 (Makes two 12-inch flatbreads) | **TOTAL TIME** 2¼ hours

1 head cauliflower (2 pounds), cored and cut into ¾-inch florets (about 7 cups), divided

1 cup chickpea flour

2 large eggs

½ cup extra-virgin olive oil, divided, plus extra for drizzling

3 garlic cloves, minced, divided

2 teaspoons chopped fresh oregano or ¾ teaspoon dried

1 teaspoon table salt, divided

6 ounces Parmesan cheese, grated (3 cups)

1¼ cups fresh parsley leaves, divided

⅔ cup jarred roasted red peppers, rinsed, patted dry, and chopped

¼ cup walnuts, toasted

1 tablespoon sherry vinegar

6 anchovy fillets, rinsed, patted dry, and chopped fine (optional), divided

¼ cup ricotta cheese, divided

Why This Recipe Works Cauliflower pizza crusts have firmly secured their place on supermarket shelves, thanks to the undeniable appeal of a vegetable-based crust. But it can be tricky to create a cauliflower crust or flatbread that doesn't either crumble or stick to the pan (or both) when you try to serve it. This cauliflower-based flatbread takes a cue from socca and farinata (pages 212 and 215) to create a strong, durable structure by incorporating chickpea flour. To add irresistible crispness, stir in a generous amount of grated Parmesan cheese, which essentially fries in the oven to create a gloriously crisp crust. Top the flatbreads with a savory red pepper romesco sauce, more cauliflower, and parsley for a vegetable-based flatbread with plenty of pizzazz (or add anchovies if desired). If you don't have a baking peel, use a rimless or overturned baking sheet to slide the flatbreads onto the baking stone. If you don't have a baking stone, you can use a preheated rimless or overturned baking sheet; however, the breads will be less crisp. Don't top the second flatbread until right before you bake it.

1 One hour before baking, adjust oven rack to upper-middle position, set baking stone on rack, and heat oven to 475 degrees. Process 4 cups cauliflower florets, chickpea flour, eggs, ¼ cup oil, two-thirds of the garlic, oregano, and ¼ teaspoon salt together in food processor until thick, smooth batter forms, about 3 minutes, scraping down sides of bowl as needed. Transfer batter to large bowl and stir in Parmesan.

2 Line baking peel with 16 by 12-inch piece of parchment paper with long edge perpendicular to handle and spray parchment well with canola oil spray. Transfer half of batter (about 2 cups) to center of prepared parchment and top with second greased sheet parchment. Gently press batter into 12-inch round (about ¼ inch thick), then discard top piece parchment. Carefully slide round, still on parchment, onto stone and bake until edges are browned and crisp and top is golden, about 12 minutes, rotating halfway through baking (parchment will darken). Transfer crust to wire rack set in rimmed baking sheet and discard bottom parchment. Repeat with remaining batter to make second crust.

3 In clean, dry food processor work bowl, process ¼ cup parsley, red peppers, walnuts, sherry vinegar, remaining garlic, and ¼ teaspoon salt until smooth, about 30 seconds, scraping down sides of bowl as needed. With processor running, slowly add 3 tablespoons oil until incorporated. (Romesco sauce can be refrigerated for up to 3 days.)

4 Heat remaining 1 tablespoon oil in 12-inch nonstick skillet over medium-high heat until shimmering. Add remaining 3 cups cauliflower florets and remaining ½ teaspoon salt and cook, stirring frequently, until florets are spotty brown and crisp-tender, 12 to 15 minutes.

5 Working with 1 crust at a time, spread half of sauce (about ⅓ cup) in thin layer over crust, leaving ¼-inch border. Scatter half of cauliflower and half of anchovies (if using) evenly over top. Place flatbread (still on wire rack in sheet) on stone and bake until warmed through, about 5 minutes.

6 Transfer flatbread to cutting board. Sprinkle evenly with ½ cup parsley, dollop half of ricotta in small spoonfuls evenly over flatbread, and drizzle with oil to taste. Slice into 8 slices and serve immediately. Repeat topping and baking for second flatbread.

Caramelized Onion Flatbread with Blue Cheese and Walnuts

SERVES 4 to 6 (Makes two 14 by 8-inch flatbreads) | **TOTAL TIME** 2 hours

2 tablespoons extra-virgin olive oil, plus extra for brushing

2 pounds onions, halved and sliced through root end ¼ inch thick

1 teaspoon packed brown sugar

½ teaspoon table salt

½ recipe Pizza Dough (page 337)

1 teaspoon pepper

1 cup walnuts, toasted and chopped coarse, divided

4 ounces blue cheese, crumbled (1 cup), divided

2 scallions, sliced thin, divided

Why This Recipe Works This rustic flatbread features jammy caramelized onions accented with pungent blue cheese and pleasingly bitter toasted walnuts. And the two variations change the flavors dramatically while still keeping those onions the center of attention. Starting them over medium-low heat encourages them to release their excess moisture, and then turning up the heat and continuing to cook them helps them become deeply browned. Adding some brown sugar enhances their natural sweetness while also helping the onions caramelize more quickly. Once you've got your onions perfected, roll out a piece of pizza dough; brush it with oil; and scatter the caramelized strands over the top, followed by the cheese and nuts. A garnish of fresh scallions adds bright flavor and color. We like to use our Pizza Dough; however, you can use 1 pound ready-made pizza dough from the local pizzeria or supermarket. If you don't have a baking peel, use a rimless or overturned baking sheet to slide the flatbreads onto the baking stone. If you don't have a baking stone, you can use a preheated rimless or overturned baking sheet; however, the breads will be less crisp.

1 Adjust oven rack to lower-middle position, place baking stone on rack, and heat oven to 500 degrees. Let baking stone heat for at least 30 minutes or up to 1 hour.

2 Heat oil in 12-inch nonstick skillet over medium-low heat until shimmering. Stir in onions, sugar, and salt. Cover and cook, stirring occasionally, until onions are softened and have released their juices, about 10 minutes. Remove lid; increase heat to medium-high; and continue to cook, stirring often, until onions are deeply browned, 10 to 15 minutes.

3 Transfer dough to lightly floured counter, divide in half, and cover with greased plastic wrap. Working with 1 piece of dough at a time (keep other piece covered), press and roll dough into 14 by 8-inch oval. Transfer dough to parchment-lined baking peel and reshape as needed. Gently dimple surface of dough with your fingertips.

4 Brush dough liberally with oil and sprinkle with pepper. Scatter half of caramelized onions, ½ cup walnuts, and ½ cup blue cheese evenly over dough, leaving ½-inch border. Slide parchment paper and flatbread onto baking stone.

5 Bake until flatbread is deep golden brown, about 10 minutes, rotating flatbread halfway through baking. (Prepare second flatbread while first bakes.) Remove flatbread from oven by sliding parchment paper back onto baking peel. Transfer flatbread to cutting board, discarding parchment. Sprinkle with half of scallions, then slice and serve. Let stone reheat for 5 minutes before baking second flatbread.

Variations

Caramelized Onion Flatbread with Potato, Goat Cheese, and Rosemary

Omit walnuts, blue cheese, and scallions. Toss 1 pound very thinly sliced unpeeled small red potatoes with 1 tablespoon water in large bowl. Cover tightly with plastic wrap and microwave until potatoes are just tender, 3 to 7 minutes. Let potatoes cool. In step 4, scatter half of potatoes and ½ cup crumbled goat cheese over each flatbread, then sprinkle each with ¼ teaspoon minced fresh rosemary.

Caramelized Onion Flatbread with Shaved Brussels Sprouts, Fontina, and Hazelnuts

Omit walnuts, blue cheese, and scallions. Toss 10 ounces trimmed and thinly sliced brussels sprouts with 2 teaspoons extra-virgin olive oil and ¼ teaspoon table salt. In step 4, scatter half of brussels sprouts; ½ cup shredded fontina; and 2 tablespoons toasted, skinned, and chopped hazelnuts over each flatbread.

Thin-Crust Whole-Wheat Pizza with Pesto and Goat Cheese

SERVES 4 (Makes two 13-inch pizzas) | **TOTAL TIME** 40 minutes, plus 1 hour resting

2 cups fresh basil leaves

7 tablespoons extra-virgin olive oil

¼ cup pine nuts

3 garlic cloves, minced

½ teaspoon table salt

¼ cup finely grated Parmesan or Pecorino Romano cheese

1 recipe Whole-Wheat Pizza Dough (page 338)

4 ounces goat cheese, crumbled (1 cup), divided

Why This Recipe Works Whole-wheat pizza dough makes this nutty-tasting crust with a crisp exterior and moist-tender interior. It may seem extreme to heat the oven at 500 degrees for an hour before baking and then preheat the broiler too before sliding the pizza into the oven, but this technique helps you achieve a pizza parlor–quality pie. Placing the pizza on the preheated baking stone near the top of the oven, rather than the usual home-oven approach of placing it near the bottom, means that the high heat of the oven reflects from the hot baking stone off the ceiling of the oven and back onto the top of the pie, browning the toppings before the crust overcooks. To complement the wheaty flavor of the crust, go tomato-free and opt for a white pizza, topping it with a basil pesto sauce and dollops of creamy goat cheese (or try one of the variations). We like to use our Whole-Wheat Pizza Dough; however, you can use 1½ pounds ready-made whole-wheat pizza dough from the local pizzeria or supermarket. The regular Pizza Dough (page 337) would be delicious here as well. If you don't have a baking peel, use a rimless or over-turned baking sheet to slide the pizzas onto the baking stone. If you don't have a baking stone, you can use a preheated rimless or overturned baking sheet; however, the crust will be less crisp.

1 Process basil, oil, pine nuts, garlic, and salt in food processor until smooth, scraping down sides of bowl as needed, about 1 minute. Stir in Parmesan and season with salt and pepper to taste.

2 One hour before baking pizza, adjust oven rack 4½ inches from broiler element, set baking stone on rack, and heat oven to 500 degrees. Remove dough from refrigerator and divide in half. Shape each half into smooth, tight ball. Place balls on lightly oiled baking sheet, spacing them at least 3 inches apart. Cover loosely with plastic coated with vegetable oil spray; let stand for 1 hour.

3 Heat broiler for 10 minutes. Meanwhile, coat 1 ball of dough generously with flour and place on well-floured countertop. Using your fingertips, gently flatten into 8-inch disk, leaving 1 inch of outer edge slightly thicker than center. Lift edge of dough and, using back of your hands and knuckles, gently stretch disk into 12-inch round, working along edges and giving disk quarter turns as you stretch. Transfer dough to well-floured baking peel and stretch into 13-inch round. Using back of spoon, spread half of pesto in thin layer over surface of dough, leaving ¼-inch border. Sprinkle with ½ cup goat cheese. Slide pizza carefully onto stone and return oven to 500 degrees. Bake until crust is well browned and cheese is partially browned, 8 to 10 minutes, rotating pizza halfway through baking. Remove pizza, place on wire rack, and let rest for 5 minutes. Slice and serve.

4 Heat broiler for 10 minutes. Repeat process of stretching, topping, and baking with remaining dough and toppings, returning oven to 500 degrees when pizza is placed on stone.

Variations

Thin-Crust Whole-Wheat Pizza with Garlic Oil, Two Cheeses, and Basil

Heat ¼ cup extra-virgin olive oil in 8-inch skillet over medium-low heat until shimmering. Add 2 minced garlic cloves; 2 anchovy fillets, rinsed, patted dry, and minced (optional); ½ teaspoon pepper; ½ teaspoon dried oregano; ⅛ teaspoon red pepper flakes; and ⅛ teaspoon table salt. Cook, stirring constantly, until fragrant, about 30 seconds. Transfer garlic oil to bowl and let cool completely. Substitute garlic oil for pesto. In step 5, omit goat cheese. Before baking, layer ½ cup fresh basil leaves over each dough round. Sprinkle ¼ cup Pecorino Romano cheese over basil, followed by 1 cup shredded whole-milk mozzarella. Bake until crust is well browned and cheese is bubbly and partially browned.

Thin-Crust Whole-Wheat Pizza with Wine-Braised Onions and Blue Cheese

Bring 1 onion, halved and sliced ⅛ inch thick; 1½ cups water; ¾ cup dry red wine; 3 tablespoons sugar; and ¼ teaspoon table salt to simmer in 10-inch skillet over medium heat. Cook, stirring often, until liquid evaporates and onions are crisp-tender, about 30 minutes. Transfer mixture to bowl, stir in 2 teaspoons red wine vinegar, and let cool completely before using. Omit pesto. Omit goat cheese. Before baking, spread ⅓ cup crème fraîche over surface of each dough round, leaving ¼-inch border. Sprinkle half of onion mixture evenly over each pizza, followed by ½ cup coarsely chopped walnuts and ½ cup crumbled blue cheese. Bake and rest as directed, then top each pizza with 2 tablespoons shredded basil.

Thin-Crust Pizza with Pumpkin, Cashew Ricotta, and Apple-Fennel Slaw

SERVES 4 (Makes two 13-inch pizzas) | **TOTAL TIME** 1¼ hours, plus 9 hours soaking and resting

Cashew Ricotta

⅔ cup raw cashews

3 tablespoons water, plus water for soaking cashews

4 teaspoons extra-virgin olive oil

1¼ teaspoons lemon juice, plus extra for seasoning

¼ teaspoon table salt

Pizza

1 recipe Pizza Dough (page 337)

3 tablespoons extra-virgin olive oil, divided, plus extra for drizzling

1 large shallot, minced

¾ teaspoon table salt, divided

1 garlic clove, minced

1 teaspoon pumpkin pie spice

1 cup canned unsweetened pumpkin puree

2 teaspoons maple syrup, divided

½ teaspoon pepper, divided

1 Granny Smith apple, cored and cut into 2-inch matchsticks

1 small fennel bulb, 2 tablespoons fronds chopped, stalks discarded, bulb halved, cored, and sliced thin

1 tablespoon cider vinegar

1 teaspoon whole-grain mustard

¼ cup dried cranberries

Why This Recipe Works The flavors and aromas of autumn in New England inspire this pizza, which uses the same high-heat baking technique as the whole-wheat pizza on page 196 to achieve a restaurant-quality crust. Here you'll use our pizza dough made with bread flour. The dairy-free yet decadent sauce blends cashew-based ricotta with a spiced pumpkin mixture. (You can use whole-milk dairy ricotta, if you prefer.) After baking, you'll top the hot pizza with a cool, textural salad of thinly sliced green apple and fennel tossed in a mustard-maple vinaigrette. Then finish these pumpkin-y pies with a tangle of bottle-green fennel fronds, jewel-like dried cranberries, and a drizzle of golden olive oil for a pizza that looks as beautiful as, well, autumn in New England. We like our recipes for Pizza Dough and cashew ricotta, but you can use 1¾ pounds store-bought dough and ⅔ cup store-bought dairy ricotta, if you like. If you don't have a baking peel, use a rimless or overturned baking sheet to slide the pizza onto the baking stone. If you don't have a baking stone, you can use a preheated rimless or overturned baking sheet; however, the crust will be less crisp. See the Seeded Pumpkin Crackers (page 154) to use up the remaining canned pumpkin.

1 **For the cashew ricotta** Place cashews in bowl and add water to cover by 1 inch. Soak cashews at room temperature for at least 8 hours or up to 24 hours. Drain and rinse well. Process cashews, water, oil, lemon juice, and salt in food processor until smooth, about 2 minutes, scraping down sides of bowl as needed. Adjust consistency with additional water as needed. Season with salt, pepper, and extra lemon juice to taste. (Ricotta can be refrigerated for up to 1 week.)

2 **For the pizza** One hour before baking, adjust oven rack to upper-middle position, set baking stone on rack, and heat oven to 500 degrees. Divide pizza dough in half and shape each half into smooth, tight ball. Space dough balls 3 inches apart on lightly oiled rimmed baking sheet, cover loosely with greased plastic wrap, and let rest for 1 hour.

3 Meanwhile, heat 1 tablespoon oil in 8-inch skillet over medium heat until shimmering. Add shallot and ¼ teaspoon salt and cook until softened, about 3 minutes. Stir in garlic and pumpkin pie spice and cook until fragrant, about 30 seconds. Stir in pumpkin and cook until darkened slightly, 3 to 5 minutes. Remove from heat and let cool slightly, about 10 minutes. Stir in cashew ricotta, 1 teaspoon maple syrup, ¼ teaspoon salt, and ¼ teaspoon pepper; set aside. Toss apple, fennel bulb, vinegar, mustard, remaining 2 tablespoons oil, remaining 1 teaspoon maple syrup, remaining ¼ teaspoon salt, and remaining ¼ teaspoon pepper together in bowl; set aside.

4 Heat broiler for 10 minutes. Meanwhile, coat 1 dough ball generously with flour and place on well-floured counter (keep second dough ball covered). Using your fingertips, gently flatten dough into 8-inch round, leaving 1 inch of outer edge

slightly thicker than center. Using your hands, gently stretch dough into 12-inch round, working along edges and giving dough quarter turns as you stretch. Transfer dough to well-floured baking peel and stretch into 13-inch round.

5 Spread ½ of pumpkin–cashew ricotta mixture over dough, leaving ½-inch border. Slide pizza carefully onto stone and return oven to 500 degrees. Bake until crust is well browned, 10 to 12 minutes, rotating pizza halfway through

baking. Transfer pizza to wire rack, sprinkle half of apple-fennel mixture over pizza, and let cool for 5 minutes. Sprinkle with half of fennel fronds and half of dried cranberries and drizzle with extra oil; slice and serve.

6 Heat broiler for 10 minutes. Repeat process of stretching, topping, and baking with remaining dough and toppings, returning oven to 500 degrees when pizza is placed on stone.

Sfincione

SERVES 4 to 6 | **TOTAL TIME** 2½ hours, plus 26 hours chilling and resting

Dough

2¼ cups (11¼ ounces) all-purpose flour

2 cups (12 ounces) semolina flour

1 teaspoon instant or rapid-rise yeast

1⅔ cups (13⅓ ounces) ice water

3 tablespoons extra-virgin olive oil

1 teaspoon sugar

2¼ teaspoons table salt

Sauce

2 onions, grated

½ cup water, room temperature

1 (14.5-ounce) can whole peeled tomatoes, drained

2 tablespoons extra-virgin olive oil

3 anchovy fillets, rinsed, patted dry, and minced

½ teaspoon dried oregano

¼ teaspoon red pepper flakes

¼ teaspoon table salt

Pizza

7 tablespoons extra-virgin olive oil, divided

1 cup panko bread crumbs

1 ounce Parmigiano Reggiano cheese, grated (½ cup)

Pinch table salt

8 ounces provolone, sliced

8 anchovy fillets, rinsed, patted dry, and sliced in half lengthwise (optional)

¼ teaspoon dried oregano

Why This Recipe Works Walk among the street vendors in Palermo, and you'll see sfincione on offer, a classic type of pizza featuring onions, anchovies, bread crumbs, and local caciocavallo cheese. Sold in bakeries, purchased on the street, and made at home, sfincione is most famous for being prepared for New Year's celebrations. The rectangular pizza's thick, soft base has a tight, even, cakelike crumb (sfincione loosely translates to "thick sponge"). The crust is pale yellow and has an almost creamy texture thanks to the semolina flour used in the dough. Spread over the top of this crust is a concentrated, complex tomato sauce bolstered by plenty of onion; a modest layer of cheese; anchovies; and a sprinkling of bread crumbs. To get the desired crumb in the crust, you'll take a three-pronged approach: Incorporating a generous amount of olive oil into the dough tenderizes it; letting the dough slowly rise in the refrigerator overnight lets flavors develop without large bubbles forming; and then rolling it out and weighting it down with another baking sheet during the second rise keeps the crumb even and tight. If you have access to caciocavallo, use a young version of that in place of the provolone. It is important to use ice water in the dough to prevent overheating during mixing. We prefer King Arthur brand all-purpose flour and Bob's Red Mill semolina flour in this recipe.

1 **For the dough** Whisk all-purpose flour, semolina flour, and yeast together in bowl of stand mixer. Whisk ice water, oil, and sugar in 4-cup liquid measuring cup until sugar has dissolved. Using dough hook on low speed, slowly add water mixture to flour mixture and mix until cohesive dough starts to form and no dry flour remains, 1 to 2 minutes. Cover bowl tightly with plastic wrap and let dough rest for 10 minutes.

2 Add salt to dough and knead on medium-low speed until dough is smooth and elastic and clears sides of bowl, about 8 minutes. Transfer dough to lightly floured counter and knead by hand to form smooth, round ball, about 30 seconds. Place dough seam side down in lightly greased large bowl or container, cover tightly with plastic, and refrigerate for at least 24 hours. (Dough can be refrigerated for up to 2 days.)

3 **For the sauce** Place onions and water in medium saucepan and bring to boil over medium heat. Reduce heat to low, cover, and simmer gently for 1 hour. Meanwhile, process tomatoes, oil, anchovies, oregano, pepper flakes, and salt in food processor until smooth, about 30 seconds. Add tomato puree to onion mixture and continue to cook, stirring occasionally, until reduced to 2 cups, 15 to 20 minutes. Transfer to bowl and let cool completely before using.

4 **For the pizza** One hour before baking, adjust oven rack to middle position, set baking stone on rack, and heat oven to 500 degrees. Spray rimmed baking sheet (including rim) with vegetable oil spray, then coat bottom of sheet with ¼ cup oil. Press down on dough to deflate. Transfer dough to lightly floured counter and dust with flour. Press and roll dough into 18 by 13-inch rectangle. Loosely roll dough around rolling pin and gently unroll it onto prepared sheet, fitting dough into

corners. Cover loosely with greased plastic, then place second rimmed baking sheet on top and let dough rise for 1 hour.

5 Remove top sheet and plastic. Using your fingertips, gently press dough into corners of sheet. Stir panko, Parmigiano, salt, and remaining 3 tablespoons oil together in bowl. Spread provolone slices over dough in even layer. Using back of spoon or ladle, spread tomato sauce in thin layer over provolone, leaving ½-inch border. Sprinkle panko

mixture evenly over sauce and dough. Lay anchovy slices, if using, evenly over panko mixture and sprinkle with oregano.

6 Place pizza in oven and reduce oven temperature to 450 degrees. Bake until bottom crust is evenly browned and cheese is bubbly and partially browned, 20 to 25 minutes, rotating sheet halfway through baking. Let pizza cool in sheet on wire rack for 5 minutes, then transfer to cutting board with metal spatula. Cut into squares and serve.

Pizza al Taglio with Arugula and Fresh Mozzarella

SERVES 4 to 6 | **TOTAL TIME** 1¼ hours, plus 18 hours chilling and resting

Dough

2⅔ cups (14⅔ ounces) bread flour

1 teaspoon instant or rapid-rise yeast

1½ cups (12 ounces) water, room temperature

2 tablespoons extra-virgin olive oil

1¼ teaspoons table salt

Vegetable oil spray

Sauce

1 (14.5-ounce) can whole peeled tomatoes, drained

1 tablespoon extra-virgin olive oil

2 anchovy fillets, rinsed

1 teaspoon dried oregano

½ teaspoon table salt

¼ teaspoon red pepper flakes

Topping

¼ cup extra-virgin olive oil, divided

4 ounces (4 cups) baby arugula

8 ounces fresh mozzarella cheese, torn into bite-size pieces (about 2 cups)

1½ ounces Parmesan cheese, shredded (½ cup)

Why This Recipe Works The singular Roman invention known as pizza al taglio is baked in rectangular pans and cut into slabs as big or as small as the buyer desires. Roman pizzerias display their many varieties behind glass in deli-style cases, where it is sold by the length and cut with scissors (al taglio means "by the cut"). This pizza has a unique crust: full of irregularly sized holes, tender and chewy in equal measure, with an audibly crisp yet delicate bottom and a complex, yeasty flavor. Sometimes the toppings are applied before the crust goes into the oven so that they can cook and brown, while sometimes the pizza can resemble an open-faced sandwich, with items such as salad greens, soft cheeses, or cured meats piled on after it comes out of the oven. You have your choice of both options with this recipe and its variations. To create the crust, this dough contains lots of water and olive oil. Because the dough is so wet, you'll fold it by hand to develop gluten rather than use a stand mixer. Then, you'll give it a long rest in the refrigerator. At that cool temperature, the yeast more slowly consumes the sugars in the flour, producing more of the desirable acids that create flavor complexity. The long rest also gives the dough time to relax for easy stretching to its final dimensions. This pizza is baked on the lowest rack of the oven, so that the bottom gets evenly browned but the top doesn't overcook. Anchovies give the sauce depth without announcing themselves, so don't omit them. We prefer King Arthur brand bread flour in this recipe.

1 **For the dough** Whisk flour and yeast together in medium bowl. Add room-temperature water and oil and stir with wooden spoon until shaggy mass forms and no dry flour remains. Cover bowl with plastic wrap and let sit for 10 minutes. Sprinkle salt over dough and mix until fully incorporated. Cover bowl with plastic and let dough rest for 20 minutes.

2 Using your wet hands, fold dough over itself by gently lifting and folding edge of dough toward middle. Turn bowl 90 degrees; fold again. Turn bowl and fold dough 4 more times (total of 6 turns). Cover bowl with plastic and let dough rest for 20 minutes. Repeat folding technique, turning bowl each time, until dough tightens slightly, 3 to 6 turns total. Cover bowl with plastic and let dough rest for 10 minutes.

3 Spray bottom of 13 by 9-inch baking pan liberally with oil spray. Transfer dough to prepared pan and spray top of dough lightly with oil spray. Gently press dough into 10 by 7-inch oval of even thickness. Cover pan tightly with plastic and refrigerate for at least 16 hours. (Dough can be refrigerated for up to 24 hours.)

4 **For the sauce** While dough rests, process all ingredients in blender until smooth, 20 to 30 seconds. Transfer sauce to bowl, cover, and refrigerate until needed (sauce can be refrigerated in airtight container for up to 2 days).

5 **For the topping** Brush top of dough with 2 tablespoons oil. Spray rimmed baking sheet (including rim) with oil spray. Invert prepared sheet on top of pan and flip, allowing dough to fall onto sheet (you may need to lift pan and nudge dough at 1 end to release). Using your fingertips, gently dimple dough into even thickness and stretch toward edges of sheet to form 15 by 11-inch oval. Spray top of dough lightly with oil spray; cover loosely with plastic; and let rest until slightly puffy, 1 to 1¼ hours.

6 Thirty minutes before baking, adjust oven rack to lowest position and heat oven to 450 degrees. Just before baking, use your fingertips to gently dimple dough into even thickness, pressing into corners of sheet. Using back of spoon or ladle, spread ½ cup sauce in even layer over surface of dough. (Remaining sauce can be frozen for up to 2 months.)

7 Drizzle 1 tablespoon oil over top of sauce and use back of spoon to spread evenly over surface. Transfer sheet to oven and bake until bottom of crust is evenly browned and top is lightly browned in spots, 20 to 25 minutes, rotating sheet halfway through baking. Transfer sheet to wire rack and let cool for 5 minutes. Run knife around rim of sheet to loosen pizza. Transfer pizza to cutting board and cut into 8 rectangles. Toss arugula with remaining 1 tablespoon oil in bowl. Top pizza with arugula, followed by mozzarella and Parmesan, and serve.

Variations

Pizza al Taglio with Prosciutto and Figs

Omit sauce ingredients as well as arugula, mozzarella, and Parmesan in topping. Spread remaining 2 tablespoons oil evenly over dough. Bake pizza as directed until bottom of crust is evenly browned and top is lightly browned in spots. Let pizza cool, then cut as directed. Top slices of pizza with 4 ounces thinly sliced prosciutto, followed by 8 thinly sliced figs and 2 ounces thinly shaved ricotta salata.

Pizza al Taglio with Potatoes and Soppressata

Decrease oil in topping to 3 tablespoons and omit arugula, mozzarella, and Parmesan. After spreading sauce over dough, lay 6 ounces thinly sliced soppressata in even layer over sauce, followed by 10 ounces thinly sliced provolone. Toss 1 pound peeled and thinly sliced small Yukon Gold potatoes with ½ teaspoon pepper and remaining 1 tablespoon oil. Starting in 1 corner, shingle potatoes to form even row across bottom of pizza, overlapping each slice by about one-quarter. Continue to layer potatoes in rows, overlapping each row by about one-quarter. Bake pizza as directed until bottom of crust is evenly browned and potatoes are browned around edges. Sprinkle pizza with 2 teaspoons chopped fresh parsley before serving.

Pide with Eggplant and Tomatoes

SERVES 6 (Makes 6 pide) | **TOTAL TIME** 1¾ hours, plus 25½ hours resting and cooling

Dough

- 3 cups (16½ ounces) bread flour
- 2 teaspoons sugar
- ½ teaspoon instant or rapid-rise yeast
- 1⅓ cups ice water
- 1 tablespoon extra-virgin olive oil
- 1½ teaspoons table salt

Topping

- 1 (28-ounce) can whole peeled tomatoes
- 5 tablespoons extra-virgin olive oil, divided
- 1 pound eggplant, cut into ½-inch pieces
- ½ red bell pepper, chopped
- ½ teaspoon table salt
- 3 garlic cloves, minced
- ½ teaspoon smoked paprika
- ¼ teaspoon red pepper flakes
- 6 tablespoons minced fresh mint, divided
- 6 ounces feta cheese, crumbled (1½ cups), divided

Why This Recipe Works This Turkish flatbread is identifiable by its signature canoe shape. Beyond that, it can be made with any number of filling combinations, as pide varies from region to region and from family to family. For this version, you'll make a simple dough with bread flour that gets a long fermentation in the refrigerator. This allows for great flavor development and creates a baked crust with a crisp exterior and pleasingly chewy interior. For the toppings, the combination of eggplant, red bell pepper, and tomatoes is a classic in Turkish cuisine. Sautéing all the vegetables together until the mixture is thickened eliminates excess moisture (meaning that you don't have to salt the eggplant before cooking). Smoky paprika and spicy red pepper flakes; a healthy amount of mint; and some briny, creamy feta accent the vegetables. Shaping the pide on individual parchment sheets makes transferring the little boats to the preheated baking stone easy and efficient. Press and roll the remaining 3 dough balls into ovals while the first set of pide bake, but don't top and shape the pide until right before baking. If you don't have a baking peel, use a rimless or overturned baking sheet to slide the pide onto the baking stone. If you don't have a baking stone, you can use a preheated rimless or overturned baking sheet; however, the crust will be less crisp. We like to use our dough here; however, you can use 1¾ pounds ready-made pizza dough from the local pizzeria or supermarket. It is important to use ice water in the dough to prevent it from overheating in the food processor. We prefer King Arthur brand bread flour in this recipe.

1 **For the dough** Pulse flour, sugar, and yeast in food processor until combined, about 5 pulses. With processor running, slowly add ice water and process until dough is just combined and no dry flour remains, about 10 seconds. Let dough rest for 10 minutes.

2 Add oil and salt to dough and process until dough forms satiny, sticky ball that clears sides of bowl, 30 to 60 seconds. Transfer dough to lightly oiled counter and knead by hand to form smooth, round ball, about 30 seconds. Place dough seam side down in lightly greased large bowl or container, cover tightly with plastic wrap, and refrigerate for at least 24 hours or up to 3 days.

3 **For the topping** Pulse tomatoes and their juice in food processor until coarsely ground, about 12 pulses. Heat 2 tablespoons oil in 12-inch nonstick skillet over medium-high heat until shimmering. Add eggplant, bell pepper, and salt and cook, stirring occasionally, until softened and beginning to brown, 5 to 7 minutes. Stir in garlic, paprika, and pepper flakes and cook until fragrant, about 30 seconds.

4 Add tomatoes; bring to simmer; and cook, stirring occasionally, until mixture is very thick and measures 3½ cups, about 10 minutes. Off heat, stir in ¼ cup mint and season with salt and pepper to taste; let cool completely before using.

5 One hour before baking, adjust oven rack 4 inches from broiler element, set baking stone on rack, and heat oven to 500 degrees. Press down on dough to deflate. Transfer dough to clean counter and divide in half, then cut each half into thirds (about 4¾ ounces each); cover loosely with greased plastic. Working with 1 piece of dough at a time (keep remaining pieces covered), form into rough ball by stretching dough around your thumbs and pinching edges together so that top is smooth. Space balls 3 inches apart, cover loosely with greased plastic, and let rest for 1 hour.

6 Cut six 16 by 6-inch pieces of parchment paper. Generously coat 1 dough ball with flour and place on well-floured counter. Press and roll into 14 by 5½-inch oval. Arrange oval on parchment rectangle and reshape as needed. (If dough resists stretching, let it relax for 10 to 20 minutes before trying to stretch it again.) Repeat with 2 more dough balls and parchment rectangles.

7 Brush dough ovals with oil, then top each with ½ cup eggplant mixture and ¼ cup feta, leaving ¾-inch border. Fold long edges of dough over filling to form canoe shape and pinch ends together to seal. Brush outer edges of dough with oil and transfer pide (still on parchment rectangles) to baking peel.

8 Slide each parchment rectangle with pide onto baking stone, spacing pide at least 1 inch apart. Bake until crust is golden brown and edges are crisp, 10 to 15 minutes. Transfer pide to wire rack, discard parchment, and let cool for 5 minutes. Sprinkle with 1 tablespoon mint, slice, and serve. Repeat with remaining 3 dough balls, 3 parchment rectangles, oil, and toppings.

SHAPING PIDE

1 Press and roll 1 dough ball into 14 by 5½-inch oval on well-floured counter. Arrange oval on parchment rectangle and reshape as needed.

2 Brush oval with oil, then top with ½ cup eggplant mixture and ¼ cup feta, leaving ¾-inch border.

3 Fold long edges of dough over filling to form canoe shape and pinch ends together to seal. Brush outer edges of dough with oil.

Adjaruli Khachapuri

SERVES 6 | **TOTAL TIME** 40 minutes, plus 2½ to 3½ hours rising

Dough

- 1¾ cups (8¾ ounces) all-purpose flour
- 1½ teaspoons sugar
- 1 teaspoon instant or rapid-rise yeast
- ¾ teaspoon table salt
- ½ cup plus 2 tablespoons (5 ounces) ice water
- 1 tablespoon extra-virgin olive oil

Topping

- 6 ounces whole-milk mozzarella cheese, shredded (1½ cups)
- 6 ounces feta cheese, crumbled (1½ cups)
- 1 large egg yolk
- 1 tablespoon unsalted butter

Why This Recipe Works In the country of Georgia, in the Caucasus region of central Asia, this cheese-filled bread is so beloved that it's the national dish. Different versions of khachapuri are shaped and filled in different ways; the adjaruli version is distinguished by its distinctive wide, flat boat shape. When the bread is still hot from the oven, the molten cheese is usually topped with an egg and butter and stirred together tableside. Diners tear off chunks of the crust to swipe into the center. This dough uses all-purpose flour, which provides enough structure to contain the oozy cheese and gives the bread a lightly chewy texture. A blend of mozzarella and feta cheeses approximates the briny, salty tang and desirable stringy texture found in the Georgian cheeses traditionally used, such as sulguni and imeruli. Stirring in an egg yolk and a pat of butter right before serving makes the filling smooth, stretchy, and ultrarich. It is important to use ice water in the dough to prevent it from overheating in the food processor. Use block mozzarella here.

1 **For the dough** Process flour, sugar, yeast, and salt in food processor until combined, about 3 seconds. With processor running, slowly add ice water and oil and process until dough forms sticky ball that clears sides of bowl, 30 to 60 seconds.

2 Transfer dough to counter and knead until smooth, about 1 minute. Shape dough into tight ball and place in greased bowl. Cover bowl with plastic wrap and let dough rise at room temperature until almost doubled in size, 2 to 2½ hours. (Alternatively, dough can rise in refrigerator until doubled in size, about 24 hours. Let come to room temperature, about 2 hours, before proceeding.)

3 Turn out dough onto lightly floured 16 by 12-inch sheet of parchment paper and coat lightly with flour. Flatten into 8-inch disk using your hands. Using rolling pin, roll dough into 12-inch circle, dusting dough lightly with flour as needed.

4 Roll bottom edge of dough 2½ inches in toward center. Rotate parchment 180 degrees and roll bottom edge of dough (directly opposite first rolled side) 2½ inches toward center. (Opposing edges of rolled sides should be 7 inches apart.)

5 Roll ends of rolled sides toward centerline and pinch firmly together to form football shape about 12 inches long and about 7 inches across at its widest point. Transfer parchment with dough to rimmed baking sheet. Cover loosely with plastic and let rise until puffy, 30 minutes to 1 hour. Adjust oven rack to middle position and heat oven to 450 degrees.

6 **For the topping** Combine mozzarella and feta in bowl. Fill dough with cheese mixture, lightly compacting and mounding in center (cheese will be piled higher than edge of dough). Bake until crust is well browned and cheese is bubbly and beginning to brown in spots, 15 to 17 minutes. Transfer sheet to wire rack. Add egg yolk and butter to cheese filling and stir with fork until fully incorporated and cheese is smooth and stretchy. Lift parchment off sheet and slide bread onto serving dish. Serve immediately.

SHAPING ADJARULI KHACHAPURI

1 After rolling dough disk into 12-inch circle, roll bottom edge of dough 2½ inches in toward center. Rotate parchment 180 degrees and roll bottom edge of dough (directly opposite first rolled side) 2½ inches toward center.

2 Roll ends of rolled sides toward centerline and pinch firmly together to form football shape about 12 inches long and about 7 inches across at its widest point.

3 After rising, fill dough with cheese mixture, lightly compacting and mounding in center.

BATTER "BAKES"

Socca with Caramelized Onions and Rosemary

SERVES 6 to 8 (Makes four 10-inch pancakes) | **TOTAL TIME** 1¼ hours

Socca

1½ cups water

1⅓ cups (6 ounces) chickpea flour

¼ cup extra-virgin olive oil, divided

1 teaspoon table salt

¼ teaspoon ground cumin

Topping

2 tablespoons extra-virgin olive oil, plus extra for drizzling

2 cups thinly sliced onions

½ teaspoon table salt

1 teaspoon chopped fresh rosemary

Coarse sea salt

Why This Recipe Works These thin, crisp, nutty-tasting chickpea pancakes will transport you right to the French Riviera, where they are popular choices for snacking on as street food or at outdoor cafés alongside a glass of chilled rosé. Traditionally, the socca batter is poured into a large cast-iron skillet and baked in a very hot wood-burning oven to make one large pancake with a blistered top and a smoky flavor, which is cut into wedges for serving. To make socca at home, you'll "bake" these supereasy smaller versions entirely on the stovetop, using a preheated nonstick skillet and flipping them to get a great crust on both sides. The smaller socca are easier to flip than one large pancake, and the direct heat of the stovetop ensures a crispy exterior on both sides, giving the socca a higher ratio of crunchy crust to tender interior. A topping of golden caramelized onions enhanced with rosemary complements these savory flat-breads. Or try the variation with Swiss chard, pistachios, and dried apricots. Both go great with that rosé.

1 **For the socca** Adjust oven rack to middle position and heat oven to 200 degrees. Set wire rack in rimmed baking sheet and place in oven. Whisk water, flour, 4 teaspoons oil, salt, and cumin in bowl until no lumps remain. Let batter rest while preparing topping, at least 10 minutes.

2 **For the topping** Heat oil in 10-inch nonstick skillet over medium-high heat until just smoking. Add onions and table salt and cook until onions start to brown around edges but still have some texture, 7 to 10 minutes. Add rosemary and cook until fragrant, about 1 minute. Transfer onion mixture to bowl; set aside. Wipe skillet clean with paper towels.

3 Heat 2 teaspoons oil in now-empty skillet over medium-high heat until just smoking. Lift skillet off heat and pour ½ cup batter into far side of skillet; swirl gently in clockwise direction until batter evenly covers bottom of skillet.

4 Return skillet to heat and cook socca, without moving it, until well browned and crisp around bottom edge, 3 to 4 minutes (you can peek at underside of socca by loosening it from side of skillet with rubber spatula). Flip socca with rubber spatula and cook until second side is just cooked, about 1 minute. Transfer socca, browned side up, to prepared wire rack in oven. Repeat 3 more times, using 2 teaspoons oil and ½ cup batter per batch.

5 Transfer socca to cutting board and cut each into wedges. Serve, topped with sautéed onions, drizzled with extra oil, and sprinkled with sea salt.

Variation

Socca with Swiss Chard, Apricots, and Pistachios

Omit onion topping. Heat 1 tablespoon oil in 12-inch nonstick skillet over medium heat until shimmering. Add 1 finely chopped onion and cook until softened, about 5 minutes. Stir in 2 minced garlic cloves, ¾ teaspoon ground cumin, ¼ teaspoon salt, and ⅛ teaspoon ground allspice and cook until fragrant, about 30 seconds. Stir in 12 ounces stemmed and chopped Swiss chard and 3 tablespoons finely chopped dried apricots and cook until chard is wilted, 4 to 6 minutes. Off heat, stir in 2 tablespoons finely chopped toasted pistachios and 1 teaspoon white wine vinegar, and season with salt and pepper to taste. Top each cooked socca with ⅓ cup chard mixture, slice, and serve.

Farinata

SERVES 6 to 8 (Makes one 12-inch pancake) | **TOTAL TIME** 1¼ hours, plus 4 hours resting

Why This Recipe Works A short but scenic train ride south from the French Riviera to the Italian Riviera brings you from socca country to farinata country. On the Ligurian coast of Italy, the golden batter for this chickpea flour pancake is poured across a wide, shallow copper pan and slid into an extremely hot wood-burning pizza oven. The delectable result—a pancake that's crispy at the edges but plush and creamy inside—is savored as a midmorning or midafternoon snack. The simple batter consists of just chickpea flour, water, and salt, but letting it hydrate for an extended time after whisking the ingredients together causes the batter to thicken and turn smooth, making for a pancake that is denser and more custardy than socca. To replicate Ligurian results without the wood-burning oven or the specialty pan, turn to cast iron. A well-seasoned 12-inch cast-iron skillet is the closest approximation to the traditional pan; after preheating, its fantastic heat retention in the oven gives the farinata a wonderfully crisped bottom and edges and an evenly cooked, tender interior. Farinata is often served plain or with just one or two simple adornments. In this version, fresh rosemary added to the skillet before pouring in the batter and a sprinkling of coarse sea salt and freshly ground black pepper to finish complement the savory cake. Garnish with more fresh rosemary, if you like.

1 cup (4½ ounces) chickpea flour

2 cups cold water

¾ teaspoon table salt

3 tablespoons extra-virgin olive oil

1 tablespoon chopped fresh rosemary

Coarse sea salt

1 Whisk flour, cold water, and salt in large bowl until smooth. Cover and let sit at room temperature for at least 4 hours or up to 24 hours.

2 Adjust oven rack to upper-middle position and heat oven to 400 degrees. Heat 12-inch cast-iron skillet over medium heat for 3 minutes. Add oil, swirl to coat evenly, and heat until shimmering. Add rosemary and cook until fragrant, about 30 seconds.

3 Whisk batter to recombine, then pour into skillet. Transfer skillet to oven and bake until top of pancake is dry and golden and edges begin to pull away from sides of skillet, 35 to 40 minutes. Remove skillet from oven and heat broiler.

4 Return skillet to oven and broil until pancake is spotty brown, 1 to 2 minutes. Let pancake cool slightly in skillet on wire rack for 5 minutes. Using thin spatula, loosen edges and underside of pancake from skillet, then carefully slide pancake onto cutting board. Season with sea salt and pepper to taste. Cut into wedges and serve warm.

Blini

SERVES 10 to 12 (Makes about 60 blini) | **TOTAL TIME** 45 minutes

Why This Recipe Works These hearty yet elegant Russian buckwheat pancakes are usually topped or filled with a variety of luxurious and flavorful elements, such as sour cream and caviar or smoked fish. (There are also sweet versions topped with jam or honey.) They come in all sizes, from plate-size versions that get rolled up around the fillings and are eaten with a knife and fork to finger-food versions that are eaten more like crostini, such as this silver dollar–size one known as oladi. While many blini are yeasted and gain a certain tanginess from the fermenting of the yeasted dough, this rendition is leavened with baking powder and baking soda, making it much quicker to prepare. Buttermilk adds tanginess to the batter to compensate for the lack of yeast. Since buckwheat flour contains no gluten, incorporating some all-purpose flour adds structure and sturdiness. Fun fact about why buckwheat is gluten-free: It isn't actually wheat at all, but rather an herb, whose seeds are ground to make flour. Top these two-bite blini with a dollop of sour cream or crème frâiche and smoked salmon or trout, plus garnishes such as capers and chopped chives or red onion (or go all out and serve them with caviar).

½ cup (2½ ounces) all-purpose flour

½ cup (2½ ounces) buckwheat flour

1 tablespoon sugar

½ teaspoon table salt

½ teaspoon baking powder

¼ teaspoon baking soda

¾ cup buttermilk

½ cup whole milk

1 large egg

4 tablespoons unsalted butter, melted and cooled, divided

1 Adjust oven rack to middle position and heat oven to 200 degrees. Line rimmed baking sheet with aluminum foil, top with wire rack, and spray rack with vegetable oil spray; set aside.

2 Whisk all-purpose flour, buckwheat flour, sugar, salt, baking powder, and baking soda together in medium bowl. In separate bowl, whisk buttermilk, milk, egg, and 2 tablespoons melted butter together. Whisk buttermilk mixture into flour mixture until just combined (do not overmix).

3 Using pastry brush, brush bottom and sides of 12-inch nonstick skillet very lightly with some of remaining melted butter; heat skillet over medium heat. When butter stops sizzling, add batter in spots to skillet using 1 scant tablespoon batter per pancake (6 to 8 pancakes will fit at a time). Cook until large bubbles begin to appear on surface of pancakes, 1½ to 2 minutes. Flip pancakes and cook until golden on second side, about 1½ minutes longer.

4 Transfer pancakes to prepared rack and keep warm, uncovered, in oven. Repeat with remaining butter and remaining batter. Let cool slightly before topping and serving. (Blini can be frozen to for up to 1 week; let them cool completely, wrap them in plastic wrap, and freeze. Thaw frozen pancakes in refrigerator for 24 hours, then spread out over baking sheet and warm in 350-degree oven for about 5 minutes before serving.)

Pajeon

SERVES 4 (Makes two 10-inch pancakes) | **TOTAL TIME** 50 minutes

Why This Recipe Works Korea's ubiquitous scallion pancake is an ideal anytime comfort food that you'll want to eat right off the pan alongside its tart, sweet-spicy dipping sauce. The filling-to-batter ratio is high in these crisp-chewy pancakes, and the scallions are typically cut into lengths, so the effect is a nest of verdant stalks bound together by the viscous batter. As it sizzles in the skillet, the pancake browns and the interior sets up soft and dense. Adding potato starch to the all-purpose flour equips the batter with more starchy material for crisping up; the chemical makeup of potato starch also helps keep the starch molecules separate after cooling so that the crust stays crispy. Since starches absorb ice water more slowly than they do room-temperature water, using ice water in the batter minimizes hydration, helping the pancakes crisp more easily during frying. Baking soda raises the batter's pH and boosts browning; baking powder opens up the crumb so that it's not gummy. Pressing the pancakes into the skillet after flipping them also encourages browning. Purchase the coarse variety of gochugaru (Korean red pepper flakes), which is sometimes labeled "coarse powder." Use a full teaspoon if you prefer a spicier dipping sauce. We prefer potato starch because it yields pajeon with the crispest exterior, but you can substitute cornstarch.

1. **For the dipping sauce** Whisk soy sauce, water, vinegar, sesame oil, gochugaru, and sugar together in small bowl; set aside.

2. **For the pancakes** Line large plate with double layer of paper towels and set aside. Separate dark-green parts of scallions from white and light-green parts. Halve white and light-green parts lengthwise. Cut all scallion parts into 2-inch lengths and set aside. Whisk flour, potato starch, sugar, baking powder, pepper, baking soda, and salt together in medium bowl. Add ice water and garlic and whisk until smooth. Using rubber spatula, fold in scallions until mixture is evenly combined.

3. Heat 2 tablespoons oil in 10-inch nonstick skillet over medium-high heat until just smoking. Stir batter to recombine. Run blade of spatula through center of batter to halve, then scrape half of batter into center of skillet. Spread into round of even thickness, covering bottom of skillet, using spatula or tongs to move scallions as necessary so they are evenly distributed in single layer. Shake skillet to distribute oil beneath pancake and cook, adjusting heat as needed to maintain gentle sizzle (reduce heat if oil begins to smoke), until bubbles at center of pancake burst and leave holes in surface and underside is golden brown, 3 to 5 minutes. Flip pancake and press firmly into skillet with back of spatula to flatten. Add 1 tablespoon oil to edges of skillet and continue to cook, pressing pancake occasionally to flatten, until second side is spotty golden brown, 2 to 4 minutes. Transfer to prepared plate.

4. Repeat with remaining 3 tablespoons oil and remaining batter. Let second pancake drain on prepared plate for 2 minutes. Cut each pancake into 6 wedges and transfer to platter. Serve, passing sauce separately.

Dipping Sauce

- 2 tablespoons soy sauce
- 1 tablespoon water
- 2 teaspoons unseasoned rice vinegar
- 1 teaspoon toasted sesame oil
- ½–1 teaspoon gochugaru
- ½ teaspoon sugar

Pancakes

- 10 scallions
- 1 cup (5 ounces) all-purpose flour
- ¼ cup (1 ounce) potato starch
- 1 teaspoon sugar
- 1 teaspoon baking powder
- ½ teaspoon pepper
- ¼ teaspoon baking soda
- ¼ teaspoon table salt
- 1 cup ice water
- 2 garlic cloves, minced
- 6 tablespoons vegetable oil, divided

Kimchi Jeon

SERVES 2 (Makes one 10-inch pancake) | **TOTAL TIME** 40 minutes

Dipping Sauce

- 5 tablespoons plus 1 teaspoon sugar
- 5 tablespoons plus 1 teaspoon soy sauce
- 5 tablespoons plus 1 teaspoon water
- 1½ teaspoons unseasoned rice vinegar
- 1 garlic clove, minced

Pancake

- ¼ cup (1¼ ounces) all-purpose flour
- 1 large egg white
- 1 cup cabbage kimchi, drained with 2 tablespoons juice reserved, chopped coarse
- 4 scallions, white parts sliced thin, green parts cut into 1-inch lengths
- 3 tablespoons vegetable oil, divided

Why This Recipe Works Kimchi is a ubiquitous condiment on the Korean table, adding spice and tang to soups, rice, and noodles and even flavoring this savory pancake. It has been said that when Korean farmers couldn't tend to their crops due to inclement weather, making kimchi pancakes was a comforting way to pass the time. Today these delicious pancakes are popular in both restaurants and homes, and the key to making them successfully is to prevent the kimchi, with its relatively high moisture content, from making them soggy. You achieve this by draining the pickled cabbage but reserving a measured 2 tablespoons of liquid for the batter. Binding the kimchi with just this liquid, one egg white, and a little flour really encourages the kimchi to shine. Scallions add more flavor and a pop of color. Flipping the delicate pancake to cook on the second side without it breaking and the kimchi falling out can be challenging, so instead, gently slide the pancake onto a plate and invert it onto another plate. This makes for a flawless flip, and you'll be able to easily slide the pancake, browned side up, back into the skillet to brown the second side. The salty-sweet dipping sauce counterbalances the kimchi's spiciness. This recipe can easily be doubled; make the pancake batter in two separate bowls and cook the pancakes in two batches.

1 **For the dipping sauce** Simmer all ingredients in small saucepan over medium heat, stirring occasionally, until thickened and reduced to about ¾ cup, about 5 minutes. Let cool completely before serving.

2 **For the pancake** Whisk flour, egg white, and reserved kimchi juice together in large bowl. Stir in scallions and kimchi until well combined.

3 Heat 2 tablespoons oil in 10-inch nonstick skillet over medium-high heat until shimmering. Add pancake batter and spread into even layer with rubber spatula. Cook until well browned around edges, about 4 minutes. Run spatula around edge of pancake and shake skillet to loosen. Slide pancake onto large plate.

4 Heat remaining 1 tablespoon oil in now-empty skillet over medium heat until shimmering. Invert pancake onto second large plate, then slide it, browned side up, back into skillet. Cook until pancake is well browned on second side, about 4 minutes. Slide pancake onto cutting board, cut into wedges, and serve with dipping sauce.

1 After browning first side, loosen pancake with rubber spatula and slide onto large plate.

2 Place second large plate face down over pancake; invert pancake onto second plate.

3 Slide pancake, browned side up, back into skillet and continue to cook.

Whole-Wheat Crepes with Creamy Sautéed Mushrooms and Asparagus

SERVES 4 (Makes 8 crepes) | **TOTAL TIME** 1½ hours

Crepes

½ teaspoon vegetable oil

1 cup (5½ ounces) whole-wheat flour

½ teaspoon table salt

2 cups milk

3 large eggs

4 tablespoons unsalted butter, melted and cooled

Filling

1½ pounds cremini mushrooms, trimmed and sliced ¼ inch thick

¼ cup water

½ teaspoon vegetable oil

1 tablespoon unsalted butter

1 shallot, minced

½ teaspoon table salt

¼ teaspoon pepper

8 ounces asparagus, trimmed and cut on bias ¼ inch thick

⅔ cup heavy cream

6 tablespoons grated Pecorino Romano cheese

½ teaspoon grated lemon zest

Why This Recipe Works Delicately nutty whole-wheat crepes make a lovely match for a rich mixture of cremini mushrooms and asparagus bound with cream and Pecorino Romano cheese. This recipe yields more crepes than you'll need for the illing, but the extras allow you to practice your batter-swirling technique. For the elegant filling, first sauté savory cremini mushrooms until they're well browned, and then add minced shallot and sliced asparagus, cooking the asparagus just until it's tender. Some heavy cream and grated Pecorino Romano make the filling luxuriously creamy, while lemon zest brightens it up. The crepes will give off steam as they cook, but if at any point the skillet begins to smoke, remove it from the burner and turn down the heat. Stacking the crepes on a wire rack allows excess steam to escape so that they won't stick together. The batter makes 10 crepes, but only eight are needed. You can substitute white mushrooms for the cremini.

1 **For the crepes** Heat oil in 12-inch nonstick skillet over low heat for at least 5 minutes. While skillet heats, whisk flour and salt together in medium bowl. In second bowl, whisk together milk and eggs. Add half of milk mixture to flour mixture and whisk until smooth. Add melted butter and whisk until incorporated. Whisk in remaining milk mixture until smooth.

2 Using paper towel, wipe out skillet, leaving thin film of oil on bottom and sides. Increase heat to medium and let skillet heat for 1 minute. Test heat of skillet by placing 1 teaspoon batter in center and cooking for 20 seconds. If mini crepe is golden brown on bottom, skillet is properly heated; if it is too light or too dark, adjust heat accordingly and retest.

3 Lift skillet off heat and pour ⅓ cup batter into far side of skillet; swirl gently in clockwise direction until batter evenly covers bottom of skillet. Return skillet to heat and cook crepe, without moving it, until surface is dry and crepe starts to brown at edges, loosening crepe from sides of skillet with rubber spatula, about 35 seconds. Gently slide spatula underneath edge of crepe, grasp edge with your fingertips, and flip crepe. Cook until second side is lightly spotted, about 20 seconds. Transfer crepe to wire rack. Return skillet to heat for 10 seconds before repeating with remaining batter. As crepes are done, stack on rack. (Crepes can be wrapped tightly in plastic wrap and refrigerated for up to 3 days or stacked between sheets of parchment paper and frozen for up to 1 month. Allow frozen crepes to thaw completely in refrigerator before using.)

4 **For the filling** Combine mushrooms and water in 12-inch nonstick skillet and cook over high heat, stirring occasionally, until skillet is almost dry and mushrooms begin to sizzle, 4 to 8 minutes. Reduce heat to medium-high. Add oil and toss until mushrooms are evenly coated. Continue to cook, stirring occasionally, until mushrooms are well browned, 4 to 8 minutes. Reduce heat to medium.

5 Push mushrooms to sides of skillet. Add butter to center. Once butter has melted, add shallot, salt, and pepper to center and cook, stirring constantly, until fragrant, about 30 seconds. Add asparagus and cook, stirring occasionally, until just tender, about 1 minute. Reduce heat to medium-low; add cream; and cook, stirring occasionally, until reduced by half, about 1 minute. Off heat, add Pecorino and lemon zest, stirring until cheese is melted and mushroom mixture is creamy.

6 Place crepes on large plate and invert second plate over crepes. Microwave until crepes are warm, 30 to 45 seconds (45 to 60 seconds if crepes have cooled completely). Working with 1 crepe at a time, spread ⅓ cup mushroom mixture across bottom half of crepe. Fold crepes in half and then into quarters. Transfer to plate and serve.

MAKING CREPES

1 Lift skillet off heat and tilt slightly away from you. Pour ⅓ cup batter into far side of skillet.

2 Turn your wrist to rotate skillet clockwise and spread batter over entire skillet bottom.

Rye Crepes with Smoked Salmon, Crème Fraîche, and Pickled Shallots

SERVES 4 (Makes 8 crepes) | **TOTAL TIME** 1½ hours

Rye Crepes

½ teaspoon vegetable oil

1 cup (5½ ounces) rye flour

½ teaspoon table salt

2½ cups milk

3 large eggs

4 tablespoons unsalted butter, melted and cooled

Filling

⅓ cup distilled white vinegar

2 tablespoons sugar

2 shallots, sliced thin

¾ cup crème fraîche

3 tablespoons capers, rinsed and chopped

3 tablespoons finely chopped chives

1½ teaspoons grated lemon zest plus 1½ tablespoons juice

¼ teaspoon table salt

¼ teaspoon pepper

8 ounces smoked salmon

Why This Recipe Works For big-personality crepes with a subtle spiciness, try rye flour. Although it contains less gluten than whole-wheat flour, it still contains enough to form sturdy crepes. Rye flour also absorbs moisture at a different rate than whole-wheat flour, so increasing the milk from the 2 cups used in the Whole-Wheat Crepes with Creamy Sautéed Mushrooms and Asparagus (page 222) to 2½ cups here makes the batter fluid enough for easy portioning and cooking. Pairing these earthy rye crepes with a smoked salmon filling takes its inspiration from classic blini toppings (see page 217 for Blini). Mixing crème fraîche with lemon, chives, and chopped capers makes for a briny, bright mixture to pair with the rich smoked salmon. Sliced shallots quickly pickled with vinegar and sugar offer a tangy contrasting crunch. The crepes will give off steam as they cook, but if at any point the skillet begins to smoke, remove it from the burner and turn down the heat. Stacking the crepes on a wire rack allows excess steam to escape so that they won't stick together. The batter makes 11 crepes, but only eight are needed. For more information on making crepes, see page 223.

1 **For the crepes** Heat oil in 12-inch nonstick skillet over low heat for at least 5 minutes. While skillet heats, whisk flour and salt together in medium bowl. In second bowl, whisk together milk and eggs. Add half of milk mixture to flour mixture and whisk until smooth. Add melted butter and whisk until incorporated. Whisk in remaining milk mixture until smooth.

2 Using paper towel, wipe out skillet, leaving thin film of oil on bottom and sides. Increase heat to medium and let skillet heat for 1 minute. Test heat of skillet by placing 1 teaspoon batter in center and cooking for 20 seconds. If mini crepe is golden brown on bottom, skillet is properly heated; if it is too light or too dark, adjust heat accordingly and retest.

3 Lift skillet off heat and pour ⅓ cup batter into far side of skillet; swirl gently in clockwise direction until batter evenly covers bottom of skillet. Return skillet to heat and cook crepe, without moving it, until surface is dry and crepe starts to brown at edges, loosening crepe from sides of skillet with rubber spatula, about 35 seconds. Gently slide spatula underneath edge of crepe, grasp edge with your fingertips, and flip crepe. Cook until second side is lightly spotted, about 20 seconds. Transfer crepe to wire rack. Return skillet to heat for 10 seconds before repeating with remaining batter. As crepes are done, stack on rack. (Crepes can be wrapped tightly in plastic wrap and refrigerated for up to 3 days or stacked between sheets of parchment paper and frozen for up to 1 month. Allow frozen crepes to thaw completely in refrigerator before using.)

4 **For the filling** Combine vinegar and sugar in small bowl and microwave until sugar is dissolved and vinegar is steaming, about 30 seconds. Add shallots and stir to combine. Cover and let cool completely, about 30 minutes. Drain shallots and discard liquid.

5 Combine crème fraîche, capers, chives, lemon zest and juice, salt, and pepper in medium bowl.

6 Place crepes on large plate and invert second plate over crepes. Microwave until crepes are warm, 30 to 45 seconds (45 to 60 seconds if crepes have cooled completely). Working with 1 crepe at a time, spread 2 tablespoons crème fraîche mixture across bottom half of crepe, followed by 1 ounce smoked salmon and one-quarter of shallots. Fold crepes in half and then into quarters. Transfer to plate and serve.

Galettes Complètes

SERVES 4 (Makes 4 crepes) | **TOTAL TIME** 1¼ hours

Crepes

- ½ teaspoon vegetable oil
- ¾ cup (3⅜ ounces) buckwheat flour
- ¼ cup (1¼ ounces) all-purpose flour
- ½ teaspoon table salt
- 2 cups milk
- 3 large eggs
- 4 tablespoons salted butter, melted and cooled

Filling

- 4 thin slices deli ham (2 ounces)
- 5½ ounces Gruyère cheese, shredded (1⅓ cups)
- 4 large eggs
- 1 tablespoon salted butter, melted
- 4 teaspoons chopped fresh chives

Why This Recipe Works On the rocky coast of Brittany, France, crepes are made from earthy, mineral-y buckwheat flour. This classic preparation has them partially folded around nutty Gruyère cheese and salty-sweet ham, with an egg cracked into the well. They're cooked until the eggs are set and then sprinkled with fresh herbs, making for a lovely presentation. Since buckwheat is naturally gluten-free, you can't use just buckwheat flour, or you'll end up with brittle crepes that tear. Blending in some all-purpose flour gives them more resilience. And though these are traditionally made one by one in a skillet, arranging four on a baking sheet and sliding them into the oven lets you serve more people at once. The crepes will give off steam as they cook, but if at any point the skillet begins to smoke, remove it from the burner and turn down the heat. Stacking the crepes on a wire rack lets excess steam escape so that they won't stick together. The batter yields 10 crepes, but only four are needed. You can double the filling amount to make eight filled crepes; prep the second batch on a second baking sheet while the first batch is in the oven. Extra crepes also freeze well, or you can stash them in the fridge for a couple days to use in the other recipes that use crepes in this chapter (or simply wrap them around some scrambled eggs). Salted butter is traditional, but you can substitute unsalted. If using unsalted butter, add an additional ¼ teaspoon salt to the batter. For more information on making crepes, see page 223.

1 **For the crepes** Adjust oven rack to middle position and heat oven to 450 degrees. Heat oil in 12-inch nonstick skillet over low heat for at least 5 minutes. While skillet heats, whisk buckwheat flour, all-purpose flour, and salt together in medium bowl. In second bowl, whisk together milk and eggs. Add half of milk mixture to flour mixture and whisk until smooth. Add melted butter and whisk until incorporated. Whisk in remaining milk mixture until smooth.

2 Using paper towel, wipe out skillet, leaving thin film of oil on bottom and sides. Increase heat to medium and let skillet heat for 1 minute. Test heat of skillet by placing 1 teaspoon batter in center and cooking for 20 seconds. If mini crepe is golden brown on bottom, skillet is properly heated; if it is too light or too dark, adjust heat accordingly and retest.

3 Lift skillet off heat and pour ⅓ cup batter into far side of skillet; swirl gently in clockwise direction until batter evenly covers bottom of skillet. Return skillet to heat and cook crepe, without moving it, until surface is dry and crepe starts to brown at edges, loosening crepe from sides of skillet with rubber spatula, about 35 seconds. Gently slide spatula underneath edge of crepe, grasp edge with your fingertips, and flip crepe. Cook until second side is lightly spotted, about 20 seconds. Transfer crepe to wire rack. Return skillet to heat for 10 seconds before repeating with remaining batter. As crepes are done, stack on rack. (Crepes can be wrapped tightly in plastic wrap and refrigerated for up to three days or stacked between sheets of parchment paper and frozen for up to one month. Allow frozen crepes to thaw completely in refrigerator before using.)

4 **For the filling** Line rimmed baking sheet with parchment paper and spray with vegetable oil spray. Arrange 4 crepes spotty side down on prepared sheet (they will hang over edge). (Reserve remaining crepes for another use.) Working with 1 crepe at a time, place 1 slice of ham in center of crepe, followed by ⅓ cup Gruyère, covering ham evenly. Make small well in center of cheese. Crack 1 egg into well. Fold in 4 sides, pressing to adhere.

5 Brush crepe edges with melted butter and transfer sheet to oven. Bake until egg whites are uniformly set and yolks have filmed over but are still runny, 8 to 10 minutes. Using thin metal spatula, transfer each crepe to plate and sprinkle with 1 teaspoon chives. Serve immediately.

Bánh Xèo

SERVES 4 (Makes 3 crepes) | **TOTAL TIME** 1¼ hours

Nước Chấm

3 tablespoons sugar, divided

1 small Thai chile, stemmed and minced

1 garlic clove, minced

⅔ cup hot water

5 tablespoons fish sauce

¼ cup lime juice (2 limes)

Crepes

1 head Boston lettuce (8 ounces), leaves separated and left whole

1 cup fresh Thai basil leaves

1 cup fresh cilantro leaves and thin stems

1 cup hot water (120 to 130 degrees)

½ cup (3 ounces) white rice flour

3 tablespoons cornstarch

½ teaspoon ground turmeric

½ teaspoon table salt, divided

3 tablespoons vegetable oil, divided

4 ounces boneless country-style pork ribs, trimmed and cut into 2-inch-long matchsticks

1 small red onion, halved and sliced thin

6 ounces medium-large shrimp (31 to 40 per pound), peeled, deveined, halved lengthwise, and halved crosswise

⅓ cup canned coconut milk

6 ounces (3 cups) bean sprouts, divided

Why This Recipe Works These Vietnamese rice flour pancakes are a spectacular jumble of flavors, textures, and temperatures, the centerpiece of which is a warm, crisp-tender, turmeric-tinted crepe punctuated with pieces of shrimp and pork. To enjoy them, you tuck pieces of the sunny-yellow pancake inside a cool lettuce leaf along with aromatic herbs and then dip the bundle into nước chấm, a tart-spicy-sweet sauce. To make the crepes, stir-fry pork and shrimp with sliced onions, push the mixture to one side, and pour in the rice flour and coconut milk batter. When it hits the hot skillet, it sizzles audibly, hence the onomatopoeic name: "Bánh" is a term for a variety of foods made primarily of starch, and "xèo" ("sss-ay-o") means "sizzling" and mimics the hiss of the batter hitting the pan. Bean sprouts are then placed onto the filled side of the crepe, which cooks until it achieves crispness on the bottom and a tender texture on top. Using hot water in the batter helps minimize the gritty texture that rice flour can have, and the cornstarch absorbs extra moisture so that the crepes crisp properly. To preserve the texture of the first few crepes while making the last one, hold them on a rack in a 275-degree oven. Stir the coconut milk thoroughly to combine before measuring. We prefer regular coconut milk here, but you can substitute light coconut milk. Buy ordinary white rice flour; glutinous rice flour will make the pancakes too sticky and soft. As is traditional, we like to serve these with Đồ Chua.

1 **For the nước chấm** Using mortar and pestle (or using flat side of chef's knife on cutting board), mash 1 tablespoon sugar, Thai chile, and garlic to fine paste. Transfer to medium bowl and add hot water and remaining 2 tablespoons sugar. Stir until sugar is dissolved. Stir in fish sauce and lime juice. Divide sauce among 4 individual small serving bowls.

2 **For the crepes** Adjust oven rack to middle position and heat oven to 275 degrees. Set wire rack in rimmed baking sheet, spray rack with vegetable oil spray, and set aside. Arrange lettuce, basil, and cilantro on serving platter. Whisk hot water, rice flour, cornstarch, turmeric, and ¼ teaspoon salt in bowl until smooth.

3 Heat 1 teaspoon oil in 12-inch nonstick skillet over medium-high heat until shimmering. Add pork and onion and cook, stirring occasionally, until pork is no longer pink and onion is softened, 5 to 7 minutes. Add shrimp and remaining ¼ teaspoon salt and continue to cook, stirring occasionally, until shrimp just begin to turn pink, about 2 minutes. Transfer mixture to second bowl. Wipe skillet clean with paper towels. Add coconut milk and 2 teaspoons oil to crepe batter and stir to combine.

4 Heat 2 teaspoons oil in now-empty skillet over medium-high heat until just smoking. Add one-third of pork mixture and heat through until sizzling, about 30 seconds. Spread pork mixture over half of skillet. Pour ½ cup batter evenly over entire skillet. (Batter poured over filling will drain to skillet surface. If needed, tilt skillet gently to fill gaps.) Spread 1 cup bean sprouts over filling. Cook until crepe loosens completely from bottom of skillet with gentle shake, 4 to 5 minutes. Reduce heat to medium-low and continue to cook, shaking skillet occasionally, until edges of crepe are lacy and crisp and underside is golden brown, 2 to 4 minutes.

5 Gently fold unfilled side of crepe over sprouts. Slide crepe onto prepared wire rack and transfer to oven to keep warm. Repeat 2 more times with remaining oil, pork mixture, batter, and bean sprouts. When final crepe is cooked, use 2 spatulas to transfer all 3 crepes to cutting board and cut each crosswise into 1¼-inch-wide strips.

6 To serve, place crepes and greens in center of table, and give each diner 1 bowl of sauce. To eat, wrap individual strip of crepe and several leaves of basil and cilantro in lettuce leaf and dip into sauce.

Đồ Chua

Serves 6

This pungent pickle is also served with Vietnamese bánh mì sandwiches and summer rolls. Cover it tightly before storing it in the refrigerator. The aroma will dissipate soon after the pickle is uncovered.

- 12 **ounces daikon radish, peeled and shredded (about 3 cups)**
- 3 **carrots, peeled and shredded (about 2 cups)**
- 1 **teaspoon plus ⅓ cup sugar, divided**
- 1¼ **teaspoons table salt, divided**
- ¾ **cup distilled white vinegar**
- ½ **cup water**

1 Combine daikon, carrots, 1 teaspoon sugar, and ½ teaspoon salt in large bowl and let sit until vegetables are partially wilted and reduced in volume by half, about 30 minutes. Meanwhile, in second bowl, whisk vinegar, water, remaining ⅓ cup sugar, and remaining ¾ teaspoon salt until sugar and salt are dissolved.

2 Transfer daikon mixture to colander and drain, pressing on solids to remove excess moisture. Add daikon mixture to vinegar mixture and toss to combine. Let sit for 30 minutes at room temperature, then serve. (Pickle can be refrigerated for up to 1 week.)

MAKING BÁNH XÈO

1 Heat oiled skillet over medium-high heat and spread one-third of pork mixture over half of skillet.

2 Pour ½ cup batter evenly over entire skillet. Spread 1 cup bean sprouts over filling.

3 Cook until crepe loosens from skillet bottom with gentle shake, 4 to 5 minutes.

4 Reduce heat to medium-low; cook until underside is brown, 2 to 4 minutes. Fold crepe in half.

Gougères with Aged Gouda and Smoked Paprika

SERVES 6 to 8 (Makes 24 gougères) | **TOTAL TIME** 1¾ hours, plus 25 minutes resting and cooling

- 2 large eggs plus 1 large white
- ¼ teaspoon table salt
- ½ cup water
- 2 tablespoons unsalted butter, cut into 4 pieces
- ½ teaspoon smoked paprika
- ½ cup (2½ ounces) all-purpose flour
- 4 ounces aged gouda cheese, shredded (1 cup)

Why This Recipe Works You might be more familiar with the sweet version of these impressively crisp and airy little pastries: cream puffs. Both begin with the same dough, pate a choux, but gougères take a decisively savory turn with the incorporation of cheese—and this version has plenty of it. Make the pate a choux by cooking water, butter, and flour until a stiff dough forms; using a smearing method to stir it helps develop the gluten. A food processor is a great tool for incorporating the eggs: It's quicker and easier than doing it by hand, and the vigorous beating causes the egg proteins to unwind, leading to a superior dough that produces lighter, puffier gougères. Beating the salt directly into the eggs also helps by changing the electrical charges on the egg proteins, letting them set up into a strong network early in the baking time. This means that the dough won't collapse under the weight of all the delicious cheese that's packed into these puffs. For the best flavor and texture, use a gouda that has been aged for about one year. To prevent overbrowning on these little pastries' bottoms, bake the gougères on the upper rack of the oven, nesting two rimmed baking sheets to create a thin air gap between them. Alternatively, you can loosely roll up an 18 by 12-inch piece of aluminum foil, unroll it, and set it in a single rimmed baking sheet. Then cover the crumply foil with a sheet of parchment paper. In step 4, if you wish, you can pipe the dough using a pastry bag fitted with a ½-inch plain tip.

1 Adjust oven rack to upper-middle position and heat oven to 425 degrees. Line rimmed baking sheet with parchment paper and nest it in second rimmed baking sheet. In 2-cup liquid measuring cup, beat eggs and white and salt until well combined. (You should have about ½ cup egg mixture. Discard any excess.) Set aside.

2 Heat water, butter, and smoked paprika in small saucepan over medium heat. When mixture begins to simmer, reduce heat to low and immediately stir in flour using wooden spoon. Cook, stirring constantly using smearing motion, until mixture is very thick, forms ball, and pulls away from sides of saucepan, about 30 seconds.

3 Immediately transfer mixture to food processor and process with feed tube open for 5 seconds to cool slightly. With processor running, gradually add reserved egg mixture in steady stream, then scrape down sides of bowl and add cheese. Process until paste is very glossy and flecked with coarse cornmeal–size pieces of cheese, 30 to 40 seconds. (If not using immediately, transfer paste to bowl, press sheet of greased parchment directly on surface, and store at room temperature for up to 2 hours.)

4 Scoop 1 level tablespoon of dough. Using second small spoon, scrape dough onto prepared sheet into 1½-inch-wide, 1-inch-tall mound. Repeat with remaining dough, spacing mounds 1 to 1¼ inches apart. (You should have 24 mounds.) Using back of spoon lightly coated with vegetable oil spray, smooth away any creases and large peaks on each mound.

5 Bake until gougères are puffed and upper two-thirds of each are light golden brown (bottom third will still be pale), 14 to 20 minutes. Turn off oven; leave gougères in oven until uniformly golden brown, 10 to 15 minutes (do not open oven for at least 8 minutes). Transfer gougères to wire rack and let cool for 15 minutes. Serve warm. (Cooled gougères can be stored in airtight container at room temperature for up to 1 day or frozen in zipper-lock bag for up to 1 month. To serve, crisp gougères in 300-degree oven for about 7 minutes.)

Variation

Gougères with Manchego and Black Pepper
Substitute Manchego for aged gouda and pepper for smoked paprika.

SHAPING GOUGÈRES

1A Scoop level tablespoon of dough and, using second small spoon, scrape onto prepared baking sheet.

1B Alternatively, fill pastry bag fitted with ½-inch plain tip with dough and pipe mounds onto prepared baking sheet.

2 Use back of spoon lightly coated with vegetable oil spray to smooth away any creases and large peaks on each mound of dough.

Blue Cheese and Chive Popovers with Blue Cheese Butter

SERVES 6 (Makes 6 popovers) | **TOTAL TIME** 1¼ hours

Why This Recipe Works Traditional popovers are just flour, milk, egg, and salt—a blank canvas to be slathered with butter or jam (sometimes both). What makes them magical is how they "pop" when they bake. And what makes *these* popovers magical is how they turn out so crisp and browned on the outside, with inner walls that are lush, custardy, and oh-so-cheesy. But it's not magic that's afoot here—it's science. The heat of the oven rapidly gels the surface of the batter so that when the moisture inside turns to steam and expands, that surface stretches without bursting, leaving a growing hollow inside. Eventually the exterior dries out enough that the protein in the eggs and flour forms a shell, halting expansion. Bread flour supplies the extra gluten-forming proteins so that this batter is stretchy enough to accommodate the expanding steam better than batter made with lower-protein all-purpose flour. Though many recipes call for preheating the pan to jump-start the "pop," it's just as effective to warm the batter with heated milk. Since there is cheese in this batter, using low-fat milk and omitting butter controls the fat content to keep the popovers crispy (save the butter for melting on top!). The steady baking temperature of 400 degrees ensures a perfect bake, so you don't have to lower the temperature after the popovers reach maximum height to prevent burning, as many recipes call for. Do not open the oven during the first 30 minutes of baking. This recipe works best in a 6-cup popover pan, but you can substitute a 12-cup muffin tin, distributing the batter evenly among all 12 cups; start checking these smaller popovers after 25 minutes.

Blue Cheese Butter

- 8 tablespoons unsalted butter, softened
- 2 ounces blue cheese, crumbled (½ cup)
- ¼ cup minced fresh chives

Popovers

- 1¼ cups (6¾ ounces) bread flour
- 3 tablespoons minced fresh chives
- 1½ teaspoons dry mustard
- ¾ teaspoon table salt
- Pinch cayenne pepper
- 1½ cups 2 percent low-fat milk, heated to 110 to 120 degrees
- 3 large eggs
- 2 ounces blue cheese, crumbled (½ cup)

1 **For the blue cheese butter** Whip butter with fork until light and fluffy. Mix in blue cheese and chives and season with salt and pepper to taste. Cover with plastic wrap and let rest to blend flavors, about 10 minutes, or roll into log and refrigerate. (Leftover butter can be refrigerated in an airtight container for up to 4 days or frozen for up to 2 months.)

2 **For the popovers** Adjust oven rack to middle position and heat oven to 400 degrees. Lightly spray cups of popover pan with vegetable oil spray. Using paper towel, wipe out cups, leaving thin film of oil on bottom and sides.

3 Whisk together flour, chives, dry mustard, salt, and cayenne in 8-cup liquid measuring cup or medium bowl. Add milk and eggs and whisk until mostly smooth (some small lumps are OK). Whisk in blue cheese. Distribute batter evenly among prepared cups in popover pan. Bake until popovers are lofty and deep golden brown all over, 40 to 45 minutes. Serve hot, passing blue cheese butter alongside. (Leftover popovers can be stored in zipper-lock bag at room temperature for up to 2 days; reheat directly on middle rack of 300-degree oven for 5 minutes.)

Dutch Baby with Burrata and Prosciutto

SERVES 4 | **TOTAL TIME** 45 minutes

Dutch Baby

- ¼ cup extra-virgin olive oil, divided
- 1¼ cups (6¼ ounces) all-purpose flour
- ½ teaspoon table salt
- 4 large eggs
- 1 cup skim milk
- 2 tablespoons chopped fresh basil, oregano, thyme, parsley, and/or tarragon, plus extra for sprinkling

Topping

- 4 ounces burrata cheese, room temperature
- ¾ cup baby arugula
- ½ teaspoon extra-virgin olive oil, plus extra for drizzling
- ½ teaspoon balsamic vinegar, plus extra for drizzling
- 1 ounce thinly sliced prosciutto, torn into bite-size pieces

Why This Recipe Works Dutch babies, traditionally made in sweet versions as a homey dessert or brunch dish, have been enjoying a welcome renaissance, and this has led to all kinds of fun with modern savory renditions such as this dramatic and impressive skillet-size pancake. It's a delicious study in contrasts: The edge of this batter cake puffs dramatically in the hot cast-iron skillet to form a tall, crispy rim with a texture similar to that of a popover, while the base remains flat, custardy, and tender, similar to a thick crepe. Dutch babies are much easier to prepare than their pomp and circumstance would suggest. Pour a simple batter of flour, egg, and milk into a skillet and bake, and then add your toppings of choice for serving. Here, a tangle of peppery arugula is overlaid with salty prosciutto and burrata cheese, itself a study in contrasting textures. You can use whole or low-fat milk instead of skim, but the Dutch baby won't turn out as crisp. You can substitute fresh mozzarella for the burrata. For a dramatic presentation, you can also garnish and slice the Dutch baby right in the skillet in step 5.

1 **For the Dutch baby** Adjust oven rack to middle position and heat oven to 450 degrees. Add 2 tablespoons oil to 12-inch cast-iron skillet; place skillet in oven; and heat until oil is shimmering, about 10 minutes.

2 Meanwhile, whisk flour and salt together in large bowl. In separate bowl, whisk eggs until frothy, then whisk in milk, basil, and remaining 2 tablespoons oil until incorporated. Whisk one-third of milk mixture into flour mixture until no lumps remain. Slowly whisk in remaining milk mixture until smooth.

3 Being careful of hot skillet handle, quickly pour batter into skillet and bake until Dutch baby puffs and turns golden brown (edges will be dark brown), about 20 minutes, rotating skillet halfway through baking.

4 **For the topping** While Dutch baby bakes, tear burrata into bite-size pieces over plate, collecting creamy liquid. Toss arugula with oil and vinegar and season with salt and pepper to taste.

5 Using pot holders, remove skillet from oven. Being careful of hot skillet handle, transfer Dutch baby to cutting board using spatula. Top Dutch baby with arugula mixture, followed by prosciutto and burrata and any accumulated liquid. Sprinkle with extra basil, drizzle with extra oil and vinegar, and season with pepper to taste. Slice into wedges and serve immediately.

Spinach and Gruyère Strata

SERVES 4 to 6 | **TOTAL TIME** 2¼ hours, plus 1 hour chilling

8–10 (½-inch-thick) slices French or Italian bread

4 tablespoons unsalted butter, softened, divided

4 shallots, minced

Pinch plus 1 teaspoon table salt, divided

10 ounces frozen chopped spinach, thawed and squeezed dry

½ cup dry white wine

6 ounces Gruyère cheese, shredded (1½ cups), divided

6 large eggs

1¾ cups half-and-half

Pinch pepper

Why This Recipe Works What's quicker than quiche, sturdier than soufflé, and combines the best qualities of both? It's strata, a layered casserole that's simple to prepare and inherently designed to be prepped ahead and served later. Strata comprises bread and cheese bathed in a custardy "batter" of eggs and milk or cream. Flavorful fillings that provide both substance and character are usually added, and the result is a puffed, golden-brown, hearty meal. Earthy spinach and nutty Gruyère cheese star here, but the bread is far from a supporting player; it's the foundation. Thick slices of French or Italian bread, dried and crisped in the oven, offer great texture, and buttering the crisped slices adds richness. Quickly sautéing the vegetables before layering them removes excess moisture and prevents the casserole from becoming waterlogged. Weighting down the assembled strata improves its texture; 1 hour is the minimum, but you can also do it overnight and bake the strata the following morning. A gallon-size zipper-lock bag filled with dried beans or rice is perfect for this purpose. This recipe can be doubled and assembled in a greased 13 by 9-inch baking dish; increase the baking time to 1 hour and 20 minutes. You can substitute any semisoft melting cheese, such as Havarti, sharp cheddar, or Colby, for the Gruyère. Use a medium-dry fruity white wine such as Sauvignon Blanc.

1 Adjust oven rack to middle position and heat oven to 225 degrees. Arrange bread in single layer on rimmed baking sheet and bake until dry and crisp, about 40 minutes, flipping slices halfway through baking. Let bread cool slightly, then spread 2 tablespoons butter evenly over 1 side of bread slices.

2 Meanwhile, melt remaining 2 tablespoons butter in 10-inch nonstick skillet over medium heat. Add shallots and pinch salt and cook until softened, about 3 minutes. Stir in spinach and cook until warmed through, about 2 minutes; transfer to bowl. Add wine to now-empty skillet and simmer over medium-high heat until reduced to ¼ cup, about 3 minutes; set aside and let cool.

3 Grease 8-inch square baking dish. Arrange half of bread slices, buttered side up, in single layer in dish. Sprinkle half of spinach mixture and ½ cup Gruyère over top. Repeat with remaining bread, remaining spinach mixture, and ½ cup Gruyère to make second layer.

4 Whisk eggs, half-and-half, pepper, reduced wine, and remaining 1 teaspoon salt together in bowl, then pour evenly over top of bread and Gruyère in dish. Cover dish tightly with plastic wrap, pressing it flush to surface. Weight strata down and refrigerate for at least 1 hour. (Strata can be refrigerated for up to 24 hours.)

5 Adjust oven rack to middle position and heat oven to 325 degrees. Meanwhile, let strata sit at room temperature for 20 minutes. Unwrap strata and top with remaining ½ cup cheese. Bake until edges and center are puffed and edges have pulled away slightly from sides of dish, 50 to 55 minutes. Let cool for 5 minutes before serving.

Pimento Cheese Featherbed Eggs

SERVES 10 to 12 | **TOTAL TIME** 2 hours, plus 6½ hours chilling and cooling

Why This Recipe Works Featherbed eggs, popularized by the late great cookbook author Marion Cunningham, is an enchanting old-fashioned name sometimes given to strata. Classic recipes usually use white sandwich bread or French bread, relying on the mix-ins to change the flavor, but here you'll make a quick homemade cornbread for a completely new flavor and texture foundation. As with other strata recipes, the cornbread still needs to be dried in some way before it's added to the mixture so that the finished casserole doesn't turn out soggy and heavy. To make the cornbread and dry it out at the same time, you'll pour the seasoned batter into a rimmed baking sheet in a ¼-inch layer rather than into the usual 8-inch square pan. Baking this thin layer for 17 minutes causes it to overbake slightly, which helps it dry out. It cools completely (and continues to dry out) in just 10 minutes and is easy to tear into pieces. Mustard and Worcestershire sauce zest up the custard, and using extra-sharp cheddar cheese and pimentos lends this strata the beloved flavors of classic Southern pimento cheese. Weighting down the assembled strata improves its texture; 6 hours is the minimum for this casserole, but you can also do it overnight and bake the strata the following morning. A gallon-size zipper-lock bag filled with dried beans or rice makes an excellent weight.

1 **For the cornbread** Adjust oven rack to middle position and heat oven to 400 degrees. Line rimmed baking sheet with parchment paper and spray with vegetable oil spray.

2 Whisk cornmeal, flour, baking powder, baking soda, pepper, salt, and cayenne together in bowl. Whisk milk and eggs together in separate bowl. Whisk milk mixture into cornmeal mixture until just combined. Pour batter into prepared sheet and spread to cover entire sheet. Bake until lightly browned and edges of cornbread pull away from sides of sheet, 17 to 19 minutes. Let cornbread cool in sheet on wire rack for 10 minutes.

3 **For the custard** Spray 13 by 9-inch baking dish with vegetable oil spray. Tear cornbread into 1-inch pieces and place in prepared dish. Add 1½ cups cheddar, pimentos, and shallots to cornbread and toss to combine. Whisk milk, eggs, mustard, Worcestershire, and salt in bowl; pour custard over cornbread mixture. Top casserole with remaining 1 cup cheddar. Cover with plastic wrap, weight down, and refrigerate for at least 6 hours. (Strata can be refrigerated for up to 24 hours.)

4 Adjust oven rack to middle position and heat oven to 325 degrees. Unwrap strata and bake until lightly browned and center registers 170 degrees, 50 minutes to 1 hour. Let cool for 15 minutes. Serve.

Cornbread

- 1 cup (5 ounces) cornmeal
- 1 cup (5 ounces) all-purpose flour
- 2 teaspoons baking powder
- ½ teaspoon baking soda
- 1½ teaspoons pepper
- ½ teaspoon table salt
- ¼ teaspoon cayenne pepper
- 1⅓ cups whole milk
- 2 large eggs, lightly beaten

Custard

- 10 ounces extra-sharp cheddar cheese, shredded (2½ cups), divided
- ½ cup plus 2 tablespoons jarred chopped pimentos
- 2 shallots, minced
- 4½ cups whole milk
- 6 large eggs, lightly beaten
- 1 tablespoon Dijon mustard
- 1 tablespoon Worcestershire sauce
- 2 teaspoons table salt

Butternut Squash and Spinach Bread Pudding

SERVES 6 to 8 | **TOTAL TIME** 2¾ hours, plus 40 minutes soaking and cooling

1½ pounds butternut squash, peeled, seeded, and cut into ¾-inch pieces (4 cups)

1 tablespoon extra-virgin olive oil

1½ teaspoons table salt, divided

1 teaspoon pepper, divided

1 (18- to 20-inch) French baguette, torn or cut into 1-inch pieces (10 cups)

3 cups heavy cream

2 cups whole milk

8 large egg yolks

2 ounces Parmesan cheese, grated (1 cup), divided

2 teaspoons minced fresh thyme

2 garlic cloves, minced

10 ounces frozen spinach, thawed, squeezed dry, and chopped

Why this Recipe Works Bread pudding is another great example of a dish that's often thought of as a dessert but also has delicious savory versions worth exploring. A savory bread pudding is similar to a strata, but often bread puddings have a higher proportion of milk or cream to eggs in their "batter," making their interiors a little softer and more custardy. This hearty rendition fits that definition; it features roasted butternut squash, earthy spinach, and Parmesan cheese bound with a garlicky custard made using both heavy cream and milk. The sturdy crumb and neutral flavor of a French baguette is the ideal match; while many recipes for bread pudding call for cubing the bread, you'll get a more pleasing texture by tearing the baguette into rustic, ragged pieces. Toasting the torn pieces to a deep golden brown enriches their flavor and gives the bread a crispness that prevents the finished dish from turning soggy. To prevent the custard from curdling in the oven, it includes just egg yolks rather than the traditional whole eggs; the fat in the yolks helps to stabilize and emulsify the custard. We prefer the flavor and texture of a high-quality French baguette here, but a conventional supermarket baguette also works.

1 Adjust oven racks to upper-middle and lower-middle positions and heat oven to 450 degrees. Toss squash with oil, ½ teaspoon salt, and ¼ teaspoon pepper in bowl, then spread out onto aluminum foil–lined rimmed baking sheet. Arrange bread in single layer on second rimmed baking sheet.

2 Place squash on lower-middle rack and bread on upper-middle rack. Bake bread until crisp and browned, about 12 minutes, stirring halfway through baking. Remove bread from oven and stir squash; continue to cook squash until tender, 10 to 15 minutes.

3 Whisk cream, milk, yolks, ½ cup Parmesan, thyme, garlic, remaining 1 teaspoon salt, and remaining ¾ teaspoon pepper together in large bowl. Stir in toasted bread and let sit, stirring occasionally, until bread softens and is beginning to absorb custard, 30 to 45 minutes. When bread is softened, stir in roasted squash and spinach.

4 Spray 13 by 9-inch baking dish with vegetable oil spray. Adjust oven rack to middle position and heat oven to 350 degrees. Pour half of bread mixture into prepared dish and sprinkle with ¼ cup Parmesan. Top with remaining bread mixture and remaining ¼ cup Parmesan. Bake until custard is just set, about 1 hour, rotating dish halfway through baking. Let cool for 10 minutes before serving.

ROLLS, BREADSTICKS & MORE

Peppery Dinner Rolls with Caramelized Onion and Smoked Paprika

MAKES 12 rolls | **TOTAL TIME** 1½ hours, plus 2½ hours rising and cooling

1 large onion, chopped

¾ cup water, divided

1 tablespoon vegetable oil

1¼ teaspoons table salt, divided

2 teaspoons smoked paprika

3 tablespoons plus 2 cups (11 ounces) bread flour, divided

½ cup whole milk, chilled

1 large egg

1½ teaspoons instant or rapid-rise yeast

2 tablespoons sugar

4 tablespoons unsalted butter, cut into 4 pieces and softened, plus ½ tablespoon melted

2 teaspoons pepper

Vegetable oil spray

Flake sea salt

Why This Recipe Works While classic American dinner rolls are the quintessential side for countless meals, adding jammy caramelized onion, robust smoked paprika, and spicy black pepper makes them anything but ordinary. These rolls are also outstandingly light and fluffy thanks to the use of a tangzhong, a cooked flour and water paste that allows the dough to absorb more water, resulting in a moister crumb. To support the weight of the onion, the dough needs a strong gluten structure, created by adding a resting period and withholding the butter until the gluten is firmly established. The shaping method is also important. Flattening each portion of dough and rolling it up in a spiral organizes the gluten strands into coiled layers, which bake up into feathery sheets. The slight tackiness of the dough aids in flattening and stretching it in step 7, so don't dust your counter with flour.

1 Cook onion, ¼ cup water, oil, and ¼ teaspoon table salt in covered 12-inch nonstick skillet over medium-high heat until water has evaporated and onion starts to sizzle, 6 to 8 minutes.

2 Uncover, reduce heat to medium-low, stir, and redistribute onion into single layer. Cook, without stirring, for 30 seconds. Stir onion, scraping up any fond from skillet, then redistribute onion into single layer. Repeat cooking, stirring, and redistributing until onion is softened, well browned, and slightly sticky, 15 to 20 minutes. Transfer onion to bowl, stir in paprika, and set aside to cool while making dough.

3 Whisk remaining ½ cup water and 3 tablespoons flour in small bowl until no lumps remain. Microwave, whisking every 20 seconds, until mixture thickens to stiff, smooth, pudding-like consistency and forms mound when dropped from end of whisk into bowl, 40 to 80 seconds.

4 In bowl of stand mixer, whisk flour paste and milk until smooth. Add egg and whisk until incorporated. Add remaining 2 cups flour and yeast. Fit mixer with dough hook and mix on low speed until all flour is moistened, 1 to 2 minutes. Let stand for 15 minutes.

5 Add sugar and remaining 1 teaspoon table salt and mix on medium-low speed for 5 minutes. With mixer running, add 4 tablespoons softened butter, 1 piece at a time. Knead for 4 minutes, scraping down dough hook and sides of bowl occasionally (dough will stick to bottom of bowl). Add cooled onion and pepper and mix on medium-low speed for 1 minute.

6 Transfer dough to very lightly floured counter. Knead briefly to form ball and transfer, seam side down, to lightly greased bowl; lightly coat surface of dough with oil spray and cover with plastic wrap. Let rise until doubled in size, about 1 hour.

7 Grease 9-inch round cake pan. Press down on dough to deflate. Transfer dough to counter (lightly oil counter and hands if dough is very sticky). Pat and stretch dough into 8 by 9-inch rectangle with short side facing you. Cut dough lengthwise into 4 equal strips and cut each strip crosswise into 3 equal pieces. Working with 1 piece of dough at a time, gently stretch and press to form 8 by 2-inch strip. Starting on short side, roll dough to form snug cylinder.

Arrange shaped rolls seam side down in prepared pan, placing 10 rolls around edge of pan, pointing inward, and remaining 2 rolls in center. Cover with plastic and let rise until doubled in size, 45 minutes to 1 hour.

8 Adjust oven rack to lowest position and heat oven to 375 degrees. Bake rolls until deep golden brown, 25 to 30 minutes. Let rolls cool in pan on wire rack for 3 minutes; invert rolls onto rack, then reinvert. Brush tops and sides of rolls with melted butter and sprinkle with sea salt. Let rolls cool for at least 20 minutes before serving.

Potato Dinner Rolls with Cheddar and Mustard

MAKES 12 rolls | **TOTAL TIME** 1½ hours, plus 1 hour resting

1 pound russet potatoes, peeled and cut into 1-inch pieces

2 tablespoons unsalted butter, cut into 4 pieces

2¼ cups (12⅓ ounces) bread flour

3 ounces sharp cheddar cheese, shredded (¾ cup), divided

2 teaspoons instant or rapid-rise yeast

1 tablespoon sugar

1 teaspoon dry mustard

1 teaspoon table salt

1 large egg, plus 1 large egg beaten with 1 teaspoon water

Why This Recipe Works When incorporated correctly in a bread recipe, hearty mashed potatoes actually give the crumb of the bread a wonderfully light texture. That's because the particular starches found in potatoes dilute gluten-forming proteins, weakening the dough's structural network and making it softer, moister, and more tender. As a bonus, the potassium naturally found in potatoes (and which infuses their cooking water) helps feed the yeast for a higher, quicker rise. We use cooked mashed russets and bread flour to create a dough with a stable structure that supports the greatest amount of spuds, producing airy, perfectly risen rolls. Sharp cheddar cheese and the warm zing of dry mustard complement the potatoes to really jazz up these rolls. Since you'll be using some of the potato cooking water in the dough, don't add salt to it. A pound of russet potatoes should yield a little more than 1 very firmly packed cup (8 ounces) of mash. For the optimum rise, the dough should be warm; if your potatoes or cooking water are too hot to touch, let them cool before proceeding. This dough looks very dry when mixing begins, but resist the urge to add more cooking water; the dough will soften as mixing progresses.

1 Place potatoes in medium saucepan and cover with water by 1 inch. Bring to boil over high heat; reduce heat to medium-low and simmer until potatoes are cooked through, 8 to 10 minutes. Transfer 5 tablespoons potato cooking water to bowl to cool; drain potatoes. Return potatoes to saucepan and place over low heat. Cook, shaking saucepan occasionally, until any surface moisture has evaporated, about 1 minute. Remove from heat. Process potatoes through ricer or food mill or mash well with potato masher. Measure out 1 very firmly packed cup (8 ounces) potatoes and transfer to bowl. Reserve any remaining potatoes for another use. Stir in butter until melted.

2 Combine flour, ½ cup cheddar, yeast, sugar, mustard, and salt in bowl of stand mixer. Add warm potato mixture to flour mixture and mix with your hands until combined (some large lumps are OK). Add whole egg and reserved potato cooking water; mix with dough hook on low speed until dough is soft and slightly sticky, 8 to 10 minutes.

3 Shape dough into ball and place in lightly greased container. Cover tightly with plastic wrap and let rise at room temperature until almost doubled in volume, 30 to 40 minutes.

4 Press down on dough to deflate. Transfer dough to clean counter and stretch into even 12-inch log. Cut log into 12 equal pieces (about 2 ounces each) and cover loosely with greased plastic.

5 Line rimmed baking sheet with parchment paper. Working with 1 piece of dough at a time, form into rough ball by stretching dough around your thumbs and pinching edges together so top is smooth. Place ball seam side down on clean counter and, using your cupped hand, drag in small circles until dough feels taut and round. Cover dough balls with plastic while rolling remaining pieces. (If dough sticks to your hands, lightly dust your fingers with flour.) Arrange rolls on prepared sheet. Cover loosely with greased plastic and let rise at room temperature until almost doubled in size, 30 to 40 minutes. While rolls rise, adjust oven rack to upper-middle position and heat oven to 425 degrees.

6 Brush rolls gently with egg wash. Sprinkle rolls evenly with remaining ¼ cup cheddar. Bake rolls until deep golden brown, 12 to 14 minutes, rotating sheet halfway through baking. Transfer sheet to wire rack and let cool for 5 minutes. Transfer rolls from sheet to wire rack. Serve warm or at room temperature.

Porcini and Truffle Crescent Rolls

MAKES 12 rolls | **TOTAL TIME** 1 hour, plus 2¼ hours rising and cooling

Why This Recipe Works Most recipes for from-scratch crescent rolls require a lot of time and effort to layer softened butter into the dough before shaping and baking, which may explain why those refrigerated canisters have such stubbornly enduring popularity. But here's an easier, faster method that yields homemade crescent rolls just as rich, buttery, and tender as the more labor-intensive traditional kind (and store-bought can't hold a candle to these beauties). It's as easy as stirring melted butter into the liquid ingredients and then combining that mixture with the dry ingredients in a stand mixer. For the over-the-top sophisticated flavor that makes these rolls a must-have anytime you're having people over, add minced dried porcini mushrooms to the dough and brush on fragrant truffle oil twice: once over the circle of dough before cutting and shaping the rolls, and then again over the golden crescents when they emerge from the oven.

1 Whisk flour, mushrooms, thyme, yeast, and salt together in bowl of stand mixer. Whisk whole egg and yolk, half-and-half, melted butter, and sugar in 4-cup liquid measuring cup until sugar has dissolved.

2 Fit mixer with dough hook and slowly add half-and-half mixture to flour mixture, mixing on low speed until cohesive dough starts to form and no dry flour remains, about 2 minutes, scraping down dough hook and sides of bowl as needed. Increase speed to medium-low and knead until dough is smooth and elastic and clears sides of bowl but sticks to bottom, about 8 minutes.

3 Transfer dough to lightly floured counter and knead by hand to form smooth, round ball, about 30 seconds. Transfer dough seam side down to lightly greased large bowl; cover with plastic wrap; and let rise until doubled in size, 1 to 1½ hours.

4 Line rimmed baking sheet with parchment paper. Press down on dough to deflate, then transfer to lightly floured counter. Press and roll dough into 15-inch circle. Brush top of dough with 1 tablespoon truffle oil and cut into 12 wedges. Working with 1 wedge at a time and starting at wide end, gently roll up each dough wedge, ending with pointed tip on bottom. Push ends toward each other to form crescent shape; transfer to prepared sheet with tip of dough underneath each roll, spacing rolls about 2 inches apart.

5 Cover sheet loosely with greased plastic and let rise until nearly doubled in size and dough springs back minimally when poked gently with your knuckle, 1 to 1½ hours. (Unrisen rolls can be refrigerated for at least 8 hours or up to 16 hours; let rolls sit at room temperature for 1 hour before baking.)

6 Adjust oven rack to middle position and heat oven to 350 degrees. Gently brush rolls with egg wash and bake until golden brown, 20 to 25 minutes, rotating sheet halfway through baking. Transfer rolls to wire rack, brush with remaining 2 teaspoons truffle oil, and let cool for 15 minutes. Serve warm.

- 2½ cups (12½ ounces) all-purpose flour
- 1 ounce dried porcini mushrooms, rinsed and minced
- 4 teaspoons minced fresh thyme
- 1 teaspoon instant or rapid-rise yeast
- 1 teaspoon table salt
- 1 large egg plus 1 large yolk, room temperature, plus 1 large egg beaten with 1 teaspoon water
- ½ cup half-and-half, room temperature
- 7 tablespoons unsalted butter, melted and cooled slightly
- ¼ cup (1¾ ounces) sugar
- 5 teaspoons truffle oil, divided

Thai Curry Butter Fan Rolls

MAKES 12 rolls | **TOTAL TIME** 1¼ hours, plus 3 hours rising

¾ cup whole milk, warm

¼ cup (1¾ ounces) sugar

1 large egg plus 1 large yolk, room temperature

1 tablespoon instant or rapid-rise yeast

3½ cups (17½ ounces) all-purpose flour

4 scallions, minced

2 teaspoons table salt

8 tablespoons unsalted butter, cut into 8 pieces and softened, plus 4 tablespoons unsalted butter, melted, divided

¼ cup Thai red curry paste

½ cup chopped fresh cilantro, divided

Why This Recipe Works If ever a roll was aptly named, it's the butter fan roll: layers of yeasty bread brushed with melted butter that fan out while baking to form rolls that are soft and tender, with faintly crisp tips. Stirring Thai red curry paste into the melted butter adds bold flavor and color, and adding scallions to the dough and sprinkling cilantro between the layers elevates these into restaurant-quality rolls that taste as amazing as they look. The basic method goes like this: Mix and knead the dough and let it rise. Then punch down the dough, roll it out, cut it into strips, butter and stack the strips, cut the strips into roll-size portions, and nestle them into muffin tins. Let the dough rise again, and then bake the rolls on the upper-middle rack (which fosters the crisp-but-not-crunchy edges). This process creates the traditional layers that are both impressive-looking and fun to pull apart when eating.

1 In bowl of stand mixer, whisk milk, sugar, egg and yolk, and yeast until sugar has dissolved, then let sit until foamy, about 5 minutes. Add flour, scallions, and salt. Fit mixer with dough hook and knead on medium-low speed until dough is shaggy, about 2 minutes.

2 With mixer running, add softened butter, 1 piece at a time. Knead until dough is smooth, about 5 minutes, scraping down dough hook and sides of bowl occasionally. Transfer dough to lightly floured counter and knead by hand to form smooth, round ball, about 30 seconds. Transfer dough seam side down to lightly greased large bowl; cover with plastic wrap; and let rise until doubled in size, 1½ to 2 hours.

3 Grease 12-cup muffin tin. Press down on dough to deflate. Transfer dough to lightly floured counter, divide in half, and cover loosely with greased plastic. Press and roll 1 piece of dough (keep remaining piece covered) into 15 by 12-inch rectangle, with long side parallel to edge of counter.

4 Using pizza wheel or sharp knife, cut dough vertically into 6 (2½-inch by 12-inch) strips. Combine 3 tablespoons melted butter and curry paste in small bowl. Brush tops of 5 strips evenly with half of butter–curry paste mixture, leaving 1 strip unbrushed. Sprinkle ¼ cup cilantro over brushed dough strips. Stack strips squarely on top of each other, brushed side to unbrushed side, finishing with unbrushed strip on top.

5 Using sharp knife, cut stacked dough strips crosswise into 6 equal stacks. Place stacks, cut side up, in muffin cups. Repeat with remaining dough, remaining butter–curry paste mixture, and remaining ¼ cup cilantro. Cover muffin tin loosely with greased plastic and let dough rise until doubled in size, 1½ to 2 hours.

6 Adjust oven rack to upper-middle position and heat oven to 350 degrees. Bake until golden brown, 20 to 25 minutes, rotating muffin tin halfway through baking. Let rolls cool in muffin tin for 5 minutes, brush with remaining 1 tablespoon melted butter, and serve warm.

SHAPING FAN ROLLS

1 Roll half of dough into 15 by 12-inch rectangle, with long side parallel to edge of counter. Using pizza wheel or sharp knife, cut dough vertically into 6 (2½ by 12-inch) strips.

2 Brush tops of 5 strips evenly with half of butter–curry paste mixture, leaving 1 strip unbrushed. Sprinkle ¼ cup cilantro over brushed strips. Stack strips on top of each other, brushed side to unbrushed side, finishing with unbrushed strip on top.

3 Cut stacked dough strips crosswise into 6 equal stacks. Place stacks, cut side up, in each of 6 muffin cups. Repeat with remaining dough, remaining butter–curry paste mixture, and remaining cilantro. Cover and let rise as directed.

Pão de Queijo

MAKES 8 rolls | **TOTAL TIME** 1¼ hours, plus 2 hours resting

Why This Recipe Works Crackly and crunchy on the outside, bready just under the crust, and gooey in the center, these little baked cheese buns are a favorite breakfast food and snack in Brazil. (They would also be great dunked in tomato sauce, stuffed with ham for breakfast, or split open for a quick sandwich.) They happen to be naturally gluten-free, because they are made with tapioca starch rather than wheat flour. Tapioca starch (also called tapioca flour) has several unique qualities that make it a great substitute for wheat flour. For example, it's low in amylose—one of the types of polysaccharides that make up starch—and therefore forms a high-viscosity paste that can trap air for light baked goods. The dough is similar to a classic French pate a choux (this is what is used for gougères and profiteroles) and relies primarily on steam rather than chemical leavening agents to create rise. This version has a little less moisture in the dough than is typical, which ensures that there is no gumminess in the finished rolls and that the pão de queijo have just the right balance of crackle and soft cheesiness.

3 cups (11¾ ounces) tapioca starch

2 teaspoons kosher salt

¼ teaspoon baking powder

⅔ cup plus 2 tablespoons whole milk

½ cup vegetable oil

1½ tablespoons unsalted butter

2 large eggs, plus 1 large egg beaten with 1 teaspoon water

3½ ounces Parmesan cheese, finely grated (1¾ cups)

3½ ounces Pecorino Romano cheese, finely grated (1¾ cups)

1 Using stand mixer fitted with paddle, mix tapioca starch, salt, and baking powder on low speed until combined, about 30 seconds.

2 Combine milk, oil, and butter in medium saucepan and bring to boil over high heat. With mixer running on low speed, working quickly, pour milk mixture over tapioca mixture and continue to mix on low speed until all ingredients are incorporated, about 3 minutes.

3 Add 2 whole eggs and mix on low speed until dough comes together; turns shiny and sticky; and clings to sides of bowl, about 8 minutes, scraping down paddle and bowl halfway through mixing.

4 Add Parmesan and Pecorino and mix on low speed until cheeses are incorporated, 30 to 60 seconds. Mix with rubber spatula to ensure mixture is fully incorporated. Remove bowl from stand mixer and press plastic wrap directly onto surface of dough. Refrigerate for at least 2 hours. (Dough can be refrigerated for up to 24 hours.)

5 Adjust oven rack to middle position and heat oven to 450 degrees. Stack 2 baking sheets and line top sheet with parchment paper. Divide dough into 8 balls (about 3½ ounces each). To form rolls, lightly dampen your hands with water and roll balls between your palms until smooth. Evenly space rolls on prepared sheet.

6 Brush egg wash over tops of rolls. Place rolls in oven and immediately reduce oven temperature to 375 degrees. Bake for 40 minutes, until rolls are deep golden brown and outer crusts are dry and crunchy, rotating sheet halfway through baking. Transfer rolls to serving platter and let cool for 5 minutes. Serve.

Garlic Knots

MAKES 12 knots | **TOTAL TIME** 1 hour, plus 2¼ hours rising, resting, and cooling

1 teaspoon plus ¾ cup water, room temperature, divided

6 tablespoons unsalted butter, divided

9 garlic cloves, minced (3 tablespoons)

2 cups (10 ounces) all-purpose flour

1½ teaspoons instant or rapid-rise yeast

1 teaspoon table salt

Coarse sea salt

Why This Recipe Works The garlic knots popular at many pizzerias are usually made from leftover pizza dough. This recipe brings these buttery, supremely garlicky bread nuggets home without any help from a pizza delivery driver. For garlic knots that are fluffier and more tender than pizza crust but still chewier than dinner rolls, the dough is made with all-purpose flour rather than the typical bread flour; kneading the dough for a solid 8 minutes provides the right elasticity to let you roll portions into ropes and twist them into their signature knot shapes. Though pizza joints sometimes use a lot of garlic powder to flavor their knots, that ends up tasting artificial. Raw garlic, on the other hand, is a little too pungent. Instead, you'll gently cook minced garlic—nine cloves of it!—in butter, then stir some of the butter and the reserved toasty garlic solids into the dough. Brushing the knots with the remaining garlic butter during baking and again just after taking them out of the oven guarantees that all your garlic cravings will be thoroughly satisfied.

1 Cook 1 teaspoon water, 1 tablespoon butter, and garlic in 8-inch skillet over low heat, stirring occasionally, until garlic is straw-colored, 8 to 10 minutes. Stir in remaining butter until melted. Strain into bowl; reserve garlic solids.

2 Whisk flour, yeast, and table salt together in bowl of stand mixer. Whisk remaining ¾ cup water, 1 tablespoon garlic butter, and garlic solids together in 4-cup liquid measuring cup. Using dough hook on low speed, slowly add water mixture to flour mixture and mix until cohesive dough starts to form and no dry flour remains, about 2 minutes, scraping down bowl as needed. Increase speed to medium-low and knead until dough is smooth and elastic and clears sides of bowl but sticks to bottom, about 8 minutes.

3 Transfer dough to lightly floured counter and knead by hand to form smooth, round ball, about 30 seconds. Place dough seam side down in lightly greased large bowl or container; cover tightly with plastic wrap; and let rise until doubled in size, 1 to 1½ hours.

4 Line rimmed baking sheet with parchment paper. Press down on dough to deflate. Transfer dough to clean counter. Press and stretch dough into 12 by 6-inch rectangle, with long side parallel to edge of counter. Cut dough vertically into 12 (6 by 1-inch) strips; cover loosely with greased plastic.

5 Working with 1 strip at a time, stretch and roll into 14-inch rope. Cover shaped ropes with plastic while stretching and rolling remaining strips. Shape 1 rope into U with 2-inch-wide bottom curve. Tie ends into single overhand knot, with 1½-inch open loop at bottom. Wrap 1 tail over loop and press through opening from top. Wrap other tail under loop and through opening from bottom. Pinch ends together to seal. Repeat with remaining ropes.

6 Arrange knots pinched side down on prepared sheet, spaced about 1 inch apart. Cover loosely with greased plastic and let rise until nearly doubled in size and dough springs back minimally when poked gently with your knuckle, 1 to 1½ hours. (Garlic knots can be refrigerated for at least 8 hours or up to 16 hours; let garlic knots sit at room temperature for 1 hour before baking.)

7 Adjust oven rack to middle position and heat oven to 500 degrees. Bake knots until set, about 5 minutes. Brush with 2 tablespoons garlic butter; rotate sheet; and bake until knots are golden brown, about 5 minutes.

8 Transfer knots to wire rack. Brush with remaining garlic butter, sprinkle with sea salt, and let cool for 15 minutes. Serve warm. (Knots can be stored in a zipper-lock bag at room temperature for up to 3 days. Wrapped in aluminum foil before being placed in the bag, the knots can be frozen for up to 1 month. To reheat, wrap the knots [thawed if frozen] in foil, place them on a baking sheet, and bake in a 350-degree oven for 10 minutes.)

SHAPING GARLIC KNOTS

1 Cut dough rectangle vertically into 12 (6 by 1-inch) strips. Stretch and roll strips into 14-inch ropes.

2 Shape 1 rope into U with 2-inch-wide bottom curve.

3 Tie ends into single overhand knot, with 1½-inch open loop at bottom.

4 Wrap 1 tail over loop and press through opening from top. Wrap other tail under loop and through opening from bottom. Pinch ends together to seal. Repeat with remaining ropes.

Parmesan Breadsticks

MAKES 18 breadsticks | **TOTAL TIME** 50 minutes, plus 2¼ hours rising, resting, and cooling

4 cups (20 ounces)
all-purpose flour

1 tablespoon instant or
rapid-rise yeast

1 tablespoon table salt

2 teaspoons onion powder

1½ cups water, room temperature

¼ cup extra-virgin olive oil

3 ounces Parmesan cheese,
grated (1½ cups), divided

1 large egg lightly beaten with
2 tablespoons extra-virgin
olive oil and pinch salt

Why This Recipe Works The best part about going to an Italian-style chain restaurant might be those satisfyingly chewy yet soft-crumbed Parmesan breadsticks that seem to keep on coming. This recipe pays homage to these iconic golden wands of bread. To ensure that the namesake flavor of the breadsticks really comes through, you'll mix Parmesan right into the dough as well as sprinkle some on top before baking. Adding a small amount of onion powder to the dough enhances the nutty taste of the cheese and further boosts the savory appeal. To achieve an easy-to-shape dough that bakes up with the perfect soft crumb, the dough is made with all-purpose flour and a generous amount of olive oil. The oil acts as a tenderizer, coating the gluten strands and preventing them from sticking to one another and forming a strong gluten network. Setting the oven to 500 degrees and brushing the breadsticks with an egg-and-oil wash ensures that the breadsticks take on a nice golden hue in the short time required to bake them through.

1 Whisk flour, yeast, salt, and onion powder together in bowl of stand mixer. Combine water and oil in 4-cup liquid measuring cup.

2 Using dough hook on low speed, slowly add water mixture to flour mixture and mix until cohesive dough starts to form and no dry flour remains, about 2 minutes, scraping down bowl as needed. Increase speed to medium-low and knead until dough is smooth and elastic and clears sides of bowl but sticks to bottom, about 8 minutes. Reduce speed to low; slowly add 1 cup Parmesan, ¼ cup at a time; and mix until mostly incorporated, about 2 minutes.

3 Transfer dough to lightly floured counter and knead by hand until Parmesan is evenly distributed and dough forms smooth, round ball, about 30 seconds. Place dough seam side down in lightly greased large bowl or container; cover tightly with plastic wrap; and let rise until doubled in size, 1 to 1½ hours. (Dough can be refrigerated for at least 8 hours or up to 16 hours; let sit at room temperature for 1 hour before shaping.)

4 Press down on dough to deflate. Transfer dough to clean counter and divide in half. Stretch each half into 9-inch log, cut each log into 9 equal pieces (about 2 ounces each), and cover loosely with greased plastic.

5 Working with 1 piece of dough at a time, form into rough ball by stretching dough around your thumbs and pinching edges together so top is smooth. Place ball seam side down on clean counter and, using your cupped hand, drag in small circles until dough feels taut and round. Cover dough balls with plastic while rolling remaining dough. Cover dough balls loosely with greased plastic and let rest for 30 minutes.

6 Line 2 rimmed baking sheets with greased parchment paper. Stretch and roll each dough ball into 8-inch-long cylinder. Moving your hands in opposite directions, use back and forth motion to roll ends of cylinder under your palms to form rounded points.

7 Arrange breadsticks on prepared sheets, spaced about 1½ inches apart. Cover loosely with greased plastic and let rise until nearly doubled in size and dough springs back minimally when poked gently with your knuckle, about 30 minutes.

8 Adjust oven racks to upper-middle and lower-middle positions and heat oven to 500 degrees. Gently brush breadsticks with egg wash and sprinkle with remaining ½ cup Parmesan. Bake until golden brown, 12 to 14 minutes, switching and rotating sheets halfway through baking. Transfer breadsticks to wire rack and let cool for 15 minutes. Serve warm. (Breadsticks can be stored in a zipper-lock bag at room temperature for up to 3 days. Wrapped in aluminum foil before being placed in the bag, the breadsticks can be frozen for up to 1 month. To reheat, wrap the breadsticks [thawed if frozen] in foil, place them on a baking sheet, and bake in a 350-degree oven for 10 minutes.)

Variations

Asiago and Black Pepper Breadsticks
Add 1 tablespoon coarsely ground pepper to flour mixture in step 1. Substitute 1 cup shredded Asiago cheese for Parmesan; add ½ cup cheese to dough in step 2 and sprinkle breadsticks with remaining ½ cup cheese before baking.

Pecorino and Mixed Herb Breadsticks
Substitute 1½ cups grated Pecorino Romano for Parmesan. Combine 1 cup Pecorino, 2 tablespoons finely chopped fresh basil, 2 tablespoons minced fresh parsley, and 2 tablespoons minced fresh oregano in bowl before adding to dough in step 2. Sprinkle breadsticks with remaining ½ cup cheese before baking.

Onion-Poppy Bialys

MAKES 12 bialys | **TOTAL TIME** 1¼ hours, plus 2 hours rising, resting, and cooling

Dough

4¾ cups (23¾ ounces) all-purpose flour

2 tablespoons kosher salt

2 teaspoons instant or rapid-rise yeast

2 cups water, room temperature

1 tablespoon sugar

Filling

3 tablespoons extra-virgin olive oil

3 onions, chopped fine

1 teaspoon kosher salt

1 tablespoon poppy seeds

Why This Recipe Works Kissing cousin to the bagel, the bialy was first brought to the United States by Jewish immigrants from Poland who settled in lower Manhattan in the early 20th century. Downtown bakeries producing the golden, chewy, onion-and-poppy-seed-filled rolls eventually became so prevalent that the Lower East Side was referred to as Bialytown. These salty-savory yeasted rolls boast puffed edges that are at once soft and chewy, and they feature a large dimple in the middle to hold the filling. Adding a generous 2 tablespoons of kosher salt to the dough results in the requisite salty flavor. Using all-purpose flour (rather than bread flour) helps keep the bialys from getting too chewy, as does incorporating two resting periods: one after portioning the dough and forming it into balls and another after shaping the balls into disks. Resting the dough gives the gluten a chance to relax and the yeast an opportunity to create bigger air pockets within the dough, ultimately producing more tender bialys.

1 **For the dough** Whisk flour, salt, and yeast together in bowl of stand mixer. Whisk water and sugar in 4-cup liquid measuring cup until sugar has dissolved. Using dough hook on low speed, slowly add water mixture to flour mixture and mix until cohesive dough starts to form and no dry flour remains, about 2 minutes, scraping down bowl as needed. Increase speed to medium-low and knead until dough is smooth and elastic and clears sides of bowl but sticks to bottom, about 8 minutes.

2 Transfer dough to well-floured counter. Using your well-floured hands, knead dough to form smooth, round ball, about 30 seconds. Place dough seam side down in lightly greased large bowl or container; cover tightly with plastic wrap; and let rise until doubled in size, 1 to 1½ hours. (Dough can be refrigerated for at least 8 hours or up to 16 hours; let dough sit at room temperature for 1 hour before shaping.)

3 Press down on dough to deflate. Transfer dough to lightly floured counter and stretch into even 12-inch log. Cut log into 12 equal pieces (about 3 ounces each) and cover loosely with greased plastic.

4 Working with 1 piece of dough at a time, form into rough ball by stretching dough around your thumbs and pinching edges together so top is smooth. Place ball seam side down on clean counter and, using your cupped hand, drag in small circles until dough feels taut and round. Cover dough balls with plastic while rolling remaining dough. Cover dough balls loosely with greased plastic and let rest for 30 minutes.

5 **For the filling** Heat oil in 12-inch skillet over medium heat until shimmering. Add onions and salt and cook until softened and golden brown, about 10 minutes. Off heat, stir in poppy seeds.

6 Line 2 rimmed baking sheets with parchment paper and lightly flour parchment. Press each dough ball into 5-inch round of even thickness and arrange on prepared sheets, spaced about 1 inch apart. Cover loosely with greased plastic and let rise until puffy, 15 to 20 minutes.

7 Adjust oven racks to upper-middle and lower-middle positions and heat oven to 475 degrees. Grease and flour bottom of round 1-cup dry measuring cup (or 3-inch-diameter drinking glass). Press cup firmly into center of each dough round until cup touches sheet to make indentation for filling. (Reflour cup as needed to prevent sticking.)

8 Divide filling evenly among bialys (about 1 heaping tablespoon each) and smooth with back of spoon. Bake until light golden brown, 15 to 20 minutes, switching and rotating sheets halfway through baking. Transfer bialys to wire rack and let cool for 15 minutes. Serve warm or at room temperature. (Bialys can be stored in a zipper-lock bag at room temperature for up to 2 days. Wrapped in aluminum foil before being placed in the bag, bialys can be frozen for up to 1 month. To reheat, wrap the bialys [thawed if frozen] in aluminum foil, place them on a baking sheet, and bake in a 350-degree oven for 10 minutes.)

SHAPING AND FILLING BIALYS

1 Press greased and floured 1-cup dry measuring cup firmly into center of each dough round until cup touches sheet to make indentation for filling.

2 Fill each bialy with about 1 tablespoon filling, smoothing with back of spoon.

Lop Cheung Bao

MAKES 10 buns | **TOTAL TIME** 1¼ hours, plus 1½ hours rising and cooling

¾ cup whole milk, warm

3 tablespoons sugar

1 teaspoon instant or rapid-rise yeast

1 tablespoon vegetable oil

2 cups (10 ounces) all-purpose flour

2 tablespoons cornstarch

1 teaspoon baking powder

⅛ teaspoon table salt

10 lop cheung

Why This Recipe Works Lop cheung bao (sometimes written as lap cheong bao) is arguably the best pig in a blanket the world has to offer. A snow-white yeasted dough is twirled around a cured Chinese sausage (lop cheung), and the buns are steamed until the dough turns fluffy and firm. The snap of the rich sausage when you bite into the pillowy, slightly sweet bun is heavenly. This recipe was developed by Jacqueline Church, who leads food and culture tours in Boston's Chinatown. Although she discovered these buns as an adult cook, she has strong memories of another savory pork and sweet bun combination that she ate growing up in Hawaii. Manapua were the islands' version of the Chinese char siu bao (see page 268) that were initially brought to Hawaii by Chinese laborers. Similar to mainland ice cream trucks, the manapua truck would arrive in her neighborhood heralded by the squeals of happy kids. When purchasing lop cheung, look for good distribution of fat throughout the sausage and some alcohol in the ingredient list; avoid sausage containing liver here. This recipe is best made in a stacking bamboo steamer basket (see page 20) set inside a skillet. Using bleached all-purpose flour will create the bright-white color that is traditional and prized for these buns; you can also use unbleached all-purpose flour, though the bao will be less bright white.

1 Whisk milk, sugar, and yeast together in 2-cup liquid measuring cup until sugar has dissolved, then let sit until foamy, about 5 minutes. Whisk in oil. Pulse flour, cornstarch, baking powder, and salt in food processor until combined, about 3 pulses. With processor running, slowly add milk mixture and process until no dry flour remains, about 30 seconds.

2 Transfer dough to lightly floured counter and knead by hand to form smooth, round ball, about 30 seconds. Transfer dough to lightly oiled large bowl, turning to coat dough ball in oil, arranging dough seam side down. Cover with plastic wrap and let rise until doubled in size, about 1 hour.

3 While dough rises, place plate in bamboo steamer basket and arrange sausages in single layer on plate. Set steamer basket over simmering water in skillet and cook, covered, until sausages are plump and color is muted, 10 to 15 minutes. (Add boiling water to skillet as needed while steaming.) Set aside plate with sausages and let cool completely. Remove basket from simmering water and set aside.

4 Cut ten 6 by 4-inch rectangles of parchment paper; set aside. Press down on dough to deflate. Transfer dough to clean counter and portion into 10 equal pieces (about 2 ounces each); cover loosely with plastic. Working with 1 piece of dough at a time (keep remaining pieces covered), form into rough ball by stretching dough around your thumbs and pinching edges together so top is smooth. Place ball seam side down on clean counter and, using your cupped hand, drag in small circles until dough feels taut and round. Cover dough balls with plastic while rolling remaining dough.

5 Working with 1 dough ball at a time (keep remaining pieces covered) and starting at center, gently and evenly roll and stretch dough into 10-inch-long rope. Wrap dough around 1 cooled sausage, starting 1 inch from 1 end of sausage (dough should wrap around sausage at least 3 times and sausage should be roughly centered on dough) and place in basket on 1 prepared parchment rectangle, tucking ends of dough underneath sausage. Cover with damp dish towel while forming remaining bao, spacing bao about 1 inch apart. Let bao sit until slightly puffy, about 20 minutes.

6 Remove damp dish towel and set covered steamer basket over cold water in skillet. Bring water to simmer over high heat and, once steam begins to escape from sides of basket, reduce heat to medium and steam until bao are puffy and firm, 10 to 15 minutes. (Add boiling water to skillet as needed while steaming.) Remove basket from simmering water and let bao cool for 5 minutes before serving.

SHAPING LOP CHEUNG BAO

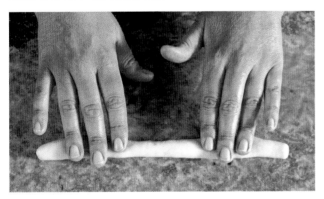

1 Gently and evenly roll dough ball into 10-inch-long rope.

2 Wrap dough rope around sausage, starting ¾ inch from 1 end of sausage (dough should wrap around sausage at least 3 times).

Char Siu Bolo Bao

MAKES 20 buns | **TOTAL TIME** 1¼ hours, plus 2¼ hours rising and cooling

Dough

- 2 tablespoons plus 2⅔ cups (13⅓ ounces) all-purpose flour, divided
- ½ cup water, room temperature
- ½ cup whole milk, chilled
- 1 large egg
- ⅓ cup plus 4 teaspoons (3 ounces) sugar
- 3½ teaspoons nonfat dry milk powder
- 2¼ teaspoons instant or rapid-rise yeast
- 1 teaspoon table salt
- 4 tablespoons unsalted butter, cut into 2 pieces and softened

Topping

- ⅔ cup plus 2 teaspoons (3½ ounces) all-purpose flour
- ¼ teaspoon baking powder
- ¼ teaspoon table salt
- 6 tablespoons unsalted butter, softened
- ⅔ cup confectioners' sugar
- 2 large eggs, beaten
- 2 teaspoons vanilla extract

1¼ pounds char siu pork (chopped if using store-bought)

Why This Recipe Works A favorite in many Chinese bakeries is a fluffy baked bun called bolo bao (pineapple bun), named for the look of its lightly crunchy topping, which is piped in a crosshatch or spiral pattern before baking. While these slightly sweet bao are typically unfilled, we took inspiration from a version served in the Hong Kong Michelin-starred restaurant Tim Ho Wan to send them over the (savory) top and stuff them with melt-in-your-mouth barbecued pork. The bao's supermoist interior is the result of adding a tangzhong, a cooked flour and water paste that gets combined with the rest of the ingredients. This superhydrated dough yields rolls that are not just moist but also fluffy because the water converts to steam in the oven, acting as a leavener. The extra water also increases gluten development to give the buns structure. We like our recipe for Char Siu Pork (page 339), but you can purchase char siu from a Chinese restaurant or Asian grocery store, if you prefer.

1 **For the dough** Whisk 2 tablespoons flour and water in small microwave-safe bowl until smooth. Microwave, whisking every 20 seconds, until mixture thickens to stiff, smooth, pudding-like consistency and registers at least 150 degrees, 40 to 60 seconds. Whisk in milk until smooth, then whisk in egg until smooth.

2 In bowl of stand mixer, whisk together remaining 2⅔ cups flour, sugar, milk powder, yeast, and salt. Add cooked flour mixture. Fit stand mixer with dough hook and mix on low speed until all flour is moistened, 1 to 2 minutes. Increase speed to medium-high and knead until dough is smooth and elastic and clears sides of bowl, 10 to 12 minutes.

3 Fit stand mixer with paddle. With mixer running on medium speed, add butter, 1 piece at a time, beating for 30 seconds after each addition. Continue to mix until butter is fully incorporated and dough is no longer shiny, 1 to 2 minutes.

4 Transfer dough to very lightly floured counter. Knead dough briefly to form ball and transfer, seam side down, to lightly greased large bowl. Cover with plastic wrap and let rise until doubled in size, 1 to 1½ hours.

5 **For the topping** Meanwhile, whisk flour, baking powder, and salt together in small bowl. Using clean, dry mixer bowl and paddle, beat butter and confectioners' sugar on medium-high speed until light, pale, and fluffy, about 3 minutes. With mixer running, gradually add eggs, then vanilla; mix until smooth, scraping down bowl as needed, about 2 minutes. Add flour mixture and mix on low speed until combined, about 30 seconds. Scrape down bowl, then fold ingredients by hand to mix fully. Transfer mixture to 1-quart heavy-duty zipper-lock bag and snip off 1 corner, making hole no larger than ¼ inch (alternatively, transfer to pastry bag fitted with ¼-inch piping tip); set aside until ready to use (do not refrigerate).

6 Line 2 baking sheets with parchment paper. Transfer dough to counter and divide into 20 equal pieces (about 1½ ounces each). Working with 1 piece of dough at a time, press dough into 4-inch round on lightly floured counter and drape in muffin

tin to form cup shape, covering each dough cup with plastic while pressing remaining dough. Fill 1 dough cup with about 1½ tablespoons char siu pork. Pull edges of dough to center and pinch tightly to seal. Transfer bun to counter, seam side down, and rotate gently to form round shape. Repeat with remaining dough cups and remaining pork. Space 10 balls evenly on each prepared sheet. Cover balls loosely with greased plastic and let rise until doubled in size, about 1 hour. Adjust oven rack to middle position and heat oven to 375 degrees.

7 Pipe about 2 tablespoons topping in tight spiral on top of each bun (topping should form circle roughly 2 inches in diameter and ¼ inch thick). Bake, 1 sheet at a time, until topping is golden brown, 14 to 16 minutes, rotating sheet halfway through baking. Transfer buns to wire rack and let cool for at least 10 minutes. Serve. (Buns can be individually wrapped in plastic wrap and frozen for up to 2 weeks [thaw frozen buns at room temperature before reheating]. To reheat, place buns on baking sheet and bake in 400-degree oven until tops are dry [but not browned] and centers are warmed through, 4 to 6 minutes.)

SHAPING CHAR SIU BAO

1 Working with one 1½-ounce piece of dough at a time, press dough into 4-inch round on lightly floured surface and drape in muffin tin to form cup shape, covering each dough cup with plastic wrap while pressing remaining dough.

2 Fill 1 dough cup with about 1½ tablespoons pork filling.

3 Pull edges of dough to center and pinch tightly to seal. Transfer bun to counter, seam side down, and rotate gently to form round shape. Repeat with remaining dough cups and remaining pork filling.

4 Pipe about 2 tablespoons topping in tight spiral on top of each bun (topping should form circle roughly 2 inches in diameter and ¼ inch thick).

Potato Knishes

MAKES 16 knishes | **TOTAL TIME** 2½ hours, plus 1¼ hours resting and cooling

Filling

2¼ pounds russet potatoes, peeled and cut into 1-inch pieces

1 teaspoon table salt, divided, plus salt for cooking potatoes

½ teaspoon pepper

1 tablespoon extra-virgin olive oil

3 onions, chopped fine

Dough

2 cups (10 ounces) all-purpose flour

1½ teaspoons baking powder

¾ cup extra-virgin olive oil, divided

½ cup water, room temperature

1 large egg, plus 1 large egg beaten with 1 teaspoon water

1 teaspoon table salt

Why This Recipe Works Knishes are the hearty, savory handheld pastries that were brought to New York in the early 20th century by Jewish Eastern Europeans. They can come in different shapes (most commonly round or square), and they can be filled with either savory or sweet fillings. Savory choices include beef, mushrooms, kasha, sauerkraut, cheese, or—as in this recipe—mashed potato and onion. The potato variety (often without onion) remains a beloved street food in New York to this day. To master the knish at home, start with a simple dough of flour, olive oil, salt, and water. Adding an egg allows the oil and water to combine, making the dough more supple, and baking powder promotes lift and tenderness. For the filling, mash high-starch russet potatoes with a whole pile of deeply browned onions for intense flavor. For efficient assembly, you will roll the dough into a very thin square and form the filling into a rope along one of its edges. A thin coating of oil on the dough prevents the layers from fusing, creating a lighter pastry. Roll the dough around the filling, slice each cylinder into individual knishes, and stand each on its end before lightly squishing to flatten it. Brushing the parchment paper–lined baking sheet with oil before arranging the knishes on it ensures crisp bottoms.

1 **For the filling** Combine potatoes and 1 tablespoon salt in Dutch oven and cover with water by 1 inch. Bring to boil over high heat; reduce heat to medium and cook until potatoes are tender, 20 to 25 minutes. Drain potatoes and return them to pot. Cook, shaking pot occasionally, until any surface moisture has evaporated, about 1 minute. Mash potatoes with potato masher until very few lumps remain. Transfer to large bowl and stir in ½ teaspoon salt and pepper.

2 Meanwhile, heat oil in 12-inch nonstick skillet over medium-high heat until shimmering. Add onions and remaining ½ teaspoon salt and cook, stirring occasionally, until well browned, about 10 minutes. Transfer to bowl with mashed potatoes and stir to combine. Let filling cool completely. (Filling can be refrigerated, covered, for up to 24 hours.)

3 **For the dough** Whisk flour and baking powder together in large bowl. Whisk 6 tablespoons oil, water, whole egg, and salt together in separate bowl. Add oil mixture to flour mixture and stir with rubber spatula until dough forms. Transfer dough to floured counter and knead until smooth, about 1 minute. Wrap in plastic wrap and let rest on counter for 1 hour. (Dough can be refrigerated for up to 4 hours; let dough come to room temperature before rolling.)

4 Adjust oven rack to middle position and heat oven to 350 degrees. Line rimmed baking sheet with parchment paper and brush parchment with 2 tablespoons oil. Divide dough in half and form each half into 4-inch square on well-floured counter. Working with 1 square at a time, roll dough into 16-inch square, covering each rolled square with plastic while rolling remaining dough. Lightly brush dough with 2 tablespoons oil, leaving 1-inch border at farthest edge.

5 Form half of filling into 1-inch log along edge of dough closest to you, leaving 1-inch border along edge and on sides. Brush far edge of dough with water. Roll dough around filling and seal seam. Trim knish log on each end so log measures 16 inches long. Place log seam side down and cut log into 8 (2-inch) pieces. Stand each knish on end and press to 1-inch thickness. Space evenly apart on prepared sheet. Repeat with remaining dough, remaining 2 tablespoons oil, and remaining filling. (Unbaked knishes can be frozen in airtight container for up to 1 month. If baking from frozen, increase baking time to 50 to 55 minutes.)

6 Brush tops and sides of knishes with egg wash. Bake until golden brown, 35 to 40 minutes, rotating sheet halfway through baking. Transfer knishes to wire rack and let cool for 15 minutes. Serve.

Variation

Potato, Pastrami, and Gruyère Knishes

Omit ½ teaspoon salt from filling. Add 2 cups shredded Gruyère cheese, 8 ounces chopped deli pastrami, 2 tablespoons yellow mustard, 1 teaspoon crushed caraway seeds, and ½ teaspoon dried dill to filling with pepper in step 1.

SHAPING KNISHES

1 Working with half of dough at a time, roll out dough into very thin 16-inch square. Brush with oil and mound half of filling evenly on dough in long rope, leaving about 1 inch clear at nearest edge and at ends.

2 Roll dough around filling and seal seam. Trim edges, place seam side down, and cut log into 8 pieces.

3 Stand each knish on end and lightly press. Place on oiled, parchment paper–lined baking sheet and brush with egg wash.

Sausage and Chive Pull-Apart Rolls

MAKES 12 rolls | **TOTAL TIME** 1½ hours, plus 2¼ hours rising and cooling

Dough

- ⅔ cup water
- ¼ cup (1⅓ ounces) plus 2¾ cups (15⅛ ounces) bread flour, divided
- ⅔ cup whole milk
- 1 large egg plus 1 large yolk
- 2 teaspoons instant or rapid-rise yeast
- 3 tablespoons granulated sugar
- 1½ teaspoons salt
- 6 tablespoons unsalted butter, cut into 6 pieces and softened

Filling

- 1½ pounds bulk pork sausage
- 1½ teaspoons pepper
- 1 teaspoon ground fennel
- 1 teaspoon ground sage
- 8 ounces sharp cheddar cheese, shredded (2 cups)
- ¼ cup minced fresh chives

Why This Recipe Works These comforting rolls are just as much at home on the breakfast table alongside eggs as they are accompanying a cozy bowl of tomato or vegetable soup at lunch or dinnertime. In fact, they're a reimagined savory version of rolled sweet breakfast buns. Instead of rolling up the enriched dough with cinnamon sugar, though, you will layer in a deeply flavorful filling of sautéed pork sausage, fennel seeds, and sage, topping that with cheddar cheese. A handful of fresh chives finishes the baked rolls. To make a tender, moist pull-apart roll, we use the tangzhong method, incorporating a cooked flour and water paste into the dough. The paste traps water, so the dough isn't sticky or difficult to work with, and the increased hydration converts to steam during baking, which makes the rolls superfluffy. Adding a resting period for the dough and withholding the sugar and salt until the gluten is firmly established strengthens the crumb and ensures that the soft bread doesn't collapse under the weight of the hearty sausage. We prefer King Arthur brand bread flour in this recipe.

1 **For the dough** Whisk water and ¼ cup flour together in small bowl until no lumps remain. Microwave, whisking every 20 seconds, until mixture thickens to stiff, smooth, pudding-like consistency that forms mound when dropped from end of whisk into bowl, 40 to 80 seconds.

2 In bowl of stand mixer, whisk flour paste and milk together until smooth. Add egg and yolk and whisk until incorporated. Add remaining 2¾ cups flour and yeast. Fit mixer with dough hook and mix on low speed until all flour is moistened, 1 to 2 minutes. Let stand for 15 minutes. Add sugar and salt and mix on medium-low speed for 5 minutes. With mixer running, add butter, 1 piece at a time. Knead for 5 minutes, scraping down dough hook and sides of bowl occasionally (dough will stick to bottom of bowl).

3 Transfer dough to lightly floured counter. Knead briefly to form ball and transfer, seam side down, to lightly greased bowl; lightly coat surface of dough with vegetable oil spray and cover with plastic wrap. Let rise until just doubled in size, 40 minutes to 1 hour.

4 **For the filling** While dough rises, grease 13 by 9-inch metal baking pan; set aside. Cook sausage in 12-inch nonstick skillet over medium heat until no longer pink, about 8 minutes, breaking up meat with wooden spoon into pieces no larger than ¼ inch. Stir in pepper, fennel, and sage and cook until fragrant, about 30 seconds. Using slotted spoon, transfer sausage to bowl and let cool completely, about 20 minutes.

5 Press down on dough to deflate. Transfer dough to lightly floured counter. Pat and stretch dough into 18 by 15-inch rectangle with long edge facing you. Sprinkle cooled sausage over dough, leaving 1-inch border along top edge. Smooth filling into even layer, then sprinkle cheese evenly over top. Gently press mixture into dough.

6 Beginning with long edge nearest you, roll dough away from you into cylinder, taking care not to roll too tightly. Pinch seam to seal and roll cylinder seam side down. Slice cylinder into 12 equal portions and transfer, cut sides down, to prepared pan. Cover tightly with plastic and let rise until buns are puffy and touching one another, 40 minutes to 1 hour. (Buns can be refrigerated immediately after shaping for up to 14 hours. To bake, remove pan from refrigerator and let sit until buns are puffy and touching one another, 1 to 1½ hours.)

7 Adjust oven rack to middle position and heat oven to 375 degrees. Bake buns until golden brown, 20 to 25 minutes. Rotate pan; cover loosely with aluminum foil; and bake until center of dough registers at least 200 degrees, 10 to 15 minutes longer. Let buns cool in pan on wire rack for 5 minutes. Place rimmed baking sheet over buns and carefully invert. Remove pan and let buns cool for 5 minutes. Place serving platter over buns and carefully reinvert. Let cool for at least 10 minutes longer before sprinkling with chives. Serve.

Za'atar Monkey Bread

SERVES 4 to 6 | **TOTAL TIME** 50 minutes, plus 2 hours rising and cooling

Why This Recipe Works Monkey bread—consisting of balls of dough baked into a round loaf or a ring-shaped loaf meant for pulling apart and eating with your hands—may be a favorite with kids, but that doesn't mean it has to be sticky and tooth-achingly sweet. This version keeps the crowd-friendly pull-apart shape but replaces the sweet stuff with the aromatic, potent spice mixture za'atar. The dead-simple approach starts with pizza dough: Divide it evenly into individual portions, roll the portions into balls, and arrange them in a round cake pan. Sprinkle the za'atar over the top and let the dough rise, then brush with oil and bake. When it comes out of the oven looking beautifully golden brown, brush on some toasted garlic oil and add a final sprinkle of za'atar and flake sea salt for the most sophisticated take on monkey bread you've ever had. We prefer our Za'atar (page 179), but store-bought za'atar works great, too; just be aware that contents of the blend may vary. We like to use our Pizza Dough, but you can use 1 pound of ready-made pizza dough from your local pizzeria or supermarket.

¼ cup extra-virgin olive oil, divided

3 garlic cloves, minced

½ recipe Pizza Dough (page 337)

3 tablespoons za'atar, divided

Flake sea salt

1 Combine 2 tablespoons oil and garlic in small bowl and microwave until garlic is fragrant, about 1 minute; set aside until ready to serve.

2 Brush 8-inch round cake pan with 1 tablespoon oil. Transfer pizza dough to lightly oiled counter and pat into 6-inch square. Divide dough into 36 equal pieces (about ½ ounce each) and cover loosely with plastic wrap. Working with 1 piece of dough at a time (keep remaining pieces covered), form into rough ball by stretching dough around your thumbs and pinching edges together so that top is smooth. Place ball seam side down on clean counter and, using your cupped hand, drag in small circles until dough feels taut and round. Place dough balls in prepared pan; sprinkle with 2 tablespoons za'atar; cover loosely with greased plastic; and let stand until dough balls are puffy and have risen slightly (about ½ inch), 1 to 2 hours.

3 Adjust oven rack to middle position and heat oven to 400 degrees. Brush tops of dough balls with remaining 1 tablespoon oil. Bake until light golden brown, 20 to 25 minutes, rotating halfway through baking. Transfer pan to wire rack and let cool for 5 minutes. Transfer bread to large plate or serving platter, brush with garlic oil, sprinkle with remaining 1 tablespoon za'atar, and let cool for 5 minutes. Sprinkle with sea salt and serve.

Pizza Monkey Bread

SERVES 6 to 8 | TOTAL TIME 1¾ hours, plus 55 minutes rising and cooling

Monkey Bread

- 1 recipe Pizza Dough (page 337)
- 4 ounces sliced pepperoni
- 3 tablespoons extra-virgin olive oil
- 1½ ounces Parmesan cheese, grated (¾ cup)
- ½ teaspoon dried oregano
- 8 (4½-inch) sticks mozzarella string cheese

Tomato Sauce

- 2 tablespoons extra-virgin olive oil
- 4 garlic cloves, minced
- 1 (28-ounce) can crushed tomatoes
- ½ teaspoon dried oregano
- ½ teaspoon table salt
- ½ teaspoon pepper

Why This Recipe Works Don't serve this to guests unless you're ready to be asked to make it again and again—it's that irresistible. You'll become an instant legend when you present this giant monkey bread, which consists of pepperoni-and-mozzarella-stuffed dough balls baked to pizza-like perfection in a Bundt pan and served with a bowl of tomato sauce for dunking nestled in the center of the ring-shaped bread. To make assembly more efficient, instead of shaping and filling each pizza-stuffed ball individually, you will form logs of dough stuffed with the fillings and then cut them into pieces. After pinching the ends of the pieces shut, the balls are ready for arranging in the pan. Mozzarella string cheese (rather than shredded cheese) is the perfect shape to roll up in the dough logs. Microwaving the pepperoni before using it renders some of its fat and prevents greasy dough, and here's a stealth trick: Brushing a bit of that luscious rendered pepperoni fat onto the outside of the balls creates a superflavorful browned crust. The simple 10-minute tomato sauce for dipping is the crowning touch. If the dough becomes slack or difficult to work with, refrigerate it for 10 minutes. Seal the open ends of the filled dough after each cut to keep the filling from leaking out. If your string cheese sticks are longer than 4½ inches, trim any overhang once you've placed the cheese on the dough. We like to use our Pizza Dough; however, you can use 1¾ pounds of ready-made pizza dough from your local pizzeria or supermarket.

1 **For the monkey bread** Line baking sheet with parchment paper and sprinkle with flour. Divide pizza dough into 2 balls. Roll each dough ball into 10 by 6-inch rectangle on lightly floured counter, then transfer to prepared sheet. Cover with plastic wrap and let sit for 15 minutes.

2 Microwave pepperoni in bowl until fat is rendered, 60 to 90 seconds, stirring halfway through microwaving. Using tongs, transfer pepperoni to paper towel–lined plate, reserving pepperoni oil in bowl (you should have about 1 tablespoon). Pat pepperoni dry with paper towels. Stir olive oil into pepperoni oil. Brush 12-cup nonstick Bundt pan with 2 teaspoons oil mixture. Combine Parmesan and oregano in separate bowl.

3 Return 1 dough rectangle to lightly floured counter and roll into 18 by 9-inch rectangle with long edge parallel to counter edge, stretching corners as needed to make neat rectangle. Starting 2 inches from long edge of dough nearest you, shingle half of pepperoni parallel to long edge. Lay 4 mozzarella sticks end to end on top of pepperoni. Sprinkle half of Parmesan mixture alongside mozzarella. Fold bottom 2-inch section of dough over filling and roll tightly toward opposite edge. Pinch seam and ends to seal. Repeat with remaining dough rectangle, remaining pepperoni, remaining 4 mozzarella sticks, and remaining Parmesan mixture.

4 Cut each log in half and pinch open ends to seal. Cut each log in half again, pinching open ends to seal. Cut each log into thirds, pinching open ends closed as you go. Place single layer of stuffed dough balls (about 6) ½ inch apart in prepared pan and brush tops and sides with one-fourth of oil mixture. Layer remaining dough balls in pan, brushing tops and sides with remaining oil mixture as you go. Cover pan with plastic and let rise at room temperature until slightly puffed, about 30 minutes. Adjust oven rack to lower-middle position and heat oven to 400 degrees.

5 **For the tomato sauce** Meanwhile, heat oil in small saucepan over medium heat until shimmering. Add garlic and cook until beginning to brown, about 90 seconds. Add tomatoes, oregano, salt, and pepper and bring to boil. Reduce heat to medium-low and simmer until slightly thickened, about 10 minutes. Remove from heat, cover, and set aside.

6 Bake until well browned, about 40 minutes, rotating pan halfway through baking. Transfer pan to wire rack and let cool for 10 minutes. Place serving platter on top of pan and invert. Let cool 10 minutes longer. Reheat sauce and transfer to serving bowl. Serve monkey bread with sauce.

SHAPING MONKEY BREAD

1 After layering pepperoni and cheese on rolled-out dough, roll rectangle into tight log and pinch to seal seam and ends. Cut each log into quarters and cut each quarter into thirds, for total of 12 pieces per log, pinching to seal open ends as you go.

2 Place single layer of stuffed dough balls (about 6) ½ inch apart in prepared pan and brush tops and sides with pepperoni oil. Layer remaining dough balls in pan, brushing tops and sides with remaining oil as you go.

Prosciutto and Fig Pinwheel Bread

SERVES 10 to 12 | **TOTAL TIME** 1½ hours, plus 3¼ hours rising and cooling

2 cups (10 ounces)
  all-purpose flour

2 tablespoons minced
  fresh thyme

2 teaspoons minced fresh sage

2 teaspoons ground fennel

1½ teaspoons instant or
  rapid-rise yeast

½ teaspoon table salt

½ cup whole milk,
  room temperature

¼ cup (1¾ ounces) sugar

2 large egg yolks,
  room temperature

8 tablespoons unsalted butter,
  softened and cut into 8 pieces

6 ounces thinly sliced prosciutto

¼ cup fig jam

1 large egg beaten with
  1 teaspoon water

Why This Recipe Works This showstopper is a stunning centerpiece for holidays—or any other special occasion. By rolling out layers of dough into rounds, adding filling and stacking them, and then cutting them partially into strips and twisting, you end up with a jaw-dropping sunburst-shaped bread. And making this showpiece is not nearly as difficult as you might think. You'll start by making an egg-enriched dough, packing in plenty of thyme, sage, and fennel for savory flavor. The layered filling involves a match made in heaven: prosciutto and fig jam. After building the filled stack of dough rounds, slice the dough into ribbons around a 3-inch circle in the center of the layered bread, then twist and pinch each ribbon around the circle before letting the bread proof again briefly, allowing any gaps to fill in organically. Brushing on egg wash before baking gives your masterpiece a beautiful sheen.

1 Whisk flour, thyme, sage, fennel, yeast, and salt together in bowl of stand mixer. Whisk milk, sugar, and egg yolks in 4-cup liquid measuring cup until sugar has dissolved. Fit mixer with dough hook and slowly add milk mixture to flour mixture, mixing on low speed until cohesive dough starts to form and no dry flour remains, about 2 minutes, scraping down dough hook and sides of bowl as needed. Increase speed to medium-low and add softened butter, 1 piece at a time. Knead for 4 minutes, scraping down dough hook and sides of bowl occasionally. Continue to knead until dough is smooth and elastic and clears sides of bowl, 10 to 12 minutes.

2 Transfer dough to lightly floured counter and knead by hand to form smooth, round ball, about 30 seconds. Transfer dough seam side down to lightly greased large bowl, cover with plastic wrap, and let rise until increased in size by about half, 1½ to 2 hours. Place in refrigerator until dough is firm, at least 1 hour or up to 24 hours. (If dough is chilled longer than 1 hour, let rest at room temperature for 15 minutes before rolling out.)

3 Press down on dough to deflate. Transfer to clean counter, cut into 4 pieces, then knead each piece to form smooth ball. Cover loosely with plastic wrap. Transfer 1 dough ball to double layer of parchment paper (keep remaining dough balls covered) on counter and press and roll dough into 12-inch circle on parchment. Shingle half of prosciutto evenly over dough. Using parchment paper as sling, transfer dough and parchment to cutting board.

4 Transfer second dough ball to lightly floured counter and press and roll into 12-inch circle. Carefully top prosciutto-topped dough round with second dough round. Microwave fig jam until loosened, about 30 seconds, then evenly brush over top dough round.

5 Transfer third dough ball to lightly floured counter and press and roll into 12-inch circle. Carefully top fig-topped dough round with third dough round. Shingle remaining prosciutto over top. Transfer final dough ball to lightly floured counter and press and roll into 12-inch circle, then lay dough round on top of stack.

6 Place 3-inch wide cookie cutter or overturned bowl in center of dough (do not press into dough). Using sharp knife positioned at 12 o'clock, cut through all 4 layers of dough and filling, starting from edge of cookie cutter and finishing at edge of dough round (be sure to cut firmly through prosciutto layers). Repeat cut on opposite side of cookie cutter, at 6 o'clock. Continue to repeat cuts around dough round to make 16 evenly spaced cuts around cookie cutter. Remove cookie cutter.

7 Grasping ends of 2 adjacent strips, twist strips twice, then twist another half turn and pinch ends together to seal.

Repeat with remaining strips. Using parchment as sling, carefully lift star and place on rimmed baking sheet (use caution as some cuts may have sliced through top parchment layer). Cover loosely with greased plastic and let rise until puffy, 40 to 60 minutes.

8 Adjust oven rack to middle position and preheat oven to 350 degrees. Brush pinwheel with egg wash and bake until golden brown, 30 to 40 minutes (if edges brown faster than center, shield edges with aluminum foil). Transfer sheet to wire rack and let cool for 15 minutes. Serve warm or at room temperature.

SHAPING PINWHEEL BREAD

1 Press and roll 1 dough ball into 12-inch round. Shingle prosciutto over dough. Press and roll second dough ball, place over prosciutto, and spread fig jam over dough. Press and roll third dough ball, place over jam, and shingle prosciutto over dough. Top stack with fourth dough round.

2 Place 3-inch-wide cookie cutter in center of dough. Using sharp knife positioned at 12 o'clock, cut through all 4 layers of dough and filling, starting from edge of cookie cutter and finishing at edge of dough round. Repeat cut on opposite side of cookie cutter, at 6 o'clock.

3 Continue to repeat cuts around dough round to make 16 evenly spaced cuts around cookie cutter.

4 Grasping ends of 2 adjacent strips, twist strips twice, then pinch ends together to seal. Repeat with remaining strips.

YEASTED LOAVES

Almost No-Knead Bread with Olives, Rosemary, and Parmesan

MAKES 1 loaf | **TOTAL TIME** 1¼ hours, plus 12½ hours rising and cooling

3 cups (15 ounces) all-purpose flour

4 ounces Parmesan cheese, grated fine (2 cups)

1 tablespoon minced fresh rosemary

1½ teaspoons table salt

¼ teaspoon instant or rapid-rise yeast

1 cup chopped pitted green olives

¾ cup water, room temperature

½ cup mild lager, room temperature

1 tablespoon distilled white vinegar

Why This Recipe Works Crusty, chewy, beautifully open-crumbed bread with briny, piney, umami-packed mix-ins can be yours with minimal effort. The promise of no-knead bread *still* seems too good to be true—but it's not. Our almost no-knead technique replaces the extended kneading and shaping required of traditional artisan-style bread baking with a higher dough hydration level (in other words, a wetter dough) and a longer resting period. During the long rest, the flour hydrates and enzymes work to break up the proteins so that the dough requires only 1 minute of kneading to help the gluten network form. You'll let the dough rest again and then bake it in a Dutch oven, an ideal environment for creating and trapping steam. The steam heats the loaf rapidly, causing the air bubbles in the dough to expand quickly and create an open crumb. As the steam condenses onto the surface of the baking bread, it causes the starches to form a thin sheath that eventually dries out, giving the finished loaf a shiny, crispy crust. To mimic the complex flavor of artisan bread, beer brings a "bready" aroma and vinegar adds tang (its acetic acid is the same acid produced during traditional dough fermentation). Use a mild lager, such as Budweiser; strongly flavored beers will make this bread taste bitter. Use a Dutch oven that holds 6 quarts or more. In step 4, start the 30-minute timer as soon as you put the bread in the cold oven; don't wait until the oven has preheated to start the timer or the bread will burn.

1 Whisk flour, Parmesan, rosemary, salt, and yeast together in large bowl. Whisk olives, room-temperature water, beer, and vinegar together in 4-cup liquid measuring cup. Using rubber spatula, gently fold olive mixture into flour mixture, scraping up dry flour from bottom of bowl, until dough starts to form and no dry flour remains. Cover bowl tightly with plastic wrap and let sit at room temperature for at least 8 hours or up to 18 hours.

2 Lay 18 by 12-inch sheet of parchment paper on counter and lightly spray with vegetable oil spray. Transfer dough to lightly floured counter and knead by hand until smooth and elastic, about 1 minute.

3 Shape dough into ball by pulling edges into middle, then transfer seam side down to center of prepared parchment. Using parchment as sling, gently lower loaf into Dutch oven (let any excess parchment hang over pot edge). Cover tightly with plastic and let rise until loaf has doubled in size and dough springs back minimally when poked gently with your knuckle, 1½ to 2 hours.

4 Adjust oven rack to middle position. Using sharp paring knife or single-edge razor blade, make two 5-inch-long, ½-inch-deep slashes with swift, fluid motion along top of loaf to form cross. Cover pot and place in oven. Turn oven to 425 degrees and bake loaf for 30 minutes (start timing as soon as loaf goes in oven).

5 Remove lid and continue to bake until loaf is deep golden brown and registers 205 to 210 degrees, 25 to 30 minutes. Using parchment sling, remove loaf from pot and transfer to wire rack; discard parchment. Let cool completely, about 3 hours, before serving. (Bread is best eaten the day it is baked but can be wrapped in aluminum foil and stored for up to 2 days. To serve, reheat in 400-degree oven for 5 to 10 minutes.)

Variation

Almost No-Knead Cranberry-Pecan Bread
Omit olives. Substitute ½ cup dried cranberries and ½ cup toasted pecans for Parmesan and rosemary.

Potato-Dill Sandwich Bread

MAKES 1 loaf | **TOTAL TIME** 2 hours, plus 4¼ hours rising and cooling

1 large russet potato (10 ounces), peeled and cut into 1-inch pieces

3 tablespoons unsalted butter, cut into 6 pieces

2⅔ cups (14⅔ ounces) bread flour

1½ teaspoons instant or rapid-rise yeast

1½ teaspoons table salt

2 tablespoons minced fresh dill

1 large egg beaten with 1 teaspoon water

Why This Recipe Works With a wonderfully downy crumb and a texture sturdy enough to stand up to all your favorite fillings, potato bread is a standout among sandwich loaves. Plenty of fresh dill ups the flavor ante in this loaf. The dough is packed with 8 ounces of freshly mashed potato, and yet the baked bread is light and fluffy. How? The starches in potatoes work to dilute the flour's gluten-forming proteins, thereby weakening the bread's structural network and making it more tender. After boiling and draining the potato, drying it out on the stovetop gives you control over how much liquid you're incorporating and ensures that you're not overhydrating the dough. This bread exhibits a lot of spring in the oven, so letting the loaf rise to only ½ inch above the lip of the pan before baking ensures that its continued rise in the oven won't lead to tearing. Slashing the loaf before placing it in the oven is another foolproof way to eliminate tears by helping the loaf expand before its crust sets. Don't salt the water in which you boil the potato. The test kitchen's preferred loaf pan measures 8½ by 4½ inches; if you use a 9 by 5-inch loaf pan, increase the shaped rising time by 20 to 30 minutes and start checking for doneness 10 minutes earlier than advised in the recipe.

1 Place potato in medium saucepan and cover with 1 inch cold water. Bring to boil over high heat, then reduce heat to maintain simmer and cook until potato is just tender (paring knife slipped in and out of potato should meet little resistance), 8 to 10 minutes.

2 Transfer ¾ cup (6 ounces) potato cooking water to liquid measuring cup and let cool completely; drain potato. Return potato to saucepan and place over low heat. Cook, shaking saucepan occasionally, until any surface moisture has evaporated, about 30 seconds. Off heat, process potato through ricer or food mill or mash well with potato masher. Measure 1 cup very firmly packed potato (8 ounces) and transfer to bowl (discard remaining mashed potato or save for another use). Stir in butter until melted and let mixture cool completely before using.

3 Whisk flour, yeast, and salt together in bowl of stand mixer. Add mashed potato mixture to flour mixture and mix with your hands until combined (some large lumps are OK). Using dough hook on low speed, slowly add potato cooking water and mix until cohesive dough starts to form and no dry flour remains, about 2 minutes, scraping down bowl as needed. Increase speed to medium-low and knead until dough is smooth and elastic and clears sides of bowl, about 8 minutes. Reduce speed to low; add dill; and mix until incorporated, about 1 minute.

4 Transfer dough to lightly floured counter and knead by hand to form smooth, round ball, about 30 seconds. Place dough seam side down in lightly greased large bowl or container; cover tightly with plastic wrap; and let rise until doubled in size, 1 to 1½ hours.

5 Grease 8½ by 4½-inch loaf pan. Press down on dough to deflate. Turn out dough onto lightly floured counter (side of dough that was against bowl should now be facing up). Press and stretch dough into 8 by 6-inch rectangle, with long side parallel to counter edge. Roll dough away from you into firm cylinder, keeping roll taut by tucking it under itself as you go. Pinch seam closed and place loaf seam side down in prepared pan, pressing dough gently into corners. Cover loosely with greased plastic and let rise until loaf reaches ½ inch above lip of pan and dough springs back minimally when poked gently with your knuckle, 20 to 30 minutes.

6 Adjust oven rack to lower-middle position and heat oven to 350 degrees. Using sharp paring knife or single-edge razor blade, make one ½-inch-deep slash with swift, fluid motion lengthwise along top of loaf, starting and stopping about ½ inch from ends. Gently brush loaf with egg wash and bake until loaf is golden brown and registers 205 to 210 degrees, 45 to 50 minutes, rotating pan halfway through baking. Let loaf cool in pan on wire rack for 15 minutes. Remove loaf from pan and let cool completely on wire rack, about 3 hours, before serving.

Whole-Wheat Quinoa Bread

MAKES 1 loaf | **TOTAL TIME** 2 hours, plus 5¾ hours rising and cooling

1 cup water, room temperature, divided

⅓ cup plus 1 teaspoon prewashed white quinoa, divided

1½ cups (8¼ ounces) bread flour

1 cup (5½ ounces) whole-wheat flour

2 tablespoons plus 1 teaspoon flaxseeds, divided

2 teaspoons instant or rapid-rise yeast

1½ teaspoons table salt

¾ cup whole milk, room temperature

3 tablespoons honey

1 tablespoon vegetable oil

1 large egg beaten with 1 teaspoon water

Why This Recipe Works Nutty quinoa and earthy flaxseeds are hearty additions to this protein-packed whole-wheat loaf. Adding some bread flour to the whole-wheat flour allows you to work a good amount of cooked quinoa into the dough, with the flour's high protein content ensuring a sturdy crumb. Simply adding raw quinoa to the dough would result in an unpleasant crunchiness, but microwaving the quinoa with some water until the liquid is absorbed softens the seeds enough to give the baked bread great chewy texture. Incorporating a small amount of oil into the dough helps coat the protein strands, making the loaf moister and more tender, and adding some honey nicely balances the earthiness of both of the seeds. Sprinkling 1 teaspoon of raw flaxseeds and 1 teaspoon of raw quinoa atop the loaf just before baking gives each slice pleasing textural contrast and crunch. The test kitchen's preferred loaf pan measures 8½ by 4½ inches; if you use a 9 by 5-inch loaf pan, increase the shaped rising time by 20 to 30 minutes and start checking for doneness 10 minutes earlier than advised in the recipe.

1 Microwave ¾ cup room-temperature water and ⅓ cup quinoa in covered bowl at 50 percent power until water is almost completely absorbed, about 10 minutes, stirring halfway through microwaving. Uncover quinoa and let sit until cooled slightly and water is completely absorbed, about 10 minutes.

2 Whisk bread flour, whole-wheat flour, 2 tablespoons flaxseeds, yeast, and salt together in bowl of stand mixer. Whisk milk, honey, oil, and remaining ¼ cup room-temperature water in 4-cup liquid measuring cup until honey has dissolved. Using dough hook on low speed, slowly add milk mixture to flour mixture and mix until cohesive dough starts to form and no dry flour remains, about 2 minutes, scraping down bowl as needed. Increase speed to medium-low and knead until dough is smooth, elastic, and slightly sticky, about 6 minutes. Reduce speed to low; slowly add cooked quinoa, ¼ cup at a time; and mix until mostly incorporated, about 3 minutes.

3 Transfer dough to lightly floured counter. Using your lightly floured hands, knead dough until quinoa is evenly distributed and dough forms smooth, round ball, about 30 seconds. Place dough seam side down in lightly greased large bowl or container; cover tightly with plastic wrap; and let rise until doubled in size, 1½ to 2 hours.

4 Grease 8½ by 4½-inch loaf pan. Press down on dough to deflate. Turn out dough onto lightly floured counter (side of dough that was against bowl should now be facing up) and press into 8 by 6-inch rectangle, with long side parallel to counter edge.

5 Roll dough away from you into firm cylinder, keeping roll taut by tucking it under itself as you go. Pinch seam closed and place loaf seam side down in prepared pan, pressing dough gently into corners. Cover loosely with greased plastic and let rise until loaf reaches 1 inch above lip of pan and dough springs back minimally when poked gently with your knuckle, 1 to 1½ hours.

6 Adjust oven rack to lower-middle position and heat oven to 350 degrees. Combine remaining 1 teaspoon quinoa and remaining 1 teaspoon flaxseeds in bowl. Gently brush loaf with egg wash and sprinkle with quinoa mixture. Bake until loaf is golden brown and registers 205 to 210 degrees,

45 to 50 minutes, rotating pan halfway through baking. Let loaf cool in pan on wire rack for 15 minutes. Remove loaf from pan and let cool completely on wire rack, about 3 hours, before serving.

Shaping Techniques for Yeasted Dough

Here are some all-purpose pointers for shaping sandwich loaves, round loaves, and torpedo-shaped loaves. For sandwich loaves, rolling the dough into a tight cylinder before transferring it to the pan enforces the gluten structure and prevents the final loaf from being misshapen, as pressing the dough flat and then folding it back together does for round loaves. And as with round loaves, the dough for torpedo loaves benefits from being pressed flat and folded inward to build structure. Then there a few more steps to complete in order to make these attractive artisan-style loaves.

SANDWICH LOAVES

1 Press and stretch dough into rectangle, with long side parallel to counter edge. Roll dough away from you into firm cylinder, keeping roll taut by tucking it under itself as you go.

2 Pinch seam closed with your fingers to secure it.

3 Place loaf seam side down in greased 8½ by 4½-inch loaf pan. Gently press dough into corners of pan.

ROUND LOAVES

1 Press and stretch dough into a round.

2 Working around circumference of dough, fold edges toward center of round until ball forms.

3 Flip dough ball seam side down and, using your cupped hands, drag dough in small circles until dough feels taut and round.

TORPEDO LOAVES

1 Press and stretch dough into a square.

2 Fold top corners of dough diagonally into center and press gently to seal. (Dough will look like an open envelope.)

3 Stretch and fold upper third of dough toward center, and press seam gently to seal. (Dough will look like a sealed envelope.)

4 Stretch and fold dough in half toward you to form a rough loaf, and pinch seam gently to seal. Roll loaf seam side down.

5 Gently slide your hands underneath each end of loaf and transfer it to prepared baking sheet or baking peel, being careful not to deflate it. Tuck edges under to form taut torpedo shape.

Everything Bagel Bread

MAKES 1 loaf | **TOTAL TIME** 1½ hours, plus 3¼ hours resting, rising, and cooling

3 cups (16½ ounces) bread flour

2¼ teaspoons instant or rapid-rise yeast

1¼ cups water, room temperature

¼ cup light corn syrup, divided

1½ tablespoons kosher salt

1½ teaspoons baking soda

3 tablespoons plus 1 teaspoon everything bagel seasoning

1 large egg beaten with 1 teaspoon water

Why This Recipe Works This bread, which has the signature chewy exterior and dense, soft interior of a fresh bagel, is wonderful toasted and spread with a schmear of cream cheese. The dough for this bread is indeed similar to a bagel dough and is made with high-protein bread flour. Kneading it for a full 10 minutes in a stand mixer develops plenty of gluten to help ensure that desired chewy texture. Then, just like traditional bagels, you boil the risen loaf before baking it. This boil, though brief, sets the crust before the bread goes into the oven, which means that the bread doesn't rise as much while baking, contributing to its signature dense interior. Adding baking soda and corn syrup to the boiling water aids in developing a shiny brown crust with great chew. Once the boiled dough is in the loaf pan, making slashes across the top allows steam to escape as it bakes. Last but not least, coating the dough with everything bagel seasoning elevates it to bagel bliss. We prefer our Everything Bagel Seasoning (page 162; double the recipe), but you can use store-bought, if you prefer. The test kitchen's preferred loaf pan measures 8½ by 4½ inches; if you use a 9 by 5-inch loaf pan, start checking for doneness 5 minutes earlier than advised in the recipe. We prefer King Arthur brand bread flour in this recipe.

1 Grease 8½ by 4½-inch loaf pan. Whisk flour and yeast together in bowl of stand mixer. Using dough hook on low speed, slowly add room-temperature water and 2 tablespoons corn syrup to flour mixture and mix until cohesive dough starts to form and no dry flour remains, about 2 minutes, scraping down bowl as needed. Turn off mixer, cover bowl with dish towel or plastic wrap, and let dough sit for 10 minutes.

2 Add salt to dough and knead on medium speed until dough is smooth and elastic, about 10 minutes. Turn out dough onto clean counter and form into ball by pinching and pulling dough edges under so top is smooth. Flip dough smooth side down.

3 Pat dough into 6-inch square and position parallel to counter edge. Fold top edge of dough down to midline, pressing to seal. Fold bottom edge of dough up to meet first seam at midline and press to seal. Fold dough in half so top and bottom edges meet; pinch together to seal. Flip dough seam side down and roll into 8-inch log.

4 Transfer to prepared pan, seam side down. Cover dough loosely with plastic lightly coated with vegetable oil spray and let rest in warm place until dough rises to lip of pan, about 1 hour.

5 Adjust oven rack to middle position and heat oven to 350 degrees. Line large plate with clean dish towel. Bring 2 quarts water to boil in Dutch oven. Once boiling, add baking soda and remaining 2 tablespoons corn syrup.

6 Gently tip dough out of pan onto counter. Lift dough, gently lower into boiling water, and cook for 45 seconds per side. Using spider skimmer or 2 slotted spoons, transfer dough to prepared plate. Gently fold dish towel over dough to wick away excess moisture on top. Let sit until cool enough to handle, about 2 minutes.

7 Spray now-empty pan with oil spray. Add 2 tablespoons everything bagel seasoning to pan and shake until bottom and sides of pan are evenly coated. Transfer dough to prepared pan, seam side down, pushing it in at edges to fit if necessary. Using sharp paring knife or single-edge razor blade, make six ¼-inch-deep slashes crosswise along surface of dough, about 1 inch apart. Brush dough with egg wash, then sprinkle with remaining 4 teaspoons everything bagel seasoning. Bake until loaf is golden brown and registers at least 200 degrees, about 45 minutes. Let bread cool completely in pan on wire rack, about 2 hours, before serving.

BOILING BAGEL BREAD

1 Boil risen dough in solution of water mixed with baking soda and corn syrup for 45 seconds per side.

2 Let boiled dough cool slightly and then transfer it to pan coated with everything bagel seasoning. Loaf may appear misshapen; that's OK.

Cranberry-Walnut Bread

MAKES 1 loaf | **TOTAL TIME** 1¾ hours, plus 5 hours rising and cooling

Why This Recipe Works Baked goods studded with tart dried cranberries and rich toasted walnuts often grace the table in the fall and winter—but these offerings are typically sweet. This sturdy yet moist torpedo-shaped sandwich bread brings these seasonal flavors to the table in savory fashion, perfect for sandwiching chicken salad or leftover roast turkey or for toasting in the morning to spread with butter or cream cheese. Mixing some whole-wheat flour with the bread flour for this loaf creates a weaker gluten network than using all bread flour; this helps yield a lighter texture in the finished bread. Plus, the whole-wheat flour really complements the earthy, faintly bitter walnuts. To prevent the bottom crust from turning too dark while baking, set the loaf on two stacked baking sheets for added insulation and bake the loaf on the middle oven rack. This browns the entire exterior evenly and beautifully.

- 2¼ cups (12⅓ ounces) bread flour
- 10 tablespoons (3½ ounces) whole-wheat flour
- ¾ cup dried cranberries
- ¾ cup walnuts, toasted and chopped
- 2 teaspoons instant or rapid-rise yeast
- 2 teaspoons table salt
- 1¼ cups water, room temperature
- 2 tablespoons packed light brown sugar
- 1 tablespoon vegetable oil
- 1 large egg beaten with 1 teaspoon water

1 Whisk bread flour, whole-wheat flour, cranberries, walnuts, yeast, and salt together in bowl of stand mixer. Whisk room-temperature water, sugar, and oil in 4-cup liquid measuring cup until sugar has dissolved.

2 Using dough hook on low speed, slowly add water mixture to flour mixture and mix until cohesive dough starts to form and no dry flour remains, about 2 minutes, scraping down bowl as needed. Increase speed to medium-low and knead until dough is smooth and elastic and clears sides of bowl, about 8 minutes.

3 Transfer dough to lightly floured counter and knead by hand to form smooth, round ball, about 30 seconds. Place dough seam side down in lightly greased large bowl or container; cover tightly with plastic wrap; and let rise until doubled in size, 1½ to 2 hours.

4 Stack 2 rimmed baking sheets and line with aluminum foil. Press down on dough to deflate. Turn out dough onto lightly floured counter (side of dough that was against bowl should now be facing up). Press and stretch dough into 6-inch square. Fold top corners of dough diagonally into center of square and press gently to seal. Stretch and fold upper third of dough toward center and press seam gently to seal. Stretch and fold dough in half toward you to form rough 8 by 4-inch loaf and pinch seam closed. Roll loaf seam side down. Gently slide your hands underneath each end of loaf and transfer to prepared sheet. Reshape loaf as needed, tucking edges under to form taut torpedo shape. Cover loosely with greased plastic and let rise until loaf increases in size by about half and dough springs back minimally when poked gently with your knuckle, 30 minutes to 1 hour.

5 Adjust oven rack to middle position and heat oven to 450 degrees. Using sharp paring knife or single-edge razor blade, make one ½-inch-deep slash with swift, fluid motion lengthwise along top of loaf, starting and stopping about ½ inch from ends. Gently brush loaf with egg wash and bake for 15 minutes. Reduce oven temperature to 375 degrees and continue to bake until loaf is dark brown and registers 205 to 210 degrees, 30 to 35 minutes, rotating sheet halfway through baking. Transfer loaf to wire rack and let cool completely, about 3 hours, before serving.

Prosciutto Bread

MAKES 2 loaves | TOTAL TIME 1¼ hours, plus 5¼ hours rising and cooling

3 cups (16½ ounces) bread flour

1½ teaspoons instant or rapid-rise yeast

1 teaspoon table salt

1 cup mild lager, room temperature

6 tablespoons water, room temperature

3 tablespoons extra-virgin olive oil

3 ounces ¼-inch-thick slices prosciutto, cut into ½-inch pieces

3 ounces ¼-inch-thick slices pepperoni, cut into ½-inch pieces

3 ounces ¼-inch-thick slices capicola, cut into ½-inch pieces

1½ teaspoons coarsely ground pepper

Cornmeal

Why This Recipe Works Prosciutto bread is an Italian American specialty that you're as likely to find in an Italian butcher shop as you are in an Italian bakery. That's because it's loaded with savory, satisfying little nuggets of cured pork. To make our version extra-meaty, we include a combination of prosciutto, capicola (also called coppa), and pepperoni. The cut of the meat is important here. The usual thin deli-style slices will wad up in the dough, but thicker slabs cut into ½-inch pieces work just right. Bread flour, with its higher protein content than all-purpose flour, forms a strong gluten structure to support all the meat morsels, and adding beer to the dough boosts the yeasty, fermented flavor of the bread without having to let it rise all day. A generous amount of black pepper adds an assertively spicy flavor backbone. We love the combo of prosciutto, pepperoni, and capicola, but you can use 9 ounces of any combination of your favorite cured meats; just be sure to have each one sliced ¼ inch thick at the deli counter. Do not use thinly sliced deli meats, as they will adversely affect the bread's texture. Use a mild lager, such as Budweiser; strongly flavored beers will make this bread taste bitter.

1 Whisk flour, yeast, and salt together in bowl of stand mixer. Whisk beer, room-temperature water, and oil together in 2-cup liquid measuring cup.

2 Using dough hook on low speed, slowly add beer mixture to flour mixture and mix until cohesive dough starts to form and no dry flour remains, about 2 minutes, scraping down bowl as needed. Increase speed to medium and knead until dough is smooth and elastic and clears sides of bowl, about 8 minutes.

3 Reduce speed to low and add prosciutto, pepperoni, capicola, and pepper. Continue to knead until combined, about 2 minutes (some meats may not be fully incorporated into dough at this point; this is OK). Transfer dough and any errant pieces of meats to lightly floured counter and knead by hand to evenly incorporate meats into dough, about 1 minute.

4 Form dough into smooth, round ball and place seam side down in lightly greased large bowl. Cover tightly with plastic wrap and let dough rise at room temperature until doubled in size, about 1½ hours. (Dough can be refrigerated for at least 16 hours or up to 24 hours. Let dough come to room temperature, about 3 hours, before proceeding with step 5.)

5 Line rimmed baking sheet with parchment paper and lightly dust with cornmeal. Turn out dough onto counter and gently press down to deflate any large air pockets. Cut dough into 2 even pieces. Press each piece of dough into 8 by 5-inch rectangle with long side parallel to counter edge.

6 Working with 1 piece of dough, fold top edge of rectangle down to midline, pressing to seal. Fold bottom edge of rectangle up to midline and pinch to seal. Flip dough seam side down and gently roll into 12-inch loaf with tapered ends. Transfer loaf to 1 side of prepared sheet. Repeat shaping with second piece of dough and place loaf about 3 inches from first loaf on sheet. Cover with greased plastic and let rise at room temperature until puffy and dough springs back minimally when poked gently with your knuckle, about 45 minutes.

7 Adjust oven rack to middle position and heat oven to 450 degrees. Using sharp paring knife or single-edge razor blade, make one ½-inch-deep slash with swift, fluid motion lengthwise along top of each loaf, starting and stopping about 1½ inches from ends. Bake until loaves register 205 to 210 degrees, 22 to 25 minutes. Transfer loaves to wire rack and let cool completely, about 3 hours, before serving.

Variation

Prosciutto Bread with Provolone

Add 5 ounces provolone, sliced ¼ inch thick and cut into ½-inch pieces, with meats in step 3.

Spicy Olive Bread

MAKES 1 loaf | **TOTAL TIME** 1¾ hours, plus 5 hours rising and cooling

Why This Recipe Works An artisan bakery–style round bread generously flavored with olives, garlic, and red pepper flakes is perfect for slicing and using to build a rustic Italian salumi sandwich. Olive bread recipes sometimes go to convoluted lengths to incorporate olives without bruising them and staining the dough, but here you'll simply knead the plain dough in a stand mixer on medium-low speed as you normally would and then reduce the mixer speed to low and slowly add the olives. The low-speed mixing is gentle enough that it doesn't beat up the olives' flesh and lead to color bleeding. To create a crust that's crisp and crackly but still delicate, you'll bake the loaf in the steamy environment of a covered Dutch oven. Almost any variety of brined or oil-cured olive works in this recipe, although we favor a mix of green and black olives.

¾ cup pitted olives, rinsed, patted dry, and chopped coarse

2 garlic cloves, minced

3 cups (16½ ounces) bread flour

2 teaspoons instant or rapid-rise yeast

2 teaspoons table salt

2 teaspoons red pepper flakes

1⅓ cups water, room temperature

2 tablespoons sugar

1 tablespoon extra-virgin olive oil

1. Combine olives and garlic in bowl. Whisk flour, yeast, salt, and pepper flakes together in bowl of stand mixer. Whisk room-temperature water, sugar, and oil in 4-cup liquid measuring cup until sugar has dissolved. Using dough hook on low speed, slowly add water mixture to flour mixture and mix until cohesive dough starts to form and no dry flour remains, about 2 minutes, scraping down bowl as needed.

2. Increase speed to medium-low and knead until dough is smooth and elastic and clears sides of bowl, about 8 minutes. Reduce speed to low; slowly add olive mixture, ¼ cup at a time; and mix until mostly incorporated, about 1 minute.

3. Transfer dough to lightly floured counter and knead by hand to form smooth, round ball, about 30 seconds. Place dough seam side down in greased large bowl; cover tightly with plastic wrap; and let rise until doubled in size, 1½ to 2 hours.

4. Press down on dough to deflate. Turn out dough onto lightly floured counter (side of dough that was against bowl should now be facing up). Press and stretch dough into 10-inch round. Working around circumference of dough, fold edges toward center until ball forms. Flip dough ball seam side down and, using your cupped hands, drag in small circles on counter until dough feels taut and round and all seams are secured on underside of loaf.

5. Lay 16 by 12-inch sheet of parchment paper on counter and lightly spray with vegetable oil spray. Transfer loaf seam side down to center of prepared parchment. Using parchment as sling, gently lower loaf into Dutch oven. Cover tightly with plastic and let rise until loaf increases in size by about half and dough springs back minimally when poked gently with your knuckle, 30 minutes to 1 hour.

6. Adjust oven rack to middle position and heat oven to 450 degrees. Using sharp paring knife or single-edge razor blade, make two 5-inch-long, ½-inch-deep slashes with swift, fluid motion along top of loaf to form cross. Cover pot, place in oven, and bake loaf for 30 minutes. Remove lid; reduce oven temperature to 375 degrees and continue to bake until loaf is deep golden brown and registers 205 to 210 degrees, 20 to 25 minutes. Using parchment sling, remove loaf from pot and transfer to wire rack; discard parchment. Let cool completely, about 3 hours, before serving.

Fig and Fennel Bread

MAKES 1 loaf | **TOTAL TIME** 4 hours, plus 11¼ hours rising and cooling

Sponge

- 1 cup (5½ ounces) bread flour
- ¾ cup water, room temperature
- ⅛ teaspoon instant or rapid-rise yeast

Dough

- 1 cup plus 2 tablespoons (6¼ ounces) bread flour
- 1 cup (5½ ounces) light or medium rye flour
- 1 tablespoon fennel seeds, toasted
- 2 teaspoons table salt
- 1½ teaspoons instant or rapid-rise yeast
- 1 cup water, room temperature
- 1 cup dried figs, stemmed and chopped coarse
- Cornmeal

Why This Recipe Works This company-worthy artisan loaf, with its sophisticated pairing of sweet, earthy dried figs and complementary fennel seeds, is ideal for accompanying cheese and charcuterie plates. Blending some rye flour into the mix along with bread flour adds even more flavor intrigue. Starting the dough with a sponge develops lots of complex flavor, and making a series of folds as the dough rises incorporates air, which gives the bread better structure and a more open crumb. We sometimes use a Dutch oven to create a humid, moist bread-baking environment, which fosters an airy crumb and a beautifully browned, crisp crust on the finished bread. Here we go a step further by preheating the Dutch oven before placing the loaf inside. The Dutch oven's heavy cast-iron construction helps the vessel retain heat effectively. In combination with the steamy covered environment, this mimics the use of a baking stone or steel and lava rocks to help achieve the rustic crumb of a bakery-quality bread. Dusting the top of the loaf with cornmeal before baking gives it a rustic finished appearance and a light crunch. While any variety of dried figs will work, we especially like the flavor of Calimyrna figs. Use light or medium rye flour; dark rye flour will be overpowering. Toast the fennel seeds in a dry skillet over medium heat until fragrant (about 1 minute), and then remove the seeds from the skillet so that the seeds won't scorch.

1 **For the sponge** Stir flour, room-temperature water, and yeast in 4-cup liquid measuring cup with wooden spoon until well combined. Cover tightly with plastic wrap and let sit at room temperature until sponge has risen and begins to collapse, about 6 hours (sponge can sit at room temperature for up to 24 hours).

2 **For the dough** Whisk bread flour, rye flour, fennel seeds, salt, and yeast together in bowl of stand mixer. Stir room-temperature water into sponge with wooden spoon until well combined. Using dough hook on low speed, slowly add sponge mixture to flour mixture and mix until cohesive dough starts to form and no dry flour remains, about 2 minutes, scraping down bowl as needed.

3 Increase speed to medium-low and continue to knead until dough is smooth, elastic, and slightly sticky, about 5 minutes. Reduce speed to low; slowly add figs, ¼ cup at a time; and mix until mostly incorporated, about 1 minute. Transfer dough to lightly greased large bowl or container, cover tightly with plastic, and let rise for 30 minutes.

4 Using greased bowl scraper (or your fingertips), fold dough over itself by gently lifting and folding edge of dough toward middle. Turn bowl 45 degrees and fold dough again; repeat turning bowl and folding dough 6 more times (total of 8 folds). Cover tightly with plastic and let rise for 30 minutes. Repeat folding and rising. Fold dough again, then cover bowl tightly with plastic and let rise until nearly doubled in size, 45 minutes to 1¼ hours.

5 Lay 18 by 12-inch sheet of parchment paper on counter, lightly spray with vegetable oil spray, and dust evenly with cornmeal. Transfer dough to lightly floured counter. Using your lightly floured hands, press and stretch dough into 10-inch round, deflating any gas pockets larger than 1 inch.

6 Shape dough into ball by pulling edges into middle, then flip dough ball seam side down and, using your cupped hands, drag in small circles on counter until dough feels taut and round and all seams are secured on underside of loaf. Place loaf, seam side down, in center of prepared parchment and cover loosely with greased plastic. Let rise until loaf increases in size by about half and dough springs back minimally when poked gently with your knuckle, about 30 minutes.

7 Thirty minutes before baking, adjust oven rack to lower-middle position, place Dutch oven (with lid) on rack, and heat oven to 500 degrees. Using sharp paring knife or single-edge razor blade, make two 5-inch-long, ½-inch-deep slashes with swift, fluid motion along top of loaf to form cross. Dust top of loaf with cornmeal.

8 Carefully transfer pot to wire rack and uncover. Using parchment as sling, gently lower loaf into pot. Cover pot, tucking any excess parchment into pot, and return to oven. Reduce oven temperature to 425 degrees and bake loaf for 15 minutes (start timing as soon as bread goes in oven). Remove lid and continue to bake until loaf is deep golden brown and registers 205 to 210 degrees, about 20 minutes.

9 Using parchment sling, remove loaf from pot and transfer to wire rack; discard parchment. Let cool completely, about 3 hours, before serving.

SLASHING A LOAF

Using sharp paring knife or single-edge razor blade, make two 5-inch-long, ½-inch-deep slashes with swift, fluid motion along top of loaf to form cross.

Caramelized Onion Bread

MAKES 1 loaf | **TOTAL TIME** 3½ hours, plus 12½ hours rising, resting, and cooling

Sponge

⅔ cup (3⅔ ounces) bread flour

½ cup water, room temperature

⅛ teaspoon instant or rapid-rise yeast

Dough

2 tablespoons extra-virgin olive oil

3 cups finely chopped onions

2 garlic cloves, minced

2 teaspoons minced fresh thyme or ½ teaspoon dried

2 teaspoons packed brown sugar

2 teaspoons table salt, divided

¼ teaspoon pepper

2⅓ cups (12¾ ounces) bread flour

1¼ teaspoons instant or rapid-rise yeast

¾ cup plus 2 tablespoons water, room temperature

2 disposable aluminum pie plates

Why This Recipe Works Savory-sweet caramelized onions pack this artisan-style loaf with deeply concentrated flavor. You'll start by making a sponge, which is simply a mixture of a portion of the dough's flour, water, and yeast that ferments for around 6 hours to develop more complex flavor; it then gets mixed into the rest of the dough ingredients. You'll load a whopping 3 cups of onions into this bread, first cooking them down with brown sugar, garlic, and thyme to a deep golden brown. Finely chopped onions work best—larger pieces will leave you with soggy pockets of uncooked dough surrounding the onions. A two-pronged approach to incorporating the onions ensures that their flavor permeates every bite: First, mix half of them with the wet ingredients at the beginning of mixing, where they'll break down during kneading. Second, add the remaining half at the end of kneading to provide great textural contrast. Yellow onions offer a good flavor and a firm texture. You can use white or red onions, but the flavor will be different. Vidalia onions have a high water content and will make the dough too wet. If you own a round banneton, you may use that instead of a towel-lined colander; either way, enclosing the proofing dough in a plastic garbage bag protects it from forming a tough skin. If you don't have a baking peel, use a rimless or overturned baking sheet to slide the bread onto the baking stone. If you don't have a baking stone or steel, you can use a preheated rimless or overturned baking sheet; however, the crust will be less crisp. This recipe uses lava rocks to achieve a bakery-style loaf. For the best texture and height, we don't recommend omitting them; see page 21 for more information on lava rocks.

1 **For the sponge** Stir flour, room-temperature water, and yeast in 4-cup liquid measuring cup with wooden spoon until well combined. Cover tightly with plastic wrap and let sit at room temperature until sponge has risen and begins to collapse, about 6 hours (sponge can sit at room temperature for up to 24 hours).

2 **For the dough** Heat oil in 12-inch nonstick skillet over medium heat until shimmering. Stir in onions, garlic, thyme, sugar, ½ teaspoon salt, and pepper. Cover and cook, stirring occasionally, until onions are softened and have released their juice, 3 to 5 minutes. Remove lid and continue to cook, stirring often, until juice evaporates and onions are deep golden brown, 10 to 15 minutes. Transfer onion mixture to bowl and let cool completely before using.

3 Whisk flour and yeast together in bowl of stand mixer. Stir room-temperature water and half of onion mixture into sponge with wooden spoon until well combined. Using dough hook on low speed, slowly add sponge mixture to flour mixture and mix until cohesive dough starts to form and no dry flour remains, about 2 minutes, scraping down bowl as needed. Cover bowl tightly with plastic and let dough rest for 20 minutes.

4 Add remaining 1½ teaspoons salt to dough and knead on medium-low speed until dough is smooth and elastic and clears sides of bowl, about 5 minutes. Reduce speed to low; slowly add remaining onion mixture, 1 tablespoon at a time; and mix until mostly incorporated, about 1 minute. Transfer dough to lightly greased large bowl or container, cover tightly with plastic, and let rise for 30 minutes.

5 Using greased bowl scraper (or your fingertips), fold dough over itself by gently lifting and folding edge of dough toward middle. Turn bowl 45 degrees and fold dough again; repeat turning bowl and folding dough 6 more times (total of 8 folds). Cover tightly with plastic and let rise for 30 minutes. Repeat folding and rising. Fold dough again, then cover bowl tightly with plastic and let dough rise until nearly doubled in size, 45 minutes to 1¼ hours.

6 Mist underside of large linen or cotton tea towel with water. Line 5-quart colander with prepared towel and dust evenly with flour. Transfer dough to lightly floured counter (side of dough that was against bowl should now be against counter). Press and stretch dough into 10-inch round, deflating any gas pockets larger than 1 inch. Working around circumference of dough, fold edges toward center until ball forms. Flip dough ball seam side down and, using your cupped hands, drag in small circles on counter until dough feels taut and round and all seams are secured on underside of loaf.

7 Place loaf seam side up in prepared colander and pinch any remaining seams closed. Loosely fold edges of towel over loaf to enclose, then place colander in large plastic garbage bag. Tie, or fold under, open end of bag to fully enclose. Let rise until loaf increases in size by about half and dough springs back minimally when poked gently with your knuckle, 1 to 1½ hours (remove loaf from bag to test).

8 One hour before baking, adjust oven racks to lower-middle and lowest positions. Place baking stone or steel on upper rack, place disposable pie plates filled with 1 quart lava rocks each on lower rack, and heat oven to 425 degrees. Bring 1 cup water to boil. Remove colander from bag, unfold edges of towel, and dust top of loaf with flour. (If any seams have reopened, pinch closed before dusting with flour.) Lay 16 by 12-inch sheet of parchment paper on top of loaf. Using 1 hand to support parchment and loaf, invert loaf onto parchment and place on counter. Gently remove colander and towel. Transfer parchment with loaf to baking peel.

9 Carefully pour ½ cup boiling water into 1 disposable pie plate of preheated rocks and close oven door for 1 minute to create steam. Using sharp paring knife or single-edge razor blade, make two 7-inch-long, ½-inch-deep slashes with swift, fluid motion along top of loaf to form cross.

10 Working quickly, slide parchment with loaf onto baking stone and pour remaining ½ cup boiling water into second disposable pie plate of preheated rocks. Bake until crust is dark brown and loaf registers 205 to 210 degrees, 45 to 50 minutes, rotating loaf halfway through baking. Transfer loaf to wire rack; discard parchment; and let cool completely, about 3 hours, before serving.

USING LAVA ROCKS

Carefully pour ½ cup boiling water into 1 disposable pie plate of preheated rocks and close oven door for 1 minute to create steam. Place loaf onto baking stone and then pour remaining ½ cup boiling water into second pie plate of preheated rocks.

Cheddar and Black Pepper Bread

MAKES 1 loaf | **TOTAL TIME** 4½ hours, plus 13½ hours rising, resting, and cooling

Sponge

⅔ cup (3⅔ ounces) bread flour

½ cup water, room temperature

⅛ teaspoon instant or
rapid-rise yeast

Dough

2⅓ cups (12¾ ounces) bread flour

1¼ teaspoons instant or
rapid-rise yeast

1¼ teaspoons coarsely ground
pepper, divided

1 cup water, room temperature

2 teaspoons table salt

8 ounces cheddar cheese,
shredded (2 cups),
room temperature, divided

2 disposable aluminum
pie plates

Why This Recipe Works This yeasted cheesy bread is decadent, featuring big cheddar flavor and a lingering finish of zesty black pepper. Its rusticity makes you want to tear it into generous chunks to dunk into a bowl of tomato soup. Making a bread this cheesy isn't as simple as just kneading the generous amount of shredded cheddar into the dough, because the fatty cheese will coat the gluten strands, preventing them from linking up into a strong network. To achieve a sturdy and flavorful crumb with pockets of melted cheese, knead just half of the cheese into the dough and then roll in the remaining cheese jelly roll–style before shaping the dough into a round loaf. Look for a cheddar aged for about one year. (Avoid cheddar aged for longer; it won't melt well.) Use the large holes of a box grater to shred the cheddar. If you own a round banneton, you may use that instead of a towel-lined colander; either way, enclosing the proofing dough in a plastic garbage bag protects it from forming a tough skin. If you don't have a baking peel, use a rimless or overturned baking sheet to slide the bread onto the baking stone. If you don't have a baking stone or steel, you can use a preheated rimless or overturned baking sheet; however, the crust will be less crisp. This recipe uses lava rocks to achieve a bakery-style loaf. For the best texture and height, we don't recommend omitting them; see page 21 for more information on lava rocks.

1 **For the sponge** Stir flour, room-temperature water, and yeast in 4-cup liquid measuring cup with wooden spoon until well combined. Cover tightly with plastic wrap and let sit at room temperature until sponge has risen and begins to collapse, about 6 hours (sponge can sit at room temperature for up to 24 hours).

2 **For the dough** Whisk flour, yeast, and ¾ teaspoon pepper together in bowl of stand mixer. Stir room-temperature water into sponge with wooden spoon until well combined. Using dough hook on low speed, slowly add sponge mixture to flour mixture and mix until cohesive dough starts to form and no dry flour remains, about 2 minutes, scraping down bowl as needed. Cover bowl tightly with plastic and let dough rest for 20 minutes.

3 Add salt to dough and knead on medium-low speed until dough is smooth and elastic and clears sides of bowl, about 5 minutes. Reduce speed to low; slowly add 1 cup cheddar, ¼ cup at a time; and mix until just incorporated, about 30 seconds. Transfer dough to lightly greased large bowl or container, cover tightly with plastic, and let rise for 30 minutes.

4 Using greased bowl scraper (or your fingertips), fold dough over itself by gently lifting and folding edge of dough toward middle. Turn bowl 45 degrees and fold dough again; repeat turning bowl and folding dough 6 more times (total of 8 folds). Cover tightly with plastic and let rise for 30 minutes. Repeat folding and rising every 30 minutes, 3 more times. After fourth set of folds, cover bowl tightly with plastic and let dough rise until nearly doubled in size, 1 to 1½ hours.

5 Mist underside of large linen or cotton tea towel with water. Line 5-quart colander with prepared towel and dust evenly with flour. Transfer dough to lightly floured counter (side of dough that was against bowl should now be against counter). Press and stretch dough into 10-inch square, deflating any gas pockets larger than 1 inch. Sprinkle remaining 1 cup cheddar evenly over dough, leaving ½-inch border. Roll dough away from you into snug cylinder. Pinch seam closed. Turn cylinder seam side up and roll away from you into snug spiral, ending with tail end on bottom. Pinch side seams together to seal. Using your cupped hands, drag dough in small circles on counter until dough feels taut and round and all seams are secured on underside of loaf. (Some cheddar may become exposed.)

6 Place loaf seam side up in prepared colander and pinch any remaining seams closed. Loosely fold edges of towel over loaf to enclose, then place colander in large plastic garbage bag. Tie, or fold under, open end of bag to fully enclose. Let rise until loaf increases in size by about half and dough springs back minimally when poked gently with your knuckle, 30 minutes to 1 hour (remove loaf from bag to test).

7 One hour before baking, adjust oven racks to lower-middle and lowest positions. Place baking stone or steel on upper rack, place disposable pie plates filled with 1 quart lava rocks each on lower rack, and heat oven to 450 degrees. Bring 1 cup water to boil. Remove colander from bag, unfold edges of towel, and dust top of loaf with flour. (If any seams have reopened, pinch closed before dusting with flour.) Lay 16 by 12-inch sheet of parchment paper on top of loaf. Using 1 hand to support parchment and loaf, invert loaf onto parchment and place on counter. Gently remove colander and towel. Transfer parchment with loaf to baking peel.

8 Carefully pour ½ cup boiling water into 1 disposable pie plate of preheated rocks and close oven door for 1 minute to create steam. Meanwhile, using sharp paring knife or single-edge razor blade, make two 7-inch-long, ½-inch-deep slashes with swift, fluid motion along top of loaf to form cross. Sprinkle top of loaf with remaining ½ teaspoon pepper.

9 Working quickly, slide parchment with loaf onto baking stone and pour remaining ½ cup boiling water into second disposable pie plate of preheated rocks. Bake until crust is dark brown and loaf registers 205 to 210 degrees, 35 to 40 minutes, rotating loaf halfway through baking. Transfer loaf to wire rack; discard parchment; and let cool completely, about 3 hours, before serving.

SHAPING CHEDDAR BREAD

1 Sprinkle cheddar cheese evenly over dough, leaving ½-inch border. Roll dough away from you into snug cylinder. Pinch seam closed.

2 Turn cylinder seam side up and roll away from you into snug spiral, ending with tail end on bottom. Pinch side seams together to seal.

3 Using your cupped hands, drag dough in small circles on counter until dough feels taut and round and all seams are secured on underside of loaf.

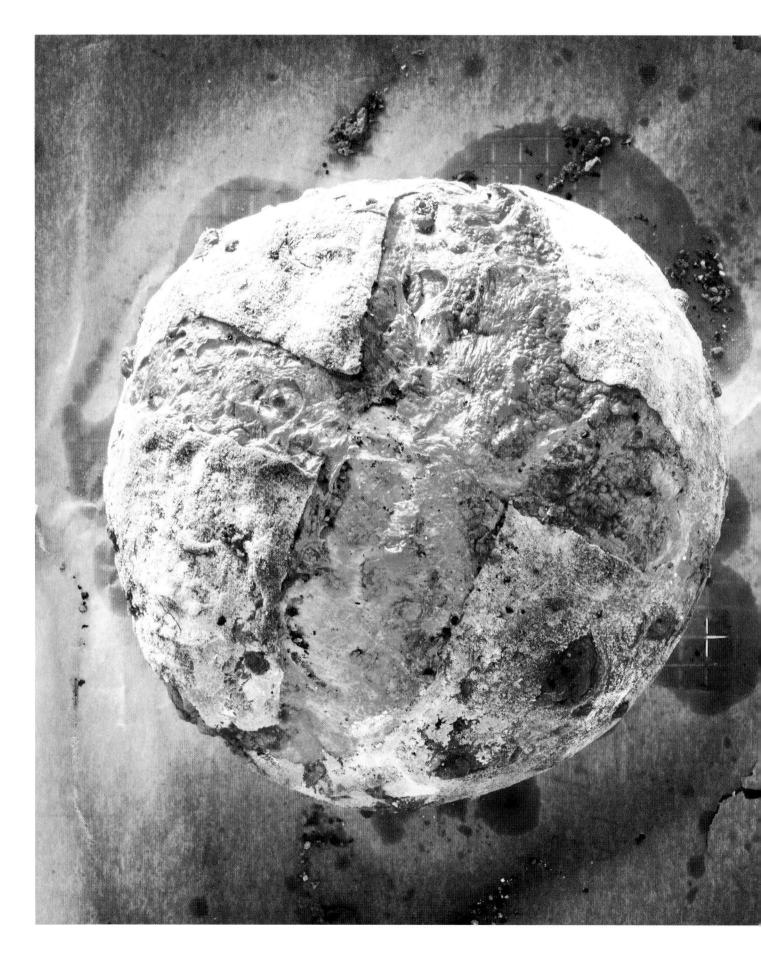

Sage-Polenta Bread

MAKES 1 loaf | **TOTAL TIME** 2¼ hours, plus 11 hours rising, resting, and cooling

Sponge

- ⅔ cup (3⅔ ounces) bread flour
- ½ cup water, room temperature
- ¼ teaspoon instant or rapid-rise yeast

Dough

- 1¼ cups plus 2 tablespoons water, room temperature, divided
- ¼ cup (1¼ ounces) plus 1 tablespoon coarse-ground polenta, divided
- 2⅓ cups (12¾ ounces) bread flour
- 2¼ teaspoons instant or rapid-rise yeast
- 2 tablespoons extra-virgin olive oil
- 4 teaspoons minced fresh sage
- 1½ teaspoons table salt

- 2 disposable aluminum pie plates

Why This Recipe Works This is unlike any "cornbread" you've ever had before. The savory corn flavor and pleasingly grainy texture of polenta make it a unique addition to an artisan-style Italian loaf. Coarse-ground polenta parcooked for just a few minutes on the stovetop contributes a soft, pillowy texture with just the right amount of chew. Since polenta increases dramatically in volume once it's cooked, you won't be able to stir all of it into the dough after kneading. Instead, you'll incorporate it in two stages, adding half to the mixer along with the sponge at the beginning of mixing and the remaining half after a brief rest, at the end of mixing. This method results in delightful pockets of cooked polenta swirled throughout the hearty loaf. Fresh sage adds herbal notes to reinforce the Italian flavor theme. Coating the loaf with dry polenta (aka cornmeal) before baking gives the baked bread a crunchy, golden exterior. Do not substitute instant polenta or prepared polenta (sold in a tube) here; either will yield a disastrous loaf. If you don't have a baking peel, use a rimless or overturned baking sheet to slide the bread onto the baking stone. If you don't have a baking stone or steel, you can use a preheated rimless or overturned baking sheet; however, the crust will be less crisp. See page 21 for more information on using a couche and flipping board. Enclosing the proofing dough inside a plastic garbage bag prevents it from forming a tough skin. This recipe uses lava rocks to achieve a bakery-style loaf. For the best texture and height, we don't recommend omitting them; see page 21 for more information on lava rocks.

1 For the sponge Stir flour, room-temperature water, and yeast in 4-cup liquid measuring cup with wooden spoon until well combined. Cover tightly with plastic wrap and let sit at room temperature until sponge has risen and begins to collapse, about 6 hours (sponge can sit at room temperature for up to 24 hours).

2 For the dough Bring ¾ cup room-temperature water and ¼ cup polenta to simmer in small saucepan over medium heat and cook, stirring frequently, until polenta is softened and water is completely absorbed, about 3 minutes; let cool completely before using.

3 Whisk flour and yeast together in bowl of stand mixer. Break cooked polenta into small pieces with wooden spoon. Stir half of cooked polenta and remaining ½ cup plus 2 tablespoons room-temperature water into sponge until well combined. Using dough hook on low speed, slowly add sponge mixture to flour mixture and mix until cohesive dough starts to form and no dry flour remains, about 2 minutes, scraping down bowl as needed. Cover bowl tightly with plastic and let dough rest for 20 minutes.

4 Add oil, sage, and salt to dough and knead on medium-low speed until dough is smooth and elastic and clears sides of bowl, about 5 minutes. Reduce speed to low; slowly add remaining cooked polenta, 1 tablespoon at a time; and mix until mostly incorporated, about 1 minute. Transfer dough to lightly greased large bowl or container, cover tightly with plastic, and let rise for 30 minutes.

5 Using greased bowl scraper (or your fingertips), fold dough over itself by gently lifting and folding edge of dough toward middle. Turn bowl 45 degrees and fold dough again; repeat turning bowl and folding dough 6 more times (total of 8 folds). Cover tightly with plastic and let rise for 30 minutes. Repeat folding, then cover bowl tightly with plastic and let dough rise until nearly doubled in size, 30 minutes to 1 hour.

6 Mist underside of couche with water and drape over inverted rimmed baking sheet. Dust couche evenly with flour, then sprinkle with remaining 1tablespoon uncooked polenta. Transfer dough to lightly floured counter (side of dough that was against bowl should now be against counter). Press and stretch dough into 10-inch square, deflating any gas pockets larger than 1 inch. Fold top and bottom corners of dough diagonally into center of square and press gently to seal. Stretch and fold upper and bottom thirds of dough toward center and press gently to seal. Stretch and fold dough in half toward you to form rough 12 by 4½-inch diamond-shaped loaf, and pinch seam closed. Gently slide your hands underneath each end of loaf and transfer seam side up to prepared couche. On either side of loaf, pinch couche into pleat, then fold remaining edges of couche over loaf to cover completely. Carefully place sheet inside large plastic garbage bag. Tie, or fold under, open end of bag to fully enclose. Let rise until loaf increases in size by about half and dough springs back minimally when poked gently with your knuckle, about 30 minutes (remove loaf from bag to test).

7 One hour before baking, adjust oven racks to lower-middle and lowest positions. Place baking stone or steel on upper rack, place disposable pie plates filled with 1 quart lava rocks each on lower rack, and heat oven to 425 degrees. Line baking peel with 16 by 12-inch piece of parchment paper, with long edge perpendicular to handle. Bring 1 cup water to boil.

8 Remove sheet with loaf from bag. Unfold couche, pulling from ends to remove pleats. Dust top of loaf with flour. (If any seams have reopened, pinch closed before dusting with flour.) Gently pushing with side of flipping board, roll loaf over so it is seam side down. Using your hand, hold long edge of flipping board between loaf and couche at 45-degree angle, then lift couche with your other hand and flip loaf seam side up onto board. Invert loaf seam side down onto prepared baking peel. Reshape loaf as needed, tucking edges under to form taut diamond shape.

9 Carefully pour ½ cup boiling water into 1 disposable pie plate of preheated rocks and close oven door for 1 minute to create steam. Meanwhile, using sharp paring knife or single-edge razor blade, make three 6-inch-long, ½-inch-deep diagonal slashes with swift, fluid motion across top of loaf, starting and stopping about ½ inch from edges and spacing slashes about 2 inches apart.

10 Working quickly, slide parchment with loaf onto baking stone and pour remaining ½ cup boiling water into second disposable pie plate of preheated rocks. Bake until crust is deep golden brown and loaf registers 205 to 210 degrees, 45 to 50 minutes, rotating loaf halfway through baking. Transfer loaf to wire rack; discard parchment; and let cool completely, about 3 hours, before serving.

Focaccia with Caramelized Red Onion, Pancetta, and Oregano

MAKES two 9-inch round loaves | TOTAL TIME 1¼ hours, plus 9½ hours resting, rising, and cooling

Sponge

- ½ cup (2½ ounces) all-purpose flour
- ⅓ cup water, room temperature
- ¼ teaspoon instant or rapid-rise yeast

Dough

- 2½ cups (12½ ounces) all-purpose flour
- 1¼ cups plus 2 tablespoons water, room temperature, divided
- 1 teaspoon instant or rapid-rise yeast
- 1 tablespoon kosher salt, divided
- 4 ounces finely chopped pancetta
- 1 red onion, chopped
- 2 teaspoons minced fresh oregano
- ¼ cup extra-virgin olive oil

Why This Recipe Works Descended from an ancient Roman flatbread, focaccia is beloved throughout Italy, and our version takes inspiration from the fundamental Ligurian recipe, adding jammy red onions, crispy pancetta, and fresh oregano. The key to focaccia is using a traditional sponge, which brings the benefits of minimal-effort slow fermentation. This mixture of flour, water, and yeast rests until its flavor grows stronger and more complex. Using an almost no-knead method mixes the ingredients without overdeveloping the gluten. Gently turning the dough over itself at regular intervals as it proofs takes the place of kneading. This technique aerates the dough to replenish the oxygen that yeast needs to work; elongates and redistributes the bubbles; and ensures a chewy, airy interior. Focaccia is often free-form, but using round cake pans and drizzling the bottoms of the pans with oil results in foolproof focaccia with a crackly bottom. Many recipes call for mixing olive oil into the dough, but coating the exterior only helps keep the insides of the breads light while adding rich flavor to the outsides, where it has plenty of impact. Sprinkling a little coarse salt into the pans means crunchy, textural salty bits on the outsides of the finished breads. If you don't have a baking stone or steel, you can use a preheated rimless or overturned baking sheet; however, the crust will be less crisp.

1 **For the sponge** Stir flour, room-temperature water, and yeast in large bowl with wooden spoon until well combined. Cover tightly with plastic wrap and let sit at room temperature until sponge has risen and begins to collapse, about 6 hours (sponge can sit at room temperature for up to 24 hours).

2 **For the dough** Stir flour, 1¼ cups room-temperature water, and yeast into sponge with wooden spoon until well combined. Cover bowl tightly with plastic; let dough rest for 15 minutes.

3 Stir 2 teaspoons salt into dough with wooden spoon until thoroughly incorporated, about 1 minute. Cover bowl tightly with plastic and let dough rest for 30 minutes.

4 Using greased bowl scraper or rubber spatula, fold dough over itself by gently lifting and folding edge of dough toward middle. Turn bowl 45 degrees and fold dough again; repeat turning bowl and folding dough 6 more times (total of 8 folds). Cover tightly with plastic and let rise for 30 minutes. Repeat folding and let dough rise 30 minutes longer. Fold dough 1 final time, then cover bowl tightly with plastic and let dough rise until nearly doubled in size, 30 minutes to 1 hour.

5 Meanwhile, cook pancetta in 12-inch skillet over medium heat, stirring occasionally, until fat is well rendered, about 10 minutes. Using slotted spoon, transfer pancetta to medium bowl. Add onion and remaining 2 tablespoons water to fat left in skillet and cook over medium heat until onion is softened and lightly browned, about 12 minutes. Transfer onion to bowl with pancetta and stir in oregano; let mixture cool completely.

6　One hour before baking, adjust oven rack to upper-middle position, place baking stone or steel on rack, and heat oven to 500 degrees. Coat two 9-inch round cake pans with 2 tablespoons oil each. Sprinkle each pan with ½ teaspoon salt. Transfer dough to lightly floured counter and dust top with flour. Divide dough in half and cover loosely with greased plastic. Working with 1 piece of dough at a time (keep remaining piece covered), shape into 5-inch round by gently tucking under edges.

7　Place dough rounds seam side up in prepared pans. Coat tops and sides with oil, then flip rounds so seam side is down. Cover loosely with greased plastic and let dough rest for 5 minutes.

8　Using your fingertips, gently press each dough round into corners of pan, taking care not to tear dough. (If dough resists stretching, let it relax for 5 to 10 minutes before trying to stretch it again.) Using fork, poke surface of dough 25 to 30 times, popping any large bubbles. Sprinkle pancetta mixture evenly over top of each loaf; cover loosely with greased plastic; and let dough rest until slightly bubbly, about 10 minutes.

9　Place pans on baking stone and reduce oven temperature to 450 degrees. Bake until tops are golden brown, 25 to 30 minutes, rotating pans halfway through baking. Let loaves cool in pans for 5 minutes. Remove loaves from pans and transfer to wire rack. Brush tops with any oil remaining in pans and let cool for 30 minutes. Serve warm or at room temperature.

Fougasse with Bacon and Gruyère

MAKES 2 loaves | **TOTAL TIME** 2¾ hours, plus 18¼ hours resting, rising, and cooling

4 slices thick-cut bacon, cut into ½-inch pieces

¼ cup (1⅓ ounces) whole-wheat flour

3 cups (15 ounces) all-purpose flour

1½ teaspoons table salt

1 teaspoon instant or rapid-rise yeast

1½ cups water, room temperature

Cornmeal or semolina flour

¼ cup extra-virgin olive oil, divided

4 ounces Gruyère cheese, shredded (1⅓ cups), divided

Why This Recipe Works Fougasse is a bread made for crust lovers, and here that crust is "stuffed" with crisp bacon and topped with nutty Gruyère cheese. Related by name and pedigree to Italian focaccia, French fougasse features a beautiful twist: After being stretched and flattened, the dough is given a series of cuts, usually in fanciful geometric patterns, to create multiple openings in the finished bread. These openings aren't just aesthetic: They dramatically increase the crust-to-crumb ratio so that nearly every bite includes an equal share of crispy crust and tender, airy interior. The cuts also help the bread bake very quickly. For this dough, you'll combine a little whole-wheat flour with the all-purpose flour for nutty flavor; sifting it to remove the bran prevents its sharp edges from cutting the long strands of gluten and compromising the bread's airy structure. You'll gently mix the dough and then fold it four times in 2 hours to produce an irregular, open crumb. Proofing it in the fridge maximizes flavor and also offers the flexibility of a bread that can be baked anytime from 16 to 48 hours after mixing and folding. To make shaping the fougasse easy, roll it out with a rolling pin, transfer it to parchment, and cut it with a pizza cutter. If you don't have a baking peel, use a rimless or overturned baking sheet to slide the fougasse onto the baking stone. If you don't have a baking stone or steel, you can use a preheated rimless or overturned baking sheet; however, the crust will be less crisp. We prefer King Arthur brand all-purpose flour in this recipe.

1 Cook bacon in 10-inch nonstick skillet over medium heat, stirring occasionally, until bacon is crisp and fat is well rendered, 6 to 8 minutes. Using slotted spoon, transfer bacon to paper towel–lined plate and set aside. Discard fat in skillet.

2 Sift whole-wheat flour through fine-mesh strainer into bowl of stand mixer; discard bran remaining in strainer. Add all-purpose flour, salt, yeast, and bacon to mixer bowl. Fit stand mixer with dough hook; add room-temperature water; and knead on low speed until cohesive dough forms and no dry flour remains, 5 to 7 minutes. Transfer dough to lightly oiled large bowl, cover with plastic wrap, and let rest at room temperature for 30 minutes.

3 Holding edge of dough with your fingertips, fold dough over itself by gently lifting and folding edge of dough toward center. Turn bowl 45 degrees and fold dough again; repeat turning bowl and folding dough 6 more times (total of 8 folds). Cover tightly with plastic and let rise for 30 minutes. Repeat folding and rising every 30 minutes, 3 more times. After fourth set of folds, cover bowl tightly with plastic and refrigerate for at least 16 hours or up to 2 days.

4 Transfer dough to lightly floured counter, stretch gently into 8-inch round (do not deflate), and divide in half. Working with 1 piece of dough at a time, gently stretch and fold over 3 sides of dough to create rough triangle with 5-inch sides. Transfer to lightly floured rimmed baking sheet, seam side down. Cover dough loosely with plastic lightly coated with vegetable oil spray and let rest at room temperature until dough is relaxed and no longer cool to touch, 30 minutes to 1 hour.

5 Adjust oven rack to lower-middle position, place baking stone or steel on rack, and heat oven to 450 degrees. Line 2 overturned rimmed baking sheets with parchment paper and dust liberally with cornmeal. Transfer 1 piece of dough to lightly floured counter and, using rolling pin, gently roll into triangular shape with 8-inch base and 10-inch sides, about ½ inch thick. Transfer dough to prepared sheet with base facing short side of sheet.

6 Using pizza cutter, make 6-inch-long cut down center of triangle, through dough to sheet, leaving about 1½ inches at either end. Make three 2- to 3-inch diagonal cuts through dough on each side of center cut, leaving 1-inch border on each end of cuts, to create leaf-vein pattern (cuts should not connect to one another or to edges of dough).

7 Gently stretch dough toward sides of sheet to widen cuts and emphasize leaf shape; overall size of loaf should measure about 10 by 12 inches. Cover loosely with plastic lightly coated with oil spray and let rest at room temperature until nearly doubled in size, 30 to 45 minutes. Twenty minutes after shaping first loaf, repeat rolling, cutting, and shaping with second piece of dough. (Staggering shaping of loaves will allow them to be baked in succession.)

8 Brush top and sides of first loaf with 2 tablespoons oil. Sprinkle loaf evenly with half of Gruyère. Using baking peel, transfer loaf, on parchment, to baking stone and bake until golden brown, 18 to 22 minutes, rotating parchment halfway through baking. Transfer to wire rack and let cool for at least 15 minutes before serving. Repeat topping and baking with second loaf.

Variations

Fougasse with Asiago and Black Pepper

Omit bacon and Gruyère. Sprinkle each loaf with 1 teaspoon coarsely ground pepper and ½ cup finely grated Asiago before baking.

Olive Fougasse

Omit bacon and Gruyère. Add 1 cup coarsely chopped pitted kalamata olives to mixer bowl with flour in step 2. Sprinkle each loaf with 1½ teaspoons chopped fresh rosemary and 1 teaspoon coarse sea salt before baking.

SHAPING LEAF-SHAPED FOUGASSE

1 Roll dough into triangular shape with 8-inch base and 10-inch sides, about ½ inch thick.

2 Transfer dough triangle to prepared baking sheet. Make 6-inch-long cut in center, leaving 1½-inch border. Make three 2- to 3-inch diagonal cuts on each side, leaving 1-inch border.

3 Gently stretch dough to widen cuts and emphasize leaf shape; loaf should measure about 10 by 12 inches.

Seeded Ficelle

MAKES 4 loaves | **TOTAL TIME** 3¼ hours, plus 18¼ hours rising, resting, and cooling

2 cups (10 ounces) all-purpose flour

1 teaspoon table salt

¾ teaspoon instant or rapid-rise yeast

¾ teaspoon diastatic malt powder (optional)

1 cup water, room temperature

3 tablespoons poppy seeds

3 tablespoons sesame seeds

2 teaspoons fennel seeds

2 disposable aluminum roasting pans

Why This Recipe Works The French word "ficelle" means "string," and its namesake loaf resembles a slender baguette made from a "string" of dough. Because it's so skinny, a ficelle maximizes the ratio of crackly crust to chewy interior. Rolling the ficelle in a mixture of poppy, sesame, and fennel seeds before baking adds more flavorful crunch. To ensure an even coating, mist all sides of the dough with water so that the seeds adhere. Adding diastatic malt powder boosts exterior browning during the loaves' short bake. This product is different from plain malt powder; it converts starches in flour to sugar to help develop crust in breads. See page 21 for more information on using a couche and flipping board. If you don't have a baking peel, use a rimless or overturned baking sheet to slide the bread onto the baking stone. If you don't have a baking stone or steel, you can use a preheated rimless or overturned baking sheet; however, the crust will be less crisp. We prefer King Arthur brand all-purpose flour in this recipe.

1 Whisk flour; salt; yeast; and malt powder, if using, together in bowl of stand mixer. Using dough hook on low speed, slowly add room-temperature water to flour mixture and mix until cohesive dough starts to form and no dry flour remains, 5 to 7 minutes, scraping down bowl as needed. Transfer dough to lightly greased large bowl or container, cover tightly with plastic wrap, and let rise for 30 minutes.

2 Using greased bowl scraper (or your fingertips), fold dough over itself by gently lifting and folding edge of dough toward middle. Turn bowl 45 degrees and fold dough again; repeat turning bowl and folding dough 6 more times (total of 8 folds). Cover tightly with plastic and let rise for 30 minutes. Repeat folding and rising every 30 minutes, 3 more times. After fourth set of folds, cover bowl tightly with plastic and refrigerate for at least 16 hours or up to 2 days.

3 Transfer dough to lightly floured counter, press into 8-inch square (do not deflate), and divide in half. Return 1 piece of dough to bowl, cover tightly with plastic, and refrigerate (dough can be shaped and baked anytime within 48-hour window). Divide remaining dough in half crosswise, transfer to lightly floured rimmed baking sheet, and cover loosely with greased plastic. Let rest until no longer cool to touch, 30 minutes to 1 hour.

4 Working with 1 piece of dough at a time (keep remaining piece covered), roll into loose 3- to 4-inch-long cylinder on lightly floured counter. Cover loosely with greased plastic and let rest for 30 minutes. Combine poppy seeds, sesame seeds, and fennel seeds in bowl. Spread half of seed mixture on second rimmed baking sheet; reserve remaining seed mixture for second half of dough. Mist underside of couche with water, drape over inverted rimmed baking sheet, and dust evenly with flour.

5 Gently press 1 dough cylinder into 6 by 4-inch rectangle on lightly floured counter, with long side parallel to counter edge. Fold upper quarter of dough toward center and press gently to seal. Rotate dough 180 degrees and repeat folding to form 8 by 2-inch rectangle. Fold dough in half toward you, using thumb of your other hand to create crease along center of dough, sealing with heel of your hand as you work your way along loaf. Without pressing down on loaf, use heel of your hand to reinforce seal (do not seal ends of loaf).

6 Cup your hand over center of dough and roll dough back and forth gently to tighten (it should form dog-bone shape). Starting at center of dough and working toward ends, gently and evenly roll and stretch dough until it measures 15 inches long by 1 inch wide. Moving your hands in opposite directions, use back and forth motion to roll ends of loaf under your palms to form sharp points. Mist loaf with water on all sides and roll in seed mixture, pressing gently to adhere.

7 Transfer loaf seam side up to prepared couche. On either side of loaf, pinch couche into pleat, then cover loosely with large plastic garbage bag.

8 Redistribute seeds on sheet into even layer. Repeat steps 5 through 7 with remaining piece of dough and place on opposite side of pleat. Fold edges of couche over loaves to cover completely, then carefully place sheet inside plastic bag. Tie, or fold under, open end of bag to fully enclose. Let loaves rise until nearly doubled in size and dough springs back minimally when poked gently with your knuckle, 30 minutes to 1 hour (remove loaves from bag to test).

9 One hour before baking, adjust oven rack to lower-middle position, place baking stone or steel on rack, and heat oven to 500 degrees. Line baking peel with 16 by 12-inch piece of parchment paper, with long edge of parchment perpendicular to handle. Unfold couche, pulling from ends to remove pleats. Gently pushing with side of flipping board, roll 1 loaf over, away from other loaf, so it is seam side down. Using your hand, hold long edge of flipping board between loaf and couche at 45-degree angle, then lift couche with your other hand and flip loaf seam side up onto board. Invert loaf seam side down onto prepared baking peel, about 2 inches from long edge of parchment, then use flipping board to straighten loaf. Repeat with remaining loaf, leaving at least 3 inches between loaves.

10 Using sharp paring knife or single-edge razor blade, make three 4-inch-long, ½-inch-deep diagonal slashes with swift, fluid motion along length of 1 loaf. Repeat with second loaf. Slide parchment with loaves onto baking stone. Cover loaves with stacked inverted disposable pans and bake for 5 minutes. Carefully remove pans; rotate loaves; and continue to bake until loaves are deep golden brown, 8 to 10 minutes. Transfer loaves to wire rack, discard parchment, and let cool for 15 minutes. Serve warm or at room temperature.

SHAPING FICELLE

1 Gently press dough cylinder into 6 by 4-inch rectangle. Fold upper quarter of dough toward center and press gently to seal. Rotate dough 180 degrees and repeat folding to form 8 by 2-inch rectangle.

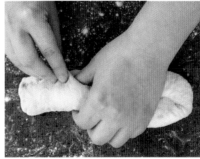

2 Fold dough in half toward you, using thumb of your other hand to create crease along center of dough, sealing with heel of your hand as you work your way along loaf. Do not press down on loaf, and do not seal ends.

Furikake Japanese Milk Bread

MAKES 1 loaf | **TOTAL TIME** 1½ hours, plus 4¾ hours resting, rising, and cooling

3 tablespoons plus 2 cups bread flour (11 ounces), divided

½ cup water, room temperature

½ cup whole milk, chilled

1 large egg

1½ teaspoons instant or rapid-rise yeast

6 tablespoons furikake, divided

2 tablespoons sugar

1½ teaspoons table salt

3 tablespoons unsalted butter, softened

1 large egg beaten with 1 teaspoon water

1 tablespoon toasted sesame oil

Why This Recipe Works A plush bread with an incredibly fluffy texture, this is no ordinary white sandwich bread. The uniquely shaped dough for Japanese milk bread (also called Hokkaido milk bread) is rolled thin and formed into tight spirals, which allows the loaf to bake up into feathery strands. Shaping the dough into two spirals before arranging them in the pan builds an orderly structure, creating this bread's gossamer-thin layers. The Japanese dough-mixing technique (now popular throughout Asia) called tangzhong works well to make a moist but not sticky dough: A simple cooked flour-water paste binds up water in the dough, resulting in a delicate and fluffy crumb in the baked loaf. While Japanese milk bread is wonderful as is, our rendition ups the flavor ante by adding furikake. This spice blend of nori, sesame seeds, bonito flakes, salt, and sugar is at once briny, earthy, nutty, and sweet. You'll add furikake to not only the dough but also the outer crust: Sprinkling the interior of the loaf pan as well as the top of the bread results in a beautiful crust that packs an umami punch and a pleasingly delicate crunch. A final brush of sesame oil on the warm baked loaf gives the bread a rich finish. We like our Furikake, but you can use store-bought, if you prefer. Just be aware that formulations can vary dramatically from brand to brand. To go all in on the nori flavor, we recommend serving slices of this bread with Nori Butter (page 5). The test kitchen's preferred loaf pan measures 8½ by 4½ inches; if you use a 9 by 5-inch loaf pan, increase the shaped rising time by 20 to 30 minutes and start checking for doneness 10 minutes earlier than advised in the recipe.

1 Whisk 3 tablespoons flour and room-temperature water in bowl until no lumps remain. Microwave, whisking every 20 seconds, until mixture thickens to stiff, smooth, pudding-like consistency that forms mound when dropped from end of whisk into bowl, 40 to 80 seconds.

2 Whisk milk, egg, and flour paste together in bowl of stand mixer until smooth. Add yeast and remaining 2 cups flour. Using dough hook on low speed, mix until cohesive dough starts to form and no dry flour remains, about 2 minutes, scraping down bowl as needed. Cover bowl tightly with plastic wrap and let dough rest for 15 minutes.

3 Add 3 tablespoons furikake, sugar, and salt to dough and mix on low speed, about 5 minutes. With mixer running, add butter, 1 tablespoon at a time, allowing each piece to incorporate before adding next, about 3 minutes total, scraping down bowl and dough hook as needed. Increase speed to medium and knead until dough is smooth and elastic and clears sides of bowl but sticks to bottom, 7 to 9 minutes.

4 Transfer dough to lightly floured counter and knead by hand to form smooth, round ball, about 30 seconds. Place dough seam side down in lightly greased large bowl; cover tightly with plastic; and let rise until doubled in size, 1 to 1½ hours.

5 Spray 8½ by 4½-inch loaf pan with vegetable oil spray. Add 2 tablespoons furikake to prepared pan and shake until bottom and sides of pan are evenly coated. Press down on dough to deflate. Turn out dough onto lightly floured counter (side of dough that was against bowl should now be facing up). Gently press and roll into 24 by 4-inch rectangle, with short side parallel to counter edge. Using pizza cutter or chef's knife, cut rectangle lengthwise into 2 equal strips.

6 Roll 1 strip of dough into snug cylinder; pinch seam closed; and place seam side down in prepared pan, with spiral against long side of pan. Repeat with remaining strip of dough, placing it adjacent to other in pan.

7 Cover loosely with greased plastic and let rise until loaf is level with lip of pan and dough springs back minimally when poked gently with your knuckle, 30 minutes to 1 hour.

8 Adjust oven rack to lowest position and heat oven to 375 degrees. Gently brush loaf with egg wash and sprinkle with remaining 1 tablespoon furikake. Bake until loaf is deep golden brown and registers 205 to 210 degrees, 30 to 35 minutes, rotating pan halfway through baking. Let loaf cool in pan on wire rack for 15 minutes. Remove loaf from pan and transfer to wire rack. Brush top and sides with oil. Let cool completely, about 3 hours, before serving.

Furikake

Makes about ½ cup

- 2 sheets nori, torn into 1-inch pieces
- 3 tablespoons sesame seeds, toasted
- 1½ tablespoons bonito flakes
- 1½ teaspoons sugar
- 1½ teaspoons flake sea salt

Process nori using spice grinder until coarsely ground and pieces are no larger than ½ inch, about 15 seconds. Add sesame seeds, bonito flakes, and sugar and pulse until coarsely ground and pieces of nori are no larger than ¼ inch, about 2 pulses. Transfer to small bowl and stir in salt. (Furikake can be stored in airtight container at room temperature for up to 3 weeks.)

SHAPING JAPANESE MILK BREAD

1 Roll 1 strip of dough into snug cylinder; pinch seam closed; and place seam side down in prepared pan, with spiral against long side of pan. Repeat with remaining strip of dough, placing it adjacent to other in pan.

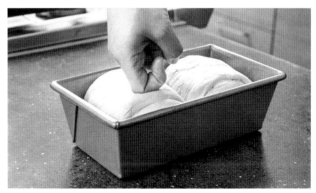

2 Cover loosely with greased plastic and let rise until loaf is level with lip of pan and dough springs back minimally when poked gently with your knuckle, 30 minutes to 1 hour.

Pizza Babka

MAKES 1 loaf │ **TOTAL TIME** 1¾ hours, plus 8¾ hours resting and cooling

Dough

- 2¼ cups (12⅓ ounces) bread flour
- 1½ teaspoons instant or rapid-rise yeast
- ½ cup whole milk
- 2 large eggs
- 1 tablespoon sugar
- ½ teaspoon table salt
- 6 tablespoons unsalted butter, cut into 6 pieces and softened

Filling

- 3 tablespoons extra-virgin olive oil
- 2 garlic cloves, minced
- ½ teaspoon dried oregano
- ¼ teaspoon red pepper flakes
- ½ cup tomato paste
- 1 teaspoon red wine vinegar
- ½ cup chopped fresh basil
- 6 ounces provolone piccante, shredded (1½ cups)
- 1½ ounces Pecorino Romano cheese, grated (¾ cup), divided

- 1 large egg beaten with 1 teaspoon water

Why This Recipe Works Babka is usually sweet, its many layers of dough swirled with chocolate, sweet cheese, cinnamon, or poppy seeds. But filling this enriched dough with savory ingredients instead makes for something truly special. The flavor inspiration for this impressive babka comes from Sicilian scaccia, a baked good featuring thin layers of unenriched dough, tomato sauce, and caciocavallo cheese in a swirled and multilayered loaf. To pack this babka filling with pizza flavor, combine tomato paste, garlic, oil, wine vinegar, oregano, and red pepper flakes. A blend of provolone piccante (aka sharp provolone) and Pecorino Romano creates superbly cheesy layers. If, when testing the bread for doneness, the thermometer comes out with a temperature below 190, try in a different spot. (Hitting a pocket of cheese may give a false reading.) The test kitchen's preferred loaf pan measures 8½ by 4½ inches; if you use a 9 by 5-inch loaf pan, increase the shaped rising time by 20 to 30 minutes and start checking for doneness 10 minutes earlier than advised in the recipe.

1 For the dough Whisk flour and yeast together in bowl of stand mixer. Add milk and eggs. Using dough hook on medium-low speed, mix until cohesive dough forms and no dry flour remains, 2 to 4 minutes, scraping down sides of bowl with rubber spatula as needed. Turn off mixer, cover bowl with dish towel or plastic wrap, and let dough stand for 15 minutes.

2 Add sugar and salt to dough and knead on medium speed until incorporated, about 30 seconds. Increase speed to medium-high and, with mixer running, add butter, 1 piece at a time, allowing each piece to incorporate before adding next, about 3 minutes total, scraping down dough hook and sides of bowl as needed. Continue to knead on medium-high speed until dough begins to pull away from sides of bowl, 7 to 10 minutes, scraping down bowl as needed.

3 Transfer dough to greased large bowl. Cover tightly with plastic and let rise until slightly puffy, about 1 hour. Refrigerate until firm, at least 2 hours or up to 24 hours.

4 For the filling Combine oil, garlic, oregano, and pepper flakes in bowl and microwave until fragrant, 45 to 60 seconds, stirring halfway through microwaving; let cool completely. Stir in tomato paste and vinegar and season with salt and pepper to taste.

5 Grease 8½ by 4½-inch loaf pan. Press down on dough to deflate, then transfer to lightly floured counter and press and roll dough into 18 by 7-inch rectangle, with short side parallel to counter edge. Spread filling over dough, leaving ½-inch border, then sprinkle basil, provolone, and ¼ cup Pecorino over filling. Roll dough away from you into firm cylinder and pinch seam and ends closed. Wrap in plastic; transfer to rimmed baking sheet; and refrigerate until firm but still supple, about 30 minutes.

6 Transfer chilled dough log to lightly floured counter with short side facing you. Using bench scraper or sharp knife, cut log in half lengthwise. Turn dough halves cut side up and arrange side by side. Gently stretch each half into 14-inch length, then pinch top 2 ends of strips together to seal. Twist strips tightly by gently lifting left strip of dough over right strip of dough. Repeat, keeping cut side up, until all of dough is twisted. Pinch bottom ends together to seal.

7 Transfer loaf, cut side up, to prepared pan, reshaping as needed to fit into pan. Cover loaf loosely with greased plastic and let rise until almost doubled in size, 1 to 1½ hours (top of loaf should rise about 1 inch over lip of pan).

8 Adjust oven rack to middle position and heat oven to 350 degrees. Gently brush loaf with egg wash; sprinkle with remaining ½ cup Pecorino; and bake until loaf is deep golden brown and registers 190 to 195 degrees, 40 to 55 minutes, rotating pan halfway through baking. Let loaf cool in pan on wire rack for 1 hour. Remove loaf from pan and let cool completely on wire rack, about 3 hours, before serving.

SHAPING BABKA

1 Press and roll dough into 18 by 7-inch rectangle. Spread filling over dough, leaving ½-inch border. Roll dough away from you into firm cylinder. Turn loaf seam side up and pinch seam and ends closed. Wrap in plastic wrap and refrigerate until firm.

2 Place chilled cylinder on counter, with short side parallel to counter edge, and use bench scraper to cut loaf in half lengthwise; turn halves so cut side is facing up.

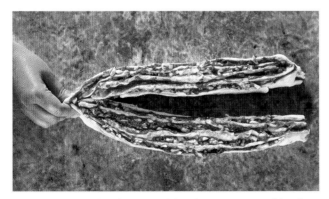

3 Gently stretch each half into 14-inch length. Line up pieces of dough side by side and pinch ends farthest away from you together to seal.

4 Lay left strip of dough over right strip of dough. Repeat, keeping cut side up, until dough pieces are tightly twisted. Pinch ends closest to you together. Transfer loaf to prepared loaf pan, reshaping as needed.

Spicy Cheese Bread

MAKES 1 loaf | **TOTAL TIME** 1½ hours, plus 3¼ hours rising and cooling

Bread

- 3¼ cups (16¼ ounces) all-purpose flour
- ¼ cup (1¾ ounces) sugar
- 1 tablespoon instant or rapid-rise yeast
- 1½ teaspoons red pepper flakes
- 1¼ teaspoons table salt
- ½ cup warm water (110 degrees)
- 2 large eggs plus 1 large yolk
- 4 tablespoons unsalted butter, melted
- 6 ounces Monterey Jack cheese, cut into ½-inch cubes (1½ cups), room temperature
- 6 ounces provolone cheese, cut into ½-inch cubes (1½ cups), room temperature

Topping

- 1 large egg beaten with 1 teaspoon water
- 1 teaspoon red pepper flakes
- 1 tablespoon unsalted butter, softened

Why This Recipe Works This softly chewy, cheesy snack bread speckled with red pepper flakes is legendary in its homeland of Wisconsin. Our homage to this bakery favorite features an eggy, challah-like dough, which bakes up appropriately soft with a thin, deeply golden crust. To incorporate enough cheese to make the bread worthy of its name—without ending up with a heavy, greasy loaf or one that loses its cheesy interior to oozing—you'll roll out the dough after its first rise, top it with cubes of cheese, roll the dough into a log to seal in the cheese, and spiral the whole thing into a cake pan for its second rise. An equal mix of provolone and Monterey Jack provides a great flavor-to-meltability ratio. Brushing the top of the dough with egg wash before baking encourages great browning and helps the extra kick of red pepper flakes cling to the top of the dough. The cake pan helps contain the cheese and also helps the bread keep its shape as it bakes up into a beautiful domed loaf. Then, to reinforce the shiny, supple crust and add the finishing touch of richness, you'll brush the top with butter after the bread comes out of the oven. If, when testing the bread for doneness, the thermometer comes out with a temperature below 190, try in a different spot. (Hitting a pocket of cheese may give a false reading.) Take the cheese out of the refrigerator when you start the recipe to ensure that it comes to room temperature by the time you need it. Otherwise, the cold cheese will prevent the dough from rising properly the second time.

1 **For the bread** Whisk flour, sugar, yeast, pepper flakes, and salt together in bowl of stand mixer. Whisk warm water, eggs and yolk, and melted butter together in liquid measuring cup. Add water mixture to flour mixture. Using dough hook on medium speed, knead until dough clears bottom and sides of bowl, about 8 minutes.

2 Transfer dough to unfloured counter, shape into ball, and transfer to greased bowl. Cover with plastic wrap and let rise in warm place until doubled in size, 1½ to 2 hours.

3 Grease 9-inch round cake pan. Transfer dough to unfloured counter and press to deflate. Roll dough into 18 by 12-inch rectangle with long side parallel to counter edge. Distribute Monterey Jack and provolone evenly over dough, leaving 1-inch border. Starting with edge closest to you, roll dough into log. Pinch seam and ends to seal, then roll log so seam side is down. Roll log back and forth on counter, applying gentle, even pressure, until log reaches 30 inches in length. If any tears occur, pinch to seal. Starting at 1 end, wind log into coil; tuck end underneath coil. Place loaf in prepared pan and cover loosely with clean dish towel. Let rise in warm place until doubled in size, 1 to 1½ hours. Adjust oven rack to lower-middle position and heat oven to 350 degrees.

4 **For the topping** Brush top of loaf with egg wash, then sprinkle with pepper flakes. Place pan on rimmed baking sheet. Bake until loaf is golden brown, about 25 minutes. Rotate pan; tent with aluminum foil; and continue to bake until loaf registers 190 degrees, 25 to 30 minutes.

5 Transfer pan to wire rack and brush bread with butter. Let cool for 10 minutes. Run knife around edge of pan to loosen bread. Slide bread onto wire rack, using spatula as needed for support. Let cool for 30 minutes before slicing. Serve warm.

SHAPING SPICY CHEESE BREAD

1 Roll dough into rectangle and cover surface with cheese cubes. Starting with longer side, roll dough into tight cylinder, trapping cheese cubes inside. Use gentle pressure to roll dough log back and forth until it is 30 inches long.

2 Starting at 1 end, wind log into coil; tuck end underneath coil. Nestle coiled dough into greased cake pan, cover with kitchen towel, and let dough rise until doubled in size.

Saffron-Rosemary Challah

MAKES 1 loaf | **TOTAL TIME** 2 hours, plus 5 hours resting, rising, and cooling

¾ cup water, divided (¼ cup boiling, ½ cup room temperature)

¼ teaspoon saffron threads, crumbled

3 tablespoons bread flour, plus 2¾ cups (15⅛ ounces)

1 large egg plus 2 large yolks

2 tablespoons extra-virgin olive oil

1¼ teaspoons instant or rapid-rise yeast

2 tablespoons sugar

1 tablespoon chopped fresh rosemary

1 teaspoon table salt

1 large egg beaten with 1 teaspoon water

Why This Recipe Works Intricately braided challah is a showstopper, and its mild, eggy flavor makes a great canvas for creative additions. While slightly sweet versions may be more common, this savory spin uses an aromatic and colorful combination of floral saffron and woodsy rosemary. Steeping the saffron threads in boiling water releases the full potential of this spice's water-soluble flavor compounds. A small amount of sugar helps create a nicely browned exterior and a tender interior texture; plus, it complements the complex flavors of the saffron and rosemary (without making the bread sweet). As with the Furikake Japanese Milk Bread (page 322), you'll use the dough-mixing technique called tangzhong, starting with a simple cooked water-flour paste to create a moist but not sticky dough. To streamline the braiding process, you'll make two three-strand braids—one large and one small—and place the small one on top of the large one. Brushing the loaf with egg wash before baking produces an evenly brown, glossy crust—the crowning touch to this gorgeous challah. Bake this loaf on two nested baking sheets to keep the bottom of the loaf from getting too dark. For an accurate measurement of boiling water, bring a kettle of water to a boil and then measure out the desired amount.

1 Combine ¼ cup boiling water and saffron in small bowl and let steep for 15 minutes. Meanwhile, whisk 3 tablespoons flour and remaining ½ cup room-temperature water in bowl until no lumps remain. Microwave, whisking every 20 seconds, until mixture thickens to stiff, smooth, pudding-like consistency that forms mound when dropped from end of whisk into bowl, 40 to 80 seconds.

2 In bowl of stand mixer, whisk egg and yolks, oil, flour paste, and saffron mixture until well combined. Add yeast and remaining 2¾ cups flour. Using dough hook on low speed, mix until all flour is moistened, 3 to 4 minutes. Turn off mixer, cover bowl with clean dish towel or plastic wrap, and let dough stand for 20 minutes.

3 Add sugar, rosemary, and salt and mix on medium speed for 9 minutes (dough will be quite firm and dry). Transfer dough to counter and lightly spray now-empty mixer bowl with vegetable oil spray. Knead dough briefly to form ball and return it to prepared bowl. Cover bowl tightly with greased plastic and let dough rise until about doubled in size, about 1½ hours.

4 Line rimmed baking sheet with parchment paper and set inside second rimmed baking sheet. Transfer dough to counter and press into 6-inch square, expelling as much air as possible. Divide dough into 2 pieces, one roughly half size of other. (Small piece will weigh about 9 ounces; larger piece, about 18 ounces.) Divide each piece into thirds and cover loosely with greased plastic.

5 Working with 1 piece of dough at a time (keep remaining pieces covered), stretch and roll dough pieces into 16-inch ropes (3 ropes will be much thicker).

6 Arrange 3 thicker ropes side by side, perpendicular to counter edge, and pinch far ends together. Braid ropes into 10-inch length and pinch remaining ends together. Transfer loaf to prepared sheet and brush top with egg wash (reserve remaining egg wash). Repeat braiding remaining ropes into second 10-inch length and place on top of larger loaf. Loosely cover loaf with plastic and let rise in warm place until loaf is puffy and increases in size by a third, 45 minutes to 1 hour.

7 Thirty minutes before baking, adjust oven rack to middle position and heat oven to 350 degrees. Brush loaf with remaining egg wash. Bake until loaf is deep golden brown and registers at least 195 degrees, 35 to 40 minutes. Let cool on sheets for 20 minutes. Transfer loaf to wire rack and let cool completely before serving, about 2 hours.

BRAIDING CHALLAH

1 Working with 1 piece of dough at a time, stretch and roll dough pieces into 16-inch ropes (3 ropes will be thicker).

2 Arrange 3 thicker ropes side by side, perpendicular to counter edge, and pinch far ends together. Braid ropes into 10-inch length and pinch remaining ends together. Transfer to prepared sheet and brush top with egg wash.

3 Repeat braiding remaining ropes into second 10-inch length. Place smaller loaf on top of larger loaf. Tuck ends underneath. Cover loosely with plastic and let rise for 45 minutes to 1 hour.

4 Brush loaf with remaining egg wash before baking.

DOUGHS & MORE

All-Purpose Double-Crust Savory Pie Dough

MAKES enough for one 9-inch pie

TOTAL TIME 15 minutes, plus 1 hour chilling

Why This Recipe Works It's hard to beat the flavor and flakiness of a pie dough made with butter, and this one is a breeze both to make in the food processor and to work with in recipes. A beaten egg adds richness and makes the dough more supple; a healthy dose of sour cream brings a slightly tangy flavor. Letting the dough rest for an hour in the refrigerator before rolling it out is a crucial step that lets the gluten relax, which leads to easier rolling and less springback in the oven. It's important that the sour cream be chilled to prevent the dough from overheating in the food processor.

- ½ cup sour cream, chilled
- 1 large egg, lightly beaten
- 2½ cups (12½ ounces) all-purpose flour
- 1½ teaspoons table salt
- 12 tablespoons unsalted butter, cut into ½-inch pieces and chilled

1 Combine sour cream and egg in bowl. Process flour and salt in food processor until combined, about 3 seconds. Add butter and pulse until only pea-size pieces remain, about 10 pulses. Add half of sour cream mixture and pulse until combined, about 5 pulses. Add remaining sour cream mixture and pulse until dough begins to form, about 10 pulses.

2 Transfer dough to lightly floured counter and knead briefly until dough comes together. Divide dough in half and form each half into 4-inch disk. Wrap each disk tightly in plastic wrap and refrigerate for 1 hour. (Wrapped dough can be refrigerated for up to 2 days or frozen for up to 2 months. If frozen, let dough thaw completely on counter before rolling.)

2 Transfer mixture to lightly floured counter and knead briefly until dough comes together. Form into 4-inch disk, wrap in plastic, and refrigerate for 1 hour. (Wrapped dough can be refrigerated for up to 2 days or frozen for up to 2 months. If frozen, let dough thaw completely on counter before rolling.)

Press-In Tart Dough

MAKES enough for one 9-inch tart

TOTAL TIME 1 hour, plus 1½ hours chilling and cooling

Why This Recipe Works Tart dough bakes up with a firmer, crisper texture than pie dough, because it contains less moisture. Without that little bit of extra moisture, though, it's harder to roll out. So this press-in dough skips the rolling; after mixing it until it just comes together, you'll sprinkle it in clumps into a tart pan and gently press it into an even layer. Using the food processor cuts the butter into the dough quickly and evenly and prevents warm hands from melting the butter. If the dough becomes too soft while you're working with it, let it firm up in the refrigerator for a few minutes. It is important to use ice water in the dough to prevent it from overheating in the food processor.

1¼ cups (6¼ ounces) all-purpose flour

1 tablespoon sugar

½ teaspoon table salt

8 tablespoons unsalted butter,
cut into ½-inch cubes and chilled

2–4 tablespoons (1–2 ounces) ice water

1 Spray 9-inch tart pan with removable bottom with vegetable oil spray. Pulse flour, sugar, and salt in food processor until combined, about 4 pulses. Scatter butter over top and pulse until mixture resembles coarse sand, about 15 pulses. Add 2 tablespoons ice water and continue to process until clumps of dough just begin to form and no powdery bits remain, about 5 seconds. If dough doesn't clump, add 1 tablespoon ice water and pulse to incorporate, about 4 pulses. If necessary, repeat with remaining 1 tablespoon ice water. (Dough can be refrigerated for up to 2 days or frozen for up to 1 month; let chilled/frozen dough sit on counter until very soft before using.)

All-Purpose Single-Crust Savory Pie Dough

MAKES enough for one 9-inch pie

TOTAL TIME 15 minutes, plus 1 hour chilling

1½ tablespoons lightly beaten egg

¼ cup sour cream, chilled

1¼ cups (6¼ ounces) all-purpose flour

¾ teaspoon table salt

6 tablespoons unsalted butter,
cut into ½-inch pieces and chilled

1 Whisk egg and sour cream together in bowl. Process flour and salt in food processor until combined, about 3 seconds. Add butter and pulse until only pea-size pieces remain, about 10 pulses. Add half of sour cream mixture and pulse until combined, about 5 pulses. Add remaining sour cream mixture and pulse until dough begins to form, about 10 pulses.

2 Press two-thirds of dough into bottom of prepared pan. Press remaining one-third of dough into fluted sides of pan. Lay plastic wrap over dough and smooth out any bumps or shallow areas using your fingertips. Place pan on plate and freeze dough until firm, about 30 minutes. (Dough-lined tart can be frozen for up to 1 month.) Meanwhile, adjust oven rack to middle position and heat oven to 375 degrees.

3 Place frozen tart shell on rimmed baking sheet. Gently press piece of greased aluminum foil against dough and over edges of tart pan. Fill tart pan with pie weights and bake until top edge of dough just starts to color and surface of dough no longer looks wet, about 30 minutes.

4 Remove sheet from oven and carefully remove foil and weights. Return sheet to oven and continue to bake until tart shell is golden brown, 5 to 10 minutes. Set sheet with tart shell on wire rack and let cool completely, about 1 hour. (Fully baked shell can sit at room temperature for up to 2 days.)

Galette Dough

MAKES enough for one 8-inch galette

TOTAL TIME 25 minutes, plus 1 hour chilling

Why This Recipe Works When making free-form galettes, the crust needs to be sturdy enough to support the fillings without the help of a pie plate yet still tender and flaky. A high ratio of butter to flour provides the best flavor and tenderest texture without compromising structure. But the real answer to satisfying structure is found in a French pastry method called fraisage, in which chunks of butter are pressed into the flour in long, thin sheets, creating lots of long, flaky layers when the dough is baked. These long layers are tender for eating yet sturdy and impermeable, making this crust ideal for supporting a generous filling. It is important to use ice water in the dough to prevent it from overheating in the food processor.

1½   **cups (7½ ounces) all-purpose flour**

½   **teaspoon table salt**

10   **tablespoons unsalted butter, cut into ½-inch cubes and chilled**

3–6   **tablespoons (1½–3 ounces) ice water**

1 Process flour and salt in food processor until combined, about 5 seconds. Scatter butter over top and pulse until mixture resembles coarse sand and butter pieces are about size of small peas, about 10 pulses. Continue to pulse, adding ice water 1 tablespoon at a time, until dough begins to form small curds that hold together when pinched with your fingers, about 10 pulses.

2 Transfer mixture to lightly floured counter and gather into rectangular pile. Starting at farthest end, use heel of your hand to smear small amount of dough against counter. Continue to smear dough until all crumbs have been worked. Gather smeared crumbs into another rectangular pile and repeat process.

3 Form dough into 6-inch disk, wrap tightly in plastic wrap, and refrigerate for at least 1 hour. (Wrapped dough can be refrigerated for up to 2 days or frozen for up to 1 month. If frozen, let dough thaw completely on counter before rolling.) Let chilled dough sit on counter to soften slightly, about 10 minutes, before rolling.

MAKING GALETTE DOUGH

Starting at farthest end, use heel of your hand to smear small amount of dough against counter. Continue to smear dough until all crumbs have been worked.

Whole-Wheat Galette Dough

MAKES enough for one 10-inch galette

TOTAL TIME 40 minutes, plus 1½ hours resting

Why This Recipe Works Using whole-wheat flour in a galette crust gives it a hearty, earthy flavor. Because whole-wheat flour contains less gluten than white flour, keeping some white flour in the dough ensures that there's enough gluten for the dough to hold its shape. However, you need to add more water to whole-wheat flour to fully hydrate it, so to prevent the white flour from absorbing that additional liquid and overdeveloping its gluten (not desirable in a galette crust), take a hands-off approach to mixing and let the flour absorb the water on its own. Barely mix the ingredients together and then chill the shaggy-looking dough briefly. The resulting dough will be remarkably supple. To punch up the crust's flaky texture and introduce more structure, you'll give the dough a series of folds to create multiple interlocking layers. You can substitute an equal amount of rye flour for the whole-wheat flour, if you like. It is important to use ice water in the dough to prevent it from overheating in the food processor.

- 1¼ **cups (6¼ ounces) all-purpose flour**
- ½ **cup (2¾ ounces) whole-wheat flour**
- 1 **tablespoon sugar**
- ¾ **teaspoon table salt**
- 10 **tablespoons unsalted butter, cut into ½-inch pieces and chilled**
- 7 **tablespoons ice water**
- 1 **teaspoon distilled white vinegar**

1 Process all-purpose flour, whole-wheat flour, sugar, and salt in food processor until combined, about 5 seconds. Scatter butter over top and pulse until it forms pea-size pieces, about 10 pulses. Transfer mixture to medium bowl.

2 Sprinkle ice water and vinegar over mixture. With rubber spatula, use folding motion to mix until loose, shaggy mass forms with some dry flour remaining (do not overwork). Transfer mixture to center of large sheet of plastic wrap, press gently into rough 4-inch square, and wrap tightly. Refrigerate for 45 minutes.

3 Transfer dough to floured counter. Roll into 11 by 8-inch rectangle, with short side of rectangle parallel to edge of counter. Using bench scraper, bring bottom third of dough up, then fold upper third over it, folding like business letter into 8 by 4-inch rectangle. Turn dough 90 degrees counterclockwise. Roll dough again into 11 by 8-inch rectangle and fold again into thirds. Turn dough 90 degrees counterclockwise and repeat rolling and folding into thirds. After last fold, fold dough in half to create 4-inch square. Press top of dough gently to seal, wrap tightly in plastic wrap, and refrigerate for at least 45 minutes. (Wrapped dough can be refrigerated for up to 2 days or frozen for up to 1 month. If frozen, let dough thaw completely on counter before rolling.) Let chilled dough sit on counter to soften slightly, 15 to 20 minutes, before rolling.

Pizza Dough

MAKES 1¾ pounds (enough for two 13-inch pizzas)

TOTAL TIME 10 minutes, plus 24¼ hours resting and chilling

Why This Recipe Works This dough produces a New York–style crust—a thin and crisp pizza crust that's both tender and chewy and that complements any toppings you put on it. Using high-protein bread flour results in a great chew, and the ratio of flour to water and yeast makes a dough that stretches thin without snapping back and that retains moisture as it bakes. You'll knead the dough quickly in a food processor and then let it proof in the refrigerator for at least a day (or up to 3 days) to fully develop its flavors. The result is worth the wait: a stretchable dough that's effortless to work with and that bakes up brown and crisp. We prefer King Arthur brand bread flour in this recipe. It is important to use ice water in the dough to prevent it from overheating in the food processor.

- 3 **cups (16½ ounces) bread flour**
- 2 **teaspoons sugar**
- ½ **teaspoon instant or rapid-rise yeast**
- 1⅓ **cups (10⅔ ounces) ice water**
- 1 **tablespoon extra-virgin olive oil**
- 1½ **teaspoons table salt**

1. Pulse flour, sugar, and yeast in food processor until combined, about 5 pulses. With processor running, slowly add ice water and process until dough is just combined and no dry flour remains, about 10 seconds. Let dough rest for 10 minutes.

2. Add oil and salt to dough and process until dough forms satiny, sticky ball that clears sides of bowl, 30 to 60 seconds. Transfer dough to lightly floured counter and knead by hand to form smooth, round ball, about 30 seconds. Place dough seam side down in lightly greased large bowl or container, cover tightly with plastic wrap, and refrigerate for at least 24 hours. (Dough can be refrigerated for up to 3 days.)

Whole-Wheat Pizza Dough

MAKES 1½ pounds (enough for two 13-inch pizzas)

TOTAL TIME 15 minutes, plus 18¼ hours resting and chilling

Why This Recipe Works Using all whole-wheat flour would result in a dry, dense pizza crust with an overwhelming flavor that would interfere with the toppings. For a great balance of wheaty flavor; a crisp bottom; and a moist, chewy interior, this recipe uses a combination of 60 percent whole-wheat flour and 40 percent bread flour. Because whole-wheat flour absorbs more liquid than white flour, adding more liquid increases the hydration of the dough, resulting in better gluten development and a great pizza-crust chew. A long rest in the refrigerator develops flavors and relaxes the gluten for better extensibility. We prefer King Arthur brand bread flour in this recipe. It is important to use ice water in the dough to prevent it from overheating in the food processor.

1½ cups (8¼ ounces) whole-wheat flour

1 cup (5½ ounces) bread flour

2 teaspoons honey

¾ teaspoon instant or rapid-rise yeast

1¼ cups (10 ounces) ice water

2 tablespoons extra-virgin olive oil

1¾ teaspoons table salt

1. Process whole-wheat flour, bread flour, honey, and yeast in food processor until combined, about 2 seconds. With processor running, add ice water and process until dough is just combined and no dry flour remains, about 10 seconds. Let dough stand for 10 minutes.

2. Add oil and salt to dough and process until it forms satiny, sticky ball that clears sides of workbowl, 45 to 60 seconds. Remove from bowl and knead on oiled countertop until smooth, about 1 minute. Shape dough into tight ball and place in large, lightly oiled bowl. Cover tightly with plastic wrap and refrigerate for at least 18 hours. (Dough can be refrigerated for up to 2 days.)

Char Siu Pork

MAKES 1¼ pounds bao filling, plus leftovers

TOTAL TIME 2 hours, plus 40 minutes marinating and cooling

Why This Recipe Works With its delightfully sticky glazed exterior and burnished edges, Chinese barbecued pork makes an irresistible filling for Char Siu Bolo Bao (page 268). This recipe is easy to make at home—and since it makes more barbecued pork than you'll need for the bao filling, you'll have plenty of bonus leftovers to add to fried rice or serve as is. Pork butt roast is often labeled Boston butt. The pork will release liquid and fat during the cooking process, so be careful when removing the pan from the oven. Pay close attention to the meat when broiling—you are looking for it to darken and caramelize, not blacken. Don't use a drawer-style broiler—the heat source will be too close to the meat. Instead, increase the oven temperature in step 5 to 500 degrees and cook for 8 to 12 minutes before glazing and 6 to 8 minutes after applying the glaze; flip the meat and repeat on the second side.

- 1 (4-pound) boneless pork butt roast, halved lengthwise, each half turned on its side, cut into 8 strips, and trimmed
- ½ cup sugar
- ½ cup soy sauce
- 6 tablespoons hoisin sauce
- ¼ cup dry sherry
- 2 tablespoons grated fresh ginger
- 1 tablespoon toasted sesame oil
- 2 garlic cloves, minced
- 1 teaspoon five-spice powder
- ¼ teaspoon ground white pepper
- ⅓ cup honey
- ¼ cup ketchup
- 2 tablespoons cornstarch

1. Using fork, prick pork 10 to 12 times on each side. Place pork in 2-gallon plastic zipper-lock bag. Combine sugar, soy sauce, hoisin, sherry, ginger, oil, garlic, five-spice powder, and pepper in medium bowl. Measure out ½ cup marinade and set aside. Pour remaining marinade into bag with pork. Press out as much air as possible; seal bag. Refrigerate for at least 30 minutes and up to 4 hours.

2. While meat marinates, combine honey and ketchup with reserved marinade in small saucepan. Cook glaze over medium heat until syrupy and reduced to 1 cup, 4 to 6 minutes. Reserve 2 tablespoons glaze and set aside.

3. Adjust oven rack to middle position and heat oven to 300 degrees. Set wire rack in aluminum foil–lined rimmed baking sheet and spray with vegetable oil spray.

4. Remove pork from marinade, letting any excess drip off, and place on prepared wire rack. Pour ¼ cup water into bottom of sheet. Cover roast with heavy-duty foil, crimping edges tightly to seal. Cook pork for 20 minutes. Remove foil and continue to cook until edges of pork begin to brown, 40 to 45 minutes. Pour pan juices into fat separator and let settle for 5 minutes. Pour off and reserve ¾ cup defatted juices; discard remaining juices.

5. Turn on broiler. Broil pork until evenly caramelized, 7 to 9 minutes. Remove sheet from oven and brush pork with half of glaze; broil until deep mahogany color, 3 to 5 minutes. Using tongs, flip meat and broil until other side caramelizes, 7 to 9 minutes. Brush meat with remaining glaze and continue to broil until second side is deep mahogany, 3 to 5 minutes. Let cool for at least 10 minutes, then cut into thin strips.

6. Chop 12 ounces pork and transfer to bowl. Combine reserved defatted juices with reserved 2 tablespoons glaze in small saucepan and whisk in cornstarch. Bring to boil over medium heat, whisking constantly, and cook until mixture is thickened and glossy, about 1 minute. Transfer to bowl with chopped pork and toss to combine. (Chopped pork filling and leftover pork strips can be refrigerated for up to 5 days; bring filling to room temperature before using.)

NUTRITIONAL INFORMATION
FOR OUR RECIPES

To calculate the nutritional values of our recipes per serving, we used The Food Processor SQL by ESHA research. When using this program, we entered all the ingredients, using weights for important baking ingredients such as flour, butter, and cheese. We also used our preferred brands in these analyses. Any ingredient listed as "optional" was excluded from the analyses. If there is a range in the serving size, we used the highest number of servings to calculate the nutritional values.

	CALORIES	TOTAL FAT (G)	SAT FAT (G)	CHOL (MG)	SODIUM (MG)	TOTAL CARB (G)	DIETARY FIBER (G)	TOTAL SUGARS (G)	PROTEIN (G)
QUICK BREADS & SCONES									
Manchego and Chorizo Muffins	290	14	8	65	550	28	0	2	10
Corn Muffins with Rosemary and Black Pepper	260	13	7	65	430	32	2	5	6
Corn Muffins with Cheddar and Scallions	320	17	10	80	520	33	2	5	9
Jalapeño and Cheddar Scones	350	20	13	85	590	34	0	7	9
Panch Phoran Scones	310	19	12	55	320	29	1	2	5
Feta-Dill Zucchini Bread with Feta Butter	300	19	12	110	560	23	0	2	9
Quick Cheese Bread	340	16	9	65	760	35	0	2	15
Quick Cheese Bread with Bacon, Onion, and Gruyère	430	24	9	70	890	35	0	2	18
Whole-Wheat Soda Bread with Walnuts and Cacao Nibs	320	12	3	5	530	45	9	4	11
Garlicky Olive Bread	360	18	5	45	680	35	0	2	14
Fresh Corn Cornbread	230	9	5	75	430	32	2	5	6
Sweet Potato Cornbread	280	12	6	100	670	39	4	9	7
Broccoli Cheese Cornbread	320	17	10	100	580	29	2	5	14
Savory Corn Spoonbread	260	15	8	125	470	26	2	8	10
Sun-Dried Tomato, Garlic, and Za'atar Biscuits	300	17	10	45	410	30	1	2	5
Rosemary and Olive Drop Biscuits	160	8	5	20	300	19	0	1	3
Mustard and Dill Drop Biscuits	160	8	5	20	350	19	0	1	3
Mixed Herb Drop Biscuits	160	8	5	20	290	19	0	1	3
Cheddar and Pimento Drop Biscuits	190	10	8	30	340	19	0	1	5
Cornmeal and Black Pepper Drop Biscuits	360	8	5	20	290	61	1	4	9
Cornmeal and Green Chile Drop Biscuits	360	8	5	20	310	62	1	4	9
Cornmeal and Sage Drop Biscuits	360	8	5	20	290	61	1	4	9

	CALORIES	TOTAL FAT (G)	SAT FAT (G)	CHOL (MG)	SODIUM (MG)	TOTAL CARB (G)	DIETARY FIBER (G)	TOTAL SUGARS (G)	PROTEIN (G)
QUICK BREADS & SCONES *(CONT.)*									
Potato Biscuits with Chives	230	12	6	20	420	26	0	3	4
Potato Biscuits with Cheddar and Scallions	260	14	7	30	470	27	0	3	6
Potato Biscuits with Bacon	290	17	8	30	510	27	0	3	6
Gruyère and Herb Buttermilk Biscuits	420	24	15	70	580	39	0	5	10
PASTRIES & PIES									
Gochujang and Cheddar Pinwheels	170	11	5	30	170	13	0	1	5
Ham and Cheese Palmiers	170	10	5	10	500	15	1	1	8
Goat Cheese, Sun-Dried Tomato, and Urfa Danish	400	27	14	65	500	29	1	2	13
Beet and Caramelized Onion Turnovers with Beet-Yogurt Sauce	310	19	8	25	570	31	2	6	7
Butternut Squash, Apple, and Gruyère Turnovers	420	27	15	60	490	37	1	10	11
Smoked Salmon and Chive Mille-Feuille	230	17	9	35	330	13	0	2	7
Spinach Pie for a Crowd	260	15	8	30	560	26	2	3	10
Deep-Dish Quiche Lorraine	600	47	25	285	590	25	0	4	19
Deep-Dish Quiche with Leeks and Blue Cheese	520	39	23	270	680	28	1	4	15
Deep-Dish Quiche with Sausage, Broccoli Rabe, and Mozzarella	520	39	23	270	700	24	1	4	19
Pizza Chiena	480	29	14	140	980	28	1	0	25
Chicken Pot Pie with Savory Crumble Topping	730	42	22	180	1080	48	2	8	38
Double-Crust Chicken Pot Pie	540	31	18	160	830	42	2	4	22
Pub-Style Steak and Ale Pie	720	40	20	210	850	31	1	2	52
Tourtière	790	55	28	165	1120	47	1	5	25
Vegetable Pot Pie	470	29	15	85	840	42	3	8	9
Cast-Iron Skillet Calzone	670	32	16	85	1770	60	0	10	37
Vegetable Stromboli	520	21	11	45	1370	59	1	9	27
Bean and Cheese Sopaipillas with Green Chile Sauce	620	36	14	50	1560	57	7	6	19
Jamaican Beef Patties	600	36	19	130	690	46	1	3	18
Poblano and Corn Hand Pies	650	35	7	65	980	67	3	2	18
Picadillo Gorditas	700	33	8	65	1330	77	8	1	28
Lamb Fatayer	330	16	5	30	520	33	1	2	13
Vegetable Samosas with Cilantro-Mint Chutney	310	14	1	0	360	40	2	2	6
TARTS & GALETTES									
Tomato and Mozzarella Tart	390	26	13	25	700	33	2	4	14
Tomato and Smoked Mozzarella Tart	400	27	13	25	720	32	2	3	15
Sun-Dried Tomato and Mozzarella Tart	390	27	13	25	720	32	2	2	14
Tomato and Mozzarella Tart with Prosciutto	400	27	13	30	890	33	2	4	16

	CALORIES	TOTAL FAT (G)	SAT FAT (G)	CHOL (MG)	SODIUM (MG)	TOTAL CARB (G)	DIETARY FIBER (G)	TOTAL SUGARS (G)	PROTEIN (G)
TARTS & GALETTES *(CONT.)*									
Asparagus and Goat Cheese Tart	450	34	14	20	490	32	2	3	12
Caramelized Onion, Tomato, and Goat Cheese Tart	480	25	10	5	760	63	8	17	11
Fennel-Apple Tarte Tatin	450	28	9	0	580	54	6	19	8
Eggplant and Tomato Phyllo Pie	410	28	8	20	800	28	3	4	10
Weeknight Spanakopita	380	26	16	120	750	22	2	3	15
Hortopita	430	27	8	85	770	36	3	4	13
Chicken B'stilla	420	24	4	165	440	27	2	4	24
Lamb Phyllo Pie	700	46	18	110	1210	43	2	10	29
No-Knead Brioche Tarts with Zucchini and Crispy Prosciutto	310	13	4.5	120	900	31	1	6	15
French Onion and Bacon Tart	320	19	10	90	490	27	1	6	7
Camembert, Sun-Dried Tomato, and Potato Tart	480	29	18	75	930	41	1	3	13
Smoked Salmon and Leek Tart	290	18	10	90	470	22	0	3	9
Potato and Parmesan Tart	390	24	13	85	510	31	1	1	9
Potato and Blue Cheese Tart	400	26	14	85	550	31	1	1	9
Corn, Tomato, and Bacon Galette	450	29	16	105	540	33	1	2	12
Fresh Tomato Galette	440	29	16	100	980	31	2	3	11
Mushroom and Leek Galette with Gorgonzola	370	23	13	75	430	34	3	4	9
Butternut Squash Galette with Gruyère	380	22	12	75	330	35	3	4	9
CRACKERS & FLATBREADS									
Seeded Pumpkin Crackers	210	9	1.5	40	180	29	3	12	5
Whole-Wheat Seeded Crackers	220	9	1.5	15	340	30	5	0	6
Whole-Wheat Everything Crackers	210	8	1.5	15	340	29	5	0	6
Gruyère, Mustard, and Caraway Cheese Coins	220	13	8	40	350	14	0	0	8
Blue Cheese and Celery Seed Cheese Coins	200	13	9	40	290	14	0	0	6
Pimento Cheese Coins	210	14	8	40	230	14	0	0	8
Mini Cheese Crackers	110	8	5	25	105	7	0	0	4
Everything Bagel Grissini	110	2	0	0	230	19	0	0	3
Piadine	340	11	1	0	370	51	0	0	7
Alu Parathas	540	24	11	45	1050	68	2	5	11
Cōngyóubing	310	19	1.5	0	500	28	0	1	5
Cheese Pupusas	560	27	13	65	2140	59	8	10	23
Tomatillo Chicken Huaraches	810	28	9	115	1080	90	13	6	52
Mana'eesh Za'atar	420	18	2.5	0	580	53	3	1	10
Lahmajun	220	9	3	20	850	25	1	2	9
Mushroom Musakhan	590	29	4	0	1280	73	10	14	15
Red Pepper Coques	460	22	3	0	980	54	2	9	9

	CALORIES	TOTAL FAT (G)	SAT FAT (G)	CHOL (MG)	SODIUM (MG)	TOTAL CARB (G)	DIETARY FIBER (G)	TOTAL SUGARS (G)	PROTEIN (G)
CRACKERS & FLATBREADS (CONT.)									
Pletzel	290	10	1.5	0	700	44	1	2	7
Pissaladière	470	13	1.5	0	820	74	5	9	12
Cauliflower Chickpea Flatbread with Romesco	170	13	3	30	400	7	2	2	9
Caramelized Onion Flatbread with Blue Cheese and Walnuts	470	24	6	15	900	54	4	12	14
Caramelized Onion Flatbread with Potato, Goat Cheese, and Rosemary	390	11	4	10	740	63	4	13	12
Caramelized Onion Flatbread with Shaved Brussels Sprouts, Fontina, and Hazelnuts	430	17	5	20	890	56	5	13	14
Thin-Crust Whole Wheat Pizza with Pesto and Goat Cheese	200	12	2.5	5	390	19	2	1	6
Thin-Crust Whole Wheat Pizza with Garlic Oil, Two Cheeses, and Basil	190	10	3.5	10	430	19	2	1	7
Thin-Crust Whole Wheat Pizza with Wine-Braised Onions and Blue Cheese	230	12	4.5	15	400	23	2	4	6
Thin-Crust Pizza with Pumpkin, Cashew Ricotta, and Apple-Fennel Slaw	420	15	2	0	440	61	4	10	11
Sfincione	660	31	8	25	1390	74	3	4	21
Pizza al Taglio with Arugula and Fresh Mozzarella	570	27	9	35	1120	55	3	2	21
Pizza al Taglio with Prosciutto and Figs	500	18	4	25	1150	65	4	11	17
Pizza al Taglio with Potatoes and Soppressata	470	19	4.5	25	990	52	2	0	18
Pide with Eggplant and Tomatoes	220	15	5	20	470	15	2	5	6
Adjaruli Khachapuri	350	17	10	80	760	33	0	3	15
BATTER "BAKES"									
Socca with Caramelized Onions and Rosemary	250	16	2	0	600	20	4	5	7
Socca with Swiss Chard, Apricots, and Pistachios	480	31	4	0	630	40	11	10	13
Farinata	110	6	1	0	230	9	2	2	4
Blini	70	3	1.5	20	170	9	1	2	3
Pajeon	370	22	1.5	0	800	37	1	2	6
Kimchi Jeon	220	11	1	0	820	28	0	20	4
Whole-Wheat Crepes with Creamy Sautéed Mushrooms and Asparagus	500	33	19	195	700	37	4	11	18
Rye Crepes with Smoked Salmon, Crème Fraîche, and Pickled Shallots	580	36	20	220	1020	41	5	16	24
Galettes Complètes	420	29	15	320	900	12	1	3	28
Bánh Xèo	410	17	5	75	1250	45	3	13	19
Gougères with Aged Gouda and Smoked Paprika	80	5	3	45	140	5	0	0	4
Gougères with Manchego and Black Pepper	90	6	4	40	150	4	0	0	4

	CALORIES	TOTAL FAT (G)	SAT FAT (G)	CHOL (MG)	SODIUM (MG)	TOTAL CARB (G)	DIETARY FIBER (G)	TOTAL SUGARS (G)	PROTEIN (G)
BATTER "BAKES" (CONT.)									
Blue Cheese and Chive Popovers with Blue Cheese Butter	390	24	14	155	610	27	1	3	14
Dutch Baby with Burrata and Prosciutto	460	27	8	215	660	36	0	3	20
Spinach and Gruyère Strata	440	29	16	260	910	18	2	6	20
Pimento Cheese Featherbed Eggs	300	15	8	160	900	26	1	7	16
Butternut Squash and Spinach Bread Pudding	530	43	25	295	730	25	3	8	14
ROLLS, BREADSTICKS & MORE									
Peppery Dinner Rolls with Caramelized Onion and Smoked Paprika	170	6	3	25	350	23	1	3	5
Potato Dinner Rolls with Cheddar and Mustard	180	4.5	3	30	250	27	1	1	7
Porcini and Truffle Crescent Rolls	170	4.5	1.5	50	210	27	0	5	6
Thai Curry Butter Fan Rolls	260	9	5	50	590	37	0	5	6
Pão de Queijo	420	25	7	80	710	37	0	1	11
Garlic Knots	140	6	3.5	15	280	18	0	0	3
Parmesan Breadsticks	360	13	3	25	970	47	0	0	12
Asiago and Black Pepper Breadsticks	370	14	3.5	30	920	47	1	0	11
Pecorino and Mixed Herb Breadsticks	360	13	3.5	30	930	47	0	0	10
Onion-Poppy Bialys	210	0	0	0	660	45	1	2	6
Lop Cheung Bao	230	10	3	20	360	28	1	6	7
Char Siu Bolo Bao	260	9	5	70	440	30	0	14	12
Potato Knishes	230	12	1.5	10	340	26	1	1	4
Potato, Pastrami, and Gruyère Knishes	310	17	5	35	550	27	1	1	10
Sausage and Chive Pull-Apart Rolls	430	23	11	110	710	34	2	4	20
Za'atar Monkey Bread	210	9	1.5	0	390	28	0	4	5
Pizza Monkey Bread	570	28	9	40	1510	64	2	12	22
Prosciutto and Fig Pinwheel Bread	230	10	6	75	500	26	0	8	8
YEASTED LOAVES									
Almost No-Knead Bread with Olives, Rosemary, and Parmesan	320	9	4	20	990	39	0	0	18
Almost No-Knead Cranberry-Pecan Bread	260	4.5	0	0	440	48	1	8	6
Potato-Dill Sandwich Bread	260	4	2.5	10	440	45	2	0	8
Whole-Wheat Quinoa Bread	270	4	0.5	0	450	49	4	7	9
Everything Bagel Bread	260	1	0	0	1070	53	2	9	9
Cranberry-Walnut Bread	350	9	1	0	590	59	4	15	10
Prosciutto Bread	180	6	1.5	10	440	22	1	0	8
Prosciutto Bread with Provolone	210	8	3	20	520	22	1	0	10
Spicy Olive Bread	260	2.5	0	0	630	47	2	3	8
Fig and Fennel Bread	170	0	0	0	590	36	3	9	5
Caramelized Onion Bread	220	3.5	0.5	0	590	39	2	3	7
Cheddar and Black Pepper Bread	280	9	6	30	180	35	1	0	13

	CALORIES	TOTAL FAT (G)	SAT FAT (G)	CHOL (MG)	SODIUM (MG)	TOTAL CARB (G)	DIETARY FIBER (G)	TOTAL SUGARS (G)	PROTEIN (G)
YEASTED LOAVES *(CONT.)*									
Sage-Polenta Bread	240	3.5	0.5	0	440	41	2	0	7
Focaccia with Caramelized Red Onion, Pancetta, and Oregano	300	11	2.5	10	700	40	0	1	9
Fougasse with Bacon and Gruyère	360	16	4.5	15	580	44	2	0	10
Fougasse with Asiago and Black Pepper	290	9	1.5	5	480	44	2	0	7
Olive Fougasse	270	8	1	0	970	42	1	0	6
Seeded Ficelle	80	1.5	0	0	150	14	1	0	3
Furikake Japanese Milk Bread	180	7	2.5	25	760	24	1	4	6
Pizza Babka	290	16	8	80	370	26	1	3	11
Spicy Cheese Bread	470	21	12	120	710	49	0	6	18
Saffron-Rosemary Challah	180	3.5	0.5	45	200	29	1	2	6
DOUGHS & MORE									
All-Purpose Double-Crust Savory Pie Dough	450	26	16	100	600	44	0	1	8
All-Purpose Single-Crust Savory Pie Dough	230	13	8	65	300	22	0	0	4
Press-In Tart Dough	240	15	9	40	190	23	0	2	3
Galette Dough	290	19	12	50	190	26	0	0	4
Whole-Wheat Galette Dough	240	9	6	25	290	33	1	2	5
Pizza Dough	310	2.5	0	0	580	59	2	1	11
Whole-Wheat Pizza Dough	280	6	1	0	680	49	5	2	9
Char Siu Pork	440	13	4	105	1730	43	0	37	36

CONVERSIONS & EQUIVALENTS

Baking is a science and an art, but geography has a hand in it, too. Flours and sugars manufactured in the United Kingdom and elsewhere will feel and taste different from those manufactured in the United States. So we cannot promise that a bread you bake in Canada or England will taste the same as a bread baked in the States, but we can offer guidelines for converting weights and measures. We also recommend that you rely on your instincts when making our recipes. Refer to the visual cues provided. If the dough hasn't "come together in a ball" as described, you may need to add more flour—even if the recipe doesn't tell you to. You be the judge.

The recipes in this book were developed using standard U.S. measures following U.S. government guidelines. The charts below offer equivalents for U.S. and metric measures. All conversions are approximate and have been rounded up or down to the nearest whole number.

EXAMPLE
1 teaspoon = 4.9292 milliliters, rounded up to 5 milliliters
1 ounce = 28.3495 grams, rounded down to 28 grams

Volume Conversions

U.S.	METRIC
1 teaspoon	5 milliliters
2 teaspoons	10 milliliters
1 tablespoon	15 milliliters
2 tablespoons	30 milliliters
¼ cup	59 milliliters
⅓ cup	79 milliliters
½ cup	118 milliliters
¾ cup	177 milliliters
1 cup	237 milliliters
1¼ cups	296 milliliters
1½ cups	355 milliliters
2 cups (1 pint)	473 milliliters
2½ cups	591 milliliters
3 cups	710 milliliters
4 cups (1 quart)	0.946 liter
1.06 quarts	1 liter
4 quarts (1 gallon)	3.8 liters

Weight Conversions

OUNCES	GRAMS
½	14
¾	21
1	28
1½	43
2	57
2½	71
3	85
3½	99
4	113
4½	128
5	142
6	170
7	198
8	227
9	255
10	283
12	340
16 (1 pound)	454

Conversions for Common Baking Ingredients

Because measuring by weight is far more accurate than measuring by volume, and thus more likely to produce reliable results, in our recipes we provide ounce measures in addition to cup measures for many ingredients. Refer to the chart below to convert these measures into grams.

INGREDIENT	OUNCES	GRAMS
Flour		
1 cup all-purpose flour*	5	142
1 cup buckwheat flour	4¼	120
1 cup bread flour	5½	156
1 cup chickpea flour	3	85
1 cup cornmeal	5	142
1 cup rye flour	5½	156
1 cup whole-wheat flour	5½	156
Sugar		
1 cup granulated (white) sugar	7	198
1 cup packed brown sugar (light or dark)	7	198
1 cup confectioners' sugar	4	113
Fat		
4 tablespoons lard	2	56
4 tablespoons (½ stick or ¼ cup) butter†	2	57
8 tablespoons (1 stick or ½ cup) butter†	4	113
16 tablespoons (2 sticks or 1 cup) butter†	8	227

* **U.S. all-purpose flour does not contain leaveners, as some European flours do. These leavened flours are called self-rising or self-raising. If you are using self-rising flour, take this into consideration before adding leaveners to a recipe.**

† **In the United States, butter is sold both salted and unsalted. We recommend unsalted butter. If you are using salted butter, take this into consideration before adding salt to a recipe.**

Oven Temperatures

FAHRENHEIT	CELSIUS	GAS MARK
225	105	¼
250	120	½
275	135	1
300	150	2
325	165	3
350	180	4
375	190	5
400	200	6
425	220	7
450	230	8
475	245	9

Converting Temperatures from an Instant-Read Thermometer

We include doneness temperatures in many of the recipes in this book. We recommend an instant-read thermometer for the job. To convert Fahrenheit degrees to Celsius, use this simple formula:

Subtract 32 degrees from the Fahrenheit reading, then divide the result by 1.8 to find the Celsius reading.

EXAMPLE
"Bake until loaf registers 205 to 210 degrees, 30 to 35 minutes."

To convert:
(1)   205°F – 32 = 173°
173° ÷ 1.8 = 96.11°C, rounded down to 96°C

(2)   210°F – 32 = 178°
178° ÷ 1.8 = 98.89°C, rounded up to 99°C

INDEX

Note: Page references in *italics* indicate photographs.